IDEAS
THAT
SHAPED
OUR
WORLD

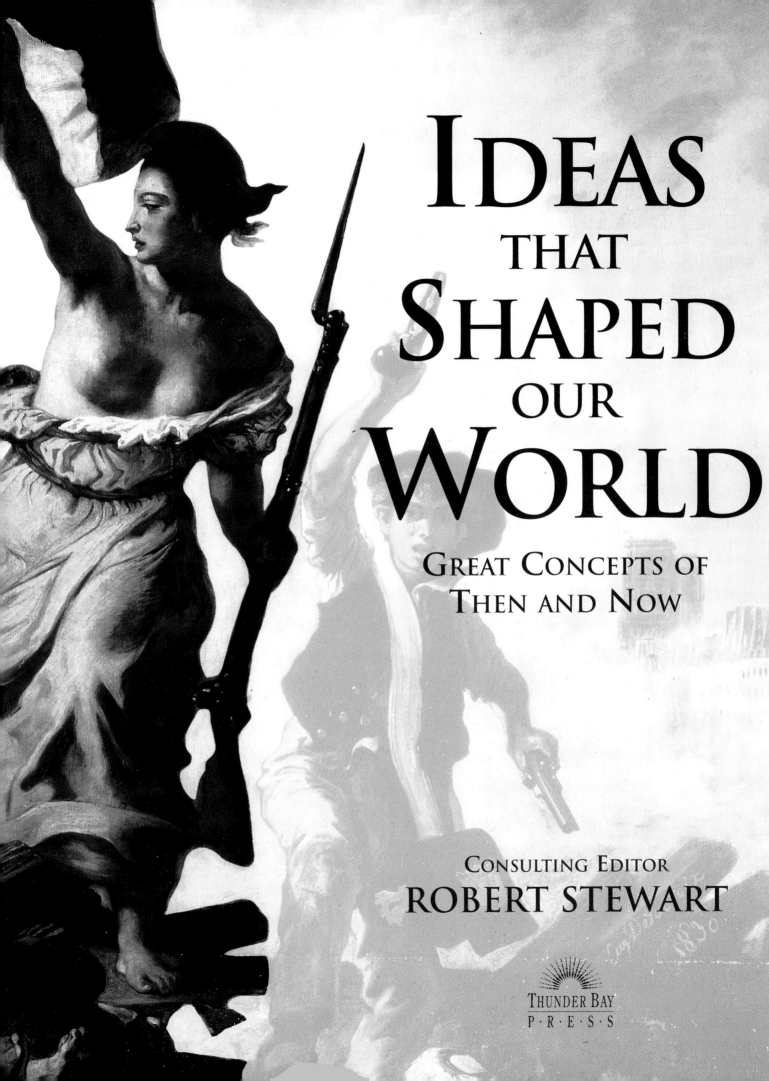

IDEAS
THAT
SHAPED
OUR
WORLD

GREAT CONCEPTS OF
THEN AND NOW

CONSULTING EDITOR
ROBERT STEWART

THUNDER BAY
P·R·E·S·S

Thunder Bay Press
5880 Oberlin Drive
Suite 400
San Diego
CA 92121-9653

Conceived, edited, and designed by
Marshall Editions
170 Piccadilly
London W1V 9DD

Library of Congress Cataloging-in-Publication Data

Ideas that shaped our world / consulting editor,
Robert Stewart.
        p. cm.
    Includes index.
    ISBN 1-57145-088-2
    1. Civilization, Modern. 2. Intellectual life—
History. 3. Philosophy—History.   I. Stewart,
Robert.   1941-
CB358.134   1997
909.82--dc219   97–8711
                                   CIP

Project editor   Christina Rodenbeck
Art editor   Vicky Holmes
Assistant editor   Charles Phillips
Designers   Kendal Osborn
                                   Kerry Quested
Picture editors   Anne-Marie Ehrlich
                                   Vanessa Fletcher
                                   Elizabeth Loving
Editorial assistant   James Rankin
Researcher   Michaela Moher
Copy editor   Jolika Feszt
DTP editors   Mary Pickles
                                   Kate Waghorn
Indexer   Laura Hicks
Production   Nikki Ingram
Production editor   Emma Dixon
Managing editor   Lindsay McTeague
Art director   Sean Keogh
Editorial director   Sophie Collins

CONTRIBUTORS

Politics and Spirituality   Robert Stewart
Philosophy   Roger Jones
Human Sciences   David Gould
The Arts   Antony Mason
Science   Nigel Hawkes

Originated in Singapore by HBM Print
Printed and bound in Italy by Chromolitho

CONTENTS

Introduction

*Without the genesis and birth of new ideas through history,
the world as we know it would not exist.*

The most enduring idea entertained by humankind in its short history is that *Homo sapiens* is the center of the universe, whether as the highest expression of God's purpose or as the pinnacle of a grand evolutionary design. That idea is sublimely wrong. We inhabit a tiny satellite of a minor star on the fringes of one of countless galaxies. We have, as a species, existed for about 250,000 years, which is to say that if the whole of planetary time were represented as a mile, humankind has been around for only the last inch or so. Descended from apes, we occupy one twig of one tiny branch on an abundant evolutionary bush that contains many limbs that are far more dominant and far more successful. Evolution operates with no goal in sight. Had not some catastrophic accident – probably the impact on the Earth of a huge meteor – wiped out the dinosaurs some 65 million years ago and thus opened up space for mammals, we would almost certainly not be here at all.

Yet none of that diminishes our sense of ourselves – for one very good reason. *Homo sapiens* is the only known species that understands those things, and for that reason alone, we may be considered the most interesting of all living creatures. We alone are capable of abstract thought.

This late modern era – the period from 1750 – has been marked by more rapid change than any time in history: change in the way we live our lives, in government, in science, and in the arts. All of these changes have come about because someone has either had a new idea

The invention of the atom bomb created the possibility of the human race self-destructing, setting in motion the Cold War and making the creation of the United Nations an absolute necessity.

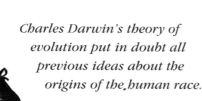

Charles Darwin's theory of evolution put in doubt all previous ideas about the origins of the human race.

or resuscitated an old one. The ideas that have shaped our world have often been ways of explaining our world. Marx's formula of lives shaped by economics explained the structure of society; Freud's discovery of the unconscious explained our dreams and our seemingly motiveless actions; Darwin's concept of evolution explained how humans dominate the planet; Rachel Carson's book *Silent Spring* explained how we are killing the planet.

All these ideas shape the information we receive every day; they inform our actions and shape our lives. Without the democracy created by French and American revolutionaries or without the computers created by mathematicians, the world we live in would be a very different one. Without the ideas of political freedom, equality, and freedom of expression, our world would certainly be a much darker place – a place without hope.

As a member of the Surrealist school, René Magritte played with the imagery of the unconscious, juxtaposing everyday objects in bizarre or unexpected ways.

The power of popular protest was demonstrated at anti-Vietnam War rallies across the United States in the late 1960s and early 1970s.

TIMELINE
3300 BC—AD 1750

As the story of human thought unfolds, it becomes clear that we have much in common with our ancestors. Throughout history, humanity has asked itself the same questions: "how did we get here?" "why do we exist?" "how does the world work?" And through time, we have come up with remarkably different answers and different methods of reaching those answers.

This timeline begins near the dawn of history, when people began to record their systems of belief, their battles, and the names of their leaders. The "cradle of civilization" was, of course, the fertile crescent – the area of the Middle East that stretches from the Nile valley, through the Holy Land, to the valleys of the Tigris and Euphrates in modern Iraq.

From about the third century BC, the story of Western civilization continues in Greece and then the Roman Empire around the Mediterranean. In the fourth century AD, the Western Empire collapsed as barbarians swept through Europe from Asia, bringing with them the Dark Ages.

Two centuries later, the followers of the prophet Muhammad created a new empire that stretched from Spain to Persia. The Arabs made great strides in science, mathematics, and philosophy, translating classical texts into Arabic. Slowly – via Spain and the Crusades – Arab learning filtered back to Europe, inspiring Europeans to open universities.

By the 15th century, Europe was flourishing economically, creating the perfect environment for the intellectual flowering of the Renaissance, which led to the Scientific Revolution of the 16th century. That in turn laid the foundations for the Enlightenment, where the main text of this book begins.

3300–2501 BC   2500–2001 BC

Politics

c.3100 BC The kingdoms of upper and lower Egypt are unified under one pharaoh, Menes.
c.2685 BC The "Old Kingdom" period of Egypt begins.

c.2500–1700 BC The Indus Valley civilization flourishes in what is now India and Pakistan.
2371–2230 BC The Mesopotamian king, Sargon I, conquers southern Mesopotamia, parts of Elam (western Iran), and Anatolia, founding the world's first empire.

Philosophy & Spirituality

c.2650 BC The Egyptian *Books of Wisdom*, collections of maxims and practical advice, are written.
c.2600 BC Egyptians begin mummifying their dead.

c.2400 BC Ptah-hotep, governor of Memphis, writes *Instructions*, the first known book of philosophy.
c.2100 BC Abraham, patriarch of Judaism, Islam, and Christianity, lives.
c.2100 BC Stonehenge, a standing stone circle, is built in Britain.

Stonehenge, Salisbury Plain, England

Human Sciences

c.3300 BC Writing is developed in Mesopotamia.
c.2900 BC The first known map is produced in Egypt.

c.2500 BC The world's first libraries are set up at Shurupak and Eresh, in Mesopotamia.
2300 BC Babylonians draw maps on clay tablets.

Art

c.3000 BC Egyptian artists use hot wax to set their colors.
c.2700 BC The *Epic of Gilgamesh* – the tale of a legendary Sumerian king in search of immortality – is written.

c.2200 BC Sumerian liturgy incorporates antiphonal forms, with choirs singing choruses and responses.
2112 BC A ziggurat – a stepped pyramid temple – is built at Ur in Sumer.

Science

c.2700 BC Chinese wear silk clothing, make bronze artifacts, and braid hempen rope.
2590 BC The Pyramid at Giza is built as a tomb for Pharaoh Cheops.

c.2800 BC Egyptian priests calculate a solar year of 365 days.

c.2500 BC Mathematical texts are produced in Mesopotamia.

The god Thoth in the underworld in the Egyptian Book of the Dead weighs a man's heart against the feather of truth

c.700 BC Sparta adopts a new constitution blending monarchy (two kings), oligarchy (five elected magistrates and a council of elders), and democracy (a legislative assembly of 9,000 citizens).
683 BC Athens rejects monarchy, choosing an elected magistrate in place of a king.
675 BC Military service becomes compulsory for the citizens of Greek city-states.
650 BC The Oracle of Apollo at Delphi, near Athens, reaches the height of its political and moral influence.
610 BC The cult of Dionysus – god of drunkenness, joy, and excess – spreads from Asia Minor through Greece.

592 BC The Greek leader Solon extends freedom to all Athenians and takes powers away from the aristocracy.
c.575 BC The caste system, which determines social status by birth, is introduced to India.
510 BC Rome abolishes its monarchy and sets up a republic, with two elected consuls supported by a Senate of magistrates.
507 BC The Greek statesman Cleisthenes introduces representative democracy to Athens, dividing the population into 10 tribes, each of which chooses 50 men by lot to attend the legislative council.

494 BC Consul Agrippa gives Rome's majority "plebeians" more powers, at the expense of the "patrician" aristocracy.
490 BC Athens defeats Persian invaders at the Battle of Marathon.
450 BC Roman law is codified for the first time in the "Twelve Tables."
404 BC Sparta defeats Athens.

399 BC Socrates goes to trial and is executed. His critical, skeptical approach was seen as a threat to tradition and the state.
332 BC Alexander of Macedon consolidates his father's empire and begins his great campaign.
331 BC Alexander conquers Egypt and lays the foundation for Alexandria.
325 BC Alexander reaches India.

202 BC Rome defeats the Carthaginian general Hannibal at Zama and becomes the foremost power in the Mediterranean region.

Alexander the Great (356–323 BC)

479–338 BC THE GOLDEN AGE OF CLASSICAL GREECE **After the Greek victory against the Persians, prosperity and stability bring a cultural flowering in Athens. Under the Athenian leader Pericles, a program of temple-building begins, and philosophy and the arts flourish.**

650 BC Greeks begin colonizing the Mediterranean.
650 BC The first coins are circulated in Lydia.
629 BC King Assurbanipal of Assyria bequeaths a 25,000-volume library to his subjects.
c.610 BC Symposia – ritualized feasting, with music, games, and intellectual discussions – are an established social custom in Greece.

c.600 BC In Persia, Zoroaster founds a monotheistic faith. He believes that good and evil are equally powerful twin spirits that divide the world between them.
600 BC In the first works of Greek philosophy, Thales of Miletus combines mythology with observations of natural phenomena.
586–538 BC The Hebrew scriptures are written down.

500 BC Greek scholar Hecataeus writes what is probably the world's first book on geography.
c.500 BC The teachings of Siddhartha Gautama, known as the Buddha, spread in India.
c.500 BC In China, Confucius teaches that man's duty is to follow the "will of heaven."
c.450 BC Sophistry, the belief that truth can only be measured by subjective experience, emerges in Athens.
429 BC Plato writes the *Republic,* marking the beginning of political theory.

387 BC In Athens, Plato founds the Academy, a school for studying philosophy.
320 BC The philosopher Pyrrho introduces skepticism.

250 BC The Hebrew Bible is translated into Greek.

290 BC A great research institute – a library and museum – is built in Alexandria.
264 BC The earliest recorded gladiator fight takes place in Rome.

c.520 BC Homosexuality is encouraged in Athens.

446 BC Herodotus writes the world's first narrative history.

A Roman gladiator fight

c.700 BC Athenian vases are painted with scenes from everyday life.
c.605 BC King Nebuchadnezzar commissions the Hanging Gardens of Babylon, a series of irrigated roof terraces considered to be one of the wonders of the ancient world.

600 BC *Aesop's Fables* are written.
580 BC On the island of Lesbos, the woman poet Sappho contributes to the flowering of Greek lyric poetry.
534 BC The first tragedies are performed at the annual festival celebrating Dionysus in Athens.

486 BC The first comedies are performed in Athens.
c.480 BC Greek sculptors start to produce genuine portraits of individual human beings, as opposed to idealized visions.
450 BC Hippodamus designs a town – Miletus – using a grid pattern.
432 BC The Parthenon is completed in Athens.
429 BC Sophocles writes the tragedy *Oedipus Rex.*

c.350 BC Aristotle's *Poetics* discusses comedy and tragedy in poetry and says that tragedy allows for the *katharsis* (purification) of pity and fear.

206 BC A guild of actors and writers is established in Rome.

570 BC Anaximander develops a systematic cosmology, depicting the world as a cylinder.
525 BC Science and mysticism are united by Pythagoras. His followers teach that understanding the universe through science leads to spiritual illumination.

410 BC On the Greek island of Cos, Hippocrates lays the foundations of western medicine.
405 BC Greek philosopher Democritus publishes the first atomic theory.

Greek comedy mask

c.350 BC Aristotle proposes six arguments to prove that the Earth is round. The idea may go back 200 years to Pythagoras.
360 BC Eudoxus, a Greek mathematician, forms the theory of planetary motion.

295 BC Euclid's *Elements* codifies classical geometry.
270 BC Aristarchus of Samos proposes that the Earth spins around the Sun.
240 BC Archimedes develops mechanics and mathematics in Sicily.

Politics

200–101 BC

149 BC Rome destroys Carthage, establishing an outpost of its empire in northern Africa.
122 BC Roman soldiers sack Corinth, bringing Greece under Roman domination.

100–1 BC

82 BC Lucius Cornelius Sulla makes the Roman Senate more powerful, but his reforms are overturned after his retirement in 79 BC.
73–71 BC Spartacus leads slaves in a widespread rebellion against the Roman government.
60 BC Rome is ruled by a triumvirate of Crassus, Pompey, and Julius Caesar.
44 BC Julius Caesar is assassinated by a group of senators who fear he will make himself king.
27 BC Rome ceases to be a republic, as Octavian assumes the title of Emperor.

AD 1–99

41 Caligula declares himself a god and is assassinated by his own bodyguards.
64 Roman authorities begin systematic persecution of Christians.
70 Jerusalem falls to Romans as the Jewish Revolt is defeated.

100–199

117 The Roman Empire reaches its greatest extent.
132 The Romans expel the Jews from Jerusalem; the expelled Jews form a diaspora throughout the Roman Empire.

The Coliseum, Rome

Philosophy & Spirituality

186 BC The Roman Senate bans Bacchanalian cults, which have become the focus for large-scale debauchery and lawlessness.
149 BC Stoicism, the pursuit of virtue through knowledge, becomes the philosophy of the Roman elite.

4 BC Jesus is born in a stable in Bethlehem.

17 Emperor worship spreads across the Roman Empire.
29–30 Jesus is crucified.
35 St. Paul is converted on the road to Damascus and becomes a missionary.
40 Philo of Alexandria integrates Judaism and Platonism.
64–70 Mark's Gospel is written.
76–80 The Gospels of Matthew and Luke are completed.
90–100 John writes his version of the Gospel.

c.50–391 ALEXANDRIA IS A GREAT INTELL[...] institute, the Mouseion, the city attracts[...] especially Jews of the diaspora. Most of th[...] also the most important center of Christia[...] first century. At the end of the fourth cent[...] and pagans lead to Alexandria's decline.

165 The cults of the Asian goddess Cybele and the Egyptian gods Isis and Horus are widespread in the Roman Empire.
175 The earliest canon of the New Testament is produced.
c.175 The Montanist heresy, based on an imminent second coming of Christ, spreads in Europe.

Human Sciences

196 BC Priests in Memphis inscribe the Rosetta Stone with phrases in Greek and hieroglyphic and cursive Egyptian texts.
c.100 BC The camel is introduced into the Saharan region of Africa.

63 BC Julius Caesar reforms the calendar, introducing a year of 365 days with an extra day every four years.
c.50 BC Julius Caesar imposes a one percent sales tax in Rome.

33 The Emperor Tiberius intervenes to stem an economic crisis caused by a shortage of coins.
80 The Coliseum is opened in Rome, entertaining the people with gory gladiator fights and Christians being torn apart by wild beasts.

Coptic Monastery of Baramus, Wadi Natrun, Egypt.

Art

c.150 BC Greek drama, now regularly performed in Rome, is extremely popular.

c.43 BC–AD 18 **THE AUGUSTAN AGE IN ROME. A flowering of literary talent, fostered by a period of peace and prosperity under the emperor Augustus. Among the period's finest writers were Virgil, Ovid, Horace, and Livy. Later eras of great literature were named after the first "Augustan Age" – notably 17th-century France and 18th-century England.**

100 BC An imperial office of music is founded in China and standardizes pitch.
c.100 BC Alexandros of Antioch carves a statue of Aphrodite, later known as the Venus de Milo, on the Greek island of Milos.
37 BC Virgil publishes the *Eclogues* or *Bucolics*, poems that celebrate the life of peasants and shepherds. These are the first pastoral poems.

2 Roman poet Ovid completes his *Metamorphoses*.
65 The Roman tragic playwright Seneca dies.
c.66 Petronius Gaius, author of the Latin prose romance *Satyricon*, dies.
85 The poet Martial publishes his *Epigrams*, short poems about Roman society and life.

120–24 The concrete-domed Pantheon is built in Rome. Roman architects were the first to use the dome on a huge scale.

Science

130 BC Greek astronomer Hipparchus makes a geocentric map of the cosmos and the first comprehensive map of the heavens.

c.80 Hero of Alexandria devises an "aelophile" – a machine that uses steam power to drive a wheel.

151 Ptolemy, author of the *Almagest* and the *Tetrabiblos*, summarizing classical mathematics and astronomy, uses lines of latitude and longitude to compile a new map of the world.
170 The Greek physician Galen formulates the concept of four "humors," which will dominate European medicine for the next 1,500 years.

Julius Caesar (102–44 BC)

c.224 The Sassanid dynasty is founded in Persia.
267 Goths pillage the Balkans and Greece.
286 Emperor Diocletian divides the Roman Empire into two halves, each ruled by an emperor: one in Rome and one in Nicomedia, in Asia Minor.

325 Constantine, emperor in the West since 312, reunites both halves of the Roman Empire.
330 The capital of the Roman Empire moves to Constantinople.
375 Huns, originally from Siberia, invade Europe.

410 Visigoths, led by Alaric, sack Rome.
451 An alliance of Romans and barbarians defeats Attila the Hun at the Catalaunian Fields.
476 Ostrogoths, led by Odoacer, depose Rome's last emperor.

532 Justinian orders 30,000 rebels to be massacred in Constantinople.
554 Justinian defeats the Goths, recapturing Italy for the Roman Empire.

605 Chinese emperors have established a strong and loyal civil service.
642 Islamic armies, having captured Jerusalem and Syria, conquer Persia and Alexandria.
661 Rebels assassinate the Muslim caliph Ali; his successor, Mu'awiyah, moves the capital to Damascus, establishing the Omayyad dynasty.

...TUAL CENTER. **Thanks to its research ...nkers from all over the Roman Empire – ...writing is still done in Greek. The city is ... theological debate by the end of the ...ry, violent clashes between Christians**

c.200 The cult of the Persian god Mithras takes hold throughout Rome.
219 The first collection and codification of Jewish oral laws, the *Mishnah*, is completed.
269 Rabbis in Tiberias publish the *Talmud*, a collection of religious commentaries and laws.
271 In Egypt, St. Anthony goes alone into the desert and becomes the first hermit. Within 10 years, communities of monks are established in Egypt.

312 Constantine is converted to Christianity.
313 By law, Christianity is tolerated throughout the Roman Empire.
325 The Council of Nicea ordains orthodox Christian doctrine.
c.360 Buddhism spreads from India to China.
397–401 St. Augustine writes the *Confessions* of his restless youth.

c.300 In Benares, Vatsayana Mallagana publishes the *Kama Sutra*, a comprehensive guide to sexual etiquette.
393 The Olympic Games are suspended; they will not be held again until 1896.

c.405 St. Jerome finishes translating the Bible from the original Greek and Hebrew into Latin (the "Vulgate" Bible).
413–427 St. Augustine writes the *City of God*.
432 St. Patrick starts to convert the Irish to Christianity.
477 Buddhism, until recently eclipsed by Taoism in China, becomes the state religion.

425 The university at Constantinople is founded. Teaching concentrates on Greek and Roman rhetoric.

c.524 Boethius writes *Consolation of Philosophy*, an immensely influential work based on the teachings of Plato.
529 St. Benedict founds a monastery at Monte Cassino in Italy, the rules of which will form the foundation of Western monasticism.
570 Muhammad is born in Mecca.

534 The Byzantine emperor Justinian completes the codification of Roman Law.
550 The church imposes a tithe, an annual tax of one-tenth of an individual's income.

622 Muhammad flees from Mecca to Medina, founding a new religion, Islam, and marking the beginning of the Islamic calendar.
651 The *Koran*, an account of Muhammad's divine revelations, is written down.
664 The Celts of Britain submit to Roman authority, ending independent Celtic Christianity.
685 Buddhism becomes the state religion of Japan.

c.660 Western Europeans learn techniques for the manufacture of paper, porcelain, and steel blades.

Greek wrestlers

The Dome of the Rock, Jerusalem

537 The church of Hagia Sophia is opened at Constantinople.
547 Cosmas Indicopleustes, a merchant from Alexandria, produces *Topographia Christiana*, an early illuminated manuscript.
563 Book copying and illustration is practiced by monks on the Scottish island of Iona.

691 The first great Islamic architectural monument, the Dome of the Rock, is built in Jerusalem.

c.260 Rampant inflation brings a devaluation of currency and a return of bartering throughout the Roman Empire.

c.280 An Egyptian mathematician named Pappus compiles a summary of all mathematical knowledge to date.

c.310 Diophantus of Alexandria outlines the elements of algebra, including the composition of formulas and the substitution of letters for unknown quantities.

425 Flavius Vegetius founds veterinary science.

c.500 In India, Aryabhata demonstrates the use of negative numbers and trigonometry.
520 Indian mathematicians adopt the decimal system.

678 Greek fire, an explosively inflammable petroleum-based mixture invented by Syrian, is first used in battle.

2000–1501 BC

c.1750 BC Hammurabi of Babylon issues a collection of laws, the *Code of Hammurabi*.
c.1700 BC The 12 tribes of Israel, led by Jacob, arrive in Egypt.
c.1567 BC Hyksos invaders are expelled from Egypt and the "New Kingdom" period begins.

c.1800 BC Babylonian priests use sheep's livers for divination.
c.1785 BC A great temple to the god Amon is built at Karnak in Upper Egypt.
c.1700 BC Egyptian dead are buried with the *Book of the Dead* – a collection of religious texts to guide them through the Underworld.

c.1500 BC A reference book for farmers is written in Sumeria.

1700 BC Artists in Crete paint frescoes depicting bull-jumping rituals in which people leap onto the backs of running animals.

2000 BC Medical texts are written in Ur.
c.1800 BC Egyptians adopt the decimal system.
1750 BC Babylonians compile tables of square and cube roots.
1550 BC Egyptian doctors produce detailed accounts of clinical cases.

1500–1001 BC

c.1430 BC The female pharaoh Hatshepsut ascends the throne of Egypt. She carries the traditional symbols of kingship, including a false beard.
c.1230 BC Moses leads the Jews out of Egypt and into the Promised Land of Israel.

Harvest time in ancient Egypt c.1400 BC

c.1500–c.1070 BC Egypt's pharaohs are buried in the Valley of the Kings, using an elaborate process of prayer and mummification.
1370 BC Pharaoh Akhenaten orders worship of a single deity – the sun god – in Egypt.
1200 BC The *I Ching*, a guide for divination, is written in China.

1100 BC Phoenicians develop an alphabetic script.

Ancient Babylonian map of the cosmos

c.1460 BC The great mortuary temple to Hatshepsut is completed in Luxor. The architect, Senemet, has designed a building that fits its site so well that it seems to grow out of the landscape. Hatshepsut's successor, Thutmose III, destroys nearly all images of his aunt after her death.
1370 BC Pharaoh Akhenaten encourages the development of realistic portraiture.

c.1400 BC Portable sundials and water clocks are invented in Egypt.
c.1150 BC The first topographical maps are produced in Egypt.

1000–901 BC

c.1000 BC King David chooses Jerusalem as the capital of a united kingdom of Judah and Israel.

953 BC King Solomon builds the first temple in Jerusalem to house the Ark of the Covenant.

1000 BC A dictionary is produced in China.
1000 BC A Babylonian map depicts the Earth as a disk enclosed by water; Babylon is at the center.

900–801 BC

880 BC The Assyrian Empire, under Assurnasipal II, stretches from the Mediterranean to the Persian Gulf.

c.870 BC Assyrians believe they must conquer their neighbors because they are engaged in a divine struggle of against evil for the sake of their god Ashur. Their wars are holy wars.

c.825 BC The port of Al Mina at the mouth of the River Orontes on the eastern Mediterranean becomes a major trading center and cultural crossroads. Eastern alphabets, cults, social customs, and philosophy begin to find their way west.

c.850 BC Homer's epic poems the *Iliad* and the *Odyssey* are composed.

800–701 BC

750–500 BC Greek city-states, such as Sparta, Corinth, and Athens, flourish. In some, government is by a king (or warrior leader), a council, and an assembly of all adult males. These governments hold the roots of modern democracy, or "rule by the people."
753 BC According to tradition, Romulus founds Rome.

c.800 BC The Celts take to cremating their dead and burying the ashes in urns.
c.700 BC The Greek poet Hesiod describes a "Golden Age," a time when the human race was perfect.

The temple at Delphi

776 BC The first Olympic Games are held by the Greek-speaking nations of the Mediterranean. The games are accompanied by a general truce between the warring city-states.
c.775 BC The Greeks adopt a 27-letter alphabet, based on a 22-letter system devised in Phoenicia.

c.750 BC Babylonian astronomers study planetary movements and eclipses.

1517–c.1550 THE REFORMATION **The religious revolution that resulted in the establishment of the Protestant churches. Dissatisfaction with the corruption of the Catholic Church and the new availability of the Bible in translation fueled new readings of the holy book. Protestantism initially emphasized the freedom of dissent. Politicians in France, Germany, England, and the Netherlands also saw the movement as a chance to challenge papal power. The counter-reformation was the Catholic Church's Draconian response to the threat of Protestantism. The result was a series of wars and massacres – including the 30 Years War (1618–48) – that continued to shake Europe well into the 17th century.**

1513 Niccolo Machiavelli writes *The Prince*, advising rulers how to gain and wield power.
1516 English statesman Sir Thomas More discusses the possibility of an ideal city-state in *Utopia*.
1517 Martin Luther, a lecturer at the University of Wittenberg, Germany posts the *95 Theses* on the door of the church at Wittenberg. These emphasize personal faith, throwing into question the importance of papal authority and precipitating the Reformation.

1533 Pope Clement excommunicates Henry VIII because he has divorced his wife Catherine of Aragon, leading to England's eventual Protestantism. Henry makes himself head of the English church.
1536 Henry VIII starts stripping the monasteries of their wealth.

1556 After a long reign Charles V, Holy Roman Emperor, hands over his empire to his brother Ferdinand and his kingdoms to his son Philip and retires to a monastery.

1579 The six provinces of the Netherlands sign the Treaty of Utrecht, a strategic alliance that allows for religious toleration. Within 10 years, Amsterdam has become the refugee capital of Europe.
1598 The Edict of Nantes grants freedom of conscience to French Protestants, bringing peace to France after 30 years of religious war.

1607 English emigrés form first North American settlement at Jamestown.
1620 The Pilgrim Fathers make landfall at Plymouth Rock.

1611 The King James translation of the Bible into English is published.
1612 Francisco Suarez, a Jesuit theologian, publishes a work that suggests that rulers only rule as a result of a "social contract" to which the people give their consent. He argued that Indians should be given the same rights as any other people.
1622 Marie de Gournay publishes *The Equality of Men and Women*.

1511 The theologian Erasmus publishes *In Praise of Folly*, in which Folly, personified by a woman, suggests that humour makes life bearable.

1540 The Jesuit order is founded. Its mission is to convert infidels.
1542 Paul III sets up an Inquisition to combat Protestantism.
1546 At the Council of Trent called by Pope Paul III, 60 Catholic bishops reject Protestant reforms.

c.1552 Religious leader John Calvin governs Geneva on the basis of his Ordinances, which regulate all aspects of the citizen's lives.

1564 The first commercial exchange in London.

Lloyd's coffeehouse, London

1571 Pope Paul IV publishes an official Index of censored books, including all Bibles that are not in Latin.

1580 Michel Montaigne, the French essayist; publishes his *Essays* – a departure from established genres.
1582 The Gregorian calendar is established by Pope Gregory XIII.
1599 The East India Company is granted the right to trade in India by Queen Elizabeth I.

1601 The Poor Laws in England make taking care of the poor a civic responsibility.
1602 The Dutch East India Company is given permission to conclude treaties, wage defensive wars, and build strongholds.
1609 The Bank of Amsterdam is founded.
1620 The first European weekly paper is printed in Amsterdam. By 1630, Amsterdam boasts more newspapers than anywhere else in Europe.

1508 Spanish settlers enslave natives in the West Indies.
1510 The first African slaves are taken to the Americas.
1513 Balboa sees the Pacific from a peak in Darien.
1522 Magellan returns from circumnavigating the globe.

the northern city states of Italy produces a flowering of rebirth of the ancient golden ages. From Italy, the the architecture and literature of the Roman Empire for Pope Julius in Rome, commission work from artists such as allow artists to reflect the world more realistically. In human body. Humanism, the idea that man creates his own of the Renaissance Man is embodied by two young kings of the poets, athletes, musicians, scholars, and statesmen.

1508 Pope Julius commissions Michelangelo to paint the Sistine Chapel.

1532 French monk François Rabelais publishes his allegorical prose satires.

1550 Vasari publishes *Lives of the Artists*, a biography of Renaissance artists – including Michelangelo, Leonardo, and Raphael – which gives them heroic status.
1561 *Gorbudoc*, the first English tragedy, is performed. Its authors are Thomas Sackville and Thomas Norton.
1562 The Accademia del Disegno, the first art school, opens in Florence.

1597 Jacopo Peri's *Dafne* is the first opera to be performed, although his *Euridice* (1600) is the first surviving example of this form.

c.1601 William Shakespeare's *Hamlet* is performed at the Globe Theatre in London.
1605 The Spanish writer Cervantes publishes *Don Quixote*, the first European novel. It satirizes the prose romance.

c.1600–c.1700 THE SCIENTIFIC REVOL
**microscope and the telescope – bro
had to go. New thinkers such as Nev**

Donatello's David

1528 Paracelsus rejects the theory of the four humors and suggests that the body is a complex chemical factory.
1543 Copernicus' *Revolutionibus Orbium Coelestium*, which suggests that the Earth moves around the Sun, is published.
1543 Andreas Vesalius, publishes the first modern book of anatomy based on dissections of cadavers.

1557 English mathematician Robert Recorde proposes the use of the = sign.
1569 Flemish cartographer and maker of globes Gerardus Mercator produces his cylindrical projection of the world.

1565 Ligorio designs a fanciful garden with follies, grottoes, and ruins for the Duke of Orsini.
c.1570 Palladio designs a series of classically inspired villas near Venice.

1609 Johann Kepler's formalizes his first and second laws of planetary motion.
1620 Galileo, Italian mathematician, physicist, and astronomist, develops the telescope to observe the stars. Later, tried for heresy by the Inquisition for refuting Aristotle's theories, he recants and spends his last years under house arrest.

1502 Peter Heinlein invents the first handheld timepiece.
1507 German cartographer Martin Waldseemuller prints the first map to show America separated from Asia.

Galileo's telescope

700–799

732 Muslim forces, having conquered Spain, are halted at Poitiers, France, by Charles Martel, king of the Franks.
768 Charlemagne becomes king of the Franks.
789 Norsemen raid Britain's southern coast, opening an era of Viking raids and colonization in Europe.

726 Emperor Leo III bans the worship of religious icons in Byzantium.
c.780 Sufism, a mystical, ascetic form of Islam, gains adherents in the Islamic world.

731 Bede, a monk at Jarrow in northern England, completes his *Ecclesiastical History* of Britain.
748 The first newspaper is printed in China.

715 The Anglo-Saxon folk epic *Beowulf* is compiled.
721 The Lindisfarne Gospels are produced by Northumbrian monks.
c.750 Gregorian chant is now regularly sung in Western monasteries.
c.768–c.880 Under Charlemagne, there begins a flowering of arts and learning known as the "Carolingian Renaissance."

760 Arabs adopt the Indian system of numerals (1, 2, 3, 4, etc.)

800–899

800 Pope Leo III crowns Charlemagne Holy Roman Emperor in St. Peter's, Rome.
841 Vikings settle in Dublin.
878 King Alfred of Wessex, England, defeats Viking invaders.

Reliquary containing Charlemagne's hand

866 John Scotus Erigena, an Irish theologian, synthesizes Christianity and Platonism in his book *De Divisione Naturae*.

809 Harun-ar-Rashid establishes the postal service in his empire.
860 Hincmar of Reims, a theologian and canon lawyer, writes a tract opposing divorce.
868 The *Diamond Sutra*, the earliest printed book still in existence, is produced in China.

851 *Silsilat al-Tarawikh*, the first book to feature tales of Sinbad the Sailor, is published.

Page of St. John's Gospel from the Lindisfarne Gospels

800 Al Batriq translates the work of Galen and Hippocrates into Arabic.
c.830 Al-Khwarizmi, a Persian mathematician, publishes *Hisab al-Jabr w-al Muqabalah*, the first major work on algebra.
833 Al Ma'mun, the Abbasid caliph, founds an observatory at Baghdad and establishes a "House of Wisdom" to translate Greek and Latin scientific texts into Arabic.
860 *Book of Artifices* – earliest extant treatise on mechanics – is written by the brothers Muhammed, Ahmad, and Hasan ibn Shakir.

900–999

930 The Althing (general court) is established in Iceland. It is the oldest national assembly.
962 The German king Otto the Great, who defeated Magyar invaders in 955, is crowned Roman Emperor.

909 A monastery is founded at Cluny, in France; the Cluniac Order will become a major reforming force in monasticism.
c.950 The Bogomil sect, which believes that the whole world is the creation of Satan, becomes widespread in Bulgaria.
993 The first Christian saints are canonized.

920 Abu Zaid Akhbar compiles *Akhbar al-Sin w-al-Hind* (Information about China and India) – a book of travelers' tales.

942 The Persian writer Al-Jahshiyan dies before completing a collection of tales originally from Iran, Greece, Arabia, and India. His work is an early version of *A Thousand and One Nights*.

900–1000 Minuscule script, introducing upper- and lower-case letters, sentences, and paragraphs, spreads among Western scholars.
c.975 Arabic numerals are adopted in the West.
980–1031 The Persian physician, Avicenna, writes the *Book of Healing* and *Canon of Medicine*.

1000–1049

1007 The word "burgess" (townsperson) is first used in a charter granting rights to a town in Anjou.
1015 Benevento, in southern Italy, is the first city to set up a commune to govern itself. Soon city-states become the norm in Italy.
1040 A "Truce of God," intended to halt private warfare, is declared in Aquitaine. Others follow.

1005 The caliph Al-Hakim founds a theological college, the Hall of Wisdom, in Cairo.
1012 The first prosecution for heresy occurs in Germany.

c.1003 In the first recorded transatlantic voyage, Leif Ericson sails from Greenland to Nova Scotia.
1012 Rice is introduced to China; it swiftly becomes a staple.
1024 The Chinese government issues the world's first paper currency.
c.1030 Chinese printers start to use movable type.

c.1005 A great age of church-building opens in Europe: in the next 100 years, magnificent cathedrals are built at Mainz, Strasbourg, Novgorod, Basel, Trier and many other cities.

1013 Al-Zahrawi writes the first Arabic treatise on surgery.
1020 Chinese sailors are known to use magnets to navigate.

1050–1099

1066 William of Normandy becomes king of England.
1077 Following his excommunication, Henry IV, the Holy Roman Emperor, submits to Pope Gregory VII.
1095 Pope Urban II declares the first crusade, a bid to make Jerusalem a Christian city by force.
1099 Crusaders capture Jerusalem and massacre its Muslim and Jewish inhabitants.

c.1050–c.1200 ISLAM AND THE SCHOLASTIC AWAKENING Western civiliz... the death of Muhammad, Islam had expanded throughout the Middle East, ... advanced civilizations of the period, offering an atmosphere of tolerance an... amalgamate the learning of previous classical and oriental thinkers. A trickl... scholars are inspired to establish the great Western universities – Paris, Oxf...

1064 A Spanish Muslim, Ali ibn-Hazm, publishes *The Final Word on Sects, Heterodoxies, and Denominations* – the first study of comparative religion.
1098 The Cistercian monastic order is founded at Cîteaux, France.

1065 The Chinese civil service starts to hold regular entrance exams.
1078 Pope Gregory VII orders his bishops to found cathedral schools.
1086 Domesday Book, a thorough survey of English landholding and wealth, is completed.

c.1010 Benedictine monk Guido d'Arezzo invents the five-line musical stave and an early version of the *do-re-mi* scale.
1066–c.1088 The first Tower of London is built.
c.1080 The Bayeux Tapestry, a 231-ft (70.5-m) long needlework record of the Norman conquest of England, is completed.

The Cistercian monastery of Vauxcelles, France, founded 1131

1130 In England, the Exchequer (treasury) keeps annual records in the form of a "pipe roll."
1146 Bernard of Clairvaux proclaims the Second Crusade.

1170 Acting on orders from the English king, knights murder Thomas Becket, the Archbishop of Canterbury.
1188 Merchants as well as nobles attend the *Cortes* of Alfonso IX of Leon.
1189 Two years after Saladin expels Crusaders from Jerusalem, Pope Gregory VIII proclaims the Third Crusade.

1204 Crusaders en route to the Holy Land sack Constantinople and take over the Byzantine Empire, sharing it out among Western nations.
1212 The Children's Crusade, made up of poor peasants and led by a 12-year-old boy, leaves Marseilles; survivors of the subsequent shipwreck are sold as slaves.
1215 King John of England signs *Magna Carta*, a charter binding him to maintain his barons' privileges and uphold the law of the land.

1258 Baghdad falls to Mongol invaders from the Far East.
1265 In England, rebel baron Simon De Montfort calls the first parliament to include knights and merchants as well as peers of the realm.

1309 Pope Clement V moves the papacy from strife-torn Italy to Avignon in southern France.

...on is profoundly influenced by the rapid rise of Islam: by 732, a century after ...rthern Africa, Spain, and into France. Muslim Spain is one of the most ...academic freedom where scholars are able to preserve, extend, and ...of this Moorish learning gradually seeps into Christian Europe, where ...d, Cambridge, Bologna.

1126–98 In Spain, the Muslim philosopher Averroës writes on Aristotle and Plato, linking Greek philosophy with Islam.
1140 Peter Abelard, an influential but unorthodox Parisian theologian and teacher, is found guilty of heresy.

1155 The Carmelite Order is founded by a group of hermits living on Mount Carmel.
1176 In Spain, Maimonides writes *Guide of the Perplexed* – a plea for a rational view of philosophy and Judaism.

1210 Francis of Assisi forms the Friars Minor, an order sworn to poverty and helping the needy.
1233 Pope Gregory IX sets up the Holy Office, or Inquisition – a church tribunal empowered to investigate heresy and enforce orthodoxy.

c.1260 In *Summa Theologiae*, Italian theologian Thomas Aquinas attempts to reconcile religious belief and astrology by accepting the influence of the planets on humans, while stressing the importance of free will.

Marco Polo arrives at Hormuz

c.1150–1250 The ideals of chivalry and courtly love enjoy a vogue among Europe's aristocracy.
1154 The *Anglo-Saxon Chronicles*, recording events in England from 880–1154, are written.
1166 Henry II of England introduces a jury system for criminal trials.

1231 Frederick II of Germany introduces gold coinage.
1241 The Baltic ports of Hamburg and Lübeck form a trading *Hansa* (association), founding the Hanseatic League.

c.1290 The guild system, whereby traders and merchants form trade associations to regulate standards and prices, is well established in Europe.
1298 Venetian traveler Marco Polo publishes an account of his travels to China.
c.1298 The spinning wheel is used to make wool yarn in England.

1310 Chinese manufacturers are using water-powered machines to make silk and iron.

c.1100 The Romanesque style of art and architecture is at its peak.
c.1125 Troubadour poets flourish in the Languedoc, southern France.
1137–44 St. Denis, the first great Gothic cathedral, is built in Paris.
1150 The temple of Angkor Wat is built in Cambodia.

c.1173 Chrétien de Troyes writes the earliest surviving versions of the legends of King Arthur.

1210 Gottfried von Strassburg writes the poem *Tristan und Isolde*.
1212 Wolfram von Eschenbach writes the German epic *Parzival*.
1236 The great narrative poem *Romance of the Rose* is written.
c.1250 Town guilds in England begin performing mystery plays in their own languages instead of Latin.

c.1265 The Gothic style of architecture, distinguished by elaborate carvings, ribbed vaults, and flying buttresses, reaches its apogee.

1306 Giotto completes his masterpiece, a fresco cycle at Padua. He ignores the rigid rules followed by his contemporaries to create a fresh, naturalistic style of painting.
1307–21 Italian poet Dante Alighieri writes the *Divine Comedy*, in which he is taken through heaven and hell by his dead beloved.
1344 Italian lyric poet Francesco Petrarch is made the Poet Laureate in Rome. His sonnets were to be highly influential on Renaissance writers.

Stained glass at Basilica of St. Denis

1175 Ptolemy's *Almagest*, with its theory that the Earth is the center of the universe, is translated into Latin.
1178 The Chinese scholar Han Chan-chi describes 27 varieties of orange in *Chu lu (Treatise on Oranges)*.
c.1180 Windmills are in use in Europe.

1204 Leonardo Fibonacci of Pisa publishes the *Liber Abaci* (Book of the Abacus), a Latin outline of Arabic mathematics.

c.1280 Magnifying glasses and eyeglasses are used in Italy.

1317 Pope John XXII bans alchemy, an early type of chemistry searching for ways to turn base metal into gold and to create an elixir of life.
1324 Cannon are made in Germany.

The Lover and his Rose from the Romance of the Rose

Politics

1350 Prague is declared the imperial capital of the Holy Roman Empire by Emperor Charles IV and Prague University is founded.
1350 Charles IV publishes "the Golden Bull," an edict declaring that his successor will be elected by a college of seven.
1377 Pope Gregory XI returns the papacy to Rome.
1377–81 Widespread peasant unrest throughout Europe results in improved conditions for peasants.
1381–82 English and French people revolt against high taxes.

1400 Bubonic plague has returned several times since 1351: 1369–71, 1390, and 1400. The population decline has resulted in labor shortages, and peasants with greater bargaining power are able to win greater freedom. By 1400, feudalism has decayed, and serfs have been replaced by free peasants in most of Europe.
1417 Outnumbered by five to one, the English defeat the French at Agincourt thanks to the longbow.
1429 17-year-old Joan of Arc leads the French to victory against the English. She was following the orders of voices that she heard in her father's garden.
1430 St. Joan is martyred.

Page from the Gutenberg Bible

1478 Ferdinand and Isabella obtain permission from the pope to launch an Inquisition. Torture and burning of Jews who had been forced to convert to Christianity begins and will continue for many years.
1492 The Spanish defeat the Muslims at their last stronghold in Spain, Granada. Three months later, all 150,000 Spanish Jews are expelled.

Philosophy & Spirituality

1380 John Wycliffe translates the Bible into English. His followers, the "Lollards," believe that people should read the Bible without the help of a priest.

1417 Pope Martin V is elected. This ends the "Great Schism" within the Roman Church, under which there were two rival popes, one at Avignon and one at Rome.

1455 Johann Gutenberg, the inventor of movable type in Europe, publishes the Gutenberg Bible in Latin, marking the beginning of the wide availability of copies of the Bible.
1470 The Italian humanist Marsilio Ficino translates Plato's *Dialogues* into Latin.

1484 Pope Innocent VIII publishes a bull deploring witchcraft in Germany, thus giving official approval to the practice of torturing and burning alleged witches.
1486 The *Malleus Malleficorum* (Witch Hammer), an encyclopedia of witchcraft, is published by two Dominican friars.

Human Sciences

c.1399 In his three-volume history, Ibn Khaldun suggests that geography influences events.

1434 One of Henry the Navigator's ships rounds Cape Bojador, opening up the west coast of Africa to exploration. The Portuguese king sent numerous expeditions to map Africa and the Canary Islands.

1484 A nautical almanac is published in Portugal.
1488 Bartolomeo Diaz rounds Cape of Good Hope.
1492 Columbus makes landfall in the New World 35 days after leaving the Canaries.
1497 Genoese explorer John Cabot claims Labrador for the English king, Henry VII.
1498 Portuguese navigator Vasco da Gama reaches India by sea.

Art

The Arnofini Wedding by Jan van Eyck

1353 Italian poet Giovanni Boccacio writes *The Decameron*, a collection of prose tales told over 10 days by a group of young people escaping the plague in the country.
1358 The Alhambra Palace is built in Granada, Spain.
1372–1433 Brunelleschi completes the cupola of Duomo at Florence.
1387–1400 Geoffrey Chaucer writes the *Canterbury Tales*, a collection of verse stories in English about a group of pilgrims.

1434 Flemish painter Jan van Eyck paints his celebrated *Giobanni Arnolfini and his Wife*. Working for wealthy patrons at the Court of Burgundy, van Eyck is one of the first artists to produce easel paintings and to paint in oils. Works of art commissioned by secular patrons rather than religious houses are a new phenomenon.
1435 The rules of perspective are systematized by Leon Alberti in *On Painting*.

c.1450–c.1550 THE RENAISSANCE The wealth and power of arts and learning called the Renaissance because it is seen as the Renaissance spreads across Europe. Artists and thinkers look back to inspiration. Great patrons, such as Lorenzo de Medici in Florence and Raphael, Leonardo, and Michelangelo. The new rules of perspective architecture, buildings are designed to reflect the proportions of the destiny, is in fact the main theme of Renaissance thinking. The ideal day, Henry VIII of England and François I of France: both are

1459 The Palazzo Medici-Riccardi in Florence, commissioned by Cosimo di Medici, is completed. Cosimo is the first great secular patron of art. His palace contains many specially commissioned works, including the sculpture *David* by Donatello.
c.1470 English writer Sir Thomas Mallory completes his prose version of the Arthurian romance, *Le Morte D'Arthur*.

1488 Michelangelo is apprenticed to artist Domenico Ghirlandaio. Before the rise of art academies in the 17th century, aspiring artists could only gain instruction through apprenticeship.

Science

1473 The first edition of Galen's work is published and becomes widely used.

1489 Johan Widman invents the mathematical symbols + and −.
1492 German navigator Martin Behaim invents the globe.

| 1625–1649 | 1650–1674 | 1675–1700 | 1700–1724 | 1725–1750 |

1649 Roman Catholic English King Charles I is deposed by Protestant rebels and executed. His death and trial put into question the concept of the divine right of kings.

1652 The Dutch settle at the Cape of Good Hope.
1653 England is governed by Oliver Cromwell, Lord Protector, a council of state and an elected parliament.
1660 By popular demand, Charles II ascends the English throne. Charles grants the people freedom of conscience and the rebel leaders an amnesty.

The Sun King, Louis XVI

1682 French King Louis XIV moves his court to Versailles.
1685 Louis XIV begins systematic persecution of Protestants.
1685 France's West Indian slaves are given certain rights – such as adequate food.
1688–89 In England, Catholic James II is replaced by Protestant William of Orange. A Bill of Rights allows parliament to vote for taxes and raise an army.

1713 The Treaty of Utrecht reshapes the map of Europe. Spain loses half of Italy to Austria.

1732 A group of handpicked debtors is sent to found a colony in Georgia.
1732 Frederick of Prussia introduces military service.
1739 Frederick the Great, under Voltaire's wing, writes the treatise *Antimachiavelli* which affirms a princely ethic founded on virtue, justice, and responsibility.

1714 Berkeley argues that the only reality is the idea of what objects are, not the objects themselves.
1718 The first Masonic Lodge is founded in London.

1644 René Descartes' *Principia Philosophiae* is published. Descartes reformulated scientific thinking in the 17th century with his attempts to describe the whole of knowledge using mathematics.

1651 English philosopher Hobbe's *Leviathan* is published.
1654 Spinoza suggest that science and the Bible can never be reconciled.
1670 Blaise Pascal's *Pensees*, a discussion of the agony of faith, is published posthumously.

1678 French philosopher Richard Simon's *History of the Old Testament* pioneers criticism of the Bible.
1690 English philosopher John Locke's *Essays* lay the epistemological foundations of modern science.

A Masonic sun woven into a German carpet

1734 Voltaire publishes his *Lettres Philosophiques*.
1739 John Wesley founds the Methodist movement, a rational approach to Protestantism.
1748 Scottish philosopher David Hume's *Enquiry Concerning Human Understanding* is published.
1750 Montesquieu's *Spirit of Laws* is published.

Rembrandt's Bathsheba Bathing

1694 The Bank of England is created.

1720 Investors rush to put money into the South Sea Company. The value of shares soars and then plummets, plunging many investors into bankruptcy.
1721 French historian Montesquieu publishes *Persian Letters*, a satirical portrait of French civilization.

1748 Pompeii is excavated, sparking public interest in ancient Rome and in archaeology in general.

1726 Anglo-Irishman Jonathan Swift satirizes European society in *Gulliver's Travels*.
1740 English writer Samuel Richardson's *Pamela*, a novel in the form of a collection of letters, is published. It influences many other "epistolary" novels.
1749 English writer Joseph Fielding's *Tom Jones* is published. It influences the development of the "picaresque" novel (from the Spanish genre of tales about a *picaro*, or rogue).

1637 Spanish writer Maria de Zayas y Sofomayor publishes early horror stories.
1642 Theaters in England are closed by the Puritans.
1648 The Académie Royale, a highly influential art school, opens in Paris. Many art academies are founded in imitation.

c.1650 Artists in Holland can – for the first time in history – work independently of patrons, producing work to be sold at auction.
1658 Molière and his troup take over the Palais Royal Theater.
1667 John Milton's epic poem, *Paradise Lost*, the story of the fall of Adam and Eve, is published.

1680 The Comédie Francaise is founded and becomes the national theater of France.

1710 Work finally completed on the Palace of Versailles, built for the French king Louis XIV. It becomes the model for a series of baroque palaces built across Europe.
1719 English writer Daniel Defoe composes *Robinson Crusoe*.

The 17th century saw a radical new approach to "natural philosophy." Technological advances – the inventions of the
w ways of looking at the world. The teachings of the ancients were reexamined and found to be inaccurate. Old assumptions
d Galileo used the evidence of their own senses to make deductions about the nature of the universe.

1735 Swedish naturalist Carolus Linnaeus' *Systema Naturae* is published. It contains his system for classifying plants into groups, depending on shared characteristics.

1628 English physician William Harvey's *Circulation of the Blood* marked the beginning of the end of medicine as taught by the Greek physician Galen, which had been accepted for 1,400 years. Harvey showed that blood must flow only to the heart and circulates continuously.

1651 Harvey suggests that babies are produced by egg and sperm.
1660 The club for scientists, the Royal Society, is founded in London.
1661 John Evelyn warns of the effects of air pollution on health in London. He suggests planting more trees.

1675 The Greenwich Observatory is founded.
1677 Dutch scientist Anton van Leeuwenhoek discovers microscopic organisms.
1687 English scientist Isaac Newton writes *Principia Mathematica*, in which he develops his three laws of motion and the universal law of gravitation and invents calculus.

1704 Newton sums up his life's work on light in *Opticks*. A byproduct of this work was the development of the reflecting telescope.
1705 Edmund Halley accurately predicts the return of the comet that bears his name.
1714 Gottfried Leibniz's *Monadology* explains a new branch of mathematics, calculus.

Sir Isaac Newton

Politics

Violent upheaval and peaceful evolution have both brought great change to the political scene in the last 250 years.

Every government, from the earliest civilizations to today, has had two main tasks: to defend its citizens from attack, and to give them a legal framework to help them live together in harmony. Yet modern governments do far more than this, among other tasks, running schools and hospitals, providing welfare, building roads, and regulating trade.

Today's political systems are a synthesis of old ideas – some of which (like democracy) date back to the city-states of ancient Greece – and new concepts. One such idea – that governments depend on the consent of the governed in a "social contract" – evolved in the 17th and 18th centuries at a time of great political upheaval, when people risked their lives in civil war and revolution to attack the authority of absolute monarchs.

The writers who formulated this theory – Thomas Hobbes, John Locke, and Jean Jacques Rousseau – were striving to analyze and explain the political realities of the day. Other thinkers provided theories which became the foundation of new types of political action. Karl Marx's vision of workers uniting to throw off the shackles of their masters inspired violent change in the Russian Revolution; it also filtered more peacefully into mainstream socialism and trade unionism.

The last 250 years have seen many political certainties crumble, such as the rule of monarchy and the right of one country to colonize others, and others rise to take their place. Freedom of speech, once a rare privilege, is now generally regarded as a human right. Democracy, if based on free elections and a genuine choice of political parties, is preferable to dictatorship, however benign; women and members of ethnic groups must be allowed to vote; the poor must have a political voice.

If universal suffrage, secret ballots, and the welfare state have transformed government, so has technology. The mass media has become hugely influential. Politicians depend on soundbites and photo opportunities created by spin doctors for the benefit of news editors. In the age of television, a good haircut may swing an election, while a single gaffe can be replayed with distorting effect. This hardly seems an appropriate culmination to the political struggles of the last few centuries, but the next millennium may see a new emphasis on older values such as truth, justice, and equality.

MAKING HISTORY Martin Luther King talks to the press in Birmingham, Alabama, in 1963.

REVOLUTION
Popular uprising or elitist coup?

Each political revolution follows its own distinctive course. But every revolution is a sharp, sudden change in the political and social order – almost always carried through by resort to arms – that leads to a permanent and more or less radical alteration of government. Revolution implies a change in the structure of society that is – in the propaganda of the revolutionaries at any rate – for the benefit of the people.

Giuseppe Mazzini (1805–72), the Italian nationalist, thought that ideas held pride of place in a revolution. "Great revolutions," he said, "are the work rather of principles than of bayonets, and are achieved first in the moral, and afterward in the material, sphere." What is certain is that every revolution is successful; if it fails, it goes down in history as an insurrection or conspiracy. Every revolution succeeds, in the end, because the forces opposed to it prove too weak to withstand it. But states are usually equipped to keep down the oppressed or the discontented. That is why there are many more failed rebellions in history than successful revolutions.

Can one detect in history a common weakness that has made some societies succumb to revolution? Probably not. Military defeat has often been a catalyst, as it was in Russia in 1917. Plato (*c.*427–347 BC) believed that every revolution stemmed from an outbreak of dissension within the ruling class. Certainly a crisis of authority afflicted the French government on the eve of the fall of the Bastille in 1789.

But before a revolution can enter the pages of history the new masters have to consolidate their authority and gain the obedience of the people – whether by assent or by force. Some revolutions, like the American rebellion against British rule that broke out in 1775, spring from the people. Popular assent is not in question. Others, like the Bolshevik coup in Russia, have either to succeed in winning over the people after the event or to impose themselves on the people by force. Usually, in fact, they have to do both.

DECLARATION OF INDEPENDENCE

Nothing shows more clearly the new respectability of revolution at the beginning of the modern era than the ringing confidence with which the framers of the American *Declaration of Independence* in 1776 proclaimed the justice of the colonists' cause. The Declaration is a statement of Enlightenment aspiration to progress, underpinned by the liberal adherence to the idea of natural rights and to the notion that government must be based on consent. In magnificent prose that has resounded down to our own time, it distilled the political theory of the Enlightenment into a few short sentences: "We hold these truths to be self-evident, that all men are created equal, that they are endowed by their Creator with certain unalienable rights, that among these are Life, Liberty, and the pursuit of Happiness. That to secure these rights, Governments are instituted among Men, deriving their just powers from the consent of the governed. That whenever any Form of Government becomes destructive of these ends, it is the Right of the People to alter or abolish it, and to institute new Government."

A FEW GOOD MEN Benjamin Franklin, Samuel Adams and red-headed Thomas Jefferson (from left to right) pause to discuss the contents of the Declaration of Independence before continuing to write it.

THE AMERICAN CONSTITUTION

The American Constitution, adopted by the 13 states of the new union in 1787, was not, by modern standards, a democratic document. Its framers agreed with John Locke (1632–1704) that the chief purpose of government was the preservation of property, and one of the forms of property that it protected was slavery. Indeed, for the purpose of deciding the size of each state's population – and therefore the number of members each should have in the House of Representatives – a slave was counted as three-fifths of a person.

In two ways, however, the constitution was revolutionary. The first was simply the fact that a whole people had shown that it was possible to devise a new society and a new form of government from scratch. More important was its republicanism, easy to take for granted now, but then genuinely radical. England had overthrown the monarchy in 1649, but the Stuarts had been restored to the throne 11 years later. All of Europe assumed that political order and good government were founded on monarchy and aristocracy.

There was no place for either in the new American constitution (the members of the upper chamber, or Senate, were elected, not chosen by accident of birth). As Thomas Paine (1737–1809), the great defender of American independence, wrote, "the romantic and barbarous distinction of men into Kings and subjects" was exploded by the system on which governments were now being founded. "The hereditary system is as repugnant to human wisdom as to human rights; it is as absurd as it is unjust."

MAN OF IDEAS Denis Diderot's wit and intelligence gave him access to Parisian high society, but it was his humble origins that gave his thinking its originality.

THE FRENCH "PHILOSOPHES"

Do ideas drive the course of history? Can books alter the direction of political events? No direct chain of causation between an idea and a political outcome can be established, but there is little doubt that the French *philosophes* of the 18th century – notably Denis Diderot (1713–84), Voltaire (1694–1778) and Jean Jacques Rousseau (1712–78) – prepared the soil and planted the seeds from which the French Revolution was to burst into life. Diderot edited that monument to radical scepticism, the vast *Encyclopédie*. Voltaire led the assault on clericalism and established religion with his famous cry, *écrasez l'infâme* ("crush the infamous thing"). Rousseau preached egalitarianism in his *Discourse on the Origin of Inequality* (1754).

The philosophes were widely read. Many of their works were passed along the sophisticated underground network that developed across Europe to thwart the censors. Their ideas and the spirit of liberty which lay behind them – known collectively as the French Enlightenment – were grounded in an unquenchable faith in the power and utility of human reason. They consistently challenged the ascendancy of outmoded traditions, superstitions and prejudices.

These philosophers were not, as they have often been portrayed, facile optimists, seduced into believing in the inevitability of moral, social, and political progress. Nor, however, did they succumb to the pessimistic conclusion that injustice and unfairness could not be overthrown. Their great work was not simply to promote the exercise of reason, but to make reason prevail in practical affairs for the improvement of mankind.

SUPREME RATIONALIST In his long career, Voltaire's fortunes rose and fell according to the political mood. At one time a favorite at court, he was forced into exile for nearly 20 years.

SEE ALSO

Liberalism · · · · · · · · · · · · · ▶
Romanticism & subjectivity · · · · · ▶
Industrialization · · · · · · · · · · · ▶

ABOLITION OF FEUDALISM

FEUDAL RIGHTS Louis XIV rides to hounds. Feudal hunting rights were among the first symbols of the old order to be abolished by the revolution.

Along with the execution of Louis XVI and the abolition of the monarchy, the most symbolic act of the French revolutionary assembly was the abolition of feudalism on August 4, 1789. Serfdom was abolished. The privileges of the seigneurial (manorial) courts were swept away, along with the seigneurial hunt, the seigneurial pigeon cote, and the seigneurial rabbit warren. Tax privileges and tax exemptions for members of the nobility were also ended.

It was not so much that France was actually a feudal state – although the feudal hangovers were irritants that had helped to produce the revolutionary mood – nor that the great landowners lost much financially by the change. What mattered was the implication that it was possible for a people to rid itself of its past and construct for itself a new society.

A new age dawned with the spreading rays of equal taxation, equal opportunity, equal justice. The notion of citizens, all equal before the law, replaced the old idea of subjects, with varying ranks assigned in a hierarchical order.

"RIGHTS OF MAN"

The phrase "rights of man," which came into common currency at the time of the American and French revolutions, grew out of the 18th-century belief that a person had natural rights simply because he existed.

Those natural rights were defined in the *Declaration of the Rights of Man and Citizens* adopted by the French revolutionary assembly in 1789 as "liberty, property, security, and the right to resist oppression." The first clause of the Declaration – "Men are born, and always continue, free and equal in respect of their rights" – was a direct echo of the writings of the Swiss-born philosopher Jean Jacques Rousseau. But another clause went a long way to undermine the notion of natural rights. "The exercise of the natural rights of every man has no limits other than those which are necessary to secure to every other man the free exercise of the same rights. And those limits are determinable only by law."

The French Declaration was a practical statement about the rights of citizens. Its focus was man-in-society, not man-as-individual. Though rooted in the idea of natural rights, it acknowledged that no person is born with rights. Rights do not exist until they are embodied in law. The French Declaration was a powerful, if indirect, statement of the truth that the foundation of liberty and freedom, of all civil society, is the rule of law.

LATIN AMERICAN INDEPENDENCE

The message of the French Revolution crossed the Atlantic and inspired a freed slave called Toussaint L'Ouverture (1746–1803) in the French Caribbean colony of St. Domingue. In 1800 he and his followers rebelled, conquering the Spanish half of the island of Hispaniola. He declared himself governor of the whole island. A large force dispatched by Napoleon Bonaparte failed to suppress the revolt, and in 1804 the new republic of Haiti was recognized – the second independent nation to arise in the New

CONQUERING HEROES In 1829, Simón Bolívar triumphantly enters Caracas, the capital of Venezuela.

World after the United States. The world was astonished by a successful slave revolt, and the example hastened the end of the slave trade.

The torch of revolution passed to the great Latin American patriots, José de San Martín (1778–1850) and Simón Bolívar (1783–1830). The generalship of these men forced Spain to relinquish most of its territories in the New World, and its place was taken, by the end of the 1820s, by the independent nations of Chile, Peru, Bolivia, Venezuela, Colombia, Ecuador, and Panama.

NAPOLEON BONAPARTE

The American wit Ambrose Bierce (1842–1914) defined a revolution as "an abrupt change in the form of misgovernment." It is widely held that all revolutions betray their instigators' idealism and end in a new form of tyranny.

To some, Napoleon was the true son of the French Revolution, who, after his rapid rise to leadership of France continued to deepen the liberalism of the revolution by his legal and administrative reforms, most famously the systemization of law into the *Code Napoléon*. But his critics argue just as strongly that Napoleon overturned the revolution. The nation-in-arms, amassed originally to defend French borders against its enemies and to carry the idea of liberation abroad, became simply the instrument of his personal ambition and the tool of his lust for conquest. By making himself emperor for life, he granted himself personal power equal to any possessed by the Bourbon kings, whose absolutism it had been the very purpose of the revolution to destroy. Monarchy, under Napoleon, was restored in new garb, and the military pursuit of *gloire* was undertaken with the same pride and instinct for territorial aggrandizement Louis XIV had shown.

> ## *"…but yesterday a King!*
> ## *…and now thou art a nameless thing:*
> ## *So abject – yet alive!"*
>
> *Lord Byron (1788–1824), "Ode to Napoleon Bonaparte"*

LIBERTY UNDER ARREST The failure of the 1848 uprisings dashed the hopes of liberals seeking to reform government throughout the German principalities.

THE REVOLUTIONS OF 1848

"When Paris sneezes," the great Austrian chancellor Fürst von Metternich (1773–1859) wrote, "Europe catches cold." In February 1848, the citizens of Paris rose in armed revolt against the government, and in the following weeks almost every European country, except Russia and Great Britain, went down the same route. Yet though thrones toppled and governments fell, by the end of 1849 order was restored. Nowhere, however, did the revolts achieve nothing.

The twin watchwords of the revolutionaries were liberalism and nationalism. Throughout Europe, liberalism made a permanent advance. In France itself, the monarchy was extinguished after its revival in 1815.

The greatest achievement occurred in Vienna, where Metternich and his repressive "system" were overthrown, although the Hapsburg emperor Franz Josef I (1830–1916) kept his throne. In the central and eastern European domains of the Hapsburgs, feudalism was nearly swept away.

NATIONALISM
The creation of a community of blood

The idea of nationalism stems from the belief that there are characteristics that separate one group of people from another. The word itself comes from the Latin *natio* for "birthplace"; hence its development into the idea of a tribal or social group based on a real or imagined community of blood. Above all, nationalism is the political principle that people of shared national characteristics should be free to bind themselves together in a sovereign, independent state.

Modern nationalism dates from the 18th century. The word was apparently first used by the German philosopher Johann Gottfried von Herder (1744–1803). It became fashionable to assert that a national identity was the product of a combination of elements that included a common ethnic ancestry, a shared historical and cultural experience, and a common language. That the emotional attachment to nationalism became prominent at the time was partly a reaction against the way Enlightenment philosophers stressed the universality of all human experience while minimizing the importance of local historical events. Napoleon's effort to bring Europe under French hegemony spurred the growth of nationalist opposition outside France.

Language has often been a crucial element in the formation of nationalist feeling. English nationality could not arise until Anglo-Saxon merged with Norman French to give birth to the English language, nor French nationality until a similar fusion had occurred between Frankish German and Latin to produce French. Whether religion holds a primary place in the formation of national identity is questionable, but it is certainly in the mix. The rise of national feeling in Europe coincided with the Reformation – when the primacy of Latin was undermined by increasing use of vernacular languages. The great Protestant reformers – Martin Luther (1483–1546) in Germany, John Knox (*c.*1513–72) in Scotland, John Calvin (1509–64) in France – appealed unashamedly to nationalist arguments.

The various components of nationalism give the inhabitants of a state a sense of apartness. So nationalism may come to encourage feelings of superiority and, in its extreme forms, engender chauvinism, xenophobia, and militarism. Undoubtedly, it has kindled wars, and for that reason people eager to combat what they see as its baleful influence have erected international bodies against it.

COMMON MEN Members of the revolutionary National Assembly stand up to suggest that the state may be a more suitable object of worship than God.

REVOLUTIONARY NATIONALISM IN FRANCE

"The world is my country," said the great 18th-century essayist Thomas Paine (1737–1809); "mankind are my brothers." In similar vein was a remark by Jean Jacques Rousseau (1712–78): "No more are there Frenchmen, Spaniards, Germans, or even Englishmen; there are only Europeans." They spoke just before the French Revolution of 1789 drowned the universalist impulse of Enlightenment rationalism in a torrent of popular nationalism.

French nationalism was a potent emotion because wrapped within it was the heady idea that the revolution was the expression of the will of the people. That the new revolutionary parliament which replaced the old Estates-General was called the National Assembly was symptomatic of the swelling of nationalist feeling.

The *grande armée* of revolutionary France, raised by the *levée en masse*, was the first in European history to approach the ideal of a people's army. The French Revolution gave birth to a number of potent symbols of nationalism: the national flag (the tricolor), the national anthem (*La Marseillaise*), and national holidays.

NATIONAL UNIFICATION OF GERMANY

Otto von Bismarck (1815–98), the architect of German unification, was the great practitioner of *realpolitik*, or politics as "the art of the possible." Great affairs of state, he said, were not to be settled by speech-making and the decisions of majorities, but by "iron and blood." War was the instrument of Bismarck's national ambitions.

His greatest achievement was to unite the numerous principalities of Germany under Prussian leadership in the North German Confederation of 1867. The new confederation was the expression of a muted nationalism. It was won by defeating Austria in war (1866), thus bringing to an end the Austrian-dominated German Confederation that had been established in 1815. "Little Germany" was Bismarck's description of the new federation, but it was far from little. In 1864 Prussian arms had already gained Schleswig-Holstein for the union. And after defeating France in 1870, Bismarck added Alsace-Lorraine to his dominions, so that when the German Empire was proclaimed in 1871, there was no doubt that it was the greatest power in continental Europe.

POWERBROKING Otto von Bismarck, probably at the time the most powerful man in Europe, leads the 1878 Berlin Congress that divided the Balkan States between Europe and the Ottoman Empire.

IRREDENTISM

Irredentism, a word derived from the Italian *irredentista* for "unredeemed," was the name of a movement begun in the late 1870s to recover for Italy the "lost territories" of Trentino, Istria, and South Tyrol. The campaign was really the last stage of the *risorgimento* ("resurrection"), the mid-19th century nationalist struggle, led by Camillo Cavour (1810–61) and Giuseppe Garibaldi (1807–82), to oust the Austrian occupiers from Italy and unify the kingdom under Victor Emmanuel of Sardinia in 1861. Venetia was absorbed into the kingdom in 1866 and Rome in 1870, but the *risorgimento* was not complete until the collapse of the Austro-Hungarian Empire in World War I and the recovery of the "lost territories" by the Treaty of St. Germain in 1919.

Irredentism was a diluted form of more purely national self-determination, bringing as it did Germans and Slovenes within Italian sovereignty and thus creating new "irredenta" for Slovenia and Germany. The term may be used to describe any such campaign as the Italian one. Germany looked upon the recovery of Alsace-Lorraine from France in the Franco-Prussian war of 1870 as the return of a province that was German in the Middle Ages.

FREEDOM FIGHTER
Contemporary commentators saw the Italian nationalist Giuseppe Garibaldi as, on one hand, a tough, passionate, little fighter (above) and on the other, an ideal romantic hero (below).

SEE ALSO

Revolution · · · · · · · · · · · · · · · ◀
Internationalism · · · · · · · · · · · ▶
The Enlightenment · · · · · · · · · · ▶
Romanticism & subjectivity · · · · · ▶

IRISH HOME RULE

No country shows better the part that religion can play as the yeast in the nationalist pudding than Ireland. The conquest and settlement of Roman Catholic Ireland by English and Scottish Protestants in the 16th and 17th centuries and the subjection of "John Bull's other island" to rule by Protestant landowners – known as the Ascendancy – was confirmed by the union of the two countries in 1801. The union produced the drawn-out campaign for independence that dominated Irish politics in the 19th century. Economic issues, especially land hunger, were also important, but it was the religious divide that brought high passion to the struggle. That struggle is not yet over.

The division of the island in 1921 into an independent Irish nation to the south, overwhelmingly Roman Catholic, and the United Kingdom province of Northern Ireland, with its majority of Protestants, has never satisfied nationalists. The fight for a united Ireland is carried on by the Sinn Fein ("Ourselves Alone") party and the terrorist organization, the Irish Republican Army (IRA).

"Too long a sacrifice
Can make a stone of the heart."

W.B. Yeats (1865–1939), Irish poet and patriot,
of the failed nationalist uprising in Dublin, Easter 1916

PAN-NATIONALISM

A powerful ingredient of political romanticism in the early 19th century was the assumption that peoples of different nationalities, as long as they spoke related languages, were joined together in one supranational family. That idea gave rise to a number of movements prefixed by the word pan, the Greek for "all."

Of these, the most important was Pan-Slavism, used by nationalists in the Balkans to win Russian backing in their struggles to throw off the Austro-Hungarian or Turkish yoke. After 1945, Russia's "Pan-Slavist mission" was a useful gloss on the imposition of communism in Eastern Europe.

"Pan-Germanism" was used by the Nazis to gain support in Germany for the absorption of Austria and the Sudetenland province of Czechoslovakia into the Third Reich. The notion of Pan-Africanism has played its rhetorical role in the recent liberation struggles against colonialism.

NOVELIST AND NATIONALIST The support of Russian novelist Fyodor Dostoyevsky (1821–88) for Pan-Slavism was a result of his broadly xenophobic outlook, which also expressed itself in an antipathy to "foreigners" resident in Russia, including Germans and Jews.

SEPARATISM

THUMBS DOWN Basque graffiti graphically displays regional hostility to both French and Spanish rule. Basque separatists have been waging a terrorist campaign against Spanish dominion since the late 1960s.

In 1918 President Woodrow Wilson (1856–1924) presented his "Fourteen Points" to the peace conference at Paris. High on the list was the principle that every people has a right to self-determination. That ideal was not everywhere upheld in the treaties that ended World War I, but it has inspired separatist movements around the world since.

Separatism – that is, a regional movement for independence from a federal or national state – has found fertile soil in Scotland, in the Canadian province of Quebec, and in the Basque region of Spain. Ruling authorities invariably offer stiff resistance to separatist campaigns, despite the fact that these call for an end to a subjection that was originally imposed, however distantly in time, by force of arms. None of the above three has yet achieved success (although a Basque republic survived briefly in 1936–37 until it was crushed by General Franco's forces).

Conquering powers that have treated the conquered people most leniently have thereby sown the seeds of separatism. The French-speaking, predominantly Roman Catholic, population of Quebec was granted its own legal and educational systems, and its own church, within the Canadian federation, as were the Scots within the United Kingdom. That limited autonomy has helped to nurture the desire for national independence. It remains to be seen whether separatism, in an age of multinational corporations and multicultural politics, is an idea that has already outlived its time.

ZIONISM

Named after Mount Zion in Jerusalem, Zionism was a movement founded by Theodore Herzl (1860–1904). In 1897, he organized the first World Zionist Council at Basel to agitate for the creation of an independent Jewish nation in Palestine. Zionism was the enemy of "assimilationism," the doctrine that Jews could work out their destinies within whatever nation they found themselves. The Zionist movement gathered strength as anti-Semitism advanced in Europe in the early decades of the 20th century.

Zionism heaped scorn on the liberal view of the Jews as a mere ethnic group. Herzl argued that the Jews had an historical cultural identity that made them (as it was put in the German context) a *Volk*, or "racial nation," with claim to the long-lost biblical homeland of Palestine. Zionism offered itself as the leash that could control the monster of anti-Semitism. The establishment of an independent Jewish state, it was argued, would win for Jews the respect of non-Jews.

But Zionism's claim that Palestine was "a land without a people for a people without a land" was false: the creation of the state of Israel in 1948 displaced hundreds of thousands of Palestinian Arabs from their homes and spawned the Palestinian nationalist struggle, led by Yassir Arafat (1929–) and the PLO (Palestine Liberation Organization). Zionism's aim of building a secure state for the Jews has yet to be achieved. Nor has its second great objective – to bring most of the world's Jews together in a single state – been fulfilled.

BREAKING RANKS Orthodox Jews demonstrate against the state of Israel, which they believe is in itself sacrilegious. They argue that, according to the Bible, the Jewish people should return to settle in Israel only when the Messiah has come.

DEMOCRACY
Government by the people

In his Gettysburg address of 1863, President Abraham Lincoln (1809–65) said that the American Civil War was a struggle to guarantee that "government of the people, by the people, for the people" should not perish from the Earth. Democracy may, technically, be nothing more than a method – the election of some sort of representative government by the people. But a true democracy is something more than an exercise to let people think that they rule the nation so that they will consent to be governed.

Democracy is, indeed, more about means than ends. The communist justification for calling the "people's republics" of postwar Eastern Europe democracies was that, since the state owned the means of production and distribution and used them for the benefit of its citizens, it served the good of the people. Of course, that defense of one-party, totalitarian systems was incompatible with Western notions of democracy.

The English philosopher John Stuart Mill (1806–73) insisted that true democracy must foster "the diffusion of intelligence, activity, and public spirit among the governed." That was also the position taken by perhaps the best modern thinker about democracy, the American political philosopher John Dewey (1859–1952), who believed that democracy promoted communication between people and led them to informed deliberation and collective action in pursuit of the improvement of society. In Dewey's view, democracy alone among political systems could give expression to a pragmatic, experimental approach to the world – one that neither bowed down before authority nor worshiped an ideal notion of absolute truth. To his way of thinking, democracy facilitated the search for usefulness by allowing individuals to exercise their responsibilities in a shared, common life.

In such a version of democracy, the place of individual "rights" is diminished in status. To exalt individual rights leads to libertarianism which, at its extreme, may be as incompatible as its totalitarian foe with the democratic spirit. To place emphasis, however, on mutual duties and shared participation leads to social democracy.

THE SOCIAL CONTRACT

PEOPLE'S CHAMPION Jean Jacques Rousseau's thesis that a people had the right to topple a bad government influenced the French revolutionaries in 1789.

The idea of a "social contract" between the government and the people has been central to debate about political systems. Three giants of philosophy provided versions of this contract.

Thomas Hobbes (1588–1679) – writing amid the turmoil of the English Civil War of the mid-17th century – said that men contracted with the sovereign to give up their freedom in return for protection. Having consented to be ruled, they were not justified in withdrawing that consent. Hobbes thus provided a defense of absolute monarchy.

John Locke (1632–1704) argued that the contract was a two-way affair. The people provisionally surrendered their freedoms but, if they were dissatisfied with their rulers, they had the right to call them to account. Locke thus provided a defense of parliamentary government and limited monarchy.

Finally, Jean Jacques Rousseau (1712–78) insisted that the social contract was made between the members of society themselves and government that failed to express the "general will" of the people was not entitled to their consent. Rousseau thus put the case for the sovereignty of the people.

REPRESENTATIVE GOVERNMENT

BOSTON TEA PARTY American colonists, incensed at high taxes, empty caskets of tea into Boston Harbor in 1773. Despite paying taxes on goods, colonists had no representatives in the British Parliament.

The phrase "representative government" is used to describe any system in which representatives are elected by the people to sit in a parliament or national assembly.

The classic theory of representation holds that, once elected, members are free to vote in the assembly according to their judgment; they are not sent to parliament as delegates mandated to carry out the wishes of their constituents. That idea was expressed by Edmund Burke (1729–97) in 1774 when he said that a representative's "unbiased opinion, his mature judgment, his enlightened conscience, he ought not to sacrifice to [his constituents]." Rousseau and Marx took the contrary view: representatives were delegates whom the people could recall if they failed to represent their constituents' opinions in the assembly.

CHARTISM

Named after the petition, or People's Charter, presented to the British House of Commons in 1838, Chartism was one of the first and largest organized mass campaigns for political reform in European history. It was a protest movement against the exclusion of the working man from participation in national politics – the Great Reform Act of 1832 essentially enfranchised sections of the middle, shop-owning class – and it was in large part a "revolt of the hungry" against long hours and woeful conditions of work in the poorly paid jobs of the new industrial age.

At the time, the British parliament was still chiefly representative of the wealthy owners of land. The Chartists sought to make it a body truly representative of the nation and therefore capable of passing legislation to benefit ordinary people.

The Charter contained six demands: the vote for all adult males, equal electoral districts, vote by secret ballot (to reduce the influence of the rich over votes), salaries for members of parliament (MPs), the removal of property qualifications for MPs (so that not only the rich could afford to enter parliament), and annual parliaments. Chartism faded away within a decade, having achieved none of its objects, but all of them except annual parliaments were eventually won.

CHILD LABOR The appalling labor conditions of this young boy – stripped naked and digging coal down a mine shaft – and others like him, drove thousands of British men to join the Chartist movement in 1838 to campaign for political reform. At the time, workers were excluded from any participation in government, and the first requisite of a seat in parliament was wealth.

TIMELINE

Universal adult suffrage
Unless given otherwise, the age of qualification is 21.

1787
Adult males (excluding black slaves) in the United States

1867
Adult males in urban seats in Great Britain

1869
Women in Wyoming state elections

1875
Adult males in France

1884
Agricultural adult males in Great Britain

1893
Women in New Zealand (first country to enfranchise women)

1917
Women in the Soviet Union

1918
Women over the age of 30 in Great Britain (lowered to age 21 in 1928)

1971
Women in Switzerland (last European nation to grant women the vote)

1971
Voting age lowered to 18 in the United States

SEE ALSO

Liberalism
The Enlightenment
Industrialization

POLITICAL PARTIES

The organization of political parties in Europe and North America was a development of the late 18th and early 19th centuries. The prevalence of revolutionary movements, and the changes to social arrangements wrought by industrialism as the 19th century went on, brought people to band together on the "left" or the "right" – terms which originated in the seating position of radicals and moderates in the French revolutionary assembly in the early 1790s.

The British Prime Minister Benjamin Disraeli (1804–81) defined party as "organized opinion," but parties are just as much organized interests: land versus the towns (a major divide in 19th-century Europe), capital versus labor, high church versus chapel, and so on. Before the rise of political parties, the center of political life was the monarch, who appointed and dismissed ministers, was ultimately responsible for public policy, and controlled the patronage which is the glue of politics. As monarchy declined in power or disappeared in Western countries, the parties rose to replace it as the engine of politics, and as the vote was extended to more and more people, and finally to all adults, parties grew in size to become the mass organizations they are today.

TYRANNY OF THE MAJORITY

"Of the three forms of sovereignty – autocracy, aristocracy, democracy – democracy," wrote the German philosopher Immanuel Kant (1724–1804), "is necessarily a despotism, because it establishes an executive power through which all the citizens may make decisions about (and indeed against) the single individual without his consent."

This alarm at a potential danger of democracy was picked up by the French writer Alexis de Tocqueville (1805–59) who, in his analysis of American democracy in the 1830s, coined the phrase the "tyranny of the majority," and by John Stuart Mill (1806–73) in England. Neither man was hostile to democracy, and each saw the threat as coming not so much from laws or direct political action, as from the stifling operation of public opinion on individual thought and behavior. The tyranny of opinion is difficult to tame. For example, homosexual relations have in the past been banned in many democratic countries, partly because of hostile public opinion. But although lawmakers need some freedom to go against public opinion in order to see justice done, their power to legislate also has to be curbed. To stop lawmakers from abusing their power to ride roughshod over the rights of the individual, many countries have adopted a bill of rights which cannot be altered by a mere vote of the majority of legislators. Great Britain, which continues to uphold the right of parliament to make whatever laws it pleases on a simple majority vote, is a notable exception.

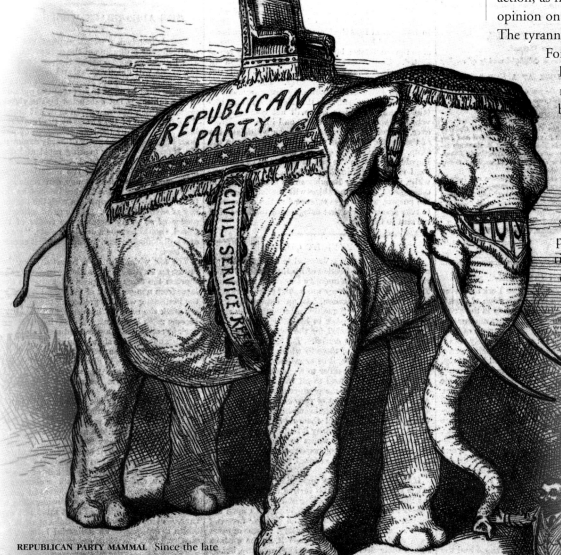

REPUBLICAN PARTY MAMMAL Since the late 19th century, cartoonists have represented the Republican Party with an elephant and the Democrats with a donkey.

REFERENDUM

FREEDOM VOTE A Zulu casts his vote in the first democratic elections in South Africa in 1994. Without a referendum the previous year, in which a majority of the white population voted to continue the dismantling of apartheid, he might still be waiting to vote.

A referendum, or plebiscite (from Greek roots, meaning "ordinance of the people"), is a vote of the electorate to approve or reject a proposal. The idea of holding referendums gained popularity toward the end of the 19th century. In the United States, the Progressives, a large movement of reformers, sought to make the referendum a permanent device of political decision-making, on the ground that it provided for "direct democracy."

Critics of the use of referendums point out that legislators are elected to make decisions, not to ask citizens to make their minds up for them. And one drawback of referendums is that a government rarely offers one to the electorate unless it is certain of having the vote go the way it wants. Referendums are most popular in Switzerland, where they are enshrined in the constitution, and where four days a year are set aside for them. The Swiss people can initiate a referendum if 50,000 people propose a change to the constitution.

CHECKS AND BALANCES

"Checks and balances" is a phrase used to describe constitutional methods of preventing one branch of government – the executive, the legislative, or the judicial – from exercising dominance over the others. The idea was originally put by the French writer Baron de Montesquieu (1689–1755), who mistakenly thought the system operated in Great Britain. In fact, in the British system, the executive (prime minister and cabinet) is drawn from the legislative majority in the House of Commons and is entirely dependent upon it. Nor does the judiciary have any independent authority to overrule parliamentary statutes.

It was the American Constitution of 1787 that provided (as it still does) for the most thorough implementation of the idea of checks and balances. There the executive (president) is elected directly and may be from a different party than the majority in the legislature (the Senate and the House of Representatives). The Supreme Court can overturn a law passed by Congress and signed by the president if it finds that law to be in violation of the constitution.

POWER STRUGGLE Midway through Democrat President Bill Clinton's first term in office (1992–96), Americans elected a Republican-dominated Senate. The ability of Senate majority leader Bob Dole (above) to block legislation put forward by Clinton (below) prevented the president from making sweeping legislative changes.

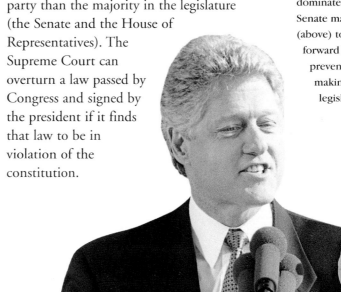

FREEDOM OF INFORMATION

SEE ALSO: *Revolution, Democracy, The Enlightenment, Moral philosophy*

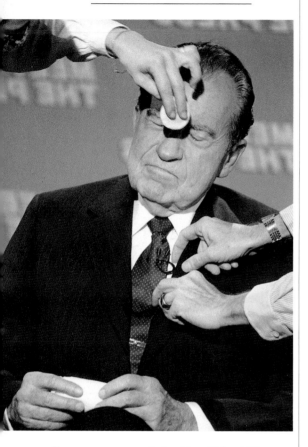

"I AM NOT A CROOK" President Richard Nixon (1913–94) gets his face powdered before going in front of the TV cameras. The Watergate affair that forced his resignation centered on the way his associates gathered secret information about his political opponents.

Knowledge is power, and secret knowledge leads to absolute power. Totalitarian systems rely on secrecy; democrats seek to dismantle it. "A large part of the prestige of dictatorships," the Bulgarian man-of-letters Elias Canetti (1905–) wrote in his study *Crowds and Power*, "is due to the fact that they are credited with the concentrated power of secrecy. In democracies a secret is dispersed among many people and its power thus weakened."

Freedom of information, meaning free access by the public to government records, has in recent years been the goal of liberals throughout the world's democracies, and legislation to effect it has been placed on the statute books of a number of countries, notably the United States, Canada, Australia, and several European countries.

Great Britain lags behind. Its records of central government are selectively available and only after 30 years. One of the chief obstacles to freedom of information, the Official Secrets Act, is no doubt necessary to protect vital interests of state, but critics charge that the act is used to shield ministers from legitimate scrutiny. Informed public debate, the bedrock of democracy, is diminished.

CIVIL DISOBEDIENCE

HISTORY MAKERS: *Henry Thoreau (1817–62), Mahatma Gandhi (1869–1948), Martin Luther King (1929–68)*

SEE ALSO: *Internationalism, Liberationism, Moral philosophy*

The phrase "civil disobedience" was first used by the New England writer Henry Thoreau in the title of his essay, *On the Duty of Civil Disobedience.*

People use civil disobedience – meaning a peaceful, nonviolent refusal to obey a law – when they believe that the law or the government cannot be changed by legal means. An individual may conduct his or her own campaign of civil disobedience. Thoreau for several years refused to pay taxes as a protest against the United States' war against Mexico and the institution of black slavery. But it is rarely effective unless it is conducted by a mass of people as an organized protest.

Mass civil disobedience was used by Mahatma Gandhi, originally in South Africa, but most tellingly in India, where in 1930 he organized a cross-country march to the sea to manufacture salt, an illegal activity. That campaign, and a similar one a decade later, did a great deal to undermine British authority in India and eventually to win India's independence.

Civil disobedience may be persuasive in intention, or coercive – for instance, to bring prisons and courts to such an overcrowded condition that the state is forced to bow to the campaigners' demands. In the 1960s, acts of civil disobedience played a major part in ending racial segregation in the United States. But some liberal democrats argue that in a constitutional society – in which reformers have the political and legal means to seek redress of grievances – the rule of law ought never to be subjected to concerted assaults.

PEACEMAKER Mahatma Gandhi puts his hands together in greeting. His efforts to free India of British colonial rule ended in success in 1948.

PROPORTIONAL REPRESENTATION

HISTORY MAKERS: *John Stuart Mill (1806–73), Carl Andrae (1812–93)*

SEE ALSO: *Democracy, Sociology*

The election by the people of members to sit in representative assemblies lies at the heart of democratic systems of government. The method of election varies throughout the world, but all methods fall into one of three categories.

The first, used in Great Britain, is popularly called "first past the post." A majority of the votes cast is not required by the winning candidate, who needs only to be at the top of the poll. That is to say, he or she requires simply a "plurality" of the votes.

The second system, used in France, is two-tiered. Any candidate who gains a clear majority of the votes cast – more than 50 percent – is elected. In constituencies where no candidate does this, the two candidates with the most votes face each other in a run-off election to determine the winner. This goes halfway to proportional representation, but it nearly always leaves supporters of minor parties underrepresented.

The object of the third election method, proportional representation, is for an elected chamber that mirrors the first preferences of the whole electorate as closely as possible. In Germany, for example, any party gaining five percent of the national vote is entitled to representation in the Bundestag (the German national assembly), and the representatives are chosen by the party from a party list. In the British and French systems, it is highly improbable that a party gaining only five percent of the vote nationally would have any candidate successful in a particular constituency.

There is no doubt that proportional representation provides a more "fair" or, at any rate, more accurate reflection of political opinion in an electorate. But critics argue that elections, at least on the national level, are more about electing a government than electing an assembly and that the first-past-the-post system, unlike systems of proportional representation, furnishes voters with a direct knowledge of the force of their votes in putting a government in place. And the elected government knows (save in the exceptional circumstance that it wins the most seats, but not the highest popular vote) that it has more first-preference backing than any other party.

OPINION POLLS

HISTORY MAKERS: *George Gallup (1901–84)*

SEE ALSO: *Democracy, Philosophy of science, Sociology*

Politicians have always found ways to canvass popular opinion, or what Benjamin Disraeli (1804–81), leader of the British Conservative Party, grandly dismissed as mere "public sentiment." But independent, organized polling of political opinion really began in 1935, when George Gallup founded the American Institute of Public Opinion.

Polling methods have become more sophisticated since then, but Gallup laid down the essential requirements of polling. The people polled must be chosen randomly. For accurate results, the pool must consist of at least 1,200 people. The sample must be a valid cross-section of the population, measured by such elements as gender, age, occupation, income, ethnic background, and the like.

Opinion polls have proliferated throughout the democratic world, but they have come under attack from critics, so that in many countries the results of polls may not be published during a specified period before an election. That infringement of free speech is justified as

BAD CALL On the day of his election victory in 1948, President Harry Truman holds up a newspaper announcing his defeat. The *Tribune* had been so confident of its poll that it went to press without waiting for the election results.

a counter to the so-called bandwagon effect, by which it is believed that people are influenced to vote for whoever is ahead in the polls or to abstain on election day if their candidate, or party, is trailing in the polls.

CONSERVATISM

Looking back in order to look forward

There have always been conservatives, people who prefer the safety of the world as it is to a new, untested way of doing things. But conservatism as a modern political force may be traced to the counterrevolutionary movement that developed in opposition to the secular, reformist program of the Enlightenment and the French Revolution. It was articulated by Edmund Burke (1729–97), among others, in his *Reflections on the Revolution in France* (1790).

Burke attacked the notion of planning society according to a blueprint. Societies grew organically out of the past, he argued. Every society was, in the somewhat mystical language favored by conservatives, "a partnership not only between those who are living, but between those who are living, those who are dead, and those who are to be born."

Conservatives distrust ideas and exalt experience and historical continuity. Traditionally they have spoken out against "big government." "A government that is big enough to give you all you want," said Barry Goldwater (1909–), the conservative Republican presidential candidate in 1964, "is big enough to take it all away."

But conservatism has always been ready to ally itself with institutions of established power and authority – the monarchy, the army, and the church, especially with the Roman Catholic church in Europe. With its roots in landed society, and its instinct for order, conservatism defends hierarchy and what it considers to be the natural division of society into classes. Though it may not be possible to say so frankly to democratic electorates, it can hardly be ignored that conservatism, opposed to egalitarianism and eager to safeguard the rights of property owners, sides with the rich against the poor.

CONSERVATIVE PARTIES

The last 200 years, marked as they have been by the advance of both democracy and industrialization, have been an era of unprecedented scope and rapidity of social and economic change in human history. To declare oneself a conservative in the face of that change has not been easy. Not surprisingly, very few political parties in the world dare to call themselves Conservative.

The Canadian party fudges the issue by calling itself the Progressive Conservative Party. Standing almost alone is the British Conservative Party, which dropped the name Tory in the 1830s (although the word is still popularly used) and which has retained the name Conservative ever since – not at all to its detriment, since, along with the American Democratic Party, it is the longest surviving and most successful political party in the world.

CHRISTIAN COALITION

MORAL OUTRAGE The Reverend Jerry Falwell denounces fellow TV evangelists Jim and Tammy Bakker who, in 1987, were caught lining their own pockets with the proceeds from their ministry.

A powerful new voice has been making itself heard in the United States during the last 20 years or so. It is the voice of the Christian Coalition, a right-wing organization devoted to seizing control of the Republican Party. It is backed by large finances and the support of zealous activists.

Its roots lie in an organization called the Moral Majority, founded by television evangelist Reverend Jerry Falwell in the late 1970s to give political expression to the discontent of Christians opposed to the elimination of Christian prayer from state schools, the proliferation of pornography, the depiction of violence on television, the extension of civil rights to homosexuals, and above all else, the legalization of abortion.

The Coalition's links with traditional conservative politics are attested to by its call for greatly reduced levels of taxation and drastic cuts in public spending (except on defense). Moreover, despite the deep religious traditions of black Americans, the Coalition is largely composed of white, middle-class voters from small-town and rural America. Falwell's organization registered more than 2 million voters between 1980 and 1984, and they contributed handsomely to Ronald Reagan's landslide victory in the presidential election of 1984. Since then, the Christian Coalition has gone from strength to strength, although it has not yet succeeded in capturing the Republican nomination for one of its own nor in turning the tide against abortion.

THE NEW RIGHT

So long as the land was the chief provider of the wealth of nations, conservatism's preference for community values and ordered paternalism over individual rights made sense. But the rapid industrialization and urbanization of the economy since the 19th century meant that conservatism had to accommodate itself to a capitalist society. And since capitalism is grounded in continual change, requiring the flux involved in neverending economic change and growth to sustain itself, conservatives have increasingly adopted both the language and the ethos of the unpredictable marketplace.

They have therefore tended to become apologists for the classical school of economic liberalism. They distrust government regulation and believe in a society in which individuals make free choices based on their own self-interest. This "neo-conservative" or "new right" approach was most wholeheartedly taken up by the Thatcherites of Great Britain and the Reaganites of the United States during the 1980s.

FARTHER TO THE RIGHT British Prime Minister Margaret Thatcher and President Ronald Reagan take a brisk walk on the White House lawn. Both took their respective countries to the right with tough economic policies, including big cuts in welfare.

SEE ALSO

Nationalism · · · · · · · · · · · · · · · ▶
Idealism vs. materialism · · · · · · · · ◀
Industrialization · · · · · · · · · · · · ◀
Macroeconomics · · · · · · · · · · · · ◀
Monetarism · · · · · · · · · · · · · · · ◀

LIBERALISM
Progress and reason

The foundation of liberalism is its reluctance to acknowledge the claims of authority on the grounds of authority alone. Liberals do not accept that institutions or ideas have a legitimate claim to be honored or obeyed simply because they are established and hallowed by custom. Liberalism, which aspires to progress in human affairs, places emphasis on the power of human reason to apply itself to problems and find solutions to them.

Liberalism is also, by its nature, inclusive. It wishes to bring everyone into the great project of the moral, intellectual, and material improvement of humanity. It is thus no accident that the parents of liberalism are the 17th-century scientific revolution and the 18th-century Enlightenment, and that its siblings are secularism and democracy.

The political term "liberal" first came into use in Spain, to describe the rebels against the antidemocratic monarchical constitution after 1815. In the 1820s, it came to be used more and more frequently in England. Only in England and its white colonies did the name eventually come to attach itself to political parties themselves, but the idea of liberalism spread across Europe as the 19th century advanced.

Liberalism was not the same everywhere, but its core was a belief in free institutions as the means to progress. Its adherents tended to be merchants who clamored for free trade; its perceived enemies tended to be the landed classes who had long held sway in politics. Among its objects were freely elected parliaments, independent judiciaries, freedom of speech and religion, the separation of church and state, and the freedom to amass and protect property. Another key concept for liberals was "careers open to talents."

Of the three great ideals proclaimed by the French revolutionaries – liberty, equality, and brotherhood – liberalism devoted itself chiefly to liberty. Liberals emphasized individual rights and individual self-expression; except when it suited them to mount mass campaigns, they distrusted collective action. Although for most of the 19th century, liberals had no truck with democracy or "one man one vote," by the late 19th century they were forced to bow to the spirit of the age and throw in their lot with universal manhood suffrage. As socialism came to the fore in the 20th century, liberalism tended to find itself a spent force. It may be, as socialism withers, that the revival of liberalism is at hand.

LIBERTY

Defining the limits of individual liberty is perhaps the fundamental function of law and politics. The basis of liberty is the absence of coercion. The extent of individual liberty is simply the extent of the area within which people can act unobstructed by others.

Yet most societies also place a high value on conditions such as justice, and in order to promote these they need to curtail individual freedom. But most liberal thinkers since the 18th century have accepted that there are certain inviolable liberties – or human rights. The Swiss-French writer Benjamin Constant (1767–1830) listed them as liberty of religion, opinion, expression, and property. The lists vary, but defining the limits of liberty is the question that defines parties and gives life to politics. Put simply, the conservative tilts toward order, the socialist toward equality, and the liberal toward freedom.

LADY LIBERTY The Statue of Liberty towers over Paris before being sent piece by piece across the Atlantic. She was a gift from the French people to mark America's first centenary (1876).

LIBERTARIANISM

In his essay of 1859, *On Liberty*, the English philosopher John Stuart Mill (1806–73) defined the foundation of liberty: "The sole end for which mankind are warranted, individually or collectively, in interfering with the liberty of action of any of their number is self-protection." The corollary was that any action was permissible, however harmful to the doer, so long as it did no harm to others. This principle lies at the heart of libertarianism, alongside another of Mill's cardinal beliefs, that the unfettered expression of opinion was a bulwark of a free and healthy society.

Censorship of any kind, whether of child pornography or of the expression of racial hostility, is anathema to libertarians. So is the belief that collective wellbeing takes precedence over individual freedom. Libertarians find themselves opposed to the utilitarian argument, powerful in the development of modern liberal and socialist parties, that individual freedom to choose may need to be sacrificed on the altar of "the greatest happiness of the greatest number." Specific objects of libertarian attack include phone-tapping and bugging, laws against drug-taking, and, especially in the United States (where a Libertarian party was founded in 1973), controls on the possession and use of guns.

PHILOSOPHER IN LOVE John Stuart Mill's work was heavily influenced by Harriet Taylor, with whom he had a long affair and married only after her husband's death.

THE NEW DEAL

HELPING HAND Democrat Franklin Delano Roosevelt meets Dust Bowl farmers during his 1932 campaign for the presidency of the United States. He beat the incumbent Herbert Hoover by a wide margin.

The New Deal implemented by President Franklin Delano Roosevelt (1882–1945) was one of the most complete political explorations of modern liberalism this century has known. Gaining the presidency while the nation was in the depths of a severe depression, Roosevelt and his "brains trust" came up with a plan that they thought would pull the country back from the brink of the abyss. The New Deal had two main aims. One was to put banking back on a firm footing – the 1929 Wall Street Crash had decimated the American financial system. The other was to find work for the millions of unemployed people.

During Roosevelt's first 100 days in office in 1933, Congress passed a number of bills designed to rescue the United States. Roosevelt imposed strict currency controls, provided cheap loans to farmers, and started huge civil-engineering works including the building of the Hoover Dam.

Typical of reactions to liberalism, historians of both the left and right criticize the New Deal. Right-wing thinkers accuse it of being statist or even socialist, while left-wing ones comment that it was simply an extension of Progressivism. What is certain is that Roosevelt's swinging reforms restored faith in American democracy at a time when fascism was casting its shadow across the European continent.

MODERN LIBERALISM

The most thorough and arresting restatement of the foundations of political liberalism has come from the American scholar John Rawls (1921–). Rawls's two basic principles are that everyone is entitled to the maximum liberty compatible with equal liberty for others, and that social and economic inequalities are justifiable only in a society which affords equal opportunity to everyone.

In *A Theory of Justice* (1971), Rawls proposed a novel method of arriving at a just society. People are to imagine themselves in an original state in which they do not know anything of their social position – income, status, education, race, gender, natural abilities. They then decide on what principles society should be organized in order to give them a just opportunity of living the good life. Rawls's argument is that people under such presumed ignorance of their own circumstances will be forced to show an equal concern for everyone else in order to make sure that their own prospects are not jeopardized.

SEE ALSO

Conservatism · · · · · · · · · · · ◄

Progressivism · · · · · · · · · · · · ▶

The Enlightenment · · · · · · · · · · ▶

Moral philosophy · · · · · · · · · · ▶

Industrialization · · · · · · · · · · · ▷

Macroeconomics · · · · · · · · · · · ▷

PROGRESSIVISM

HISTORY MAKERS: *Theodore Roosevelt (1858–1919)*
SEE ALSO: *Referendum, Liberalism*

Between 1890 and 1914, reformers called Progressives tried to rid American politics and industry of corruption. Two developments that came about during the "gilded age" of U.S. history that followed the end of the Civil War in 1865 angered the Progressives. One was the rise to dominance of political party bosses and party machines. To counter their influence, Progressives sought to establish the regular use of referendums, primary elections to select presidential candidates, and the right of the people to fire public servants.

The Progressives' other chief grievance was the economic power of the captains of industry who had foisted monopoly capitalism on the people during America's industrial leap forward after 1865. Progressives called on government to break up the cartels that dominated American big business, to regulate industry, and to pass laws to protect the people from the results of unchecked laissez-faire economics.

DEFENDER OF THE PEOPLE Teddy Roosevelt, U.S. President 1901–09, often wore Western dress on his hunting trips. The Progressive Party was founded to support his unsuccessful campaign for re-election in 1912.

POPULISM

HISTORY MAKERS: *Juan Perón (1895–1974) and Eva Perón (1919–52)*
SEE ALSO: *Totalitarianism*

CROWD APPEAL Eva Perón, wife of Argentinian President Juan Perón, was so adored by the people of Argentina that attempts have been made to have her canonized by the Pope.

Populism was originally the name for two agrarian reform movements, one in Russia and the other in the U.S. Each drew inspiration from an imagined golden age in a pastoral past.

The 19th-century Russian campaign to build a society on the communal traditions of the peasantry went by the name of *narodnichestvo*, or "populism." It was eventually overwhelmed by the Bolshevik revolution of 1917. In the United States, the People's Party, which flourished in the 1890s, appealed to the antipathy felt by small producers and farmers to big business.

More generally, however, populism has come to signify any overt political appeal to popular passions – usually combined with an attack, however veiled, on the establishment and often exhibiting a distinctly xenophobic tinge. One of the outstanding examples in the 1990s has been Jean-Marie Le Pen's right-wing movement in France.

ANARCHISM

HISTORY MAKERS: *Pierre-Joseph Proudhon (1809–65), Peter Kropotkin (1842–1921)*
SEE ALSO: *Revolution, Socialism*

Anarchism, whose intellectual heyday at the end of the 19th century stemmed from the writings of Pierre-Joseph Proudhon and Peter Kropotkin, is founded on the belief that all state authority is coercive and therefore invalid. "Property is theft," Proudhon declared, and since the chief aim of government was the protection of property, no form of government could be justified except the form of constant self-government proposed by anarchism.

Political anarchism insists that all decisions should be taken by the whole community and that the community must not assume any authority – by right of majority will – to impose its decisions on individuals. As a system, it is therefore inappropriate for any but the smallest groups of people. Nevertheless, anarchist assassination attempts unnerved governments across Europe in the lead-up to World War I.

SAFE HAVEN At the end of the 19th century, Britain was a refuge for political dissidents from all over Europe, including anarchists.

MULTICULTURALISM

SEE ALSO: *Revolution, Sociology*

BROTHERHOOD OF MAN People from a variety of cultures rub shoulders at London's annual carnival in Notting Hill. Started by a homesick West Indian teacher in the 1960s, the carnival is now Europe's biggest street festival.

The key notion of multiculturalism is that moral concepts and values are only relative. The apologist for multiculturalism finds it impossible to identify one kind of life as the best. Given the variety that characterizes human societies, there can be no common moral or political language. What is right for one society may be wrong for another, and what is right for one section of a society may be wrong for another section.

This way of thinking – much influenced by the rise of social anthropology in our century – represents a break with the traditional search by political philosophers for a definition of such terms as "freedom" and "justice." There is no place in the strict multiculturalist vision for the French revolutionaries' proclamation of the universal rights of man. In its place is the pluralist acknowledgment that people are bound – for historical, geographical, sexual, and a host of other reasons – to occupy incompatible spheres, to follow their own customs and practice their own rituals, to adopt conflicting moral codes and languages.

Multiculturalism thus urges not simply the toleration, but the celebration, of differences. It has not yet come to occupy center stage in the political world, not even in the United States, where it is strongest – at least in the lip-service paid to it. Instead, the American government has made the winning of universal human rights around the globe a high priority of foreign policy.

GLASNOST AND PERESTROIKA

HISTORY MAKERS: *Mikhail Gorbachev (1931–)*

SEE ALSO: *Marxism, Totalitarianism, Freedom of information*

During General Secretary Mikhail Gorbachev's leadership of the Soviet Union in the second half of the 1980s, *glasnost*, the Russian for "openness to public scrutiny," and *perestroika*, meaning "restructuring," were key concepts in the liberalization of Soviet administration and society. Gorbachev's program of reform also included the gradual introduction of market forces into the economy.

The political restructuring included the election, in 1989, of a new parliament (to which one-third of the

FREE ENTERPRISE *Babushkas* in a Moscow market sell hand-whittled chess pieces, icons of the Virgin Mary and Russian dolls. Allowing private street traders to operate on a small scale was part of Gorbachev's reforms.

GOODBYE TO ALL THAT Mikhail Gorbachev was more popular abroad than in the Soviet Union. Economic difficulties, notably a food shortage in 1990–91, hastened his fall from power.

deputies were elected by free popular vote from an open field of candidates) and the relinquishing of much central economic planning to local bodies. In the elections many Communist Party candidates were defeated, including members of the Politburo, the party's political committee.

Glasnost centered on legal reforms, new laws to provide for press freedoms, and the right to public assembly and freedom of conscience. A small but telling example of its effect was a decree of 1988 that ended the old Soviet practice of encouraging people to inform anonymously against their neighbors for dishonest dealings.

Gorbachev may have intended to preserve communist rule by relaxing it. But the instability that followed his reforms and the aspirations to democracy that they encouraged hastened the demise of communist authority throughout the Soviet empire and the eventual collapse of that empire itself. Gorbachev lost the leadership of the Soviet Union in 1991.

SOCIALISM
Economics and inequality

"From each according to his abilities, to each according to his needs." That classic formulation of socialism was uttered by the French radical Louis Blanc (1811–82) in 1840. The roots of modern socialism lie a little farther back, in the Enlightenment's concern for human progress and in the response to social problems and economic inequalities thrown into relief by the rise of industrialism.

"Happiness," the French revolutionary Louis de Saint-Just (1767–94) wrote in 1791, "is a new idea in Europe." The pursuit of happiness became, in the program of utilitarians like the English reformer Jeremy Bentham (1748–1832), not an individual quest, but a collective one. Utilitarians held that the great test of all legislation should be whether it increased or diminished "the greatest happiness of the greatest number." To meet that test, according to socialists, governments needed to intervene in social and economic arrangements. They had to declare war on the injustices, inequalities, and class divisions that were the inevitable result of industrial capitalism.

The word "socialism" itself first made its appearance in the 1830s in England and France, and then as now it covered a wide variety of opinions and projected remedies for the ills of society. Certain key beliefs, however, were broadly accepted by people who called themselves socialists. The fundamental proposition of socialism has always been that production is a function of all members of society and that the rewards of production are therefore due to all. Socialists exalt cooperative effort above individual entrepreneurship and believe that the state should take possession, or ownership, of the means of production in the interests of society as a whole. The state should also take steps to guarantee the fair redistribution of wealth to the individual members of society. The aim is the elimination of class distinctions.

An abiding debate among socialists has always been whether a classless society organized on socialist principles can be brought about through the ballot box – or whether the powerful institutions of capital and private property can be toppled only by revolutionary violence.

CHRISTIAN SOCIALISM

"Christian socialism" can be used loosely to denote the views of anyone who believes that the teachings of Christ point toward collective action to improve the lot of the weak, the oppressed, and the poor. Specifically, however, the term refers to two movements.

The first was the attempt by certain individuals in mid-19th-century Great Britain, notably Charles Kingsley (1819–75) and Frederick Maurice (1805–72), to persuade the Church of England to adopt a social and education policy for the benefit of the working classes. The second movement, arising in Austria and other European states, sought to give practical political expression to two papal encyclicals of the late 19th century – *Rerum novarum* and *Quadragesimo Anno* – which attempted to counter the challenge of socialism by proposing a Christian corporate state with legislative protection for the rights of labor.

Christian socialism was therefore essentially a conservative program. Socialism itself, by its aspiration to create an earthly paradise, is often seen as inherently incompatible with Christianity. Hence the position taken by Pope Pius XI (1857–1939) that "religious socialism, Christian socialism are expressions implying a contradiction in terms."

FOUNDERS

The two men who have the greatest claim to be regarded as the founding fathers of modern socialism are the French social scientist Claude-Henri de Rouvroy Saint-Simon (1760–1825) and the British cotton master and reformer Robert Owen (1771–1858).

Saint-Simon devoted his intellectual life to analyzing the nature of industrial society and the relationships between prevailing systems of belief and the structure of societies. He believed that liberalism was too wedded to individual rights to be able to ameliorate the condition of the working classes and to give the producers of wealth, the laborers, their just rewards. This would not occur until society's existing rulers – the great landowners and the clergy – were replaced by a new class of scientists, intellectuals, artists, and producers and until a new religious spirit united them in the effort to direct all activity toward the common good.

Owen was more practical. At his cotton mills at New Lanark, Scotland, and briefly at New Harmony in Indiana, he established cooperative communities and sought to put into practice his vision of a society in which ownership and control of the means of production were communal. Owen also argued that money should be replaced as a medium of exchange by a barter system in which goods were distributed according to need. He believed that character and behavior were determined by environment. Like Saint-Simon, he was drawn to the conclusion that a new society based on cooperative socialist principles could be created only on the base of a reinvigorated Christian morality.

SCRAPS FROM THE RICH MAN'S TABLE Poor women collect food left over after the Lord Mayor's Banquet in Victorian London. Socialism was proposed as a solution to the striking inequality between the destitute and the wealthy.

LABORERS' LEISURE At Robert Owen's cooperative New Lanark community, cotton-mill workers and their families could learn new skills after working hours.

SEE ALSO

Marxism · · · · · · · · · · · · · · · · · · ▶
The Enlightenment · · · · · · · · · · ▶
Moral philosophy · · · · · · · · · · · ▶
Industrialization · · · · · · · · · · · · ▶

TRADE UNIONS AND SYNDICALISM

Trade unionism, the organized gathering together of workers to give them the strength of numbers to battle for higher wages, shorter hours, and better working conditions, was a response to industrialism and took root first of all in the world's first industrial society, Great Britain. There the ban on collective action by workers was lifted in 1825 and almost at once trade unions sprang into life.

All over Europe, workers followed the British example and by the end of the 19th century, trade unions were legal in almost every Western country. The chief weapon of trade unionists was the strike, and the growth of trade unionism gave rise to a branch of socialism known as syndicalism. It took its name from the French word for a trade union, *syndicat*, and its heyday was the two or three decades following the formation in France of the Confédération Générale du Travail in 1895. The movement was especially strong in France, Belgium, Italy, and Spain, and in Mexico and Argentina.

Syndicalists sought to bring the ownership and management of industry into direct workers' control – in opposition to those socialists who wanted to place public ownership in state hands – and to bypass the state by establishing a federation of workers' units. They advocated the use of industrial sabotage and strikes, especially general strikes, to achieve their political end. Their antipathy toward the state linked them with anarchists, and the movement has often gone by the name of anarcho-syndicalism.

SOCIAL DEMOCRACY

The term "social democracy" was originally used to distinguish the revisionist socialism adopted by the German Social Democratic Party in 1875 from Marxism. Its program reflected the ideas of Ferdinand Lassalle (1825–64) and Eduard Bernstein (1850–1932). They accepted that under universal suffrage, a free state could develop socialism, whereas strict Marxism denied that the state, being itself an instrument of class domination, could be a neutral instrument of social change.

They recommended the "fair distribution" of the fruits of production, whereas Marxism had no place for moral values such as "fairness," which had no independent existence outside their economic determinants.

"Social democracy" was at first indistinguishable from "democratic socialism." But in post-1945 Europe it has come to mean a position that accepts a mixed economy (the combination of public and private ownership) and believes that, with government intervention in the operations of the free market, social justice may be achieved. This tempered socialism, which owed much to the analysis of the English economist John Maynard Keynes (1883–1946), abandoned the war against capitalism.

"Workers of the world, unite!"

Karl Marx (1818–83)

FABIANISM

MARRIED TO THE JOB Beatrice (1858–1943) and Sidney Webb (1859–1947), leading lights in the Fabian Society, warm their hands at the fire. Together they made groundbreaking social surveys of London's poor.

Fabianism is a strand in socialist thought that advocates patient reliance on the slow processes of education and legislation to usher in the socialist society. The term derives from the Fabian Society, founded in London in 1884 by middle-class intellectuals such as George Bernard Shaw (1856–1950) and Sidney and Beatrice Webb. It was named after the Roman general Fabius Cunctator ("the delayer," *d.* 203 BC), who in his campaign against the Carthaginian military leader Hannibal (247–182 BC) rejected attack in favor of a war of attrition and harassment.

Fabians stood out against a revolutionary path to socialism and placed their faith in universal suffrage and what Sidney Webb called "the inevitability of gradualness." The Fabian position has become the dominant one in democratic socialist parties throughout the Western world. They believe that by persuading voters of the justice of socialism, society can be transformed at the ballot box.

In the eyes of the original Fabians, educating the populace required cadres of professionals, chosen by merit and democratically accountable, to lead the people. Fabianism has thus suffered from the charge of being elitist.

THE LAND QUESTION

"It will, generally, be found," Benjamin Disraeli (1804–81) wrote, "that all great political questions end in the tenure of land." Most democratic socialists have shied away from the nationalization of land or of food production, but one American reformer agreed with Disraeli that landownership was the key to social and economic relationships.

In 1879 the social critic Henry George (1839–97) published a book called *Progress and Poverty* to demonstrate that chronic poverty in expanding capitalist societies and economic cycles of growth and depression were both attributable to fluctuations in the value of property and therefore in rents. The financial speculation that those fluctuations encouraged was conducted by wealthy individuals for their own benefit. As an antidote to that symptom of national ill-health, George proposed that a single tax be laid on land values and that taxes on earned income be abolished.

Although his plan had some links with socialist thought – the single tax would create a common property in, though not ownership of, the land – it was intended to provide an incentive to entrepreneurship and individual enterprise in a free labor market. No country ever adopted George's proposal, although in many countries a single tax on real property values has been used as the means of raising revenue for local government.

END OF THE TENANCY A 19th-century landlord turns down his tenant's application for a renewed lease.

TIMELINE

British trade unionism
Trade unionism arose first in Great Britain.

1824
Great Britain lifts ban on trade unions.

1833
Robert Owen organizes the Grand National Consolidated Trades Union, a cooperative venture meant to unite masters and workers.

1868
Trades Union Congress formed as representative organization for all trade unions.

1875
Peaceful picketing in support of a strike is legalized.

1893
Trade unions join with socialists to form the Labour Party.

1906
Trade Disputes Act grants unions immunity from damages caused by strike action.

1926
General strike lasts nine days and ends in defeat for the miners.

1979–84
Acts of parliament make secondary picketing illegal and compel unions to call a strike only after a postal ballot of members.

MARXISM
When economics determines everything

Everything that Karl Marx (1818–83) wrote and thought stemmed from his conviction that all human activity was economically determined. Though he was intensely interested in politics, Marx believed that political activity – just like religion, morality, culture – took its form from the economic system that gave it birth. And through all the centuries of human history – especially under the economic system of Western capitalism as it operated when he was writing, in the middle decades of the 19th century – one theme stood out: class warfare and the exploitation of one class by another.

"The history of all hitherto existing society," Marx wrote in the *Communist Manifesto* (1848), "is the history of class struggles." He argued that the struggle between the landed aristocracy and the bourgeoisie (or the capitalist employer class) had already resulted in the victory of the bourgeoisie. The coming struggle would pit the bourgeoisie against the proletariat (or the wage-earning, employed class). This battle was inevitable because the workers were bound to rebel against their economic exploitation.

By "exploitation," Marx meant primarily the difference between the value of what the workers produced and the value of their wages. That difference was, of course, profit. The search for profits produced two great defects in the capitalist economy. The first was overproduction. Factories worked at full capacity so as to be profitable – they produced more goods than the wage earners could afford to buy; markets became choked and the assembly lines had to slow down. In other words, a cycle of boom and slump was built into the capitalist system. A corollary was that capitalism depended upon a "reserve army of the unemployed," ready for work when a period of boom required extra labor.

Capitalism was therefore doomed to destruction in the revolution that would install "the dictatorship of the proletariat." That dictatorship would be a brief affair, lasting only during the transition from capitalism to communism, after which society would enter a new life. Class warfare would be no more, for there would be only one class, the producing class. And in the absence of class conflict, there would be no need for a coercive state. The state would "wither away" as the fraternity of communism established itself. In Marx's theory the Enlightenment dream of bringing heaven down to Earth reaches its extreme conclusion.

THE COMMUNIST MANIFESTO AND HISTORICAL MATERIALISM

In the midst of the revolutionary turmoil that convulsed most of Europe in 1848, Karl Marx and his colleague Friedrich Engels (1820–95) wrote the *Communist Manifesto*.

It opened with the arresting statement that a specter was haunting Europe – "the specter of Communism." And it ended with the exhortation that has become one of the most famous phrases of our time: "The proletarians have nothing to lose but their chains. They have a world to win. WORKERS OF THE WORLD, UNITE!"

It may seem odd for Marx – whose theory, as it developed over the next few decades, proclaimed the inevitability of proletarian victory – to call upon the workers to force the issue. Surely they had only to wait for history to work out its purpose. In fact, Marx was never the thorough-going economic determinist that he sometimes appeared to be. In his *Provisional Rules of the International Working Men's Association*, written in 1864, he argued that "the emancipation of the working classes must be conquered by the working classes themselves" and advocated that the masses take control over their destiny.

Toward the end of his life, Engels was eager to put the record straight. "According to the materialist conception of history, the production and reproduction of real life constitutes in the last instance the determining factor of history. Neither Marx nor I ever maintained more. Now, when someone comes along and distorts this to mean that the economic factor is the sole determining factor, he is converting the former proposition into a meaningless, abstract, and absurd phrase. The economic system is the basis, but the various factors of the superstructure, the political forms of the class struggles and their results...political, judicial, philosophical theories...all these exercise an influence upon the course of historical struggles and in many cases determine for the most part their form."

Since its first publication in 1848, Marx and Engels's *Manifesto* has been translated into nearly every language in the world, and although Marx's opinions may no longer be as widely admired as they were in the past, his influence on political thought remains pervasive.

FATHER OF REVOLUTIONS Karl Marx provoked very different responses from people. At Marx's funeral his friend Engels said he was the "best-hated" man of his time, yet he also died "beloved by millions."

BOLSHEVIKS AND MENSHEVIKS

REVOLUTIONARY ELITE The Red Army Command that led the successful October Revolution in 1917 grew out of Lenin's early supporters, the Bolsheviks.

At its 1903 convention, the Russian Social Democratic Party – a Marxist organization devoted to the overthrow of Tsarism – found itself embroiled in a row between Vladimir Lenin (1870–1924) and Julius Martov (1873–1923), cofounders of the party newspaper, *Iskra* ("Spark"). They were opposed on two issues. The first was the structure of the party itself. Martov envisioned a mass revolutionary party, organized along democratic lines, whereas Lenin was determined to lead a small revolutionary elite. Lenin's view won the day by a small majority because, for unrelated reasons, the members of a Jewish group who would have voted against him had recently withdrawn from the meeting.

The second issue was the choice of who should staff the paper. When party members voted to elect *Iskra*'s staff, Lenin's candidates again defeated Martov's by a whisker. What at first appeared to be a couple of unimportant votes in fact opened up a permanent split in the party. From that time, Lenin's supporters became known as *bolsheviki* (men of the majority) and Martov's followers as *mensheviki* (men of the minority).

Lenin's small band of Bolsheviks were eventually to carry out the revolutionary coup that gave birth to the Soviet communist state in 1917. It remained a tactic of both Lenin

and his successor Joseph Stalin (1879–1953) to brand opponents within the Communist Party as Mensheviks, a taunt that was often enough to justify their "liquidation."

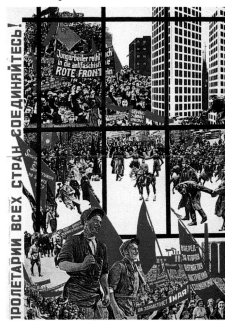

OCTOBER REVOLUTION Soviet propaganda portrayed the 1917 revolution as a popular uprising, although it was really a coup.

SEE ALSO

Socialism · · · · · · · · · · · · · · · · · ◀

Totalitarianism · · · · · · · · · · · · ▶

Idealism vs. materialism · · · · · · · · ▶

MARXISM-LENINISM

Marx believed that capitalism, by bringing into existence the industrial, urban proletariat, contained the seeds of its own demise: the workers would rise up against their exploitation by capitalist employers. Marx supposed that the revolution, when it came, would be a mass revolt.

Lenin, practically involved in the business of making the revolution in largely peasant, agrarian Russia, took a different line. In *What Is To Be Done?* (1902) he wrote that the history of every country demonstrated that "the working class, exclusively by its own effort, is able to develop only trade union consciousness." The workers' imaginative horizons were, in Lenin's view, limited by their own economic and social circumstances – hence the need for a revolutionary (and implicitly intellectual) vanguard to develop revolutionary class consciousness. "Vanguardism" became a justification for allowing the revolutionary leaders, blessed by superior insight, to dictate every detail of party policy and strategy from above. Marxism-Leninism, which became the model for Communist parties throughout the world, thus laid the grounds for totalitarianism.

Lenin's other major divergence from Marx was to argue that imperialism was the death throes of capitalism. Therefore an imperialist power like tsarist Russia, though still a peasant society, was as ripe for revolution as a society that had been sufficiently industrialized to produce the class warfare between a bourgeoisie and an urban proletariat that Marx said was essential for revolution.

COMRADE LENIN Lenin and Stalin mix with members of the Communist Party. Idealized images of Lenin were a favorite with Soviet artists in the 1920s and 1930s.

SOCIALIST REALISM

BREAD FOR THE HUNGRY A Soviet poster in the Socialist-Realist manner shows what the starving masses need. This style of art was perhaps used most successfully in posters and children's books.

For the first two decades of the 20th century, Russian artists were at the cutting edge of Modernism. In the euphoria of the Bolshevik victory, modern art seemed to be presented with a unique opportunity to play its part in forging a new society. Admittedly, the minister for education and the arts announced that art should be used for "agitprop" – agitation and propaganda to spread the revolutionary creed. But he also recalled from Munich the émigré Russian painter Vasily Kandinsky (1866–1944), hailed as the first abstract painter, to oversee art education. Yet as Soviet rule slid toward totalitarianism, artistic freedom fell by the wayside.

Totalitarian regimes seek not simply to coerce citizens into obedience, but also to control their minds. Socialist Realism became the official painting style: a figurative manner devoted to portraying heroic men and women working in fields and factories. Modernism, denounced as the degenerate art of capitalist imperialism, was driven from the field – with the result that it is difficult to bring to mind a Russian painter of note from the Stalinist era.

MAOISM

The revolution that brought the communists, led by Mao Tse-tung (1893–1976), to power in China in 1949 was essentially a revolt of the peasantry against foreign occupation. But Mao wished the revolution to be a triumph for his brand of Marxism. That meant rejecting Marx's view that a revolution could be achieved only by an industrialized proletariat and ignoring Lenin's dependence upon a revolutionary elite.

Mao offered the Chinese peasantry a form of socialism based on what he called the "mass-line" theory of leadership. Leaders and led were to educate each other in tiny groups – or "cells." Throughout China, that is what

THIRD WORLD HERO Chairman Mao writes at his paper-strewn desk. He showed that the concepts of Marxism could be applied in any country in the world.

happened. The needs of the peasants were catered for, and in return the peasantry listened to the communists.

Mao attacked Stalinism for impoverishing the peasantry, curtailing popular participation in society by handing economic control to the central party, and for pretending socialist society had no contradictions. But in fact Mao increasingly followed Stalin's model: the party line was everything, and dissent was crushed.

THE CULTURAL REVOLUTION

In 1957 Mao announced that the Communist Party was to let "a hundred flowers blossom" in China. Apparently, in order to show that Marxism could tolerate free discussion and thereby consolidate support for the revolution, he invited people to air their views. The initiative backfired. So strenuous and widespread was dissent, so damning the criticism of party officials, that Mao was forced to retreat and once more clamp down on freedom of expression.

Another interpretation is that he had announced the Hundred Flowers Campaign simply to tempt dissidents into the open – as he put it in a little-known speech of 1957, to bring "snakes out of lairs." Whatever the true explanation, Mao launched a "socialist education movement" in 1962 to bring "rightists," or "capitalist roaders," back into line. By 1965 this had developed into the full terror of the Cultural Revolution.

Armed with Mao's Little Red Book – an anthology of his sayings – Red Guards roamed the countryside ferreting out enemies of socialism. Schools and universities were closed, and opponents of the regime – suspected or actual – were humiliated, tortured, and, in thousands of instances, executed. By 1967, China faced civil war, and the Red Guards'

INTERNAL EXILE A band of urban students goes off to be "re-educated" by the peasantry in a propaganda poster from the Cultural Revolution.

GIRL WORKER The virtues of manual labor and the evils of intellectuals were drummed into teenagers, who turned on their teachers, sometimes torturing and even executing them.

intimidation of peasants and workers was bringing agricultural and industrial production to untenably low levels. Mao therefore recalled the Red Guards, reopened the schools, and sent millions of young people to be "educated" by working among peasants in the countryside. In 1969 the Cultural Revolution was declared to be over.

ALIENATION

HISTORY MAKERS: *Karl Marx (1818–83)*

SEE ALSO: *Industrialization, Sociology*

THE MODERN CONDITION Marx argued that capitalism alienated the worker from the products of his mind and body by making them the property of the capitalist owner.

The idea of alienation derived directly, as much of Marx's thought did, from the writings of the philosopher Georg Hegel (1770–1831). Hegel believed that individuals and societies developed through history by a series of alienations, beginning, for each individual, in the gaining of an awareness of separate identity from the mother.

Hegel thought that human history was working itself out as the closing of the gap – or alienation – between individual and universal consciousness. In the union of the two, which Hegel described as absolute self-consciousness, alienation would be eradicated. Marx rejected the psychological basis of Hegel's scheme, which located alienation in consciousness. Instead he found the roots of alienation in the economic substructures of society.

Unlike the rest of the animal kingdom, human beings could overcome the tyranny of providing for basic needs and express themselves creatively in the things that they produced. But capitalism denied men and women the opportunity for creative production and pitted workers against one another in a competitive system. Since capitalist alienation was economically induced, the individual could not overcome it by his or her own efforts. The modes of production, distribution, and exchange could be changed, and alienation banished, only by class action.

FIVE-YEAR PLANS

HISTORY MAKERS: *Vladimir Illyich Lenin (1870–1924), Joseph Stalin (1879–1953)*

SEE ALSO: *Marxism, Capitalism*

"Socialism," Lenin told the 1920 Congress of Soviets, "is Soviet power plus the electrification of the whole country." In other words, the commanding heights of the economy were to be controlled by the party chiefs in the interest of the rapid industrialization of the Soviet empire. In fact, Lenin's New Economic Policy, introduced in 1921, allowed for private ownership and trading, and for prices to be determined by the market.

Industrialization proceeded too slowly, however, for "socialism in one country" to be achieved. In 1928 Stalin reverted to wholesale nationalization and appointed a central commission, Gosplan, to produce five-year plans for heavy industry and agriculture.

Central planning worked. Although wages remained low and consumer goods were virtually unobtainable, by 1939 the U.S.S.R. held third place in the world's industrial tables behind the U.S. and Germany. Workers who exceeded their quotas were hailed as national heroes and called Stakhanovites, after the astoundingly overachieving coal miner Alexei Stakhanov.

PERMANENT REVOLUTION

HISTORY MAKERS: *Leon Trotsky (1879–1940), Che Guevara (1928–67)*

SEE ALSO: *Revolution, Marxism, Internationalism*

After the Russian Revolution of 1917, Lenin had expected Bolshevism to spread rapidly from Russia to Germany and other parts of Europe; indeed in Lenin's theory, it was crucial for the success of Soviet communism that it was not left isolated in a capitalist world. But when Marxist revolutions failed to materialize elsewhere, Stalin fell back on "socialism in one country": the communist utopia could be built without allies. Leon Trotsky never accepted this idea. He held to the views that he had expounded in his 1906 publication, *Results and Prospects* (written after the failed 1905

POLITICAL TRAVELER Argentine-born Che Guevara helped Fidel Castro's coup in Cuba before trying to export Marxist revolution to African and South American countries.

revolution). By "permanent revolution," Trotsky really meant "unbroken revolution." Unlike Marx and Lenin, he believed that a socialist, proletarian revolution could simply grow out of a democratic, non-socialist one. Trotsky's opposition to "socialism in one country," his insistence that the revolution must be carried abroad, and an international Marxist movement maintained, was one of the causes of his expulsion from the Soviet Union and his eventual assassination in Mexico by Stalin's agents.

In the West the term "Trotskyism" came into vogue during the years of Cold War to mean nothing more precise than communist infiltration of democratic socialist parties to subvert them to revolutionary Marxist ends.

COLLECTIVIZATION

HISTORY MAKERS: *Joseph Stalin (1879–1953), Mao Tse-tung (1893–1976)*

SEE ALSO: *Marxism, Capitalism*

A vital part of the Communist Party's economic plan for the U.S.S.R. was the forced collectivization of agriculture. Collectivization was as much a demonstration of socialist hostility to the private landowners, the kulaks, as it was the product of economic analysis showing that communal farming would be more productive than private.

In 1929 Stalin announced that the time had come to pass from "the policy of restricting the exploitative tendencies of the kulaks to the policy of eliminating the kulaks as a class." Troops moved into the countryside, individual farms vanished, and peasants and kulaks were moved to cooperative farms. According to the most recent estimates, between 6.5

LOST GENERATION Peasant children at a work camp are bundled up against the bitter cold.

and 10 million kulaks were dispossessed of their land, especially in the wheat-growing region of the Ukraine (a center of resistance to Bolshevism in the civil war of 1918–20). Most of them were transported to the northern and eastern parts of the U.S.S.R., and many ended up in the infamous labor camps of the Gulag Archipelago. The result was famine, and the death total from starvation, transportation, and imprisonment rose to nearly 15 million by the early 1930s.

Mao repeated the mistake in China – by 1957 more than 90 percent of farms had been collectivized – and the results were no less cruel. Assisted by Mao's worthless advice on farming methods, collectivization plunged China into a famine that cost 27 to 30 million lives by starvation between 1959 and 1961.

GREAT LEAP FORWARD

HISTORY MAKERS: *Mao Tse-tung (1893–1976)*

SEE ALSO: *Marxism, Capitalism*

In the 1950s, the Chinese economy, under a five-year plan on the Soviet model (priority for heavy industry, nationalization, and central control), expanded more rapidly than at any previous time in the 20th century. Even

so, it failed to keep pace with Western production. Mao initiated a series of campaigns to appeal to the people to work ever harder.

The first of them, the Great Leap Forward announced in 1958, marked a return to Mao's ideal of decentralized, communal socialism, mixing agriculture with small-scale, local industry. But it set ridiculously high targets – steel production was to surpass that of the United States in only four years – so that, in effect, China's lack of capital and resources was to be made good by exploiting the masses. What happened was a dismal failure, one hidden from the population by lies (false reports of droughts and floods were used to explain the famine). Exhortation gave way to coercion, and the rural labor force was brought to the point of exhaustion. In 1961 Mao retired temporarily, and the Great Leap Forward was abandoned.

STARVATION DIET A man gnaws desperately at a tree trunk to try to gain some sustenance. Millions were reduced to eating anything they could find during the Great Leap Forward.

IMPERIALISM
Power, prestige, and loot

Empires are as old as the hills, or almost. It is difficult to escape the conclusion that the prime motive for empire has been economic. Rome depended upon the wheat fields of the eastern Mediterranean, and the empires of the New World came into being during the Renaissance because of Europe's restless search for a sea passage to the riches of the East, a search that resulted in the accidental discovery of the Americas.

On the other hand, the scramble for Africa in the latter decades of the 19th century at times seemed to be merely a race among the European powers for the prestige and power that the acquisition of overseas territory conferred. And the quest for raw materials and markets was often masked by the activities of Christian missionaries.

Whatever the motive, imperialism always entailed, in one form or another, the subjection of native peoples to meddling interference and foreign rule. Racism was implicit in modern imperialism, and apologists for European rule over "inferior" peoples eagerly drew on classical precepts. Cicero, for one, had justified Roman rule over the "barbarians" by pointing out that "servitude in such men is established for their welfare."

A debate has flourished as to whether the gains of imperialism – such as the construction of railroads and other forms of economic infrastructure, or the establishment of democratic institutions – have outweighed the evident losses in wealth, traditions, self-respect, and lives. One thing is certain: without Europe's empires, the slave trade would never have left its deep stain on the heritage of Europe and the Americas. Nor would the natives of North America, the Aborigines of Australia, and the Xhosa people of southern Africa have come so close to extinction.

"THE WHITE MAN'S BURDEN"

The phrase "the white man's burden" is the title of a poem published in 1899 by the English writer Rudyard Kipling.

"Take up the White Man's burden –
Send forth the best ye breed –
Go, bind your sons to exile
To serve your captives' need;
To wait in heavy harness
On fluttered folk and wild –
Your new-caught, sullen peoples,
Half-devil and half-child."

It was the during the high tide of late Victorian imperialism that the supposed civilizing mission of European peoples in the "less advanced" parts of the world reached its peak. Few Europeans knew anything of Africa and Asia, and most of those who did found it convenient to forget that both Africa and Asia had boasted magnificent civilizations while Europe was still a backwater of the Roman and post-Roman world.

Imperialist officials, working alongside traders and God-fearing missionaries, were to bring less fortunate peoples out of the shadows of history and into the light of European liberal democracy and Christianity.

LOCAL COLOR British residents ride in a magnificent procession of the Mogul court in 18th-century India. Britain gained a foothold on the subcontinent with the East India Trading Company. It was not until the 19th century that India officially became part of the Empire – "the jewel in the crown."

ECONOMIC IMPERIALISM

GUNBOAT DIPLOMACY British naval power defeated China in the war of 1840–42. It began when the Chinese banned the lucrative British opium trade.

The first systematic analysis of the economic underpinnings of imperialism came from the English scholar J.A. Hobson (1858–1940). In his book *Imperialism: a Study* (1902) – the inspiration for Lenin's attack on capitalist imperialism – he suggested that overproduction and accumulated surplus capital, combined with low wages and a depressed home market, forced industrialists to look abroad for exports and investment markets.

To secure these markets, governments had to assert control over distant regions. For example, in the 17th and 18th centuries, English laws tried to restrict enterprise in the American colonies to the supply of raw materials for the mother country.

No single theory can explain all the imperial activity in the world; but no other explanation with the force of the Hobson/Leninist one has yet been offered.

THE MONROE DOCTRINE

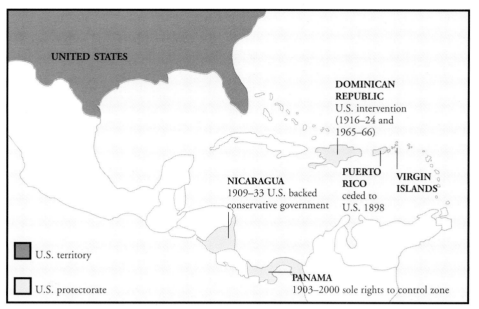

UNITED STATES

DOMINICAN REPUBLIC U.S. intervention (1916–24 and 1965–66)

PUERTO RICO ceded to U.S. 1898

VIRGIN ISLANDS

NICARAGUA 1909–33 U.S. backed conservative government

■ U.S. territory

□ U.S. protectorate

PANAMA 1903–2000 sole rights to control zone

EXPANDING THE UNION After the Civil War, U.S. growth focused on Central America, but other additions were the Philippines in 1898 and Hawaii in 1900. Alaska, settled in the 1880s, was declared U.S. territory in 1912.

The ink on its constitution had barely dried when the United States took its first steps toward building a North American empire. In 1803 the U.S. bought from France a vast tract of land lying west of the Mississippi and stretching from the Gulf of Mexico to what is now the Canadian border – the Louisiana Purchase. In 1812 it attempted to conquer British North America (Canada), but was defeated by the British, and in 1845 it brought Texas into the Union after a war against Spanish Mexico. This opened the way for expansion to the Pacific, which was completed by the admission of California in 1850.

The achievement of arms and money gave rise to the idea that the United States had a natural right to the territory of the New World or, at the very least, a moral duty to be its protector. In 1823 President James Monroe (1758–1831) asserted that the United States would tolerate no future European colonization in the Western hemisphere and that it would interpret any attempt by a European power to exercise influence there as an unfriendly act.

This – the Monroe Doctrine – was an unexceptional statement of national security interests. But as the United States grew in strength and confidence, it became the fashion to claim God's blessing for unchecked American expansion.

SEE ALSO

Liberationism · · · · · · · · · · · · ▶
Internationalism · · · · · · · · · · · · ▶
Moral philosophy · · · · · · · · · · · ▶
Economics · · · · · · · · · · · · · · ▶
Industrialization · · · · · · · · · · · · ▶

THE BRITISH EMPIRE

Half the globe, as it appeared in British atlases, was once red, and the sun never set on the British Empire. At first the British government was as much a follower as an instigator of colonial and imperial projects. British control over large parts of India in the late 18th century was established, not by foreign office officials, but by the East India Company. Of course, the company formed part of the British "establishment" and was, except in a technical sense, as much an organ of the British state as any government department.

It is salutary to remember that in India, as later in Africa, the British government was drawn, often reluctantly, into administrative roles in the wake of commercial enterprise. But it is equally true that a cardinal element in the long series of wars against France fought by Great Britain throughout the 18th century – five major conflicts in all – was the deliberate quest for mastery of the seas, therefore of maritime trade, and therefore of overseas markets and territory.

A major defense of imperialism was that "trade followed the flag." The American experience disproved the notion, for Anglo-American trade continued to flourish after the United States won its independence in 1783. Even so, the final victory over France at Waterloo in 1815 put the seal on Great Britain's rise to preeminence and its position, a source of national pride for more than a century to follow, as the world's greatest imperial power.

THE SLAVE TRADE

The institution of slavery, which came down to modern Europe from ancient times, depends upon people's willingness to look upon a human life as a piece of property, entirely at the disposal of its owner. That this is so was demonstrated when slavery was abolished in all the lands possessed by Great Britain by an act of Parliament of 1833. Abolition was accompanied by the payment of compensation to slave owners; none was offered to the slaves.

Great Britain was the first country to abolish the slave trade (1807) and slavery itself, and its initiative rang the death knell of a pattern of trade that had flourished since 1500, when the first slaves – supplied by local slave-traders – were transported from the west coast of Africa to Spain's new Caribbean colony of Hispaniola. Thousands of Africans, crowded like cattle in the airless bowels of sailing ships, lost their lives in the dreaded "middle passage." It got its name from its central position in what was known as the

"Teach your subordinates that we are all British gentlemen engaged in the magnificent work of governing an inferior race."

Richard Southwell Bourke, Earl of Mayo, Viceroy of India (1822–72)

ACCEPTED PRACTICE
African slaves, under the supervision of a white man, work in a boiling house – where raw sugar-cane is turned into sugar, molasses, and rum – on the Caribbean island of Antigua. The New World economies that produced sugar, cotton, and tobacco were entirely dependent on the exploitation of slave labor.

TIMELINE

Major European seizures of territory in the Far East

In some instances, imperial rule passed to other Western nations.

1520
Timor (PORT)

1565
Philippines (SPA)

1604
Borneo (NETH)

1649
Sumatra (NETH)

1755
Java (NETH)

1819
Singapore (GB)

1828
New Guinea (NETH)

1841
Sarawak (GB)

1842
Hong Kong (GB)

1846
Brunei (GB)

1877
North Borneo (GB)

1852
Burma (GB)

1863
Cambodia (FRA)

1893
Laos (FRA)

triangular trade that went from Europe to Africa's "slave coast," to the sugar and tobacco colonies of the New World, and then back.

Brazil was the most voracious consumer of African slaves, taking in about four million before the trade was ended in 1870. In all, it is estimated that about 15 million Africans were taken into slavery across the Atlantic during more than three centuries of European imperialism in the New World.

THE RUSSIAN EMPIRE

From its tiny beginnings as Kievan Rus in the 10th century, Russia grew over the centuries to become the largest continental empire – one continuous land mass – in history. The great era of empire building was the 18th century, when Peter the Great (*r.*1682–1723) and Catherine the Great (*r.*1762–96) established Russian ascendancy in the eastern Baltic and, in wars with Turkey, appropriated large chunks from the waning Ottoman Empire in the south. The imperial adventure was renewed in the mid-19th century when the "Russian Bear" overran what remained of Caucasian independence and made startling inroads into central Asia. By 1865 the Russian Empire extended as far as the Pacific and the borders of China and Afghanistan.

Running throughout the whole period of expansion was a debate about whether Russia should model itself on the West – democratic, increasingly secular, and technologically progressive – or whether it should nourish its traditions as a landlord-dominated, Orthodox autocracy. In the climactic moment of modern Russian history, it was the West that seemed to have won: in 1917 Western Marxism vanquished Tsarism. But the habit of autocracy proved durable (although the Church was dismembered).

After 1945 Russian imperialism was given a free hand in Eastern Europe. The collapse of the Soviet Empire after the fall of the Berlin Wall in 1989 and the retreat of communism have left the future of Russia one of the great imponderable questions of modern politics.

TOTALITARIANISM

States run by thought police

Totalitarianism is usually considered to be a modern phenomenon, a complete political system exhibited most starkly by Germany under the Nazis, Italy and Spain under the Fascists, and the Soviet Union and China under the Communists. Total authority over every citizen has been made easier to exercise in an era of mass politics, sophisticated means of policing, and rapid communication.

Every totalitarian regime is a dictatorship in which the rule of law is virtually suspended, and the most vital department of state is the secret police. But totalitarianism is more than a dictatorship. Although totalitarian regimes demand obedience and enforce it by terror and intimidation, what distinguishes them is that they crave assent. Their goal is to penetrate the minds of their citizens to such an extent that the whole nation becomes ideologically one, without the possibility of dissent. By bringing everything within the orbit of the party – by making every action and every thought political – politics is eliminated.

The writer Jung Chang (1952–   ) has described totalitarianism in action in a passage from *Wild Swans*, her memoirs of life in Mao's China. "The Party's all-round intrusion into people's lives was the very point of the process known as 'thought reform'. . . Every week a meeting was held for those 'in the revolution.' Everyone had both to criticize themselves for incorrect thoughts and be subjected to the criticism of others . . . Meetings were an important means of communist control. They left people no free time, and eliminated the private sphere." Thus totalitarian regimes set themselves against individualism – the notion that the best society is one that gives every individual the greatest opportunity for the development of his or her powers and the pursuit of his or her happiness – which since the Renaissance has been the philosophical foundation of European civilization.

NIETZSCHE AND THE "ÜBERMENSCH"

The German philosopher Friedrich Nietzsche (1844–1900) announced the death of God and worried about the nihilism that he believed would follow from it. He believed that traditional Western, Christian morality was inadequate for the coming crisis, because it appealed to "herd instincts" and exalted "slave morality". The "enhancement of life" required a greater emphasis on creativity. He argued that the play of forces that made up earthly existence had no goal or final purpose, and what raised one person above another was "the will to power." The future therefore belonged to those human beings capable of raising themselves by their creativity above the herd. A person of that type he called an *übermensch*, or "superman." It is easy to see why the Nazis found such ideas, crudely represented, attractive. But Nazism drew far more on evocations of Teutonic mythology – found, for example, in Wagner's operas – (much admired by Hitler) than it did on the complex ideas of Nietzsche.

ANTI-SEMITISM

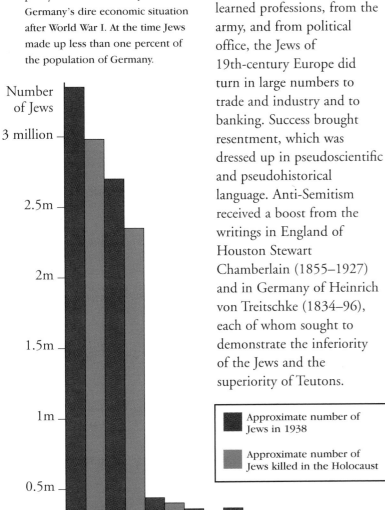

PROPAGANDA OF HATE Part of Nazi policy was to blame the Jews for Germany's dire economic situation after World War I. At the time Jews made up less than one percent of the population of Germany.

Semites include Hebrews, Assyrians, and Arabs. But hatred of, or prejudice against, the Jews specifically – which has waxed and waned since the foundation of Christianity – goes by the misnomer of anti-Semitism. One strand derives from the crude assertion that "the Jews crucified Christ." In modern times the chief charge has been that Jews are somehow uniquely engaged – at other people's expense – in money making. Excluded from the learned professions, from the army, and from political office, the Jews of 19th-century Europe did turn in large numbers to trade and industry and to banking. Success brought resentment, which was dressed up in pseudoscientific and pseudohistorical language. Anti-Semitism received a boost from the writings in England of Houston Stewart Chamberlain (1855–1927) and in Germany of Heinrich von Treitschke (1834–96), each of whom sought to demonstrate the inferiority of the Jews and the superiority of Teutons.

Number of Jews

- ■ Approximate number of Jews in 1938
- ■ Approximate number of Jews killed in the Holocaust

Poland, Russia, Hungary, Czechoslovakia, Germany, Netherlands, France, Austria, Greece, Yugoslavia, Romania, Belgium, Bulgaria

"GENERAL WILL"

MACHINE OF TERROR The glee with which the Parisian mob greeted the mass executions that took place during the Terror (1793–94) could be seen as a negative expression of the "general will." In all, 17,000 people were executed within the space of 11 months.

Jean Jacques Rousseau (1712–78) expounded his idea of the "general will" in *The Social Contract* (1762). The general will was not simply the will of the majority, nor the sum total of the wills of all the individuals in a society. It was a nebulous thing, the will to bring about the highest common good of what he called the "moral and collective body" of the community. This abstract, complicated idea led, in Rousseau's mind, to the democratic recognition of the sovereignty of the people.

A difficulty arises, however, when it comes to giving practical expression to the general will. Someone has to decide what the general will is and how to implement it. Rousseau argued that everyone must be compelled to obey the general will and thus "be forced to be free."

Some critics of Rousseau's thought have found in its implicitly anti-pluralist, anti-individualist strain a foretaste of the totalitarian temperament that runs from the French revolutionary leader at the time of the Terror, Maximilien Robespierre (1758–94) – who announced that "our will is the general will" – to Joseph Stalin and Adolf Hitler.

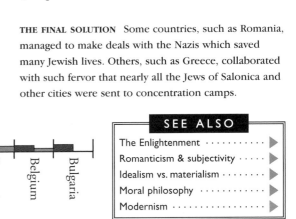

THE FINAL SOLUTION Some countries, such as Romania, managed to make deals with the Nazis which saved many Jewish lives. Others, such as Greece, collaborated with such fervor that nearly all the Jews of Salonica and other cities were sent to concentration camps.

SEE ALSO
The Enlightenment
Romanticism & subjectivity
Idealism vs. materialism
Moral philosophy
Modernism

JAPAN'S "DARK VALLEY"

The rise to power of the military in Japan during the 1930s was marked by the very features that characterized totalitarianism in the West – xenophobia, an antipathy to democracy, and a desire for territorial expansion. Right-wing sympathizers especially disliked the Westernizing of Japanese society that had taken place since the demise of the shoguns and the samurai and the beginning of the "enlightened" Meiji era in 1867.

Extremist nationalist societies, like Kokusuikai (National Purity Society) and the terrorist organization Ketsumeidan (League of Blood), joined forces with the higher ranks of the army and navy in a campaign of propaganda and assassination that eroded the institutions of parliamentary democracy and relegated the emperor to the status of a puppet. By 1932 the army, simply ignoring the government, had conquered the part of mainland China known as Manchuria (which became Manchukuo) and large parts of Mongolia.

Japan entered the *kurai tanima*, or "dark valley," an era of repression and censorship at home and rabid aggression abroad. In 1936 Japan allied itself with Nazi Germany and the Axis powers and overran northern China. Its imperialist ambitions were scarcely masked by a declaration that it wished to create a "Greater Co-Prosperity Sphere" in Southeast Asia.

After it attacked Pearl Harbor in 1941, Japan seemed unbeatable – taking control of Hong Kong, Malaya, Singapore, the Dutch East Indies, and the Philippines, and by seizing Burma and Papua New Guinea, imperiling India and Australia – until defeat in 1945 brought the dark days to an end.

"Japan's best course is to beat China to her knees"

Japanese Prime Minister Konoe Fumimaro (1891–1945) in 1937

DEGENERATE ART

"CORRUPT AND DEGENERATE" The works of Emil Nolde were condemned by the Nazis. He was forced into internal exile and banned from painting, although he continued to practise his art illegally.

Dictators are obsessed by cleanliness. Purge after purge – of civil servants, of the army, of universities, of their own parties – takes place in the ceaseless endeavor to remove all traces of impurity from their fiefdoms. In 1937 Adolf Hitler opened the Great German Art Exhibition at Munich. It was held in a new building, templelike in structure and neoclassical in style, that was intended as Nazism's riposte to the prevailing International Style of Western architecture – the style of the Bauhaus and of Le Corbusier.

In his opening address, Hitler declared that the Nazis were going to "wage a merciless war of destruction against the last remaining elements of cultural disintegration," the works of modernist artists that were "not capable of being understood in themselves but need some pretentious instruction book to justify their existence."

A day later, a "Degenerate Art" exhibition opened, also in Munich. It was mounted by the Nazis to denounce distortions of form and color, to revile the religious paintings of Emil Nolde (1867–1956) and Max Beckmann (1884–1950) as blasphemy, to expose immorality – in short to "demonstrate the common root of political and cultural anarchy" in esthetic experimentation. The public flocked to see it; by comparison the exhibition of German worthies excited little interest. Over the next two years, public galleries were emptied of modernist canvases, and thousands were either sold to help fill the Nazi war chest or burned in public.

"MEIN KAMPF"

RACIAL HATRED A small boy and his parents walk past an anti-Semitic poster in Vienna – a city which before the war had a prosperous Jewish population. Hitler's envy of Viennese Jewry helped form his political ideology.

Adolf Hitler's monumental *Mein Kampf* (My Struggle) was written while he was in prison for his part in the Munich putsch, or attempted coup of 1923. Its autobiographical sections are a melodramatic account of his personal battle to rise above odds stacked against him. It is also, in passage after wearying passage, a sustained calumny of the Jews.

But two elements of the book hold great interest. The first is Hitler's analysis of the power of propaganda and the techniques required to make it effective – the one original intellectual achievement of his life. The second is the articulation of Hitler's resolve to make *lebensraum*, or "living space," for the Aryan race by carving out a slave empire in the East – absorbing the German-speaking people of Austria and the Czech Sudetenland, and imposing Nazi rule over Poland and Russia.

"Nature," he wrote, "knows no political frontiers. She begins by establishing life on this globe and then watches the free play of forces. Those who show the greatest courage and industry are the children nearest to her heart and they will be granted the sovereign right of existence."

THE CORPORATE STATE

The idea of the corporate state is particularly associated with Benito Mussolini (1883–1945), leader of the Fascist movement which came to power in Italy in 1922. In the corporate state all self-governing associations, all business interests were to lose their individuality and independence. Mussolini defined the concept in an entry that he wrote for the *Enciclopedia Italiana*. "No individuals nor groups (political parties, labor unions, classes) exist outside the State. For this reason Fascism is opposed to Socialism, which clings rigidly to class war in the historic evolution and ignores the unity of the State, which molds the classes into a single moral and economic reality."

Yet it was not for nothing that Adolf Hitler (1889–1945) called his movement "national socialist"; both Nazism and Fascism shared with socialism a desire to give control of the economy to the central government. Socialism purported to do so in the name of the people: nationalization was depicted as "public ownership." Fascism offered strict control of foreign exchange; of the allocation of raw materials; of investment, and disciplined regulation of the work force, both industrial and agricultural; and of prices, wages, and profits – all in the name of the mystical state. The corporate state turned out to be, in the 1930s, little more than the subordination of all activity to the task of putting Germany and Italy on a war footing.

POWER AT THE CENTER Benito Mussolini believed that in the final analysis the state itself acted as the national corporation; in theory, this allowed all classes a role in economic production.

GENOCIDE

The American novelist Upton Sinclair (1878–1968) defined fascism – in its generic, not specifically Italian, sense – as "capitalism plus murder." Violence is inherent in a totalitarian regime because terror is one of the regime's weapons and the silencing of dissent one of its necessities.

Genocide – the systematic elimination of a race of people – is not a necessary corollary of dictatorship. But it is useful for a dictator to be able to throw blame on others, to divert discontent toward a scapegoat: throughout history, demagogues have pointed to "the enemy within." Saddam Hussein (1937–) of Iraq has used Kurdish groups in the northern part of his country in this way, and threatened them with annihilation.

For a policy of genocide to be successful, the ground has to be well prepared. The English novelist Aldous Huxley (1894–1963) wrote: "When particular men and women are thought of merely as representatives of a class, which has previously been defined as evil and personified in the shape of the devil, then the reluctance to hurt or murder disappears."

The mass slaughter of the Jews by the Nazis did not begin until the Nazis had hammered home to the German people the message that the Jews were responsible for all the ills of German society. Jews were endlessly vilified, in words and pictures, as nothing better than vermin. Who would not wish to rid a society of disease-carrying rats?

The elimination of the Jews, called the "final solution," was pursued with such resolve because the Nazi leader Adolf Hitler did actually believe what he said – as page after page of his autobiography *Mein Kampf* (1925–27) testifies. The Jews were not simply a scapegoat. In Hitler's mind, and in the mind of the anti-Semites who rallied to him, the Jews were an evil presence, polluting Germany's Aryan stock and standing in the way of the racial supremacy that was Germany's destiny.

CAMBODIAN HORROR Dry bones bear witness to the slaughter by the Khmer Rouge in the 1970s of 1.5 million Chinese, Vietnamese, Laotian, Thai, Indian, and Pakistani people because they were not of "pure" Khmer stock.

PROPAGANDA

YOUNG MINDS ON FIRE Blazing artwork calls youthful Germans to a Nazi rally. Ex-journalist Joseph Goebbels (1897–1945) was Nazi Party minister of propaganda from 1933 and waged a ruthless war of words on its behalf.

For most of its history, "propaganda" was a perfectly respectable word – it appears blamelessly in the name of the Congregatio de Propaganda Fide, a committee appointed by the papacy in 1622 to propagate the Christian faith. In the 20th century, it has sometimes come to mean little more than a pack of lies.

The origin of this shift appears to have been the reporting of invented enemy atrocities during World War I, especially by the *Daily Mail* in England. The intensive use of propaganda has been a hallmark of totalitarian regimes. Hitler explained the psychology of the "big lie" in *Mein Kampf*: "In the big lie, there is always a certain force of credibility; because the broad masses of a nation are always more easily corrupted in the deeper strata of their emotional nature than consciously or voluntarily, and thus in the primitive simplicity of their minds they more readily fall victim to the big lie than the small lie, since they themselves often tell lies in small matters, but...it would never come into their heads to fabricate colossal untruths."

FRANCO'S SPAIN

The Spanish Civil War of 1936–39 was a microcosm of the great political debate that raged for most of the 20th century between totalitarianism and liberal democracy. From it, the Nationalist cause, supported by matériel from Nazi Germany, emerged victorious.

The dictatorship of General Francisco Franco (1892–1975) lasted for 36 years. It is commonly described as fascist, and Franco's attempt to build a Spanish economy on the principles of autarky, or self-sufficiency, without recourse to foreign investments or credits was modeled on the Italian example. Franco's movement was essentially one of conservative reaction, authoritarian in the extreme, to the fledgling parliamentary democracy of the Second Republic, established in 1931. Franco skillfully united under his leadership the Falange, with its street-fighting "Blueshirts," the church, and the monarchists.

But whereas Bolshevism and Nazism were dynamic, forward-looking movements, and their rise and fall were matters of supreme importance to the whole world, Franco's was a local achievement in the Spanish backwater.

FIGHTERS AGAINST FRANCO Political conviction drove young men from many backgrounds and countries to volunteer for the International Brigade in its struggle against the Nationalist forces in the Spanish Civil War.

THE CULT OF PERSONALITY

One of the great pillars of the Nazi state – perhaps in the end the most important – was the *Führerprinzip*, the "leader principle." From the moment in 1921 when Adolf Hitler assumed the leadership of the German Workers' Party and added the words National Socialist to its title, he made it plain that the party must do whatever he wanted or do without him. By 1923 he was demanding to be saluted. When the Nazis came to power in 1933, the greeting "Heil Hitler" was declared to be "the German greeting" and made compulsory for all public officials; the Nazi salute was made mandatory during the singing of the national anthem.

The cult of personality, the transformation of a political leader into a national savior, was fostered in order to cleanse Germany of political activity and political ideas. Above all factions and group associations, the Führer, according to a 1939 publication expounding Nazi "constitutional law," was "the bearer of the collective will of the people."

The Soviet leader Joseph Stalin (1879–1953) was as devoted to the cult of personality as Hitler, but he had to overcome the Communist Party's tradition of collective leadership. It is hard to imagine, had Nazism survived Germany's defeat in 1945, a successor to Hitler publicly denouncing his cult of personality as the Communist Party secretary general Nikita Khrushchev (1894–1971) did Stalin's at the party congress in 1956.

PEOPLE'S CHOICE Leaders who inspire personality cults are not always tyrants. Cory Aquino was democratically elected the Philippine president in 1986.

LIBERATIONISM
The unchaining of the oppressed

For as long as there have been rulers, there have been oppressors. Indeed, for most of history, the many have been oppressed by the rich and powerful few. Liberation politics of the modern era seeks to bring the plight of the oppressed – especially in the supposedly liberal democracies of the affluent West – onto the political agenda. The aim is to gain equal personal and legal status and equal economic and employment opportunities for those who do not seem to get a fair chance in society.

Each of the three most prominent liberation movements – on behalf of blacks in predominantly white societies, of homosexuals in predominantly heterosexual societies, and of women in male-dominated societies – has had two strands: the effort to raise the social consciousness and self-respect of members of the oppressed group; and the campaign to enlist those members in the struggle to persuade or compel society to do them justice.

The most contentious element in liberation politics is the role of "positive discrimination," or "affirmative action," by which is meant setting minimum quotas for women and minorities, especially in the workplace and in educational institutions. Advocates of positive discrimination argue that equality will never be achieved for groups left far behind unless a level playing field, or something approaching it, is artificially established. Opponents point out that positive discrimination robs its intended beneficiaries of self-esteem, distorts the measurement of real progress, and is a form of unacceptable discrimination against those individuals – not members of the oppressed group – to whom equal opportunity and appointment on merit is denied.

BLACK POWER

Black Power became the name for the militant branch of the Civil Rights movement in the United States that flourished briefly in the late 1960s and early 1970s. The origin of the movement is traced to the call by Stokely Carmichael (1941–) in 1966 for civil rights agitators to turn their backs on the assimilationist goal and nonviolent methods of Martin Luther King (1929–68).

Advocates of Black Power wanted racial separatism, always with the threat of violence. Their leaders did much to raise the self-esteem of American blacks. The two foremost organizations within the movement were the Black Panthers and the Black Muslims, the latter were raised to prominence by the rhetoric of Malcolm X (1925–65).

FEMINISM

FOOD FOR THOUGHT Feminist graffiti deface – and update – a poster advertising a brand of beer.

Women's struggles to gain social, economic, and political equality with men undoubtedly lie deep in history, obscured by the tradition of historical writing that has flowed from male pens. The modern movement of feminism, however, is usually traced to the late 18th century, to the formation of women's political clubs in Paris in the wake of the French Revolution and to the nascent campaign for female suffrage, especially associated with the publication in 1792 of *Vindication of the Rights of Women* by the English writer Mary Wollstonecraft (1759–97).

Feminists in the 19th century were largely occupied with gaining for women the right to vote, property rights in marriage, and the right to be educated. Contemporary feminism in the West, arising strongly in the United States in the 1960s, has made male patriarchy in all its aspects the focus of attack and has raised the issue of gender discrimination in a wide variety of fields beyond the political and economic – linguistic studies, psychoanalysis, history, and many others. Feminism has become both a tool of analysis and a practical program.

Some of the objects of the feminist movement – achieved to varying degrees in different parts of the world – have been legal recognition of a woman's right to abortion, to equal pay with men for equal work done, and to equal division of property on divorce. Feminists have fought to dismantle the patronizing Victorian pedestals on which men put them, in the process making male emancipation from inhibiting preconceptions an important ingredient of the feminist agenda.

GAY LIBERATION

In the 1960s and 1970s most Western nations decriminalized sexual activity between consenting male adults. That victory for homosexuals ushered in gay liberation movements throughout the West.

Being invisible, at least compared with women and blacks, gay people had not suffered the same degree of overt discrimination. The main effort of gay liberation has been to raise the self-esteem of homosexuals, to eradicate the shame that the culture has taught them to feel and so banish fears of disclosure.

Whether people should be "outed" (their homosexuality brought to public knowledge) without their consent has divided the movement. Arguments in favor of outing are that the gain in making known the sexuality of worthy citizens or celebrities outweighs any private distress and that to shy away from it is to admit that homosexuality is shameful. Gay liberation also has a number of legislative objectives, among them being the equal recognition in law of married homosexual couples, and equal age of consent with heterosexuals.

OUT AND PROUD Marchers in the first Gay Pride march parade through the streets of New York City in 1973.

TIMELINE

Decriminalization of homosexuality

1961
All nonviolent consensual sex activities between adults in private are decriminalized in 24 states.

1971
Homosexual acts are decriminalized in Austria.

1978
Homosexual acts are decriminalized in Spain. The age of consent is set at 12.

1979
Homosexuality is no longer classed as a disease in Sweden.

1981
Law prohibits discrimination against gays and lesbians in Norway.

1988
Male homosexual acts are decriminalized in Israel. Previously, a 10-year prison sentence had been possible.

1989
In Denmark, legislation allows homosexuals to engage in a "registered partnership," with a status similar to marriage.

1992
Homosexual acts in the army are decriminalized in Switzerland.

SEE ALSO

Liberalism · · · · · · · · · · · ◄
Moral philosophy · · · · · · · · · · · ►

INTERNATIONALISM
A global perspective

Internationalism is a relatively recent idea. Narrowly defined, it refers to the recognition that all nations are bound together in a collective enterprise that calls for cooperative action. It has gained force from the shrinking of the world – thanks largely to modern methods of rapid communication – into a "global village."

For most of the 20th century, Europe's bloody divisions and the post-1945 Cold War between the capitalist West and the communist eastern bloc distracted Western minds from the greatest of international issues – the gaping economic disparity between rich and poor nations. The abandonment of communism in most of Eastern Europe, beginning in 1989, brought the end of the Cold War and so removed the framework for the conduct of international relations. Meanwhile, the material advance of the Pacific Rim countries threw the established economic order into disarray.

The pressures on international action nevertheless remain the same: disease, pollution, and the rapid growth of population in the poor countries of the world, making water, housing, food, jobs, and education scarce. Pessimists foresee a weakening of social systems in those countries and the collapse of states; optimists look forward to continuing improvement on the back of free-market practices and economic interdependency between rich and poor nations.

THE INTERNATIONAL

Most international organizations seek to pool the resources or unite the purposes of nation-states for their mutual benefit. The International, a working men's association founded by the German theorist Karl Marx (1818–83) in 1864, was intended to override national boundaries and unite men and women solely on the basis of class.

From the beginning, the movement's high hopes foundered on wrangling between its left-wing factions, most notably in the early years between Marxists and anarchists – a running quarrel that resulted in the dissolution of the First International in 1876. The Second International was formed in 1889, but it fell victim to the patriotic nationalism of 1914.

The International's call to working men to refuse to fight in the "capitalist war" fell on deaf ears, and the knell of the movement was sounded when the German Socialist Party voted almost unanimously for war credits to finance the Kaiser's military requirements. Lenin wrote: "Internationalism (kindly note) consists in the workers of all countries shooting at each other in the name of the 'Defense of the Fatherland.'"

TALKING PEACE Members of the United Nations discuss the growing violence in the Congo (now Zaire) in 1964.

INTERNATIONAL LAW

AFTER WAR, JUSTICE With associates, Alfred Krupp (far left), owner of the German Krupp armaments firm, faces prosecution at the Nuremberg War Trials in 1947. The men were charged with aiding the Nazi war effort.

In 1899 a Permanent Court of Arbitration was established at an international conference at The Hague. It was empowered to hear international disputes when at least one nation from each side agreed to arbitration. The International Court of Justice, established by the United Nations in 1945, now presides in cases of international law. It is competent to handle disputes arising from the interpretation of treaties and conventions, to judge where there have been breaches of international law, and to assess reparations.

The content of international law is nebulous, but is generally held to include customary practices by nations, as well as the articles of treaties, conventions, and protocols. Some jurists also include "principles" of law relating to human rights. There is no body of law to which all countries pay homage, although member states of the United Nations are required to uphold its regulations. Nor is there any method of enforcing the law except by the action of public opinion, economic or other sanctions – or resort to war.

Many jurists maintain that there is no such thing as international law. For instance, the Nuremberg hearings in 1945–48, which sentenced Nazi war criminals to death or imprisonment, rested on flimsy legal foundations. The judgments were enforceable only because of the strength of world opinion.

THE UNITED NATIONS

Fifty years have passed since the founding of the United Nations (UN) in 1945. It is not a world government and does not aspire to be one: it is a meeting place for nation-states. Its two fundamental purposes remain to provide a forum for resolving international disputes and through its agencies to promote improved living standards throughout the world and thus eliminate some causes of conflict.

However, one important change has occurred in the UN's practices. Until recently, it had always refrained from intervening in disputes, especially in internal disputes, unless invited to do so by a member state. In Somalia and Rwanda in the 1990s, that inhibition was overcome.

Reformists are pressing for more generous funding of the UN by member states, for a permanent peacekeeping force, and for the expansion of the number of permanent members in its Security Council (currently the United States, Russia, France, Britain, and China) to make it more representative of the contemporary world.

BANNER OF UNITY One of the United Nations' key functions is to safeguard world peace, but it faces an uncertain future unless solid criteria are established governing when and how it will intervene in disputes.

INTERNATIONAL ORGANIZATIONS

NATO The North Atlantic Treaty Organization was created by Western countries who had allied in April 1949 to counter the military threat of the Soviet Union and its allies. Founder members included the United States, France, Britain, and Italy. West Germany joined in 1955 and Spain in 1982.

Warsaw Pact Defense alliance signed by the U.S.S.R., Bulgaria, East Germany, Czechoslovakia, Hungary, Poland, Romania, and Albania in May 1955.

EEC The European Economic Community was established under the Treaty of Rome in 1957 to remove trade barriers and provide for mobility of capital and labor. Original members were Belgium, France, Luxembourg, the Netherlands, Italy, and West Germany. Britain, Denmark, and Ireland joined in 1973; Greece, Portugal, and Spain in the 1980s.

The Commonwealth Some British colonies that had become self-governing dependent states were joined in the British Commonwealth of Nations in 1931. The word "British" was dropped in 1946.

SEE ALSO
Nationalism
Imperialism
Liberationism

MULTINATIONAL CORPORATIONS

THE GLOBE IN ITS GRIP Shell promoted this vision of itself as the world's foremost oil company in the 1920s. The oil business – dependent on mineral-rich countries for its raw materials – demands a global approach.

Multinational corporations have two outstanding characteristics: an element of joint ownership across national boundaries and some sort of coordinated international management. They began to emerge at the end of the 19th century because, for their own benefit and profit, large corporations wished to control rival companies in foreign countries and also wanted to overcome barriers to trade – such as protective tariffs – by manufacturing in countries to which they would otherwise export.

One important motive for corporations in the high-wage West to become multinational is the desire to exploit the low-wage labor market in other parts of the world. A common criticism of the spread of multinationals is that they undermine national sovereignty and, by placing themselves beyond the easy reach of governments – in such matters as taxation and the control of capital transfers – pose a threat to democratic accountability. Some critics also bemoan the erosion of cultural distinctiveness that follows from the dispersion of identical products, above all American ones, throughout the world.

INTERPOL

Interpol, the International Criminal Police Organization, was founded at Vienna in 1923. It was dissolved in 1938 when Austria was absorbed into the German Reich, and founded again in Paris after the war. The present headquarters are in Lyon in central France.

Popular imagination peoples the world with Interpol agents; in fact, the organization is essentially a clearing house for information about criminals, and about methods of detection and prevention. Interpol enables the police forces of the sovereign nations which belong to it – now more than 130 – to combat international crime more readily. By far the most important crimes that Interpol tackles are smuggling – above all of drugs and precious metals – and fraud, especially forgery and the counterfeiting of paper money. Interpol depends heavily for its effectiveness on the agreement between nations to uphold extradition treaties allowing for the transfer for trial of suspected criminals from one country to another.

International cooperation ended a 20-year manhunt in August 1994 when the terrorist Illich Ramirez Sanchez, nicknamed Carlos the Jackal, was arrested in the Sudan and brought to France by Interpol. Sanchez, a Venezuelan-born Marxist activist, was wanted for the murder of two French special agents in Paris in 1975, as well as for several other terrorist attacks in Western Europe that were linked to Middle Eastern governments. In 1992 a French court had sentenced him, in his absence, to life imprisonment for the killing of the special agents.

INTERNATIONAL FUGITIVE Carlos the Jackal evaded capture for two decades before he was seized in Khartoum by Sudanese and French authorities with Interpol help in 1994. This mug shot was taken in 1975 at the height of his notoriety after the successful kidnapping of 81 OPEC delegates in Vienna. Three died and seven were wounded but Sanchez and the other five terrorists negotiated an undisclosed ransom for the lives of the hostages and escaped by plane to Algeria.

GENEVA CONVENTION

LIFELINE In 1994 Red Cross food and medical aid was the difference between life and death for thousands of refugees abandoning their homes in Rwanda, Central Africa. The refugees were members of the Hutu tribe who were fleeing slaughter at the hands of the rival Tutsi tribe in Rwanda.

The Geneva Convention is the collective name for a series of international agreements, made between 1864 and 1949, which taken together have established a code of practice for the treatment of wounded combatants in war, those who minister to them, and prisoners of war. The first convention, signed at Geneva, established the Red Cross, an international agency to help people captured or wounded in war. The convention also called for immunity from attack for all hospitals and encampments for the sick and wounded, for the impartial and humane treatment of all combatants, and for the recognition of the Red Cross symbol (a red cross on a white background) and the protection of all medical corps and their assistants who wore it.

The Hague Convention of 1907 added to those provisions the treatment of prisoners of war (POWs). Signatories to the convention undertook to treat POWs humanely, to guarantee that information about POWs would be available and visits by neutrals allowed. A 1949 agreement extended the regulations to include a guarantee of adequate food, the unhindered delivery of relief supplies for POWs, and a ban on the use of torture to extract information from them.

AMNESTY INTERNATIONAL

Founded in London in 1961, Amnesty International was part of the international movement to protect and extend basic human rights throughout the world. In 1948 the United Nations had adopted its Universal Declaration of Human Rights, whose 30 articles listed what international opinion considered to be the basic social, economic, civil, political, and human rights of every individual in the world, but the implementation of the Declaration is not binding upon UN member states.

Amnesty International, which is independent of the UN and of the British government, merely seeks to publish accounts of violations of human rights and to exert the pressure of public opinion to end those violations. It works for the release of people imprisoned because of their political or religious convictions, fair trials for political prisoners, and the eradication of torture and extrajudicial executions. It also campaigns for the abolition of capital punishment throughout the world. Its work is largely dependent upon voluntary contributions.

> *"Everyone has the right to freedom of thought, conscience, and religion."*
>
> *United Nations Declaration of Human Rights, 1948*

PEACEMAKER Peter Berenson, the English lawyer who founded Amnesty International, was awarded the Nobel Prize for Peace in 1977. His organization is famous for its letter-writing campaigns, in which Amnesty members ask political leaders to rectify individual human-rights abuses.

BALANCE OF POWER

SEE ALSO: *Internationalism*

Throughout history, rulers and states have sought to maintain peace and stability by pursuing the objective of a "balance of power." Especially in Europe during the century from 1815 to 1914, it was the aim of the great powers to prevent any one of them from gaining enough military superiority to threaten the independence of the rest. The diplomacy of that era ended in the division of Europe into two antagonistic groupings – the Triple Alliance (Germany, Austria-Hungary, and Italy) and the Triple Entente (Great Britain, Russia, and France).

The outbreak of World War I in 1914 seemed to demonstrate the ineffectiveness of the idea as the guiding light of diplomacy, and in the interwar years, 1918–39, the objective broadened into the more general one of "collective security." Treaties, such as the Locarno Pact of 1925 (in which the Western European powers "guaranteed" the existing frontiers between France, Belgium, and Germany) and the Paris Pact of 1928 (in which 67 signatory nations renounced war as an instrument of policy), were grounded in the argument that mutual agreement to forswear war would make it impossible for one nation to break out of the system in defiance of all the others. But the system required all parties to agree on what was aggression and to contain it even when their national interest was not directly involved.

The feebleness of the system was demonstrated during the crisis provoked by Germany's invasion of Czechoslovakia in 1938, when the British prime minister Neville Chamberlain (1869–1940) remarked, "how fantastic, incredible it is that we should be digging trenches and trying on gas masks here because of a quarrel in a faraway country between people of whom we know nothing."

Collective security had failed, and after 1945 it was replaced by the idea of nuclear deterrence.

NUCLEAR DETERRENCE

HISTORY MAKERS: *Nikita Khrushchev (1894–1971), John F. Kennedy (1917–63)*

SEE ALSO: *Physics*

Diplomacy by threat of force, the basis of all international relations, was given sinew by the manufacture and stockpiling of nuclear weapons by the United States and the Soviet Union after 1945. The threat became, for the first time in history, one of speedy mutual destruction and even of the annihilation of life on this planet. Soviet and American strategists had to contend with the knowledge that no "first strike" with nuclear weapons could deliver a knockout blow and that each of them possessed a "second-strike" nuclear capacity that guaranteed retaliation against the aggressor. "Mutual assured destruction," or MAD as it came to be called, was the basis of the theory that nuclear weapons were a deterrent to war.

Hence there took place the most expensive arms race in history, a race in which both sides insisted that they were building up their store of nuclear weapons in order not to have to use them. At the same time, the effectiveness of nuclear weapons as deterrents relied on the belief that the other side would use them. This inherent paradox led Robert McNamara (1916–), a powerful Cold Warrior in the Kennedy administration, to remark after he had left office that "one cannot fashion a credible deterrent out of an incredible action."

MUSHROOM CLOUD The atom bomb's distinctive explosion has become a symbol for the end of the world, because an escalating nuclear war would make the globe uninhabitable for humans. Much publicized nuclear testing, such as this French explosion in the Pacific, has become part of the game of nuclear deterrence, as more and more countries join the nuclear club.

UNILATERALISM

HISTORY MAKERS: *Bertrand Russell (1872–1970), Bruce Kent (1929–)*
SEE ALSO: *Global economics, Physics*

BAN THE BOMB In April 1963, 14,000 supporters took part in a CND protest march between the British government's atomic weapons research center in southern England and London.

The philosopher Bertrand Russell drew an analogy between relying on nuclear deterrence to prevent war and asking humanity to walk to eternity on a tightrope – humanity was bound to fall off. The Campaign for Nuclear Disarmament (CND) – of which Russell was a prime mover – was founded in Great Britain in 1958.

The movement reached the peak of its influence in Great Britain at the Labour Party conference of 1960, when a resolution in favor of unilateral disarmament – disarmament by one country without waiting for reciprocal action by other countries – was carried. But the view that disarmament could be achieved only by multilateral agreements and that unilateralism was too risky prevailed in ruling circles.

CND spread to North America and continental Europe, but its influence ebbed as a series of test bans and nonproliferation treaties in the 1970s and 1980s seemed to demonstrate the effectiveness of multilateralism.

TERRORISM

SEE ALSO: *Internationalism*

Many types of violence are popularly referred to as terrorism, from political assassination to guerrilla warfare; the British government defined terrorism in the 1989 Prevention of Terrorism Act as "the use of violence for political ends." Such a broad definition robs the term of meaning. Freedom-fighters, for instance, are not terrorists unless they use the weapon of terrorism. Acts of terrorism, properly understood, must inspire a general terror by their random and indiscriminate targeting of victims.

The assassination of President John F. Kennedy (1917–63) was not an act of terror: it made no one fearful for life beyond the highest-ranking politicians in America. The hijacking of planes and the bombing of public places may, depending upon the motive behind them, be acts of terror because they instill in people a general dread.

Acts of terror are rarely intended to achieve direct results. Since terrorism is almost always the weapon of the weak, its purpose is frequently simply to gain attention for a cause. The Palestine

TERRORISTS ON TRIAL Following a series of bloody attacks, leaders of the Italian Red Brigade were tried in Turin and imprisoned in 1978.

MASKED MURDERER One of the terrorists who attacked the Israeli Olympic team peers down from an Olympic village balcony before continuing with the slaughter of 11 athletes.

Liberation Organization celebrated the bombing of the 1972 Olympics as "like painting the name of Palestine on top of a mountain that can be seen from the four corners of the Earth."

Terrorism is condemned by governments, but the Zambian leader Kenneth Kaunda (1924–) once asked people to ponder which was preferable, "the selective brutality of terrorism or the impartial horrors of war."

ISOLATIONISM

HISTORY MAKERS:

George Washington (1732–99), James Monroe (1758–1831), Woodrow Wilson (1856–1924)

SEE ALSO: *Revolution, Imperialism, Internationalism*

NOT AN AMERICAN WAR Woodrow Wilson successfully campaigned for re-election as President in 1916, largely on the basis that he had kept the United States out of World War I by establishing the country's neutrality.

The American historian Richard Hofstadter (1916–70) once wrote, with some irony, that the United States was the only nation to have begun with perfection and aspired to progress. Certainly, a belief in the virtue of the New World and the corruption of Europe ran powerfully in early American history. That sentiment has colored the conduct of American international relations ever since.

There is a hint of what later became known as isolationism in some remarks of the first American president, George Washington, in 1787. Europe, he cautioned, had "primary interests" remote from the interests of the United States, which should deter the U.S. from implicating itself by artificial ties in the "combinations and collisions of her friendships or enmities." President James Monroe sounded the same note in an 1823 address – an argument later known as the Monroe Doctrine.

The high tide of isolationism was reached in the first half of the 20th century. It lay behind the United States' very late entry into World War I – made only in 1917 when Germany, having agreed to stop sinking neutral shipping, resumed doing so. It was also behind the Senate's refusal to ratify American membership of the League of Nations after the war, and the unwillingness to enter on the Allied side in World War II until it was provoked by the Japanese attack on Pearl Harbor in December 1941.

Yet isolationism has never been a governing passion in American foreign policy, as American commitment to NATO and American military intervention in crises all over the world since 1945 bear testimony.

McCARTHYISM

HISTORY MAKERS: *Joseph McCarthy (1909–57)*

SEE ALSO: *Marxism, Totalitarianism*

The term "McCarthyism" entered the political language in the 1950s as a byword for guilt by association combined with smear by innuendo. In the early days of the Cold War, the American senator Joseph McCarthy whipped up a "red scare" with his accusations of heavy communist infiltration of the State Department. In addition, he used congressional investigations to make charges against public officials and private citizens (especially in the media and films). He often had little or no evidence, and he himself was protected by congressional immunity from being sued for slander.

McCarthyism led to demands for loyalty oaths and security checks on employees and to the "blacklisting" of people suspected of being communist sympathizers – often known as "fellow travelers." The atmosphere of suspicion and distrust that was created in government and academic circles blighted many promising careers.

One of the consequences of McCarthyism was the elevation in status and authority of the congressional House Un-American Activities Committee. The committee was originally formed with the specific purpose of investigating people who might be supposed to have pro-Axis sympathies during World War II. The exertions of that committee (denounced from the outset by liberals) led to the establishment of the Subversive Activities Control Board and the Communist Control Act of 1954, which, against the grain of the constitutional protection of free speech, outlawed the Communist Party in the United States.

CULTURAL POLICEMAN Senator Joe McCarthy (left, at microphone) saw communism as a threat to the American way of life.

THE COLD WAR

HISTORY MAKERS:

*Joseph Stalin (1879–1953),
Nikita Khrushchev (1894–1971),
John F. Kennedy (1917–63)*

SEE ALSO: *Marxism, Internationalism*

KEEPING CAPITALISM AT BAY Workers erect the Berlin Wall to separate the communist eastern section of the German city from its western part, controlled by the Americans and British.

"Let us not be deceived," the American financier Bernard Baruch (1870–1965) said in a speech of 1947; "we are today in the midst of a cold war." Almost overnight, the phrase entered the political vocabulary to describe the economic, geopolitical, and ideological confrontation between the capitalist United States and its allies in NATO, and the communist Soviet Union and its satellite states in the Warsaw Pact.

Soviet strategy appeared to focus on the encouragement of communist revolutions throughout the world. The principal object of American foreign policy became the "containment" of communist "aggression." According to the popular "domino theory," when one state succumbed to communist insurrection, adjoining states tumbled in the same direction. American armed intervention in Korea in the early 1950s and in Vietnam in the 1960s followed from that theory. But the Cold War also meant that the suzerainty of the Soviet Union behind the "iron curtain" that divided Eastern from Western Europe was tacitly acknowledged: NATO connived at the Soviet suppression of national revolts in Hungary in 1956 and in Czechoslovakia in 1968.

Perhaps the most arresting episode in the Cold War was the Cuban Missile Crisis of 1962. After the Soviet premier Nikita Khrushchev had ordered the installation of nuclear warheads in Cuba, the Americans gave him an ultimatum to remove them and positioned ships around Cuba in a naval "quarantine." The world appeared to be on the brink of nuclear war, but the Soviets backed down.

The pursuit of détente – policy aimed at easing relations between the two sides – lowered the intensity of the Cold War in the 1960s. With the dismantling of the Berlin Wall in 1989 it could be said to have finally ended.

DIVIDED CITY A man peers through the brickwork of the Berlin Wall. The Wall, which put neighbors on different sides of an arbitrary line, became a poignant symbol of the Cold War.

INTERNATIONAL LANGUAGE

HISTORY MAKERS: *Ludwig Lejzer Zamenhof (1859–1917)*

SEE ALSO: *Liberationism, Internationalism*

Perhaps the most ambitious proposal to bring all the peoples of the world together in peace and harmony is the one to unite them by a common language. There have been modest precedents. Medieval Christendom was bound together by one official language, Latin, in which all international affairs were conducted. But the mass of the population, the peasants – who had scarcely heard of the next county, let alone distant Rome – conversed in their local dialects. Briefly, in the 17th and 18th centuries, French established itself as the language of polite society from Moscow to Madrid. But it was only in the late 19th century that schemes to invent an artificial language for the whole world arose.

At least 50 such languages have been promoted – the best known being Esperanto, which was devised by a Polish eye doctor, Ludwig Zamenhof, in 1889. Each language has prided itself on the simplicity and regularity of its spelling and grammar. But the great drawback of artificial languages – most of them derived from Romance (Latin-based) languages – is the difficulty of devising a vocabulary to fit the diverse cultural traditions of Africa, Polynesia, the Far East, and Europe.

Moreover, an invented language has an inherent need to remain static; otherwise the emergence of local variations would eventually lead to the development of whole new languages, destroying the very purpose of the exercise. But static languages are dead languages, useless things for everyday communication. An international language is unlikely to be adopted. Far more probable, for the foreseeable future, is a continuation of the spread of English as the unofficial *lingua franca* for most of the world.

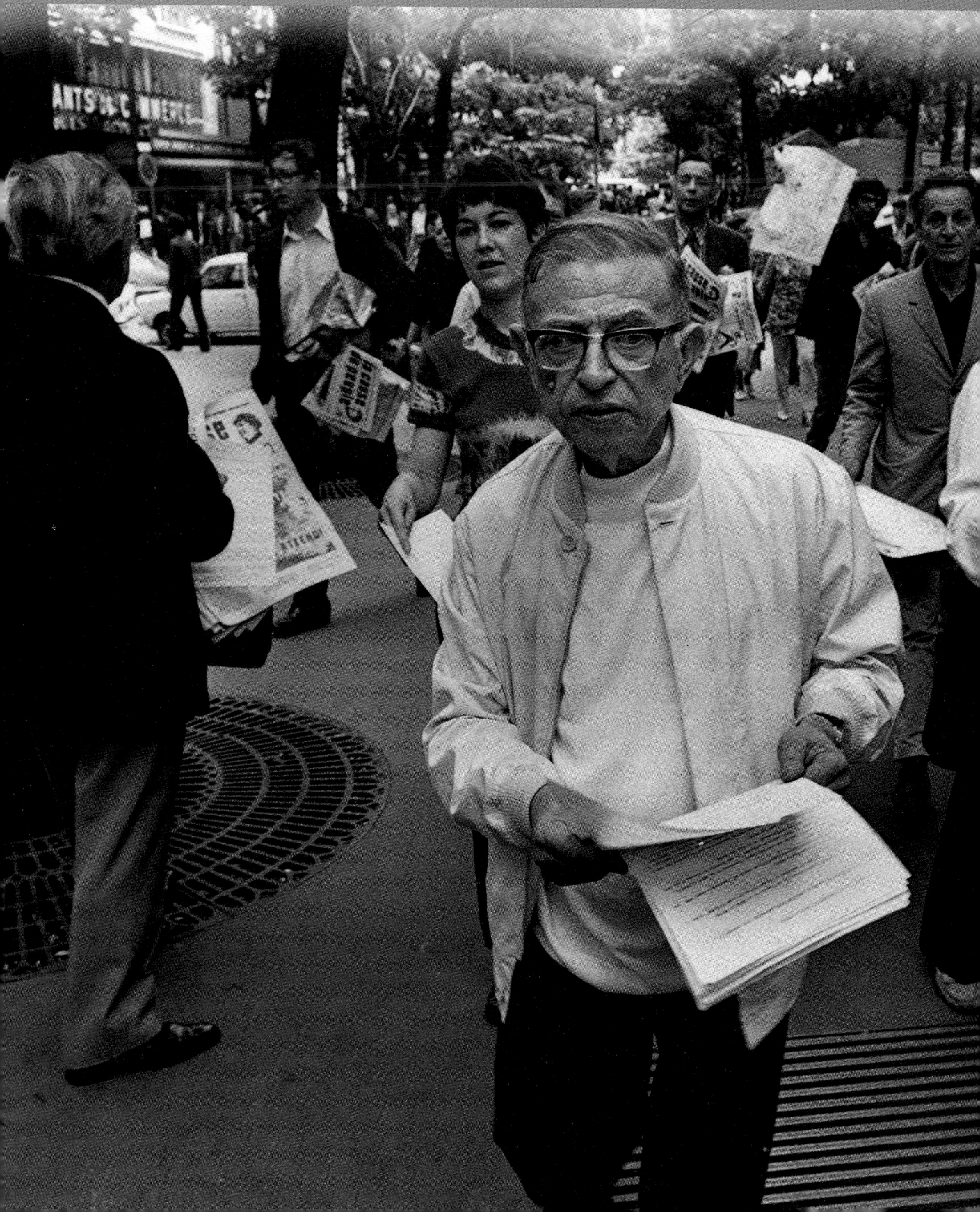

Philosophy & Spirituality

The tension between reason and imagination, the rational and the irrational has exercised thinkers for generations.

The term philosophy is derived from the Greek words *philos* (lover) and *sophia* (wisdom). And the founders of the Western tradition are the ancient Greeks, notably Socrates, Plato, and Aristotle. They asked general questions such as "What is the nature of reality?" rather than specific questions like "Is this a loaf of bread?" Using logic and rational argument to prove their points, they set both the agenda and the methods for philosophy down to the present day.

The influence of the Greeks was felt through the eras of the Roman Empire and medieval Christianity. Modern philosophy began in the 17th century with René Descartes, who started again from first principles. But modern philosophy did not progress in the same way as the natural sciences of the same period. Rationalists thought that knowledge could be gained by the use of reason alone, whereas scientists preferred the experimental method. Materialists argued that reality is ultimately composed of matter, idealists that reality is primarily spiritual.

After the Enlightenment, the philosophy of continental Europe diverged from that of the Anglo-American world. "Continental" philosophy emphasized questions of existence and subjectivity. The Anglo-American school, by contrast, argued that philosophy could tell us little or nothing about the human condition, its role was to clarify concepts and be a handmaiden to science.

Today, philosophers are trying to bridge the gap between the analytic and continental schools. Philosophy is still as fresh and unpredictable as it has always been.

As for spirituality, Friedrich Nietzsche's announcement of God's death was premature. But it seems unlikely that Western society will ever have quite the same relationship with the supernatural as it did before the Enlightenment. What also seems certain is uncertainty; Western religion is in a period of transition. Who knows what the next millennium will bring?

IDEAS IN ACTION Jean-Paul Sartre and Simone de Beauvoir demonstrate against the French presence in Algeria in 1965.

THE ENLIGHTENMENT

Reason challenges tradition

The characteristics of the Enlightenment were a belief in science and the experimental method, and in the use of reason to solve problems. The conviction that education could be a catalyst for social change was matched by trust in the integrity of the individual. Scepticism about received ideas meant the doctrines of the church were examined afresh – and often dismissed as superstition. Political systems were also questioned, leading to demands for more comprehensive political representation. These new attitudes paved the way for the American and French revolutions.

The core period of the Enlightenment was the second half of the 18th century, but the battle of ideas that led to the Enlightenment began in the 17th century. The English essayist Francis Bacon (1561–1626) advocated the use of scientific method, and the French mathematician René Descartes (1596–1650) proposed a critical rationalism. The Enlightenment was the culmination of a movement away from the authority and dogmatism of the medieval period.

Medieval philosophy combined Christian beliefs with the ideas of the Greek thinkers Plato (*c.*428–348 BC) and Aristotle (384–322 BC). In the medieval world, philosophers respected their predecessors and accepted their methods. If a new discovery about nature contradicted one of Aristotle's principles, for example, it would probably have been assumed that it was the discovery that was in error.

Enlightenment thinkers, however, were not content to accept appeals to Aristotle's authority. Scientists were using experimental methods to examine nature – and this could not be done without rejecting some of Aristotle's assumptions about the world. This gradual erosion of theories that had previously been treated as facts had consequences in fields other than science. No longer did the justification for monarchy seem so clear, nor the existence of God so certain.

Few of the philosophical questions posed during the Enlightenment have been completely laid to rest, but that seems to be the nature of modern philosophy, which attempts to answer – as far as possible – unanswerable questions. It is the attempt that is important. The same debates about God, morality, and science continue to the present day.

RATIONALISM

A rationalist is a philosopher who believes that we can gain knowledge by the use of reason alone, without reference to the external world. Rationalism has a long history in philosophy, but René Descartes was the first modern rationalist. He felt that philosophy should move away from the beliefs of the medieval scholars and put itself on firm foundations.

In order to establish these foundations, Descartes decided to start from scratch and assume that he knew nothing for certain. He realized that he could not doubt that he was thinking, as doubt is a type of thought. Without any reference to the external world, he was sure that he had found a basic truth that could not be questioned. Of course, once he realized that he was thinking, he could no longer doubt that he existed – because something must be doing the thinking. This allowed him to build up a philosophical system based on thought alone.

Once Descartes had reintroduced critical questioning into philosophy, the scene was set for the 100-year debate that was to lead to the Enlightenment in the 18th century.

REASON HOLDS THE KEY René Descartes refused to accept the truth of any received notion or proposal that could not be proved by rational argument.

EMPIRICISM

NATURAL EXPERIMENT American empirical scientist and statesman Benjamin Franklin (1706–90) invented the lightning conductor following this outdoor trial in 1752.

Empiricism is the belief that all knowledge comes from experience. The "empirical world" is the world of the senses – that is, the world we can see, feel, touch, hear, and smell.

The English philosopher John Locke (1632–1704) thought that the human mind at birth is a *tabula rasa* (blank tablet), on which experience writes the general principles and details of all knowledge. This was completely opposite to the rationalists. A rationalist would attempt to find knowledge by thought alone, but an empiricist would use the methods of the experimental sciences. It was not until the work of Immanuel Kant that empiricist and rationalist strains were brought together.

THE ENCYCLOPEDISTS

The *Encyclopédie ou Dictionnaire Raisonné des Sciences, des Arts et des Métiers* was published in 17 volumes between 1751 and 1765. The French philosopher Denis Diderot (1713–84) was the main editor. He was a committed empiricist and wrote on philosophy, religion, political theory, and literature. He was highly critical of the church's influence on ideas.

The French writer Voltaire (pen name of François Marie Arouet; 1694–1778) also edited and contributed to the encyclopedia. He was critical of the clergy, the king, and the privileges of the nobility. Jean Jacques Rousseau (1712–78), the French philosopher and novelist, wrote on music and political economy. Later he quarreled with Diderot and came to regard the encyclopedia as the work of the devil.

Rousseau was not alone. In 1752 and 1759, the Jesuits managed to suppress publication, although in each case for only a short period. Diderot, however, remained firm, and by 1772 a further 11 volumes of plates were published. Diderot's ambition "to change accepted habits of thought" was largely successful.

EVERYTHING WE KNOW The writers of the *Encyclopédie* wanted to promote scientific thought by making correct information available. Their belief in the power of knowledge epitomized the spirit of the Enlightenment.

TIMELINE

1684
Isaac Newton proposes his theory of gravitation.

1690
John Locke publishes his influential *Two Treatises of Government*, arguing that if governments offend against natural law they should be overthrown.

1739–40
David Hume anonymously publishes his empiricist *A Treatise of Human Nature*.

July 4, 1776
The inhabitants of England's American colonies declare their independence.

August 26, 1789
The revolutionary French National Assembly issues the *Declaration of the Rights of Man and the Citizen*. These include liberty and equality.

1787
The United States Constitution is drawn up.

SEE ALSO

Revolution ·············▶
Nationalism ············▶
Idealism vs. materialism ·······▶
Philosophy of science ·······▶
Neoclassicism ···········▶

THE ANALYTIC/SYNTHETIC DISTINCTION

We judge some statements to be true or false in relation to facts in the world – for example, that you are now reading this book. This is called by philosophers a synthetic truth. Other statements we judge to be true due to the meanings of the words involved. We can know that the sentence "All bachelors are unmarried" is true without having to carry out a survey of bachelors, because the sentence is true by definition. It is an analytic truth.

Synthetic truths are "truths of fact" and analytic truths are "truths of reason." We use empirical methods to verify synthetic statements and rationalist methods for analytic statements. Immanuel Kant was the first to use the terms "synthetic" and "analytic." He pointed out that all analytic truths are necessary; they could not have been otherwise. If the definition of a bachelor is an unmarried man, then all bachelors are unmarried. Synthetic statements are not necessary. It is not necessarily true that you are reading this book – you could be reading a photocopy.

In philosophy, it is important to make the analytic/synthetic distinction. If you argue that a thing is true, you should be clear whether you are saying something about the empirical world or are clarifying the meanings of words.

KILLER LOGIC If murder is defined as "wrong killing," then it must be bad. This is an analytic truth – proved by reason rather than experience. But some types of killing, for example in self-defense, may not qualify as murder.

KANT

MASTER'S TABLE Immanuel Kant (far right) leads a discussion at home in Königsberg, where he taught logic at the University for 27 years. During his lifetime, Kant's work was influential across Europe and, in the centuries following his death, it has been the key to philosophical debate.

The German philosopher Immanuel Kant (1724–1804) is one of the great figures in the history of philosophy and was probably the most important thinker of the Enlightenment period. He tried to combine rational and empirical strands in his work and wrote about a wide variety of subjects, including the natural sciences, metaphysics (what reality is), morality, and religion.

He was impressed with the progress in the natural sciences since the time of the English scientist Isaac Newton (1642–1727). It seemed to him that philosophy, by contrast, was muddled and riddled with disagreement. So he made it his aim to find out whether philosophy could say anything at all.

Kant thought that philosophy should investigate how people understand the world. One of his conclusions was that people make sense of the world through categories such as space and time. We impose these categories on objects; they are a property of our understanding rather than of the objects.

Kant's moral philosophy started from the idea that all human beings are rational and free to make choices. He went on to argue that it is possible to draw up universal moral laws. An important project for Kant was to find a sound philosophical basis for belief in God, but he was forced to conclude that all philosophical attempts to prove God's existence were unsatisfactory. Whether God existed was a question of faith rather than reason.

DETERMINISM

The rise of science that preceded the Enlightenment led to a renewed interest in the ideas of determinism, which had been a source of debate in ancient Greek times. Determinism proposes that all events are the results of previous causes. If we heat a bar of iron and the bar expands, we can say that the heat is the cause of expansion.

The idea of a physically determined universe was associated with Isaac Newton. This is sometimes called "the billiard-ball view" of nature: a billiard ball will move only when acted on by another force, such as another ball hitting it. If we could measure the velocity and angle of the first ball, we could predict with some accuracy the movement of the second.

The philosophical problem comes with human beings. If we accept the empirical view that human beings are organized systems of matter, and that our minds are formed as a result of experiences, then we may want to explain human behavior in terms of cause and effect. If we knew enough about the biological make-up of an individual, her early childhood, and the social and historical circumstances into which she was born, perhaps we could predict all her actions. From this point of view, belief in free will becomes untenable: a person may appear to have made a free choice, but this is only because we are ignorant of all the causal factors.

This is as much a problem for the present day as it was for the thinkers of the Enlightenment: if there is no such thing as free will, then we cannot apply moral concepts such as good and bad. Morality can only exist where there is choice – that is, where a person could have done otherwise. Of course, if we believe that human nature is something other than the result of previous causes, we may argue that people do have responsibility for their actions.

CAUSE AND EFFECT Enlightenment scientists knew, from the way the body works, that stimulus leads to response. Some philosophers took on the idea, arguing that an individual's life was determined by his or her experiences.

LOGIC

HOW TO FIND YOUR WAY Logic acts like a compass, revealing the reality beneath appearances. You may want to believe an argument because you like what you hear; logic tells you whether it is properly reasoned.

Good philosophy must be based on reasoned arguments. Logic can be understood as the science of proper reasoning: what separates a good argument from a bad one. A useful way to understand what makes arguments good or bad is to divide them into two types: deductive and inductive.

In a deductive argument, the conclusion is said to be true if it follows from the premises (starting statements). The best-known form of a deductive argument is the syllogism, the simplest of which consists of two premises and a conclusion:

Premise 1   All philosophers are wise.
Premise 2   Socrates is a philosopher.
Conclusion   Therefore, Socrates is wise.

However, if the first premise were "some philosophers are wise," we could not be sure that Socrates was wise – he might have been one of the philosophers who was not. Deductive logic does not appeal to empirical evidence: as long as the premises are true and the argument is valid, it follows that the conclusion must be true.

Inductive logic is concerned with making generalizations about the empirical world based on observation. It is closely connected with experimental science (an experiment is a particular type of observation). Let us say we are interested in the personality of people with different astrological signs and we observe that Virgos are neat. We may want to make a generalization based on this. However, although our observations may back up this generalization, we cannot be sure that it applies to all Virgos, only to those we have observed. There may be Virgos in the future, or in some other country, who are not like that.

ROMANTICISM & SUBJECTIVITY
Nature, art, and the individual imagination

The Romantic period was in many ways a backlash against the Enlightenment that preceded it. The Enlightenment's emphasis on a mechanical, deterministic universe left little room for the freedom and creativity of the human spirit.

The self, creativity, imagination, and the value of art were emphasized by Romantics – in contrast to the Enlightenment's emphasis on rationalism and on science, with its claims to describe the world from no particular viewpoint. In a Europe riven by revolutions and war, the certainties of the Enlightenment had already been shown to be false. Philosophically, Romanticism represented a shift from the certainty of science to the uncertainty of imagination – from the objective to the subjective.

The biggest influence on the philosophy of Romanticism, however, was the German professor Immanuel Kant (1724–1804), who led a life so sedate and orderly that it was said the people of Königsberg could set their watches by him. The move from the objective to the subjective is a result of Kant's idea, presented in *A Critique of Pure Reason* (1781), that human beings do not see the world directly but through a number of categories. Kant proposed that we do not directly see "things-in-themselves," but we only understand the world through our human point of view. Imagine three people looking at a landscape, one a farmer, another a property developer, and the third an artist: the farmer would see the potential for raising crops and livestock; the property developer, the chance to build houses; and the artist, the subtleties of color and form. None of them would see the landscape objectively.

The Romantic emphasis on the individual was reflected in ideas of self-realization and in a turning to nature. The English poet William Wordsworth (1770–1850) thought that the individual could directly understand nature without the need for social artifice, that salvation was achieved by the solitary individual rather than through political movements.

NOBLE SAVAGE

BORN GOOD Rousseau's notion of the "noble savage," a human being untainted by civilization and therefore good, contradicted the Christian idea of original sin, which asserted that humans are born wicked and therefore all natural impulses are base.

"Man was born free, and he is everywhere in chains," the French philosopher Jean Jacques Rousseau (1712–78) wrote in 1762. He thought that civilization fills people with unnatural wants and seduces them from their true nature and original freedom.

In his novel *Emile* (1762), he described the education of a free being encouraged to develop through self-expression his natural nobility and liberty of the spirit. The same year, in the *Social Contract*, he attempted to describe a society in which this natural nobility could flourish. The society would be based on a contract in which each individual would give all his or her rights to the community, but all collective decisions would be based on a direct democracy – with each member having a chance to vote on every issue. As all would be involved in decision-making, this contract would be legitimate.

The state would represent the common good, or the "general will." The general will is not to be confused with the "will of all." The will of all is what individuals think they want and includes selfish motives; the general will is what people would want if they were rational and therefore it is good.

If an individual does not want to obey the general will, Rousseau argued, he or she must be "forced to be free." To obey what is best for all is to maximize the freedom of each.

ART AND IMAGINATION

The German philosopher Friedrich Wilhelm Joseph von Schelling (1775–1854) agreed with Kant that the only thing of which we have direct knowledge is consciousness. The external world is simply an adjunct to what is most real: the mind. Through art the mind can come to full awareness of itself.

The English poet Samuel Taylor Coleridge (1772–1834) was fascinated by the psychology of artistic creativity and dissatisfied with the empiricist idea that the mind was merely a passive absorber of impressions. After reading Schelling and other idealists, he found a way to criticize what he saw as the Enlightenment's "over-mechanical" view.

The mechanical view is that the mind is simply the sum of its experience. Coleridge believed that the mind functions more like an organism than an engine: an organism can be creative, but it is difficult to see how an engine could create poetry. Coleridge felt that his version of idealism could be reconciled with his Christian beliefs and argued that Kant's moral theories were in tune with Christian sentiments.

INSPIRATION As a poet, Coleridge was convinced that the human mind can be receptive to visions that go beyond personal experience. The concept of the poetic muse, granting visions to the writer and usually personified as a young woman, goes back at least as far as the Greek poet Homer.

"GEIST" OR ABSOLUTE SPIRIT

NEW AGE DAWNING Hegel believed firmly in the progress of history, as the absolute spirit moved toward self-knowledge – a state which he believed was imminent in the 19th century.

Georg Hegel (1770–1831) was the most influential of the German idealist philosophers, perhaps the most important philosopher after Kant. He became a professor at Heidelberg in 1816 and was Professor of Philosophy at Berlin from 1818 until his death.

Like other idealists, he agreed with Kant that the mind is not simply a passive absorber of the external world but actively organizes it. As the mind cannot know things-in-themselves, what becomes real is *Geist* (literally mind, spirit, or soul in German). Hegel said: "The Real is the Rational and the Rational is the Real." For Hegel, each person's individual consciousness, or mind, is really part of a greater *Geist*, or Absolute Spirit – it is just that the individual does not realize this. If we understood that we were part of a greater consciousness, we would not be so concerned with our individual freedom; we would agree to act rationally in a way that did not follow individual caprice. By following the Real or the Rational, each individual would achieve self-fulfillment.

Hegel saw *Geist* developing through history, each period having a *Zeitgeist* (spirit of the age). These stages would eventually reach the *telos* (Greek for "end") of self-understanding, when *Geist* would come to know itself. It is only when *Geist* comes to know itself that we can be free, since it is only possible to be free if we understand reality. If we do not understand reality we cannot make a free judgment; we struggle in vain against what we do not understand.

SEE ALSO

Marxism · · · · · · · · · · · · · · · · ◄
The Enlightenment · · · · · · · · · · ◄
Poststructuralism · · · · · · · · · · ►
Romanticism · · · · · · · · · · · · · · ►

IDEALISM VS. MATERIALISM

The forces of destiny

Philosophy in 19th-century Europe became increasingly idealistic following the work of Immanuel Kant (1724–1804). While philosophers still disagreed with one another about almost everything, Kant's remarks that through science our understanding of the phenomenal world – the world of appearance – was progressing still held true.

A prominent successor to Kant was the German philosopher Georg Hegel (1770–1831), who developed the theory of dialectics in which opposing ideas were synthesized. Two interpretations of Hegel's work spawned different groups: the Old Hegelians who uncritically accepted Hegel's views, and the Young Hegelians who wanted to continue the revolution of ideas using Hegel's dialectics. The Germans Ludwig Feuerbach (1804–72) and Karl Marx (1818–83) were the most influential of these Young Hegelians.

Hegel thought that he had reconciled philosophy with religion in his work *Idea of Absolute Mind* (1807). But for Feuerbach, who believed in an empirical and materialist philosophy, religion was an example of an alienated consciousness. Feuerbach believed that man creates God in his own image, and then falls down and worships his own creation. This God is an idealized human – and by removing these ideal qualities from ourselves and projecting them onto a religious object, we are estranging or alienating ourselves from our own essence, or being. While Feuerbach saw religion as a reflection of the way society is structured but seemed content to leave society as it was, Marx wanted to radicalize society: "The philosophers have only interpreted the world in various ways; the point is to change it."

Hegel was not the only important post-Kantian philosopher. The German philosopher Arthur Schopenhauer (1788–1860) – a contemporary of Hegel – thought that the ultimate reality is not *Geist*, but will. Schopenhauer's work influenced the young Friedrich Nietzsche (1844–1900), who developed the theme of will. For Nietzsche, the "will to power" is the basic driving force of human nature and philosophy. Psychoanalysis would not be the same without the influence of these two great thinkers.

DIALECTICS

THE END OF HISTORY Georg Hegel believed that the human mind had progressed through history from consciousness to self-consciousness, through reason, spirit, and religion to absolute knowledge – a state exemplified by himself.

The reason for the progress of history, Georg Hegel argued, was so that *Geist* – the world spirit – should eventually come to know itself. He called this process "dialectical" – a starting position (the thesis) proves to be inadequate and so throws up its opposite (the antithesis). Because both these positions are unsatisfactory, progress can only occur when a superior understanding (the synthesis) takes place.

An anachronistic example helps to understand the dialectic. Say you have a motorcycle, but only a limited understanding of how it works. The point of a motorcycle is to enable you to travel (the thesis). You begin in a state of ignorance; all you know is how to drive your motorbike. Sooner or later, you will run out of fuel. The bike will stop, the opposite of traveling (the antithesis). It is only when you come to understand that the way the motorcycle works includes the notion of refueling (you understand the bike at a higher level, achieving a synthesis) that you can get it to work.

DIALECTICAL MATERIALISM

Marx took from Hegel the notion of dialectical historical development, but for Marx it was societies that were developing rather than *Geist*. Marx asserted the need to start from the "real" empirical world to produce a scientific understanding of history. History, he argued, progresses through a number of epochs, each having a particular economic arrangement. Examples of epochs include feudalism (an economy based on land ownership) and capitalism (characterized by wage labor and the existence of capital).

Marx thought that each epoch contained economic contradictions that could only be resolved by movement to a new economic form. According to his dialectical analysis of capitalism, the thesis is the growing productive force – technology and the workplace becoming more efficient – and the antithesis is the unemployment and poverty created by the factory system. The synthesis would be a revolution to replace capitalism with socialism.

Marx's most important contribution to philosophy – rather than social theory – is his theory of ideology: that dominant ideas in every epoch reflect the economic system. In liberal capitalist societies, the emphasis on notions of individual freedom are seen by Marx to be a consequence of the economic free market. Individuals who have been seduced by this notion are said to have "false consciousness."

CLASS WAR Karl Marx believed that, in the long run, a better society would result from the conflict he saw between the social classes in Victorian England.

"WILL" TO "WILL TO POWER"

While Arthur Schopenhauer accepted that Kant's "things-in-themselves" were unknowable in general, he thought people did have knowledge of one thing-in-itself: the self. The self, he argued, is a manifestation of "will." By "will" he meant energy or force. He is often referred to as a philosopher of pessimism since he thought that the will had no purpose or aim: it was blind striving. He felt that existence entails suffering.

Schopenhauer believed that there are three ways in which man can attempt to overcome this blind will and achieve salvation. The first is to develop sympathy for others; the second is to develop philosophic understanding; and the third is to contemplate works of art. This last route has been the most influential.

For Nietzsche, the "will to power" was the most basic human drive. Unlike Schopenhauer, he thought that the will to power is a creative force and that human beings

APOLLO Nietzsche's idea that people have godlike potential has been a major influence on New Age religion and psychoanalysis.

could progress to a new level of being. Nietzsche was critical of all philosophy since the Greeks, and particularly of Christianity. He said people had separated two aspects of themselves: the Dionysian (celebratory and unconscious) and the Apollonian (conscious and rational). It is only when creative individuals express their will to power by synthesizing these elements that they can progress.

Nietzsche was critical of philosophy that claimed to show a final truth. All truths for Nietzsche were interpretations of the world, necessitated by biology.

SEE ALSO

Romanticism & subjectivity · · · · ◄
Existentialism · · · · · · · · · · · · · ►
Modern spirituality · · · · · · · · · · ►
Psychology · · · · · · · · · · · · · · · ►
Industrialization · · · · · · · · · · · · ►

MORAL PHILOSOPHY

How do we decide what is right or wrong?

For most people, morals are sets of rules that ought to be obeyed; they tell us what is right or wrong. Moral philosophers want to discover how these rules are justified, and the logical consequences of moral or ethical beliefs.

Two significant ethical systems emerged in the wake of the 18th-century Enlightenment. The first of these was that proposed by the German philosopher Immanuel Kant (1724–1804). It was based on rationality and attempted to show how any rational being would agree to universal moral laws. Its influence has been enormous, and modern philosophers still use Kant's ideas as a starting point for any discussions on morality. The other was Utilitarianism, proposed by British philosopher Jeremy Bentham (1748–1832). Bentham believed that he had found a scientific approach to morality based on happiness.

Critical philosophers of the 19th century were less certain that universal moral values could be upheld. For the German Karl Marx (1818–83), morality and ethics were part of bourgeois ideology: sets of ideas that ignored the exploitative economic arrangements of society and contributed to "false consciousness." Friedrich Nietzsche (1844–1900) looked at the origins of morality and, like Marx, saw moral systems as arising from the interests of social groups. For Nietzsche, individuals had to go beyond accepted morality to create a new morality for themselves.

In the 20th century, there has been growing pessimism about the possibility of a universal moral system. The French philosopher Jean-Paul Sartre (1905–80) emphasized the subjective judgments that an individual must make in order to create his or her own moral code. Anglo-American philosophers have wondered whether philosophy can say anything meaningful at all about what is right or good. For these analytic philosophers, the role of philosophy is to analyze how people use moral concepts, rather than to say what morality ought to be. Writers like the English professor A.J. Ayer (1910–89) suggested that moral statements simply express the moral sentiments or attitudes of the individual and that philosophy has no way of evaluating which set of moral statements is best.

CATEGORICAL IMPERATIVE

Immanuel Kant believed that an action was moral if it could be universalized. If a person wanted to know if telling a lie on a particular occasion were justifiable, he or she should imagine what would happen if everyone lied.

He saw people as rational and autonomous moral agents and argued that a moral act was one that was consistent with the "categorical imperative." One formulation of this was: "Always aim to treat humanity, whether in yourself or in others, as an end in itself, never merely as a means." What Kant meant by this is that a person should not be used as a means to another's happiness; if we use someone as a means to our own ends then we have removed that person's autonomy.

PUNISHMENT
All inmates were to be visible from the center of Jeremy Bentham's prison.

UTILITARIANISM

MORAL DILEMMA Does the pleasure of the audience justify the pain of the bull?

In Britain Jeremy Bentham and John Stuart Mill (1806–1873) developed the moral theory known as Utilitarianism. It aimed to give a method of moral judgment based on experience rather than dogma.

Bentham thought that an action was good if it increased pleasure, bad if it increased pain. An action or law would be good if it produced "the greatest happiness for the greatest number." He developed a "happiness calculus" in order to calculate the consequences of any action or law in terms of pleasure or pain. Using these principles he designed a prison called the panopticon where punishment would be measured out according to the amount of pain caused by the offender.

The Scottish historian Thomas Carlyle (1795–1881) called Utilitarianism "pig philosophy" as it appeared to base the goal of ethics on the swinish pleasures of the multitude. In the light of this criticism, J.S. Mill refined Bentham's theory by suggesting that there were higher and lower pleasures, and that the higher pleasures were preferable. As he put it: "better to be Socrates dissatisfied than a fool satisfied." By lower pleasures, Mill meant pleasures of the flesh; by higher pleasures, pleasures of the intellect. One consequence of Mill's modification was that it was no longer possible to use Bentham's "happiness calculus."

THE GENEALOGY OF MORALS

For German philosopher Friedrich Nietzsche, there were two basic types of morality: "master morality" and "slave morality." By this he meant that moral codes arise from people's social origins. In master morality the noble is good, and heroism, courage, and individual greatness are emphasized. Slave morality is the morality of the weak. What harms the weak is called "evil," and what helps them is called "good."

Nietzsche thought that each individual needs to create her own moral system; the point of morality is to allow each person to sublimate and control her passions in order to emphasize the creativity inherent in her being.

MISTRESS OF HER PASSIONS Nietzsche identified Christian ethics with "slave morality," which he believed to be inferior to "master" morality, exemplified by the aristocratic code of honor of the ancient Greeks.

"BAD FAITH"

The French philosopher and writer Jean-Paul Sartre was an atheist and believed that individuals have no objective way of formulating morality. If we follow a moral system or religion, we are acting in "bad faith" by denying that we have the responsibility for determining our own choices.

Like Nietzsche, Sartre believed that it is the individual who needs to create his or her own moral code. He thought that individuals should act authentically – that is, make choices based on the understanding that they are responsible for creating themselves.

SEE ALSO

The Enlightenment · · · · · · · · · · ◄
Romanticism & subjectivity · · · · · ◄
Existentialism · · · · · · · · · · · · · · ►
Sociology · · · · · · · · · · · · · · · · · ►

GOD
The limits of philosophical argument

The 18th-century Enlightenment was a time of rationalism, and one far-reaching consequence of this was the undermining of Christian faith among the educated classes. This effect was unintended because the project of many Enlightenment philosophers was to prove the existence of God using reason. For example, the Frenchman René Descartes (1596–1650) and the German Gottfried Leibniz (1646–1716) were convinced that God's existence could be shown by reason to be necessary.

Philosophers of the later 18th century such as the German Immanuel Kant (1724–1804) continued this struggle to justify faith in God in terms of human reason. But in the 19th century, writers began to argue that logical thought was no help in debating God's existence and examining faith. The Dane Søren Kierkegaard (1813–55) and the German Friedrich Nietzsche (1844–1900) took opposite positions. Kierkegaard studied theology and, although opposed to much organized Christianity, was a committed religious thinker. He argued that people

should embrace God even if rationally it seemed an absurdity. Nietzsche was determinedly anti-Christian and proclaimed that it was time for people to create a new mode of being, with human creativity rather than God at its center.

For the German philosophers Ludwig Feuerbach (1804–72) and Karl Marx (1818–83), religion was a projection of the human essence onto an ideal: they argued that, far from being the creator of man, God is man's own creation – no more than an invention of human consciousness. Marx also believed that religion was part of an ideology that encouraged the oppressed to accept their fate. He wrote: "Religion is the sigh of the oppressed creature, the sentiment of a heartless world, and the soul of soulless conditions. It is the opium of the people."

DEATH OF GOD

Friedrich Nietzsche argued that the concept of God is a human creation, and that once we are aware of the fact we can no longer base our religious and moral beliefs on any notion of a divine external reality. "God is dead," he proclaimed; the time had come for people to create a new set of values. In many ways this argument was the inevitable conclusion of an increasing anthropocentrism – placing man at the center of the world – that had been implicit in philosophy since the work of Kant. If we view our existence through human categories, then our concept of God must itself be a human creation.

The French existentialist philosopher Jean-Paul Sartre (1905–80) accepted God's death. Much of his writing was an attempt to look at the human condition in a world without a prime mover who could have provided a basis and structure for the understanding of being. Anglo-American analytic philosophers of the 20th century have tended to agree that philosophy may help us clarify religious concepts, without giving us a secure foundation for religious belief.

FAITH AND REASON

In the era when René Descartes was arguing that the workings of human reason revealed God's existence, the French mathematician Blaise Pascal (1623–62) took an entirely practical approach. He argued that, on the basis of probabilities, it would be foolish to live as if God did not exist. Pascal's proposition was that God either exists or he does not. If we believe in God and he exists, we will be rewarded with eternal bliss in heaven. If we believe in God and he does not exist, then at worst all we have forgone is sinful pleasure.

If we do not believe in God and he does exist, we may enjoy a few sinful pleasures – but we may face eternal damnation. If we do not believe in God and he does not exist, our sins will not be punished. Would any rational gambler think that the experience of a few sinful pleasures is worth the risk of damnation?

In the 18th century, Immanuel Kant tried to show how philosophy could prove the existence of God. However, his other work showed that people cannot know reality

IN GOD'S HOUSE A central part of the religious impulse is the desire to focus on mystery. Philosophers have struggled to accommodate the human need to understand with this inclination to worship.

directly as a "thing-in-itself"; what is real in itself is beyond human experience – even if God exists, people cannot know Him.

Kant thought that a Christian could have faith in God, and that this faith would be consonant with reason. Given that human beings have the autonomy to create moral values, it would not be irrational to believe in a God who gives purpose to the moral realm.

Kant's countryman Georg Hegel (1770–1831) thought that the God of religion is an intuition of absolute spirit, or *Geist*. Hegel's *Geist* is not like the God of Christianity, traditionally considered to be transcendent – outside human consciousness. For Hegel, God is immanent and, since history is the process of *Geist* coming to know itself, we are all part of *Geist* – or God.

The Danish philosopher Søren Kierkegaard believed that reason has no place in faith since God is beyond reason. He did not think that it is rational to believe in God – but a person should have faith in God anyway.

PROOF OF GOD'S EXISTENCE

There are many traditional "proofs" for the existence of God, but three are particularly important. The first is known as the argument from design. Philosophers using this argument suggest that the intricate mechanisms of the universe – from the orbits of the planets around the Sun to the arrangement of the cells in your fingernails – could not have developed simply by chance. They must have been designed – and the being that designed them is God.

The second proof is known as the ontological argument. Philosophers using this argument propose that God is the perfect being and that, if He lacked existence, He would not be perfect, therefore He must exist.

The third proof of God's existence is known as the cosmological argument. Its supporters say that everything that exists has a cause, but that there must at some time have been a cause prior to all other causes. This "prime mover" or first cause is necessary to explain existence. The first cause is God.

SEE ALSO
Philosophy of mind · · · · · · · · · ▶
Modern Christianity · · · · · · · · ▶
Modern spirituality · · · · · · · · · ▶

ANALYTIC PHILOSOPHY
Words and meaning

To analyze means to break something down into its constituent parts. Analytic philosophy, which has been important in the English-speaking academic world since the beginning of the 20th century, attempts to analyze the meaning of statements and concepts.

In the wake of the German philosopher Immanuel Kant (1724–1804), a split occurred between Anglo-American academic philosophy and the philosophy practiced on the European continent. In the early 19th century, "continental" philosophy went in an idealist direction under Georg Hegel (1770–1831). It took an existentialist turn via Friedrich Nietzsche (1844–1900) and Martin Heidegger (1889–1976), and entered a less certain phase with poststructuralism. By contrast, Anglo-American analytic philosophers saw the German philosopher Gottlob Frege (1848–1925) as the most important thinker since Kant.

Frege was influential in the philosophy of mathematics, logic, and language. He thought that analysis of the underlying logic of sentences would allow us to judge their "truth value." The British philosopher Bertrand Russell (1872–1970) combined Frege's logical insights with an empiricism derived from the Scottish philosopher David Hume (1711–76). Russell argued that meaningful sentences were those that, when analyzed, corresponded to reality.

In the mid-20th century, linguistic philosophers such as the Briton Gilbert Ryle (1900–76) – influenced by the later work of one of Russell's students, the Austrian Ludwig Wittgenstein (1889–1951) – argued that many of the traditional problems of philosophy could be dissolved simply by studying language as it is used. But by the 1970s, philosophers began to show more interest in the philosophy of mind and the application of analytic methods to wider issues in politics, ethics, and the nature of philosophy itself.

The American Richard Rorty (1931–) has used the methods of analytic philosophy to deconstruct – or break down – its assumptions. Rorty is influenced as much by Heidegger as he is by Wittgenstein, and his approach echoes the ideas of the poststructuralists. The future may see the concerns of analytic and continental philosophy converge.

LOGICAL ATOMISM

The British philosopher Bertrand Russell believed that the grammar of ordinary language was misleading. He argued that the world was composed of "atomic facts" and that statements, if true, would correspond to these facts. Any true statement could be broken down into these components, in the same way that any material can be broken down into atoms. One of philosophy's tasks was to analyze propositions to reveal their "proper logical form."

Russell thought that terms such as "the average man" could lead to confusion. In the sentence, "the average woman has 2.6 children," the term "average woman" should be understood as a logical construction. The term is not an atomic fact, but a complex mathematical statement. Russell thought that terms like "the state" and "public opinion" were also logical constructions, and that philosophers were mistaken in treating these concepts as though they really existed.

CRITICAL EYE Bertrand Russell took a sceptical view of accepted beliefs and of human pretensions to certainty. A controversial figure, he was twice imprisoned; once for pacifism and once for antinuclear campaigning.

THE PICTURE THEORY OF MEANING

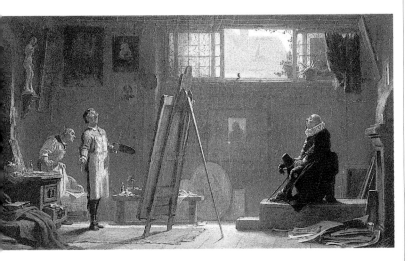

HOLD A MIRROR UP TO NATURE For many centuries artists were judged on the accuracy with which they represented the real world. Wittgenstein argued that we should use a similar test in evaluating our use of language.

Ludwig Wittgenstein came to study under Russell at Cambridge University in 1912 and contributed to his tutor's theory of logical atomism. Wittgenstein's *Tractatus Logico-Philosophicus* was published in 1921. In it, he put forward the picture theory of meaning. A picture may mirror reality by showing arrangements of objects; Wittgenstein argued that sentences, if they are to mean anything, must mirror reality in the same way that a picture does. Sentences contain names that refer to objects or states of affairs in the world. Through analysis, a true statement can be shown to consist of elementary particles that picture the world and logical constants such as "and," "if," "not," and "or." A sentence that does not picture the world is devoid of meaning.

If only statements that picture the world – statements about facts – are meaningful, then statements about ethics or religion and much of philosophy, strictly speaking, have no meaning. Of course, this applies as much to Wittgenstein's own ideas in the *Tractatus* as to other ideas. He likened his propositions to a stepladder; a reader who understood could move on from the arguments just as a man could discard a ladder once he had climbed to the point he was trying to reach.

LOGICAL POSITIVISM

The Vienna Circle consisted of a group of philosophically minded scientists and logicians. The German Moritz Schlick (1882–1936) was the official leader. Other members included the Austrians Kurt Gödel (1906–78) and Otto Neurath (1882–1945) and the German Rudolf Carnap (1891–1970). The Circle, which was influenced by the work of Frege and Russell, was active from the mid-1920s. But Schlick's assassination by a deranged student in 1936, together with the growing hostility of the Nazis, forced it to disperse.

For the Vienna Circle philosophers, only verifiable statements were meaningful; as Schlick put it, "the meaning of a proposition is the method of its verification." Statements about God, ethics, art, or metaphysics were, for them, nonsense.

This emphasis on logic and positivism – the view that knowledge must be based on observation or empirical data – was a reaction against the idealism that had been influential in German philosophy. Georg Hegel, an idealist, had proposed that philosophy's role was to outline the self-awareness of *Geist*, the universal mind or spirit; the Vienna Circle thinkers, by contrast, saw philosophy as a handmaiden to science, and argued that philosophers should be content simply to clarify concepts.

REALITY SPEAKS Mass observation – a form of research developed in the 1930s – valued facts over political or social theory. Cameras, observers, and interviewers were sent into the heart of working-class communities in England and amassed a hoard of empirical evidence.

SEE ALSO

Idealism vs. materialism ········◄

Poststructuralism ···········◄

Sociology ················►

THE MIRROR OF NATURE

MIND-BENDING VISION Richard Rorty argues that because we are constantly interpreting reality in different ways, the human mind does not simply reflect the real world; but also distorts it.

Richard Rorty (1931–) is an American philosopher who was trained in the analytic tradition, but, unlike many of his contemporaries, he has been influenced as much by the existentialists Jean-Paul Sartre (1905–80) and Martin Heidegger (1889–1976) as by the analytic philosophers' traditional mentor, Ludwig Wittgenstein (1889–1951).

Rorty argues that ever since Descartes' "invention of the mind," philosophy has tried to provide solid foundations for our understanding of the world. For example, Immanuel Kant (1724–1804) thought that we interpret the world through timeless, universal categories. He distinguished between a mirrored natural world and a mirroring non-natural mind. Philosophy's purpose, according to Kant, was to expose the shape of this mirror. But for Rorty, human understanding is not based on some objective structure of "mind," because we interpret the world through a variety of paradigms.

If there is no objective philosophical standpoint, then the idea that philosophy should be seen as the "queen of sciences" – clarifying what counts as knowledge – is unsustainable. Rorty argues that the aim of philosophers should be "to help their readers, or society as a whole, break free from outworn vocabularies and attitudes, rather than to provide 'grounding' for the intuitions and customs of the present."

THE PRIVATE LANGUAGE ARGUMENT

Since Wittgenstein's death there has been much discussion about his assertion that there could not be a "private language." Philosophy since Descartes has been built on the assumption that the most secure knowledge is based on our private experience; indeed, Descartes' distinction between the mental and the material rests on this notion.

Wittgenstein saw language as a rule-governed social activity. He thought that it was incomprehensible to imagine an individual creating his own private language. How would this person know, when he used a word, that he was using it correctly? To rely on his own memory would be "as if someone were to buy several copies of the morning newspaper to assure himself that what it said was true." As this individual has no way of externally checking the way he is using a concept, he cannot be said to be using a language.

If a private language is not possible, then the rug has been pulled from under the feet of modern philosophy's Cartesian foundations. Meaning is no longer understood as private or individual, but as public and social. The individualistic first-person certainty that underlies both rationalist and empiricist approaches to philosophy is in error.

A SOCIAL LIFE The hero of *Robinson Crusoe* (1720) by English novelist Daniel Defoe created a small piece of Europe on a desert island. His private experience of the wilderness was filtered through his social understanding – the shared beliefs and thought patterns of European civilization.

LANGUAGE GAMES

In the 1930s, Wittgenstein became critical of his earlier picture theory of meaning. In his later work, he uses a tool metaphor for language: the meaning of a word is no longer its relation to some atomic fact, it is in its use.

We use language in a variety of ways, to talk about science, religion, or art. In his later work, Wittgenstein does not agree with the logical positivists that only scientific statements have meaning: science is only one way to talk about the world, only one "language game." A language game reflects a human activity. In addition to a scientific language game, we can participate in a religious language game, an esthetic language game, or many others. Words derive their meaning from the function they perform within the language game.

Words no longer have a particular essence or refer to a particular object. A word may have a variety of usages. What these different usages have in common Wittgenstein calls a "family resemblance." Members of a family bear a resemblance to one another, but no two members of a family (apart from identical

FAMILY LIKENESSES Lions and domestic cats, members of a common family, look different but similar. Ludwig Wittgenstein argued that some words used in widely different contexts have an underlying similarity.

twins) look exactly alike. The same is true for the use of words. The word "game," for example, is used to talk about board games, card games, Olympic games, soccer games, etc. These games do not hold one essential quality in common, rather there are overlapping and crisscrossing similarities.

Wittgenstein thought that philosophical problems arise when "language goes on vacation," that is, when we take a word and try to look at it in isolation from its language game. If we try to define the essence of beauty or knowledge, instead of seeing how these concepts are used in context, we will become confused. The job of philosophy for the later Wittgenstein is therapeutic: "The philosopher's treatment of a question is like the treatment of an illness." The "illness" in question is the bewitchment of intelligence by language.

PHILOSOPHY OF MIND
Theories of consciousness

The debate about what it means to be conscious and what is meant by the concept of mind or soul is fundamental to modern philosophy. But from Greek and Roman times to the 17th century, most philosophy centered on theological problems. Questioning the existence of one's soul or consciousness was seen as questioning the works of God, and was tantamount to heresy. The subject lay dormant for centuries until the French philosopher René Descartes (1596–1650) asked himself: how do I know I exist?

The two most important philosophers to discuss the mind before Descartes were the Greeks Plato and Aristotle. Plato (c.428–348 BC) thought that what we really are is our soul, and that this soul will survive after death – indeed, he saw death as the release of the soul. He therefore believed that soul and body are distinct substances: bodies die, but souls are immortal. Aristotle (384–322 BC) thought that the soul and the body are essentially related. The soul is not a separate substance, but an arrangement of stuff, or material substance, of which the body is made. As Aristotle once said, "If an ax had a soul, its soul would be cutting." For Aristotle, individual immortality seemed impossible.

These arguments have been used to re-examine the meaning of the mind from the 18th-century Enlightenment to the present day. The German philosopher Gottfried Leibniz (1646–1716) suggested that mind and body only appear to interact: in reality there is no relation between the two substances, but God has pre-established a harmony so that minds and bodies do not fall out of sync.

The English scientist T.H. Huxley (1825–95) believed that the mind is a product of the physical brain: if a man thinks that he wants some chocolate, this may be because his stomach is sending messages to his brain because his blood-sugar level is low; consciousness is simply a reflection of biology – and when the body dies, the mind dies with it.

Recent philosophers are interested in the possibility of artificial intelligence. For example, a thermostat may be said to have three beliefs: it is too hot in here, it is too cold in here, and the temperature is just right. Could it be that human beings are just more sophisticated machines?

DUALISM

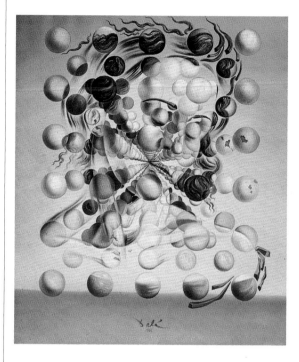

MIND OVER BODY René Descartes based his philosophy on the premise that his thinking mind was undeniably conscious. He also believed that his mind could interact with his material body, via the pineal gland in the brain.

René Descartes is called a dualist because he thought that mind and body are distinct substances: mind is conscious and nonspatial, and body is spatial but not conscious. The problem with this is that it is difficult to see how two different substances interact. With his *Meditations on Philosophy* (1641), he proved to his own satisfaction that his mind – or soul – must exist. As doubting involved thought, and thought needed a consciousness to think it, he could not doubt the existence of his mind: *cogito ergo sum,* "I think therefore I am."

But Descartes did think that it was possible to doubt the existence of his body. He argued that during a dream, he often believed a situation to be real, yet when he woke up he would find it had no basis in reality. Therefore he could not believe in his body simply because it was there. He pointed out that it was also possible to imagine that a malicious demon could be fooling him into believing that he had a body. To resolve the conundrum of whether or not his body really existed, he argued that the only way he knew he had a body was because God exists and God would not allow a malicious demon to fool him.

IDENTITY THEORY

In opposition to Descartes, identity theory suggests that mind and body are not two different substances that interact, but that both are attributes of one substance. First proposed by the Dutch philosopher Baruch Spinoza (1632–77), the theory put forward a way out of the problems of dualism and has again become popular in the 20th century.

The current version of the theory is that the mind is the brain and the brain is the mind. Consciousness is the individual's experience of the brain, and a scientist can observe brain processes which correspond to conscious experience.

Think of pain. If you stub your toe, you will be aware of pain. On a physical level, your central nervous system is sending messages from your toe to your brain. Descartes' dualism raised a problem – if body and soul are separate, how do they interact? Identity theory seems to solve this by suggesting that there is only one substance, and because there is only one, there is no problem of interaction.

SEAT OF HUMAN CONSCIOUSNESS Supporters of the identity theory argue that human thoughts and feelings have no substance beyond chemical processes in the brain.

With complex concepts the matter is more complicated, however. Say I am thinking of the concept of freedom or of Paris in the springtime, and so are you. Is it likely that both of us have the same physical parts of the brain occupied by this thought, or that a scientist using a brain scanner could read our thoughts?

BEHAVIORISM

The behaviorist approach solves the mind-body problem by simply rejecting the concept of "mind." As science can only deal with the observable – and as the mind is not observable – nothing can be said about the mind. Psychologists are not denying that we have consciousness, but are saying that from a scientific point of view only behavior can be analyzed.

The British philosopher Gilbert Ryle (1900–76) developed this approach. He suggested that the confusion about mind and body arises because of the way in which we use the word "mind." When we refer to someone as intelligent, we are in fact making judgments about that person's behavior – that they acted intelligently on a particular occasion. Intelligence therefore does not refer to some hidden private entity; for Ryle, mind is simply a term referring to types of behavior or dispositions to behave.

There are two main problems with this approach. First, what is interesting for most of us about mind or consciousness is our awareness of it, rather than our behavior. Second, it is not clear that all mental states have corresponding behavior. What behavior is associated with hearing a tune, or remembering your fifth birthday? From an observer's point of view, the behavior associated with both types of mental activity may appear identical.

MESSAGE FROM THE OTHER SIDE Spiritualists believe not only that mind and body are separate, but also that the mind, or soul, lives on after death. Members of many religions share the belief in an immortal soul.

SEE ALSO
The Enlightenment · · · · · · · · · · ◄
Idealism vs. materialism · · · · · · · · ◄
Medicine · · · · · · · · · · · · · · · · · ►

EXISTENTIALISM
Subjective experience and self-made values

The roots of existentialism lie in the work of the Danish philosopher Søren Kierkegaard (1813–55) in the first half of the 19th century. He criticized the philosophical system of Georg Hegel (1770–1831), which analyzed being (or existence) in an abstract and impersonal way. Kierkegaard was more concerned with the individual's subjective experience of human existence.

The German phenomenologist Edmund Husserl (1859–1938) was also influential in the development of methods that were later used by the existentialists. A phenomenologist is interested in things as they appear to consciousness, rather than the things-in-themselves on. Husserl's emphasis on the individual's subjective consciousness was continued in the 20th century as existentialism developed.

One of Husserl's students, Martin Heidegger (1889–1976), was interested in the "question of being." He thought that Western philosophy had been obsessed with the problem of knowledge. For Heidegger, the individual as being-in-the-world was characterized by action and anxiety: knowing the world is not our primary way of being in the world. His most fundamental question was: why should anything exist at all, when it does not have to? Although Heidegger claimed he was not an "existentialist," his influence on Sartre and the existentialist movement is undeniable.

The French philosopher Jean-Paul Sartre (1905–80) is probably the best-known existentialist. Sartre thought that there is no fixed human nature or essence and so the individual has to choose his or her being. This choice brings with it responsibility. Those who do not choose, but base their lives on pre-arranged moral and philosophical systems are said to be acting in bad faith.

Existentialism in the 20th century reflects the loss of certainties in the postmodern world. If there are no clear philosophical answers to the question of existence, then each individual has to design his or her own life as a project.

LITERATURE AND DRAMA

Existentialist literature and drama blossomed in France in the mid-20th century. Sartre's autobiographical novels *Nausea* (1938) and *The Wall* (1938) and his writings on atheistic existentialism influenced a number of other writers – notably Albert Camus (1913–60).

Camus – journalist, novelist, philosopher, and one-time actor – argued that life is essentially absurd: the modern world is full of injustice; millions work in repetitive, exploitative jobs. He believed that we should rebel against these absurdities by refusing to participate in them. In his two celebrated novels set in French Algeria – *The Stranger* (1942) and *The Plague* (1947) – an alienated hero moves through a hostile world.

A style of drama has been dubbed Theater of the Absurd after Camus' use of the word to label the meaninglessness of existence. The minimalist and repetitive activity in plays such as *The Bald Soprano* by the Romanian-born dramatist Eugène Ionesco (1912–) highlight the lack of an underlying order to life.

LIFE IS ABSURD Denied freedom by the sand in which she is buried, Winnie, female lead in the bleak comic drama *Happy Days* by Samuel Beckett (1906–89), remains obsessed with her possessions.

THE SOLITARY WANDERER

A PLACE FOR GOD Søren Kierkegaard believed that religious faith was central to an authentic existence. His Christian brand of existentialism has been a great influence on theologians in the 20th century.

Søren Kierkegaard led a brilliant but turbulent life. His intellectual precocity was recognized by his father, who educated him before he moved on to the University of Copenhagen where he studied for 10 years.

As a young man, Kierkegaard began to feel that he would always be an outsider. In 1837, he fell in love with 14-year-old Regine Olson, to whom he became engaged. After much inner turmoil, however, he broke off the engagement, convinced that his fate was to be the "exception," the lonely wanderer.

Kierkegaard thought that philosophers who claimed that philosophy could show us the ultimate nature of spirit were deluded. Hegel claimed to have overcome paradox, but Kierkegaard was not convinced. Existence, for Kierkegaard, was paradoxical. The individual must find his or her own spiritual path, not through the comfortable dogmatic rituals of the established church or the pseudoclarity of Hegelian dialectics, but through action that is conscious of religious conviction.

"EXISTENCE PRECEDES ESSENCE"

Jean-Paul Sartre was one of the leaders of a left-wing intellectual movement in France after World War II, co-founding the journal *Les Temps Modernes* with Maurice Merleau-Ponty (1908–61) and Simone de Beauvoir (1908–86). Unlike Kierkegaard, Sartre was an atheist. Because God does not exist, he argued, there is no "essence," or predefined human nature. Human existence or being differs from the being of objects in that human being is self-conscious. This self-consciousness also gives the human subject the opportunity to define itself. Individuals create themselves by making self-directed choices.

But Sartre felt that human existence is self-conscious without being predefined. As autonomous beings, humans are "condemned to be free": they are compelled to make future-directed choices. These choices induce anxiety and uncertainty. If we, as individuals, simply follow custom or social expectations in order to escape this angst, we have escaped the responsibility of making our own choices, of creating our own essence. We have acted in bad faith.

To act authentically, he argued, each individual must take responsibility for his or her future. We cannot choose the gender, class, or country into which we are born, but we can choose what we make of them. We are free to create our own interpretation of ourselves in relation to the world, to create a project of possibilities, of authentic actions as the expression of freedom.

IDEAS AND BEER Jean-Paul Sartre (wearing glasses) takes the lead in a café discussion in 1958. Members of the "left-bank" intellectual circle headed by Sartre were famous for holding philosophical meetings in cafés on the southern bank of the River Seine in Paris.

SEE ALSO

The Enlightenment · · · · · · · · · ◄
Romanticism & subjectivity · · · · · ◄
Poststructuralism · · · · · · · · · · ►

PHILOSOPHY OF SCIENCE
Logic or experimental proof?

The shift in Western thought from medieval to modern was underpinned by science. But a 200-year battle had to take place between the Christian church and emerging empiricism before the Enlightenment could flourish.

The church espoused a number of received ideas, notably that the Greek philosopher Aristotle (384–322 BC) had been right about the nature of the universe. The Polish astronomer Nicolas Copernicus (1473–1543) challenged the church's view that the Earth was at the center of the universe. He suggested that observational evidence showed that the Earth orbited the Sun. The English philosopher Francis Bacon (1561–1626) argued for the use of experiment rather than deduction as a way to increase knowledge. In 1632, the Italian astronomer and physicist Galileo Galilei (1564–1642) dared to agree with Copernicus and was hauled up before the Inquisition, the church tribunal to combat heresy. His subsequent house arrest and recantation were enough to put the brakes on scientific discovery in Italy for 100 years.

In an attempt to reconcile the church with science, the Frenchman René Descartes (1596–1650) tried to prove the existence of God using rational argument. But this alliance of rationalism and belief in God did not survive for long. In the following generation, the English scientist Isaac Newton (1642–1727) made great advances in physics based on empirical methods, which were extremely influential on the philosophers of the Enlightenment. Immanuel Kant (1724–1804) thought that Newton's laws could be shown to be true by reason and that the scientific approach could explain the phenomenal world (the world of appearances). Following on from this, the Frenchman Auguste Comte (1798–1857) argued that human thought developed through a number of stages: first, mythical and religious; then, metaphysical; and finally, a positive stage characterized by the systematic collection of observed facts. He thought that these positivist methods should now be turned to the investigation of society and developed a new area of study – sociology.

In the 20th century, the empirical method supported by Comte came under scrutiny. From the 1930s, philosophers looked for new ways to describe the scientific method.

FALSIFICATION

NEW EVIDENCE Before the first black swans were introduced into Europe from New Zealand, a deductive scientist might have argued that all swans were white because she had never seen a black one.

The Austrian-born philosopher Karl Popper (1902–94) was critical of the inductive methods used by science. He took the argument put forward by the empiricist David Hume (1711–76), who had suggested that there were logical flaws with induction. Hume said that all inductive evidence is limited: we do not observe the universe at all times and in all places. We are not justified therefore in making a general rule from this observation of particulars. No matter how many observations are made that confirm a theory, there is always the possibility that a future observation could refute it. Induction cannot yield certainty.

Popper was also critical of the empiricist view that we can objectively observe the world. He argued that all observation is from a point of view, and indeed that all observation is colored by our understanding. The world appears to us in the context of theories we already hold: it is "theory-laden."

An alternative scientific method he proposed was based on falsification. However many confirming instances there are for a theory, it only takes one counterobservation to falsify it. Science progresses when a theory is shown to be wrong and a new theory is found that better explains the phenomena. For Popper, the scientist should attempt to disprove his or her theory rather than continually attempt to prove it. He argued that science can help us approach the truth, but we can never be sure that we have the final explanation.

PARADIGMS

The American philosopher Thomas Kuhn (1922–) argued that scientific progress did not come simply in stages based upon neutral observations. Like Popper, he thought that all observation is theory-laden. Scientists have a world view, or paradigm. Each paradigm is an interpretation of the world, rather than an objective explanation.

For Kuhn, the history of science is characterized by revolutions in scientific outlook. Scientists accept the dominant paradigm until anomalies are thrown up. At that point, the scientists begin to question the basis of the paradigm itself, new theories emerge that challenge the dominant paradigm, and eventually one of these new theories becomes accepted as the new paradigm.

The American philosopher Paul Feyerabend (1924–) thought that the superiority of the modern scientific method should not be assumed. He argued that what will count as knowledge in the future may have paradigms we cannot yet know, and we should not attempt to forbid future intellectual enterprise by attempting to define one dominant paradigm of knowledge.

SCIENCE AND THE POSTMODERN WORLD

In the 20th century, the theory of relativity propounded by German-born physicist Albert Einstein (1879–1955) overthrew the paradigm based on Newton's observations which had been dominant since the Enlightenment. This change made philosophers aware that the fundamentals of a scientific understanding were not a static unchanging set of natural laws, but human interpretations of phenomena as much dependent on the community in which they surfaced as on the nature of reality itself.

Scientific explanation could no longer be looked upon as objective and neutral. At the boundaries of science, new paradigms are emerging to challenge the current orthodoxy, and so it is an open question as to how the science of the next century will develop.

POINT OF VIEW What you see may change according to what you are looking for – and scientists may be unable to grasp evidence that contradicts their world view or scientific paradigm. These two images of the Gare St. Lazare in Paris reflect (left) the intensely personal vision of Impressionist painter Claude Monet (1840–1926) and (below) the news values of a photographer recording a strike by Parisian public servants in December 1945.

SEE ALSO

The Enlightenment · · · · · · · · · · ◄
Analytic philosophy · · · · · · · · · · ◄
Sociology · · · · · · · · · · · · · · · ►
Physics · · · · · · · · · · · · · · · ►

POSTSTRUCTURALISM
Where everything is relative

By the mid-20th century, there were a number of structural theories of human existence. The Swiss linguist Ferdinand de Saussure (1857–1913) suggested that meaning was to be found within the structure of a whole language rather than in the analysis of individual words. For Marxists, the truth of human existence could be understood through economic structures. Psychoanalysts attempted to describe the structure of the psyche. In the 1960s, the structuralist movement, based in France, attempted to synthesize the ideas of Marx, Freud, and Saussure. They argued that individuals are shaped by linguistic, sociological, and psychological structures over which they have no control.

Originally labeled a structuralist, the French philosopher and historian Michel Foucault (1926–84) came to be seen as the most important representative of the poststructuralist movement. He agreed that language and society were shaped by rule-governed systems, but he disagreed with the structuralists on two counts. First, he did not think that there were unchanging structures that explained the human condition, and second, he thought that it was impossible to survey the situation objectively. Jacques Derrida (1930–) developed deconstruction as a technique for analyzing texts. Influenced by Heidegger and Nietzsche, Derrida suggests that all text has ambiguity, and because of this a final and complete interpretation is impossible to attain.

Poststructuralism and deconstruction can be seen as the theoretical formulations of the postmodern condition. Modernity, which began intellectually with the Enlightenment, attempted to describe the world in rational, empirical, and objective terms. It assumed that there was a truth to be uncovered, a way of obtaining answers to the question posed by the human condition. Postmodernism does not exhibit this confidence – reason itself is now seen as a particular historical form, as parochial in its own way as the ancients' explanations of the universe in terms of gods.

The postmodern subject has no rational way to evaluate a preference in relation to judgments of truth, morality, esthetic experience, or objectivity. As the old hierarchies of thought are torn down, a new clearing is formed on the frontiers of understanding: quite what hybrids of thought will metamorphose, interbreed, and grow in this clearing is for the future to decide.

GENEALOGY OF KNOWLEDGE

Michel Foucault attempted to analyze the "discursive practices" that claim to reveal knowledge – for example, histories of particular periods or of science. But rather than analyze these practices in terms of their truth value, he chose to examine their history or genesis. He said that he was attempting to perform an "archaeology" of knowledge to show the history of truth claims.

In his later work, he borrowed the "genealogical" approach from Nietzsche, and from Marx his analyses of ideology. Foucault sought to show how the development of knowledge was intertwined with the mechanisms of (political) power. Unlike Marx, Foucault had no belief in a deep underlying truth or structure: he held that there was no objective viewpoint from which one could analyze discourse or society.

Foucault focused on the way that knowledge and the increase of the power of the state over the individual has developed in the modern era. In his *Histoire de la Sexualité* (History of Sexuality, 1976–84), he argued that the rise of medical and psychiatric science has created a discourse in which sexuality is considered to be instinctual and mysterious. This discourse became accepted as the dominant explanation, and its assumptions began to seep into the discourse of the everyday. In this way, human subjects' experience of their own sexuality is shaped and controlled by the discourses that purport to explain it. In short, the search for knowledge does not simply uncover preexisting "objects," it actively shapes and creates them.

Foucault does not offer any all-embracing theory of human nature. He was critical of "meta-theory" – beliefs that claimed to give an exclusive objective explanation of reality. For Foucault, there is no ultimate answer waiting to be uncovered. The "discursive practices" of knowledge are not independent of the objects that are studied, but must be understood in their social and political context.

CULTURAL HIERARCHIES

Poststructural criticism has had far-reaching effects on academia because it has undermined the notions of good or bad art, good or bad taste. If everything is subjective, how do we know if Shelley was a better poet than John Lennon? How do we know that a little diamond is more tasteful than a big rhinestone? The idea of a cultural hierarchy – for example, that certain books are part of the "canon," a body of works of the highest quality that carries literary tradition from one generation to the next – has been central to Western teaching for centuries, although historically, the structure of this hierarchy has always been subject to fashion.

Casting aside the idea of a cultural hierarchy has had an enormously liberating effect on academics. They have been able to write about subjects, such as pop music, that before would have been considered too trivial to be worthy of serious study. Conversely, poststructural criticism leaves behind it a vacuum. Left without the tools to discriminate between good and bad art, without the structure of high- and lowbrow art, the critic has no role – all criticism becomes meaningless.

ROOM FOR POP STARS? Even the most traditional universities have opened their doors to poststructural and deconstructionist analysis and embraced study of subjects far removed from the canon. But tradition remains powerful in university life – especially in determining the status of academic institutions.

DECONSTRUCTION

IT'S A (WO)MAN'S WORLD The meanings at play in a text may contradict each other. The German-born film actress Marlene Dietrich (1904–92) – here in *Morocco* (1930), directed by Josef von Sternberg (1894–1969) – has an unsettling screen presence because her acting transmits subtly confusing signals: although remaining within her scripted character, she exhibits a type of frank sexuality generally reserved for the male lead actor. This works against the accepted ways of representing male-female relations in Hollywood films of the period. In *Morocco*, while dressed in male drag, she interacts with another woman as a man would in a love scene – and with remarkable intensity.

For Jacques Derrida, language or "text" is not a reflection of the world. Text structures our interpretation of the world. Following the German philosopher Martin Heidegger (1889–1976), Derrida thinks that language shapes us: texts create our understanding of reality. Derrida sees the history of Western thought as based on opposition: good vs. evil, mind vs. matter, man vs. woman, speech vs. writing. But these oppositions are defined hierarchically: the second term is seen as a corruption of the first, the terms are not equal opposites.

Derrida thought that all text contained a legacy of these assumptions, and as a result, these texts could be reinterpreted with an awareness of the implicit hierarchies. Derrida does not think that there is an end point of interpretation, a truth; all texts exhibit "*differance*": they allow multiple interpretations. Meaning is diffuse, not settled. Textuality always gives us a surplus of possibilities, yet we cannot stand outside of textuality in an attempt to find objectivity.

One consequence of deconstruction is that certainty in textual analyses becomes impossible. There may be competing interpretations, but there is no uninterpreted way one could assess the validity of any of these. Instead of basing philosophical understanding on undeniable truths, the deconstructionist turns the settled bedrock of rationalism into the shifting sands of a multiplicity of interpretations.

SEE ALSO
Multiculturalism ············ ◀
The Enlightenment ··········· ◀
Modern spirituality ·········· ▶
Sociology ················· ▶
New Romantics ············· ▶

MODERN CHRISTIANITY

The church's authority under fire

Christianity is in decline in the West – even in the United States, which has the highest figures for attendance at worship of any Western nation. An opinion poll conducted in 1991 revealed that only 58 percent of Americans thought religion played an important part in their lives, compared with 75 percent in 1952.

It is impossible to uncover the collective opinions of medieval populations, but the apparent unity of pre-Reformation Christendom is impressive. In the 16th century, the Reformation emphasized the individual's relationship with God, opening the door to the fragmentation of Christianity – and many sects have risen and fallen since. The consequence has been an erosion in the confidence of any one believer, or the members of any one sect, that their beliefs are the only true beliefs. That loss of certainty has undermined religious belief itself.

At the same time, religious faith has struggled against the powerful current of progress in the physical sciences. It is not simply that theories such as Darwinian evolution or the origin of all things in a "Big Bang" of creation seem to be irreconcilable with biblical accounts. More important, contemporary society has found that the claims of religion fail to meet the rigorous standards of evidence that science has accustomed people to expect.

In the contemporary world, the loss of authority suffered by organized Christian churches has led many people into all manner of beliefs – astrology, scientology, various forms of Eastern-derived mysticism, and the whole range of activities labeled New Age. The future will reveal whether those manifestations of the religious impulse have power to endure.

NATURAL THEOLOGY

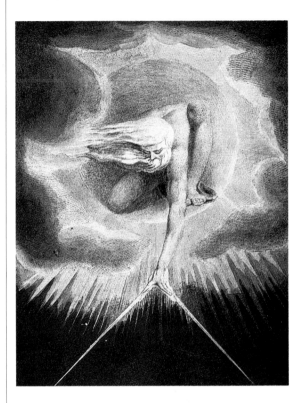

FROM ON HIGH Thomas Aquinas reacted against an older tradition – founded by the Tunisian-born Augustine (354–430) – which held that human knowledge of God was a result of divine intervention.

Natural theology, or deism – the belief that one can come to know of God's existence through rational processes, not by divine revelation – has its roots in the 13th century, in the work of the Italian philosopher Thomas Aquinas (1225–74). He rested his case for the existence of God chiefly on the argument that creation must have had a "first cause." But the full flowering of deism was to occur during the Age of Reason.

In the mid-17th century, René Descartes (1596–1650) attempted to prove God's existence by the exercise of pure reason, and in the following century French philosophers stripped belief of supernaturalism. In the minds of deists, God became the great mechanic-inventor who set the workings of the universe in motion and then withdrew. The evidence for God's existence was to be found in the design of the universe and in the working of natural laws such as gravity.

The deists' God did not intervene in human history – through miracles such as the Virgin Birth, for example – nor respond to prayer, nor call the dead to an afterlife.

CRISIS OF FAITH

"Action will furnish belief, but will that belief be the true one?" That was the troubled response of the English poet Arthur Hugh Clough (1819–61) to the advice to overcome religious doubts by the practice of church rituals. Clough's crisis of faith was a commonplace among 19th-century intellectuals, who were assaulted by the evolutionists' picture of nature "red in tooth and claw" and by the work of biblical revisionists who tore supernaturalism from the Scriptures and, in liberal versions of the life of Jesus, left Christ himself bereft of divinity.

"There lives more faith in honest doubt," wrote the English poet laureate, Lord Tennyson (1809–92), "believe me, than in half the creeds." Some overcame their doubts; many more, adrift in a rising tide of secularism and declining church attendances, took refuge in agnosticism. The "don't know" attitude of the agnostic was scorned only by the boldest of men, such as the English mathematician and atheist W.K. Clifford (1845–79), who declared human freedom to be the "sacred thing." His creed was "to recognize the enormous and fearful difference between truth and falsehood, right and wrong, and how truth and right are to be got by free enquiry and the love of our comrades for their own sake and nobody else."

HEAR OUR PRAYER Despite the onslaughts of science and the spread of atheism and agnosticism among intellectuals, the desire for belief in a fatherly God who would listen to and answer an individual's prayers remained widespread throughout the Victorian age and beyond.

PAPAL INFALLIBILITY

BEYOND DISPUTE Members of the Catholic church accept that the Pope – considered to be a descendant of the apostle Peter and Jesus Christ's representative on Earth – can assume absolute authority in certain pronouncements.

The doctrine of ultramontanism ("beyond the mountain") – a 19th-century statement of the belief that the papacy was the ultimate authority, commanding loyalty from Roman Catholics ahead of their allegiance to national states – was a warmed-up leftover from the medieval quarrel between popes and emperors. But support for the idea was strong enough in France and Germany to encourage the church's Vatican Council of 1870 – summoned by Pope Pius IX (r.1846–78) – to proclaim that the pope was incapable of error when he spoke in his official capacity on matters of faith and morals.

The doctrine does not attribute supernatural mental powers to the pope; nor does it assert that God speaks to him directly to provide answers to specific questions. What is more, it does not mean that every official papal statement is infallible. A statement is infallible only if the pope defines it as such. For instance, *Humanae Vitae* – the 1968 encyclical condemning the use of birth control – did not claim to be infallible.

SEE ALSO

Socialism ·····················
The Enlightenment ···········
Existentialism ················
Modern spirituality ···········

THEOSOPHY

HISTORY MAKERS: *Helena Blavatsky (1831–91), Henry Olcott (1832–1907), Annie Besant (1847–1933)*

SEE ALSO: *Modern spirituality*

CROWD-PULLING CHARISMA Madame Blavatsky's "miracle meetings" and seances attracted huge audiences – some reputedly 100,000 strong.

The Theosophical Society was founded by the Russian émigré Helena Blavatsky in New York in 1875. Its objective was to revive spirituality in the West by bringing together strands of Eastern mysticism and the occult. Theosophy was, in fact, a somewhat comical hodgepodge of ideas, including communication with spirits, reincarnation, and alchemy.

Its purpose was ostensibly to fill the gap created by many people's loss of traditional Christian faith – Madame Blavatsky herself was at war with the Christian church, which she wished to see overthrown – but its true message was deeply and overtly antiscientific, specifically anti-Darwinian. Underlying theosophy was the belief that pure spirit was a sufficient cause of a host of events, ranging from remote communication between individuals to the advance programing of whole historical epochs by celestial influences.

Theosophy also had a political message – internationalist, pacifist, socially progressive. Some believe that it was the spawning ground of the 20th-century revival of supernaturalism and superstition, or, at least, that its popularity was the most salient symptom of that approaching revival.

ECUMENICISM

SEE ALSO: *Modern Christianity*

The word "ecumenicism" derives from the Greek for "the inhabited world" and is used to describe a variety of initiatives to reunite the world of European Christendom, split since the Reformation of the 16th century into communicants of the Roman church and the members of various Protestant denominations. Although there have been some overtures to the Orthodox church of the East, the ecumenical impulse has largely restricted itself to Western European Christian traditions.

Ecumenicism had close ties with advocates of social reform from its beginnings in the 19th century, when Evangelicals in the established church in England cooperated with Baptists and Congregationalists in the fight against slavery and appalling conditions in industrial factories. One of the first fruits of that collaboration was the YMCA (1844). Later came the International Missionary Council, which eventually became the present-day World Council of Churches.

Today the chief objective is to break down barriers between the Roman and non-Roman churches, but obstacles to harmony – differences over doctrinal matters such as the Eucharist and other sacraments, and ecclesiastical matters such as priestly celibacy and the ordination of women – are so great that it is difficult to foresee a substantial narrowing of the divide between Rome and Protestantism.

CHRISTIAN SCIENCE

HISTORY MAKERS: *Mary Baker Eddy (1821–1910)*

SEE ALSO: *Modern spirituality, Medicine*

The Church of Christ, Scientist, was founded by Mary Baker Eddy in 1879 in Boston, Massachusetts. It rests on the principles of divine healing and the conception of the material world's unreality that was enunciated in her book *Science and Health with Key to the Scriptures* (1875), which is the acknowledged primer of the sect.

It remains a tiny, almost exclusively American, church. There is no central organization; each branch of the church is entirely self-governing and self-supporting. Christian Science holds that illness is, like sin, conquerable only in the mind. Its followers therefore eschew the assistance of medical doctors to fight against disease.

QUEST FOR WELLBEING Mary Baker Eddy's own ill health led to her interest in medicine and her eventual recourse to faith healing.

FUNDAMENTALISM

HISTORY MAKERS: *John Scopes (1901–)*

SEE ALSO: *Conservatism*

SCIENCE VS. RELIGION Schoolteacher John Scopes stands between defense and prosecution lawyers during his trial in Tennessee in 1925. Scopes was fined $100 for teaching the theory of evolution in school.

Christian fundamentalism began as a reaction against liberal Protestant theology of the 19th century, which eroded belief in the literal truth of the Bible. Fundamentalists believe that the Scriptures are the revealed word of God and are therefore true in all their elements – including supernatural and miraculous events.

They do not accept that the Bible is ever allegorical. Hence, Darwinian evolution becomes akin to blasphemy, and in some southern states, a campaign to ban the teaching of evolution in state schools continues.

Fundamentalists also refuse to countenance any suggestion that the thoughts expressed in the Bible and the phraseology of those thoughts are a reflection of social and political conditions in the early Christian era and therefore open to changing interpretations as conditions change through history. That attitude allows fundamentalists to cite passages from the Bible to support, for example, unrelenting hostility to homosexuals and, less virulently perhaps, to women.

The use of the term Islamic fundamentalism in the West is usually misleading, since in most instances it refers not to a literal reading of the Quran, but to a resurgence of the theocratic tradition of Islam in which the state and the faith are inseparable.

LIBERATION THEOLOGY

HISTORY MAKERS: *Jean-Bertrand Aristide (1953–)*

SEE ALSO: *Socialism, Marxism*

Liberation theology is scarcely what the name suggests. It has little to do with theology (the study of the nature of God), except insofar as it draws upon the understanding of Christ as the liberator who brought succor to the oppressed and the poor. It is essentially a political movement – deeply influenced by Marxism – which seeks to transform the Catholic church into an instrument of social change in order to improve conditions among the poor in underdeveloped countries.

It first manifested itself in South America in the 1960s before spreading to parts of Africa. The Vatican seemed originally to be somewhat receptive to its argument: Pope Paul VI's encyclical of 1967, *Populorum Progressio*, spoke out against the widening gap between rich and poor nations, but the Roman hierarchy has since retreated, apparently frightened off by a grassroots movement in which lesser clergy and laity joined to fight oppression, notably against General Pinochet's dictatorship in Chile and on behalf of the Sandinista National Liberation Front in Nicaragua.

The strength of liberation theology lies especially in its establishing of "base-communities," organizations of local people to promote self-help activities and propagate radical politics. It also gains adherents in Latin America by its opposition to American economic imperialism and to the intrusion of American television evangelism.

CONTRAST In cities like Rio de Janeiro in Brazil, the enormous gap between rich and poor – created partly by unchecked capitalism, corruption, and exploitation – is a reminder of why Marxism is still seen to be a viable political alternative in parts of Latin America.

MODERN SPIRITUALITY
The age of Aquarius

In the last quarter of the 20th century, anyone in the West in search of a religion can choose from a huge variety of sources – from Tibetan Buddhism to Celtic Christianity. Spirituality is a booming industry: books, tapes, workshops, and seminars promoting a heady variety of methods of reaching enlightenment are proliferating at an enormous rate. And any seeker is free to pick and mix, as well as pick and choose. There is no ban on performing a Hindu ceremony in the morning and going to a synagogue in the evening. This freedom of individual choice is probably the logical outcome of the Reformation and the Enlightenment – the first emphasized personal responsibility to God and the second scepticism toward dogma and traditional hierarchy.

Despite the fragmentation of belief, certain strong influences are common to modern spirituality: the religions of the East – in particular, Buddhism and Hinduism; Europe's own non-Christian religious heritage; and psychoanalysis. The central purpose of all the new "religions," except for the world-rejecting cults, is the development of the self. The self is, of course, a problematic concept. But it is safe to say that modern spirituality regards the self in much the same way as Christians see the soul. It is the semimystical essence of being.

Another important influence has been feminism. While religion was an important public function, it remained an almost exclusively male domain. But with its absorption into the realm of the personal and private – traditionally associated with women – religion has become increasingly feminized. The gods and religious leaders of the new age are not exclusively male.

Eclecticism leads to a great deal of tolerance, but too much tolerance also leads to a lack of discrimination. If everything is a matter of personal preference, how do we determine the difference between right and wrong?

NEW AGE

New Age is a label used to describe a wide variety of groups and individuals loosely linked by the fact that they all believe humanity to be on the threshold of a new spiritual era. The movement is characterized by antipathy to dogma and institutions. New Age ideas have many sources – from physics to the Tibetan *Book of the Dead* – but one of the key influences is the psychoanalytic theories of Swiss psychiatrist Carl Jung (1875–1961). With its emphasis on the irrational, individualism, and nature, the New Age is certainly a spiritual offspring of 19th-century Romanticism.

The movement emphasizes the superiority of the intuitive over the rational and the importance of exploring both the personal and collective unconscious, so encouraging individuals to find sacredness within themselves. To make sense of the unconscious, practitioners may use astrology, dreams, tarot cards, the Jewish cabbalah (an occult philosophy derived from readings of the Hebrew scriptures), or the *I Ching* (a book of ancient Chinese philosophy). The goal for most is personal "integration" – reconciling disparate parts of the personality to achieve "wholeness." The "feminine," which many New Agers believe has been neglected over the

OUT OF THE PAST Pre-Christian religions have been born again in the New Age. The Druids were a line of mystical priests in ancient Britain and France.

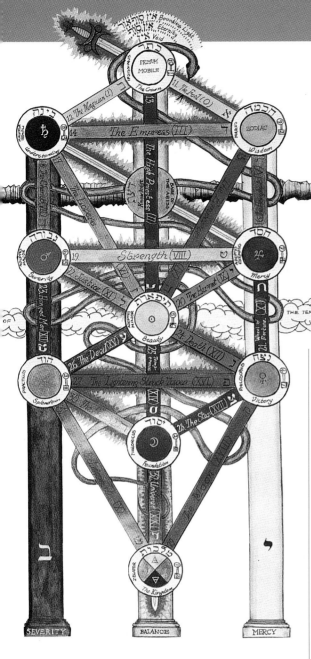

SECRETS FOR SALE Cabbalic esoterics are explained in modern artwork. In the Middle Ages when the doctrines of the cabbalah were refined, knowledge was truly a source of power; today it is a commodity.

past few millennia, is encouraged to flourish. Ecology is strongly emphasized, and James Lovelock's Gaia theory – that the Earth functions as a single organism – has had a big impact. New Age experiments such as The Farm in the United States and Findhorn in Scotland are attempts to set up spiritually and ecologically utopian communities.

CULTS

The 1970s saw the rise of cults such as the Unification Church ("the Moonies") founded by the Korean Reverend Sun Myung Moon in 1954; the Hare Krishnas; the Church of Scientology; and most infamously the People's Temple, which ended in mass suicide in the jungles of Guyana – to name just a few. These cults fall into two main categories – world-affirming or world-rejecting movements.

World-rejecting movements, such as the Moonies, see the world as an essentially evil place. They put little value in the individual and require self-denial. These movements are hierarchical; the leader is seen as closer to God than the congregation.

World-affirming movements do not have set rituals, a distinct dogma, or any hierarchy. Their loose structure and more permissive approach to the spiritual has meant that they have had far more impact on the general culture. These movements – such as EST and the Church of Scientology – see the world as an essentially good place: the problem with life is simply that people have not realized their full potential. It is the role of the cult to help people discover their inner worth.

MEDITATION

Meditation has always been a common practice among members of religious communities, but since the 1960s it has become widely practiced by lay people. This is largely due to the growing influence of Buddhism and Hinduism on Western spiritual life.

Meditation differs from prayer in that the object is to find inner stillness rather than importune an outside power. In the 1960s, a technique developed by Maharishi Mahesh Yogi, Transcendental Meditation (TM), was made fashionable by the British pop group The Beatles. In TM, a Sanskrit word or phrase, a mantra, is repeated over and over so that the conscious mind can be stilled and the user can find a deeper level of awareness. Most other techniques of meditation are similar to TM, although some involve undertaking some kind of physical exercise.

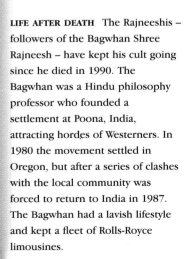

LIFE AFTER DEATH The Rajneeshis – followers of the Bagwhan Shree Rajneesh – have kept his cult going since he died in 1990. The Bagwhan was a Hindu philosophy professor who founded a settlement at Poona, India, attracting hordes of Westerners. In 1980 the movement settled in Oregon, but after a series of clashes with the local community was forced to return to India in 1987. The Bagwhan had a lavish lifestyle and kept a fleet of Rolls-Royce limousines.

SEE ALSO

God · · · · · · · · · · · · · · · · · ◀
Modern Christianity · · · · · · · · · ◀
Ecology · · · · · · · · · · · · · · · · ▶

Human Sciences

The formal study of human behavior has grown from nothing to become a major group of disciplines.

P ride of place in the curriculum of Europe's medieval universities was held by the course of studies known as *literae humaniores,* or "humane studies," covering what were considered the cornerstones of Western civilization: Greek, Latin, philosophy, and literature. The Industrial Revolution and the Enlightenment brought social and cultural changes that inspired a new interest in studying human behavior. The new formal disciplines that developed, including economics, sociology, anthropology, and psychology, form the core of what have become known as the social, or human, sciences.

The use of the word "science" here is significant. All the human sciences rest on the notion that it is possible to analyze and predict human behavior, in much the same way as the behavior of matter can be predicted by physicists and chemists. The challenge lies in the fact that people – unlike chemicals in a test tube – do not always follow simple behavioral rules. The human family is far too diverse. Economists have identified the mechanisms that determine price, value, and trade, but can only hazard a guess at the effect of recession, currency fluctuations, or interest rate changes on the individual decisions that make up a nation's economic behavior.

The evolution of human sciences has been a story of increased intimacy with the human soul. Economics, the first human science, is concerned with financial transactions; anthropology seeks to systematize the astonishing diversity of cultures, languages, and social structures. Sociology tries to relate such structures to individual behavior, while psychology, the newest of the disciplines, attempts the ambitious task of mapping the human mind itself.

Human scientists have applied scientific methods – such as observation and controlled experiments – to our behavior with varying degrees of success. Their ideas have certainly been enormously influential. The modern fascination with self-knowledge and individualism stems from Jungian psychology, while market research and marketing – both essential functions of modern businesses – rely on a melange of economics, sociology, and psychology. It remains uncertain, however, whether these new disciplines will ever attain the status of true sciences, since science itself still seems to be far from explaining how the mind works. Nevertheless, they have certainly enhanced our understanding of ourselves.

THE HUMAN FAMILY The crowded beach at Coney Island, New York, in 1929.

PHYSICAL ANTHROPOLOGY
Measuring the human race

Modern anthropology has its roots in the European colonization of the New World. The appearance, customs, and beliefs of America's indigenous peoples impressed and excited European intellectuals of the age of discovery. Reports of "noble savages" stimulated the thinkers of the Enlightenment to formulate rudimentary theories about what distinguishes human beings from the rest of the animal kingdom, and what it means to be human.

In the 19th century, Charles Darwin's theories of evolution provided a crucial stimulus to the study of man, posing a challenge to biologists to find out more about human origins. Scientists and philosophers were also eager to apply the evolutionary model to other fields, including the development of civilization and culture. Today's anthropology has two distinct but closely related strands. "Physical" anthropology focuses on man's place in nature – the ancestry, development, genetic, and other characteristics of the human species. "Social" or "cultural" anthropology examines the way people live – their customs, relationships, and beliefs.

Physical anthropologists view man as a biological phenomenon, dissecting our species with all the tools of anatomy, physiology, and zoology. For much of this century, they have concentrated on the way physical traits differ from population to population. Such "trait mapping" reveals, for example, that the natives of Scandinavia, the Baltic, and the eastern part of Britain are more likely to have blonde hair and blue eyes than are people from the rest of Europe. It can also reveal the continuing process of physiological adaptation to the environment: through natural selection, Tibetan villagers have become better at living in high altitudes, and Sahara nomads have adapted for life in hot, dry conditions.

The discovery of DNA – the chemical that carries genes – in 1953 was a breakthrough for anthropology. The main thrust of research concentrates on studying genetic patterns and connections between different populations around the world. Anthropologists can also compare genes extracted from ancient remains with modern genes. Ultimately, these techniques could provide new evidence about our origins and the way humanity populated the face of the Earth.

ANTHROPOMETRY

Measuring human physical characteristics – anthropometry – was the main research activity of early anthropologists. These studies led Johann Blumenbach (1752–1840), widely regarded as the founder of physical anthropology, to declare in 1781 that there were five human types: Caucasian, Mongolian, Ethiopian, American, and Malay. Dozens more such classification schemes, most now outdated, followed.

A major focus for the early anthropometrists was the skull. Cranial capacity, jaw structure, the angle of the brow, and other criteria were doggedly analyzed, usually for proof of the superiority of one race over another. These techniques were adopted in Nazi Germany, where calipers, protractors, and rulers were used to detect signs of "racial degeneracy." These theories are now discredited, for they depend on the belief that all members of a given group have the same characteristics – an assumption belied by the enormous range of variations within each group.

However, anthropometry remains a vital research tool for paleontologists engaged in the search for the origins of the human species. Variations in bone structure and size are vital clues to our prehistoric roots.

SKULL SKILLS Early anthropology sometimes spilled over into superstition. Phrenology, fortunetelling by the bumps on a person's head, was legitimized with scientific jargon and sold by ordinary charlatanry.

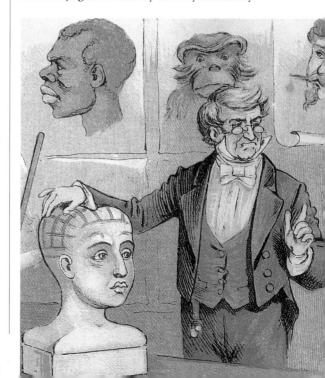

EUGENICS

CRIMINAL TYPES The claim by Italian anthropologist Cesare Lombroso (1836–1909) that criminals could be identified by their anatomical and physiological characteristics led to sometimes ludicrous attempts at photographing criminals looking appropriately wicked.

The study of human heredity and genetics has driven many people to contemplate whether the stock of people – like that of horses, cattle, or flowers – could be improved by selective breeding. It was the British scientist Francis Galton (1822–1911), a cousin of Charles Darwin, who coined the term eugenics in 1883 to describe the improvement of mankind by artificially influencing the process of natural selection.

The aim of eugenics is to influence the transmission of genetic material by helping positive traits to pass on to the next generation and preventing, or discouraging, negative traits. Some aspects of eugenics have now become widely accepted. Down's Syndrome, caused by a genetic abnormality which affects around 1 in 700 births, can be detected during pregnancy, and its incidence has been reduced by offering the choice of abortion to affected parents.

But eugenics also raises serious ethical questions, especially when it becomes a matter of social policy. Few would agree with Galton and his followers, who envisaged a system under which criminals and the physically handicapped would be compulsorily sterilized, while celibate geniuses could be forced to breed for the good of society. The horror of the Nazi Holocaust – genocide and baby factories set up in the name of a bogus racial theory – has irreversibly tainted the acceptability of eugenics as a form of social engineering.

PALEOANTHROPOLOGY

It seemed probable that Adam was man's common ancestor until 1856, when workmen quarrying limestone in the Neander valley, near Düsseldorf in Germany, dug into a cave and unearthed a handful of bones, which at first were not even recognized as human. Later examination showed that they included part of a woman's skull: a woman with a very low and heavy brow, a receding forehead, and a brain bigger than ours.

Other finds followed elsewhere in Europe and in southern Africa, and it became clear that "Neanderthal man," although a different species from *Homo sapiens*, nevertheless walked upright, lived in caves, used language, and followed a special ritual for burying the dead. It is now known that Neanderthal man was a relatively recent arrival, flourishing from around 400,000 BC until his sudden disappearance some 40,000 years ago. The Neanderthals were an archaic human species. Whether they were direct ancestors, or whether they represent the evolutionary dead end of a parallel branch of the human family tree, the continuing quest for man's ancestors has become one of the great scientific detective stories of our time.

In recent years, much attention has been focused on southern and eastern Africa, where a succession of fossil finds has provided occasionally startling evidence about our ancestors. Early hominids – that is, humanlike animals with large brains and an upright gait – are now thought to have evolved between 3 and 6 million years ago. *Homo erectus*, who knew how to make fire and flint tools, and was the direct ancestor of *Homo sapiens*, made his appearance some 1.6 million years ago. The knowledge that our own species is a mere 250,000 years old makes human beings a very recent arrival on the planet.

DISTANT COUSIN The remains of Neanderthals have been found all over Europe, but the reason for the sudden disappearance of these early hominids remains mysterious. Some anthropologists speculate that they were wiped out by our ancestors, the Cro-Magnons.

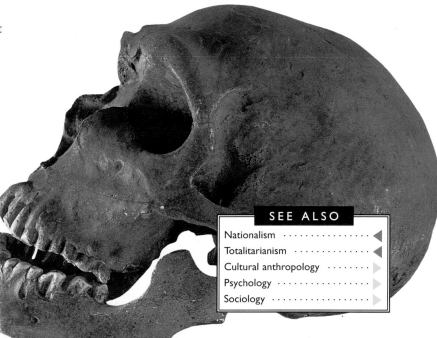

SEE ALSO

Nationalism · · · · · · · · · · · · · · ◄
Totalitarianism · · · · · · · · · · · · ◄
Cultural anthropology · · · · · · · · ►
Psychology · · · · · · · · · · · · · · · ►
Sociology · · · · · · · · · · · · · · · · ►

CULTURAL ANTHROPOLOGY
Manners and customs of the human family

The idea that the story of civilization is one of constant progress appeared in the 18th century, as industrialization brought wealth and confidence to Europe. Travelers' tales of life in Asia, Africa, and South America offered glimpses of customs and religions quite unlike those of Christian Europe. "Primitive" artifacts brought back from the Pacific and Africa were compared with the elegance of the Renaissance. Scholars seized on these differences to confirm that society had evolved from barbarism to an advanced state of culture.

The combination of intellectual fascination and pure curiosity about other cultures gave birth to what we now call cultural, or social, anthropology – the study of different societies through their customs, institutions, religious beliefs, family life, moral framework, and other aspects. In 1890, the Scottish anthropologist Sir James Frazer (1854–1941) published *The Golden Bough*, a study of comparative religion, which proposed a model of culture that focused successively on magic, religion, and finally, science. Frazer's work inspired generations of anthropologists and profoundly influenced many poets, philosophers, and artists.

The first anthropologists compiled their theories from travelers' tales and other reports, but in the late 19th century scholars started making field trips to study people by living among them. In 1883, the American geographer and physicist Franz Boas (1858–1942) led a scientific expedition to Baffin Island, in northeastern Canada. His fascination with local Inuit culture outstripped his geographical curiosity, and the expedition became the first anthropological field trip. In his later work with Native Americans, Boas developed an empirical approach, based on observation and statistical data.

By composing a picture of the way people live and examining the beliefs and customs that have been passed down from generation to generation, anthropologists explore the complex interfaces between neighbors, strangers, and relatives, and between man and the natural world. By uncovering the frameworks that sustain society, they allow us to see ourselves more clearly – and to realize that the jungle hunter of Borneo and the car-driving, apartment-dwelling city slicker are both hostages of custom and society.

ETHNICITY

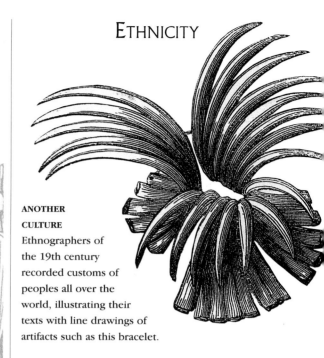

ANOTHER CULTURE Ethnographers of the 19th century recorded customs of peoples all over the world, illustrating their texts with line drawings of artifacts such as this bracelet.

One side effect of the cultural differences revealed by anthropologists has been a heightened awareness of ethnic and cultural identity. Much of Western society is now multi-ethnic, with Turks in Germany, Indians and West Indians in Britain, and North Africans in France and Spain making important contributions to society. Even within nations, regional separatism often falls along ethnic lines – as seen in Catalonia, the Basque country, Quebec, and Scotland.

Although race, religion, and national origin play a unifying role, the hallmark of ethnic identity is the social transmission of a distinctive lifestyle and beliefs from generation to generation. Studies of Polish, Italian, and Greek communities in the United States have shown the extent to which traditions from the homeland have survived and been adapted to life in a new land, often helped by continuing ties to relatives abroad.

Anthropologists also trace the way such transplanted communities settle in to their surroundings. Assimilation – intermarriage and the abandonment of old practices in order to blend in with the host population – is one of the key processes. Another is acculturation, the exchange of practices and beliefs between distinctive cultures ending in the predomination of one or the other.

RITUAL

The liturgy followed in a church, shaking hands with a stranger, and saying "cheers" before drinking are all familiar rituals. For anthropologists, the term "ritual" is applied to patterns of behavior that are symbolic, rather than actually achieving anything. Dignitaries who "lay" foundation stones with a silver trowel are well aware of this distinction.

The French anthropologist Charles-Arnold Kurr van Gennep (1873–1957), writing in 1909, coined the phrase "rites of passage" to describe the rituals that mark major milestones such as puberty and marriage, and lesser ones such as new year. Van Gennep identified three stages to these rites of passage: separation (from other people, or from their previous condition), transition (a period in limbo), and incorporation (taking on new status).

Every culture has its own rites of passage. Death, the most disruptive and frightening of all life's transitions, is an especially fertile area for ritual. The Irish symbolically laugh in the face of death by holding a wake; in many parts of the world, ritual wailing provides a way for survivors to express grief.

ALL IN THE FAMILY The elaborate edifice of kinship sets up a system of reciprocal obligations, such as the duty of parents to look after their children when they are young, and of children to look after their elderly parents. The relaxation of such obligations and the narrowing of kinship networks in industrial societies has been blamed for the perceived lack of social cohesion and discipline in the West.

FUNCTIONALISM

A community – be it an extended family, a village, or a large city – is a kind of organic being, like an animal or a human. Its members are like organs that perform different functions to keep the organism alive. Functionalism aims to figure out how each individual contributes to the overall functioning of society. It does this by piecing together all the elements and patterns detected by anthropologists and examining the consequences – both deliberate and unintended – of individual actions.

The function of an object, a law, or a custom is determined not by its practical use, but by its social or cultural role. For example, in practical terms, an ax is a tool to chop wood, but seen in terms of function, it makes farmland available by felling trees and keeps people warm by providing firewood. The function of customs is largely a matter of interpretation. The early evening stroll that is a feature of life in Mediterranean towns is more than a chance to relax in the cool of the evening after a hot day. Young people may use it to make friends or find a partner, while for elderly people, a tacit function is probably to reassure others that they are alive and well.

KINSHIP

Scottish clans, royal dynasties, and the Mafia all derive their power from the rights and obligations of kinship. Kinship systems govern inheritance, marriage, and succession, making them an agent of social regulation.

Anthropological researchers have developed various methods of categorizing kinship. Two people are kin if they share a common ancestor or are descended from each other. But kinship is not just a matter of being related by blood; marriage adds a layer of relatives, and beyond the extended family godparenthood is a form of artificial kinship. In a wider sense, kindred can include friends as well as relations. The point at which close kin become distant kin varies from culture to culture.

SEE ALSO

Nationalism · · · · · · · · · · · · · · · ◄
Physical anthropology · · · · · · · · ◄
Sociology · · · · · · · · · · · · · · · · ▶

FIELD WORK

The way a community works cannot be studied in a laboratory, so the only place for anthropologists to conduct their research is in the field. Until the end of the 19th century, however, most anthropologists relied on information supplied by travelers, missionaries, government officials, and others. The first serious field trips were undertaken in the 1890s.

But the field trips to the Trobriand Islands made between 1915 and 1918 by the British academic Bronislaw Malinowski (1884–1942) marked a radical departure in anthropological methods. Unlike his peers, who had ventured into remote settlements from research stations or local towns, Malinowski pitched his tent among the huts of Omarakana. Cut off from the amenities of the town and from the company of other Europeans, Malinowski immersed himself in the life of the village for a year at a time, learning the language, making friends, and taking part as far as possible in village activities.

This made field work not just a scientific quest, but a total experience, a kind of rebirth which all anthropologists find emotionally taxing and sometimes traumatic. Malinowski described this encounter as "a strange, sometimes unpleasant, sometimes intensely interesting adventure" which allows the student of society to penetrate the mental life of another society, its ideologies, and its beliefs. Field work brought a new depth of understanding to the study of other cultures.

GOING NATIVE The young Margaret Mead (1901–78) sits between two Samoan girls during an expedition to the South Seas (1925–26). Her writings on anthropology helped to popularize the discipline.

STRUCTURALISM

Perhaps because the French scholar Claude Lévi-Strauss (1908–) was a philosopher as well as an anthropologist, his contribution to anthropology had repercussions throughout the world of ideas. Lévi-Strauss was no field worker: he found ample inspiration in the mass of material gathered by others.

Lévi-Strauss proposed that we understand the world around us by dividing it into manageable and namable segments, called classes. Our principal method of creating these categories is to identify polarities: sounds can be loud or soft; things can be hot or cold. Even complex scientific categorizations, such as the periodic table, are based on the same idea of "oppositeness."

When we create cultural artifacts (pictures, music, political systems, and myriad other things), we unconsciously reflect this way of seeing nature. A structuralist analysis of such artifacts can therefore provide an entry point to understanding the deep structures of our own minds, and even of our very souls.

Western society, with its rapid communications and artificial environments, covers these deep structures with a thick veneer of cultural "noise." Lévi-Strauss reasoned that it would be easier to reach these universal processes by studying myths, the key literary artifacts of ancient and technologically unsophisticated peoples. In his massive study *Mythologiques* (1964–71), he found a series of polarities that ran through world mythology, revealing the core structures of human discourse: the pure and the impure, the loyal and the treacherous, the friendly and the hostile, the raw and the cooked, and so on. The apparent differences between, say, ancient Greek and Plains tribal myths mask the fact that they have the same structure and therefore, ultimately, the same meaning. Structuralism is a versatile concept and was embraced by many academics in the 1970s and 1980s. It has been applied successfully to history, literary criticism, philosophy, and psychology.

"LANGUE ET PAROLE"

RULES OF THE GAME To communicate with his audience, an actor relies on a complicated mix of emphasis, gesture, and expression – as well as the audience's and the players' mutual understanding of the laws of a language.

The study of anthropology has given rise to new ways of looking at language, among the most influential of which have been the theories of the Swiss linguist Ferdinand de Saussure (1857–1913). Saussure's posthumous publication, *A Course in General Linguistics* (1916), viewed language as a system of signs (words) which carry no intrinsic meaning but derive their meaning from the way they relate to other words. In order to transmit useful information instead of gobbledygook, speakers generate the right words, put them in order, and add a layer of more subliminal signifiers such as intonation, style, and rhetoric.

The central Saussurian thesis is that language has two components. *Langue* (language) comprises the rules, structure, and vocabulary of language – the linguistic conventions understood by speaker and listener; *parole* (speech) is the fluid stringing together of words used in actual communication – the act of speaking or writing. Saussure was far more interested in *langue* than *parole*. By separating the structure of language from the act of language, Saussure unwittingly laid the foundations for one of the major intellectual developments of the 20th century: structuralism.

UNIVERSAL GRAMMAR

Children start talking when they are very young and they learn the rules of language without the benefit of formal teaching, grammar books, or dictionaries. This extraordinary feat roused the interest of the American linguist Noam Chomsky (1928–), who produced a series of revolutionary ideas about language during the 1950s and 1960s.

Chomsky proposed that humans are born with an in-built ability to use language, just as birds are born with the ability to fly. Children's capacity to derive, from the limited variety of sentences offered by their parents, all the rules for forming all the sentences they might speak throughout their lives, is biologically and anatomically hard-wired into the brain. He suggested that this fact, in turn, might be expected to influence the nature of language itself.

A careful study of the underlying patterns, or "deep structures" of many languages – living and dead – revealed that there is indeed a universal grammar that could be a sign of biological origins. The same grammatical structures recur, and most languages depend heavily on syntax – word order. "To be or not to be" means something, but "Be be or to not to," the same words assembled without syntax, is meaningless.

If the brain truly is built to learn language, the implications are immense. Is it possible to think without words? What do universal grammar and deep structures reveal about the architecture of the mind? Is creativity derived from an innate ability to improvise endless variations from a minute sample?

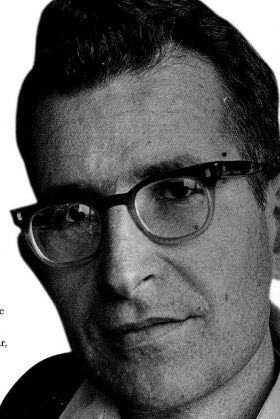

INNATE HUMANITY Noam Chomsky's fame is due to his political activism as well as his academic career. In the 1960s, he was an outspoken opponent of the Vietnam War, and since then he has been a thoughtful critic of American foreign policy.

PSYCHOLOGY
Mapping the human mind

By the late 19th century, scientists understood many of the more complex workings of the human body and had carefully anatomized the brain, but the nature of the human mind remained a mystery. Many respected doctors clung to the pseudoscientific beliefs of phrenology, a study based on the supposition that the shape of the skull influenced character and mental abilities. Mental illness was little understood and might even be dismissed as "lunacy" – madness brought on by the action of the moon.

The study of hysteria – in which patients suffer from physical symptoms such as paralysis or deafness without any organic cause – supplied the key to our current understanding of the mind. The story begins with Jean-Martin Charcot (1825–93), professor of nervous diseases at the Salpêtrière Hospital in Paris, who pioneered the use of hypnosis to treat hysteria. Charcot would put patients into a trance and deliver a series of hypnotic suggestions which made them feel better, and eventually dispelled their symptoms altogether. The process fascinated one of Charcot's students, a 29-year-old Viennese neurologist named Sigmund Freud (1865–1939). In particular, Freud noticed that on awakening, Charcot's patients had no recollection of what had been said to them. Their problems were rooted in the unconscious mind, reached via hypnosis.

Freud took Charcot's teachings on hypnosis back to Vienna and started to work closely with another physician, Josef Breuer (1842–1925). One of their cases, that of "Anna O," was to form the foundation of modern psychology. Breuer was able to cure Anna's split personality and hysteria by encouraging her to recall her past under hypnosis. By reliving the moment at which a particular symptom first appeared, Anna managed to free herself from it.

Breuer and Freud outlined their "talking cure" for nervous illness in *Studies in Hysteria* (1895). The book's central premise is that we tend to repress painful or shameful memories, which may later cause inner conflicts and manifest themselves as obsessions, phobias, or other psychological problems. The remedy is to bring these memories out into the open, where they can be analyzed and so put to rest.

THE UNCONSCIOUS

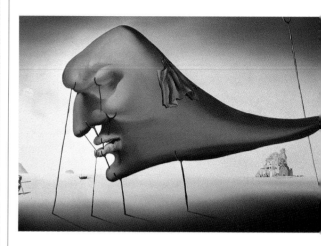

IN THE LAND OF DREAMS Exploration of the unconscious has inspired great works of art throughout this century, like *Sleep* by Salvador Dali (1904–89).

Modern psychotherapy and clinical psychology are based on a model of the mind with several components. For Freud, the mind fell into the conscious (readily accessible material such as people's names or faces), the preconscious (material that lurks below the surface, but can be brought to mind, such as distant memories), and the unconscious (an inaccessible area containing ideas which have been repressed, and therefore cannot emerge into consciousness). Dreams, which emerge when the conscious mind's grip on the psyche is dormant, are a vital route into the deepest reaches of the psyche.

Carl Jung added the concept of the collective unconscious, a storehouse of cultural ideas and memories that we inherit from our ancestors and that finds expression not just in dreams, but also in the form of myths and legends.

FREUD

The ideas of Sigmund Freud have become touchstones for our times. His discovery that we have an unconscious mind capable of influencing our conscious behavior revolutionized the way people perceive themselves and others. Many of his expressions – Freudian slips (mistakes in speech or action which reveal subconscious thoughts), Oedipal tendencies, penis envy, the ego and the id, repression, and sublimation – have entered common parlance, even if people are not always quite sure what they mean. And while Freud's obsession with sexual matters might seem misguided, it made him an unwitting prophet of the permissive society, that social explosion of the 1960s which continues to resonate today.

JUNG

The Swiss psychiatrist Carl Gustav Jung (1875–1961) created his own set of principles: analytical psychology. Jung's premise was that conflicting inner drives hinder our ability to reach an instinctive goal of personal wholeness. Jungian therapy aims to set up communication between the conscious and unconscious minds. Once they are in touch, they can work together. Jung's emphasis on self-development and his personal fascination with religion and myth, which lent a mystical cast to his thinking, led to his posthumous adoption as a guru of the "New Age."

OEDIPAL SPLIT Between 1907 and 1913, Freud (left) and Jung (above) collaborated closely – with Freud firmly in the role of mentor. When Jung dared to disagree with him about the primacy of sexuality in the human psyche, Freud saw this as a betrayal, and never forgave the younger man.

SEE ALSO

Romanticism & subjectivity ·····◄
Philosophy of mind ··········◄
Modern spirituality ·········◄
Modernism ················►

LIBIDO

When a newborn child takes its first gulp of air, it is acting in accordance with the demands of the libido, or life force – the overriding drive to survive. In so far as its ultimate aim is to reproduce the species, this instinctive energy is closely related to sexuality – hence the use of the word in common parlance to denote an individual's sex drive.

Freud's view was that the libido manifested itself in a series of different stages. In the first year or so of life, infants exclusively find physical gratification via the mouth, whether by suckling at the breast, sucking the thumb, or eating dirt. The focus then moves to the anus, as children learn to control their bowels, and then (from the age of three or so) becomes "phallic" – centered on their own penis or clitoris. With adulthood, the libido focuses on another person in a mature ("genital") sexual relationship. Jung emphasized the creativity of the libido, which he believed was capable of expression through religion, work, or other interests, as well as in sex.

Freud thought that the libido is counterbalanced by a death instinct, responsible for human aggression and all destructive behavior. He said that the history of civilization was the story of the struggle between these conflicting drives.

ARCHETYPES

Jung's studies of dreams and of world mythology revealed a set of characters and situations that recur across cultures, and throughout history. These images also appeared in the dreams and inner thoughts of Jung's patients – primordial images derived from the collective unconscious.

For example, the Greek goddess Demeter, the Hindu Parvati, and the ancient Egyptian Isis all represent an ideal (or archetype) of fecund womanhood which Jung called "the Mother." Other archetypes can be defined by their situation: the story of Hercules faced with the 12 labors is a clear invocation of the Hero archetype, but then so, too, is a dream of struggling to complete a crossword. Wherever there is a challenge to overcome, the Hero is involved.

Two especially significant archetypes are derived from each individual's experience of the opposite sex. The animus represents the "man-as-such," the essential image of maleness; the anima is its female counterpart, the "woman-as-such." Romantic love is the man's quest for his anima (as personified by a lover) and the woman's for her animus.

Archetypes also appear in the form of symbols and numbers. Thus, the circle or mandala symbolizes wholeness, and the swastika, an ancient Indian symbol, dynamism and energy. The appearance in dreams of all such symbols should, said Jung, be carefully monitored as a sign of progress toward individuation.

QUEEN OF THE NIGHT The moon in the Tarot pack is represented by a beautiful woman. In nearly all mythology, the moon is female – a maiden when she is new, pregnant when she is full, and a crone as she wanes.

MOTHER'S MILK A baby's first experience of sensual pleasure is sucking at his mother's breast. According to Freud, this initial attachment can lead to all kinds of problems, including the infamous Oedipus Complex – in which boys see their father as a sexual rival for their mother. This view is falling out of fashion as it becomes clear that Freud's interpretation of the human psyche was very much a product of his times.

FREE ASSOCIATION

Freud's major innovation in treatment techniques remains at the core of modern psychiatry. While the analyst listens, the patient speaks a series of words or ideas as they come to mind, without intervention or censorship. This method, known as association, is intended to let patients approach anxieties gradually, liberating them from the task of consciously constructing an account of their problem.

Two main techniques are employed. In free association (favored by Freudian psychoanalysis), the patient treats each new association as a stepping stone to the next one. So, for example, the chain of ideas "sun – moon – lake – fish – swimming – vacation – beach" might lead to fond memories of childhood friendships formed on vacation, and thence to more personal matters such as first love, early sexual experiences, or family tensions.

Jungian psychotherapists believe that this "chain" of ideas takes the person being analyzed too far from the original thought, and prefer to use direct association. In this method, the patient returns to the initial thought, generating a web of associations. Hence "ivy – climbing – ivy – brickwork – ivy – cemetery" and so on might bring to light feelings of sorrow that need to be laid to rest.

DEER OR FOOTPRINT? In Hermann Rorschach's (1884–1922) test, people are asked what they see in a series of inkblots and their responses supposedly give the analyst insight into the psyche.

DREAM INTERPRETATION

NIGHTMARE In every culture, dreams are deemed significant, whether as harbingers of evil or as a window into the world of the spirits.

For modern psychoanalysts, dreams represent a means of accessing the inner self – as Freud said, "The interpretation of dreams is the royal road to a knowledge of the unconscious activities of the mind." Freud believed that the obscure and bizarre content of our dreams is there to shield us from the disturbing revelations which would otherwise wake us up.

For Jung, the elaborate symbolism of dreams served as confirmation that they were precious glimpses of the unconscious.

COMMON PSYCHOANALYTIC TERMS

Id, ego, and superego According to Freud, the three parts of the human psyche. The id is the unconscious level that drives our desires. The ego is the conscious level of the mind that constructs a view of reality. The superego is what in former times might have been known as conscience, and its role is to restrain the primitive drives of the id.

Neurosis Feeling or behavior that interferes with the ability to live a normal life. Neuroses can broadly be divided into hysteria (i.e., physical symptoms), anxiety (e.g., phobias), and obsessive-compulsive disorders (e.g., performing elaborate rituals to defuse imaginary threats).

Repression The selective forgetting of painful memories and uncomfortable emotions, which nevertheless continue to exist in the unconscious. Psychoanalysis attempts to uncover and deal with repressed parts of the psyche.

Complex Set of repressed ideas or emotions that influence psychological development. Well-known examples include the Oedipus complex and the inferiority complex.

Psychosis Mental disorder severe enough to render a patient incapable of living a normal life. Psychoses are characterized by an inability to separate fantasy from reality, manifesting itself in the form of hallucinations and delusions. The blanket term "schizophrenia" is often used to describe a wide variety of psychoses.

Freudian slip A slip of the tongue or a physical accident that reveals a person's inner conflicts or desires.

Gestalt (German for configuration) A branch of psychology which stresses that the mind should be considered as a single entity, not as a set of responses.

INTROVERSION AND EXTROVERSION

"I WANT TO BE ALONE" Actress Greta Garbo (1905–90) was a classic introvert, even though she made a career in the most over-exposed profession on earth.

Whether someone is an extrovert or an introvert depends on how he or she directs their libido, or life force. Extroverts' attention is devoted to other people, producing an outgoing personality that enjoys company and likes to share life with others – albeit on an often superficial level. Introverts are more solitary and self-reliant, often looking inward to the world of the unconscious. Their friendships are probably fewer, but deeper.

These concepts are at the heart of Jung's pioneering work on classifying personality types. He went on to identify further sets of polarities – for example, one might be a "thinker" or a "feeler" – but the model of introvert and extrovert has become important in recruitment, training, and many other areas. In practice, everyone has both introvert and extrovert tendencies, although one or the other usually predominates.

LEDA AND THE SWAN The mortal Leda's passionate encounter with the divine swan is an archetype of submission and dominance.

INDIVIDUATION

Jung said that everyone is born with a particular character and set of instincts, based on the "collective unconscious." Each individual then develops aims and aspirations. The process of individuation – of realizing these aims and reconciling inner conflicts in the search for inner wholeness and personal development – is the central concept of Jungian psychology.

Jungian therapy is concerned with engineering a series of psychological transformations in order to achieve individuation. These can be encouraged both by analyzing the personal unconscious using techniques like free association, and by accessing the collective unconscious. Analysands are therefore encouraged to study myths which feature appropriate archetypes, and to measure their progress by checking for the appearance of particular archetypes in dreams. Individuation is, indeed, as much a spiritual quest as a psychological one: personal integration and development require the participation of the soul as well as the mind.

> *"A man who has not passed through the inferno of his passions has never overcome them."*
>
> *Carl Gustav Jung (1875–1961)*

INDIVIDUAL PSYCHOLOGY

SMALL AND VULNERABLE Alfred Adler argued that children and babies are intensely aware that they are weaker and less capable than adults.

Alfred Adler (1870–1937) developed a remarkably simple model of human behavior. Everyone, he said, starts life by feeling inadequate: children know that they are weaker than adults. This knowledge develops into an inferiority complex. Success in later life depends on compensating for this and developing feelings of self-esteem instead.

The way individuals fit in with society and the environment is crucial to this process. People need to feel valued at work and in their relationships. Genuine friendships, loving families, successful partnerships, and physical fitness all play a part in psychological health. Today's fascination with lifestyle owes much to Adler's revelation that we can define ourselves by how we interact with the world.

BEHAVIORISM

Not all psychology concerns itself with delving into the unconscious. The famous experiment devised by Ivan Pavlov (1849–1936) revealed a simple mechanism of learned behavior: if you ring a bell when you feed a dog, eventually the dog will start salivating at the sound of the bell, even when no food is available. He called this phenomenon the "conditioned response."

The Behaviorist School, founded in 1914 by the American psychologist John B. Watson (1878–1958), is based on the premise that humans, too, are governed by conditioned responses. Rejecting the theories of Freud and his successors as abstract hypotheses that cannot be proved scientifically, behaviorists seek to assess the human mind using laboratory techniques.

In practice, it is impossible to reduce the mind to stimulus and response. It may be relatively easy to see why the sound of running water induces the desire to urinate, or even why cocktail parties seem to make people feel thirsty. But the erotic power of a poem or the melancholy air of a particular place are psychological events far too complex to be quantified in this way.

SCIENCE OF THE NERVOUS SYSTEM Ivan Pavlov applied his theories of the conditioned response in animals to human behavior. Developed in the United States after World War II, Pavlovian experiments produced disturbing results – including showing that humans could easily be trained to torture one another.

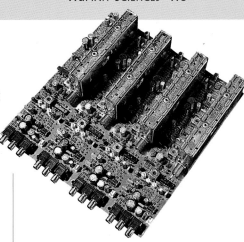

ELECTRONIC BRAIN The question of whether computer chips can have "consciousness" is still a live issue.

COGNITIVE PSYCHOLOGY

Cognitive psychology proposes a model of the mind as a kind of computer: a mechanism for analyzing, storing, processing, and reusing information acquired from the senses. By surveying human "information processes" (for example, conducting memory tests and measuring attention spans), cognitive psychology has gained important insights into memory, problem solving, perception, and other mental processes. The study of language as a cognitive process has become a separate discipline, known as psycholinguistics.

Cognitive psychology has become influential in other fields, especially computing, where scientists are trying to create neural networks – computers that "think" like people do. Robots can be trained to recognize objects by following a model of human pattern recognition, and the structure of computer memory, with its easy-access, short-term component and its store of seldom-used data, mimics our own.

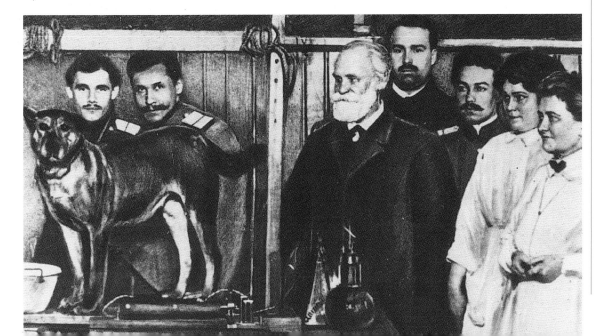

SOCIOLOGY
A person's place in the world

Sociology is the study of the development and functioning of human society. Initially, philosophers such as the Frenchmen Charles de Montesquieu (1689–1755) and Henri de Saint-Simon (1760–1825) and the Scot Adam Ferguson (1723–1816) sought to describe different societies in terms of the political, economic, and other institutions that gave them shape. Historians dispute whether this makes them the first sociologists or just important precursors, but there can be no doubt that the Frenchman Auguste Comte (1798–1857), Saint-Simon's secretary for seven years, coined the word sociology in 1839 and was the first to delineate its subject matter and methods. Comte, an eccentric genius, synthesized a mass of ideas from other thinkers to formulate his extremely complex system of "positive philosophy," explained in his *Cours de philosophie positive.*

Comte believed that there were three stages in human progress: theological, which offered supernatural explanations for earthly phenomena; metaphysical, which concentrated on abstract forces; and positive, the final enlightened stage of science. He divided sociology into the two strands that remain at its heart: "statics" – the study of the social and cultural institutions that bind society together – and "dynamics" – the study of social change or progress.

POSITIVISM

Comte was confident that if sociologists used the same methodology as chemists, physicists, and other scientists (conducting experiments, gathering empirical data, and so on), they would reveal a set of scientific laws governing human behavior and relationships. Such laws have proved elusive. It is easy to gather statistical information about a social phenomenon, such as juvenile delinquency or divorce. It is harder to find out what it means: asking a vandal why he smashed a window, or a divorcée why her marriage broke down, may not yield an answer capable of scientific analysis. The respondents may not even know the answer themselves.

Nevertheless, positivism – the belief that social phenomena are subject to laws – was hugely influential and contributed much to the optimistic character of the age. If science could discover the way people behaved en masse, it would help governments and lawmakers to craft social policies that worked. The prospect of harnessing the methods of science to solve social problems continues to hold a wide appeal.

SOCIAL DARWINISM

SURVIVAL OF THE FITTEST Jay Gould (1836–92), the 19th-century railroad magnate, fought his way to the top using a mixture of deceit and utter ruthlessness.

Positivism asserted that science could penetrate the mysteries of society. Evolution proposed a scientific framework for change. Combine these two fashionable mid-19th century ideas and one result is "social Darwinism" – the view that societies evolve through a process of struggle resulting in the survival of the fittest.

In fact, the idea was unveiled by the British philosopher Herbert Spencer (1820–1903) in 1852, seven years before Charles Darwin published his theory of evolution. Spencer believed that evolution was a universal transforming principle, equally applicable to the unfolding of a flower and the history of the universe. The common theme was the tendency over time to move from a homogenous and incoherent condition to a differentiated and tightly structured one.

Spencer's ideas provided an ideological backdrop to the rising tide of nationalism in Europe. The politicians of the Great Powers were comforted by the idea that war, invasion, and economic rivalry were legitimate means of national evolution. The ruling classes could be complacent in the belief that they were more evolved than those they ruled. Colonialists were reassured that by conquering "primitive" peoples, they were merely exercising the prerogative of a socially advanced species.

"ANOMIE"

Sociology must describe not only the ingredients of society, but also how they combine to make a whole. The first plausible explanation of how the social recipe works was proposed by Emile Durkheim (1858–1917), professor of sociology at the Sorbonne.

For him, what gave society its cohesion was a system of shared beliefs, values, and ideas. These could be based on religion, nationalism, or other factors, but were always moral in character. The question of how such values collapse and are replaced during periods of social change was a major field of inquiry for Durkheim. The breakdown of values results in "anomie" – a condition of social lawlessness and personal disorientation. In his study of suicide (1897), Durkheim proposed that the absence of social norms caused personal suffering, and he suggested ways to inculcate new agents of solidarity. Chief among these was for people to form groups by occupation.

Many of his conclusions are no longer accepted, but his rigorous research methods and approach to theory brought a firm structure to what had up to this time been a rickety framework of vague concepts.

MODERN CONDITION Edvard Munch (1863–1944) painted *The Scream* (1893), probably the best-known image of alienation in the world, in the same decade that Durkheim published his study of suicide.

TIMELINE

1748
Montesquieu outlines the theory that a nation's lifestyle is shaped by its culture in *Défense de l'esprit des lois*.

1767
Adam Ferguson publishes *An Essay on the History of Civil Society*, the first coherent account of social structures and how they change.

1830–42
Auguste Comte publishes *Cours de philosophie positive*, advancing sociology as the newest and most sophisticated of sciences.

1844
Friedrich Engels conducts a wide-ranging survey of industrial workers in Manchester, England.

1885
Charles Booth starts researching the first major empirical study in sociology, 17 volumes entitled *The Life and Labour of the People in London*.

1912
In *The Elementary Forms of the Religious Life*, Emile Durkheim argues a close relationship between moral values and social structures.

1937
Talcott Parsons publishes *The Structure of Social Action*, laying the foundations for a grand theory of social systems.

SEE ALSO

Nationalism · · · · · · · · · · · · · ◄
Poststructuralism · · · · · · · · · ◄
Evolution · · · · · · · · · · · · · · · ▶

CHARISMA

CHOSEN MAN John F. Kennedy campaigns for the presidency in 1960. JFK's fame rests partly on his undoubted charisma – he was the youngest ever president when elected at 44 in 1961 – but partly also on the mystery surrounding his assassination in Dallas on November 22, 1963.

The achievements of the German sociologist Max Weber (1864–1920) are remarkable for two reasons: first, his work has a breathtaking scope and complexity, and second, most of it dates from the period of semiretirement he started at the age of 40 following a nervous breakdown.

Weber's most famous ideas are contained in two phrases that have passed into common usage: "charisma" and "Protestant work ethic." Charisma, from the Greek word for "gift," was primarily a theological concept, referring to divine grace bestowed by God on saints and holy men. For Weber, however, great leaders also had charisma insofar as they seemed to derive their authority from a higher source. The awe in which citizens held leaders such as the French Emperor Napoleon Bonaparte (1769–1821) and President John F. Kennedy (1917–63) can be ascribed to charisma – and that is what sets them apart from their counterparts such as French President Georges Pompidou (1911–74) and President George Bush (1924–).

The Protestant Ethic and the Spirit of Capitalism was the title of an essay published by Weber during 1904–5. He traced a link between the Calvinistic depiction of work as a religious calling and the development of an enterprise culture in which capitalism thrives. This ideology, said Weber, had subsequently been detached from its roots – with the ironic result that it is most evident today in largely non-Christian societies such as China.

Another major area of investigation for Weber was bureaucracy, which he deemed the key development in Western civilization. The term, with its connotations of anonymity and rigidity, is usually used pejoratively. For Weber, however, it represented an ideal arrangement, capable of imposing order on a chaotic world via its centralized authority and strict rules of procedure.

FRANKFURT SCHOOL

The Frankfurt School is the name given to a group of sociologists and philosophers attached to the University of Frankfurt's Institute for Social Research, which was founded in 1923. Their project was to apply Marxist theory to 20th-century society. But they were against the materialist approach of communist states such as the U.S.S.R., taking more interest in Marx's debt to the idealism of the German philosopher Georg Hegel (1770–1831). This concern with alienation and consciousness led naturally to an interest in psychoanalysis and the writings of Sigmund Freud (1856–1939).

The institute itself was closed down by the Nazis in 1933. The following year, the director, Max Horkheimer (1895–1973), set up a new establishment in New York City, where he worked until the school returned to Germany in 1949.

The critical theory of Horkheimer, Theodor Adorno (1903–69), and Herbert Marcuse (1898–1979) was influential in the 1970s, but since then the Frankfurt School has moved on under the aegis of Jürgen Habermas (1929–), whose Marxist critique of society extends to language and communication as well as the more material factors. The work of the school also influenced poststructuralists such as the Frenchman Jacques Lacan (1901–81).

ICON OF THE COUNTERCULTURE Marcuse argued that mass culture was dehumanizing and that if workers were unwilling to resist it, then others – such as students – might do so. He was a hero of the 1960s student radicals.

SOCIAL SYSTEMS

PRIVILEGE STANDS OUT Boys from the exclusive English public school of Eton are deaf to taunts as they wait outside Lord's cricket ground in 1937. They have been taught not to care what members of the wider society think.

The Harvard sociologist Talcott Parsons (1902–79) was a controversial figure. In a discipline that stresses empirical proof, he constructed an edifice of compelling but untestable theories around a core of apparent contradictions.

His first major work, *The Structure of Social Action* (1937), proposed that sociology's main concern should be to study how participants in society adapt to their surroundings, fit in with their neighbors, and pursue goals. But in *The Social System* (1951), he argued that society was only explicable as a system, and that individual actions must be seen in terms of the contribution they make to the system as a whole. This latter approach saw society as a series of institutions that were sometimes in harmony, sometimes in conflict, and always in a state of flux. Social stability, he argued, depends on core values (for example, the need to educate the young) and behavioral norms – standards of conduct from which deviance is punishable by social ostracism or force of law, or is correctable by other means.

Parsons's ideas have been very influential. In the 1960s he was accused of having a conservative bias and of neglecting the study of social change. The 1970s saw him produce a more rounded theory that blurred the distinction between individual and society and took a sociological approach to human life in general.

COMMUNITY / COMMUNITARIANISM

Everyone, even people who refuse to participate in communal activities, lives in a community. Indeed, many people belong to several communities defined by activity or mutual interest: one might join a resident's association, a church, a social club, or a parent-teacher association. All these institutions bring together under a system of common rules human beings who occupy the same territory. Communities are the key local level of social interaction – the stepping stone between family and nation.

In the late 20th century it has become fashionable to lament the passing of the community, and for politicians to promise a return to lost community values. It is certainly a diminishing force in Western society, where the perceived restrictions of community life are in conflict with the key values of individualism, choice, and freedom. In the 1980s, the combination of political and social concern about the disintegration of social cohesion gave birth to a new social and intellectual movement: communitarianism.

The main themes of communitarianism – as proposed by one of its founders, the American academic Amitai Etzioni (1929–) – are that people are shaped by the values and cultures of communities, and that individual rights must be counterbalanced by social responsibilities. The movement aims to redress a balance that is seen as tilted too far toward personal autonomy and away from community values, while proposing a redefinition of the very concept of community more suited to a modern, pluralistic society.

PEACE IN OUR STREET London schoolchildren celebrate the end of World War I at a street party in July 1919. Many modern politicians and writers argue that such community celebrations bound people together and reinforced individuals' sense of social responsibility.

MASS SOCIETY

HERD INSTINCT City rush hours are a direct result of the conformity that a mass society forces on its members. Most people have common hours of work and relaxation, so they all have to travel at the same time.

Everyone wears jeans and T-shirts; everyone likes to watch movies; everyone goes to work at 9 A.M. and goes home at 5 P.M.; everyone wants a new car, yet is worried about global warming. Such a society, a mass society, is molded by the collective preferences, opinions, and activities of the majority, rather than by values based on tradition or handed down from above. Today, most industrialized nations are mass societies.

Democracy and the mass media play a pivotal role in such a society. Television, newspapers, and radio convey both information and prepackaged opinions to the public. The masses digest and regurgitate this information, bounce it back at politicians (via the media again), and pronounce their verdict at regular intervals at the ballot box. Hence in a mass society, the balance of power is tilted toward ordinary people rather than a selected elite, and public consensus becomes an important consideration in government.

Mass society also has its disadvantages. Mass consensus transfers judgment to people who are not qualified or competent to judge. It can come perilously close to mob rule, where the herd instinct and the lowest common denominator hold sway over common sense. For example, sensational reporting of hideous crimes such as murder and child abuse can whip up a public fury and thirst for revenge (fueled by a vulgar prurience) capable of hindering justice.

The deadening effects of conformity and routine are also open to criticism. The French phrase *metro, boulot, dodo* – commute, work, sleep – sums up the drabness of a society without roots or traditions, with a thin veneer of mediocre culture supplied by the mass media. People whose values conflict with mass values face exile or alienation.

GLOBAL VILLAGE

The world watched as American astronaut Neil Armstrong set foot on the moon in 1969; the world shared the drama of the 1991 Gulf War; the world gossiped about retired American football star O.J. Simpson as he stood trial for the murder of his wife in 1995. Thanks to television, people all over the planet simultaneously experienced and reacted to a distant event.

This phenomenon, the "global village," was identified in 1960 by the Canadian sociologist Marshall McLuhan (1911–80). The instant, global coverage of radio and television, said McLuhan, renders meaningless the traditional physical boundaries of villages and cities: via the mass media, the whole world comes to us. McLuhan would have been impressed by global TV channels such as MTV and CNN, and fascinated by the instantaneous media of the 1990s – the fax and the Internet. The global village is shrinking, and our links with the other members of the community are growing stronger.

ONE WORLD A Kayapo Indian in Amazonian Brazil has much the same pay-phone technology as is used in big-city systems in Paris or New York.

MASS MEDIA

AS SEEN ON TELEVISION In the modern era, the lives of distant figures such as the British royal family only have reality for the public through media representation. Prince Charles's ill-fated marriage to Lady Diana Spencer in 1981 was a spectacular television and newspaper event.

Most of us take the existence of television, radio, magazines, newspapers, movies, and books – the impersonal media of mass communication – for granted. The influence of these mass media on modern society, and the way they have transformed our culture, is especially impressive when one considers how recent an innovation the mass media is.

The era of mass communication began in 1814, when the London *Times* installed a steam-driven printing press built by two German engineers, Frederick König and André Bauer. This machine could print over a thousand copies an hour, five times as many as a manual press. Rapid improvements in printing and typesetting technology throughout the 19th century ushered in an age of cheap, mass-circulation newspapers and magazines. Motion pictures, radio, and record players became popular in the 1920s; television reached a mass market in the 1950s, and many people bought video recorders, cable, and satellite television in the 1980s. The 1990s saw the advent of the World Wide Web – a collection of computer documents that can be accessed via the Internet.

Because the means of production – such as television studios and printing presses – are expensive, the mass media is essentially one-way roads of communication. The professional communicators of the mass media are physically separated from their audiences, and members of the audience are separated from one another. The only mode of real-time interaction is to take it or leave it: to turn off the television, leave the theater before the end of the movie, or throw away the newspaper or magazine.

Marshall McLuhan addressed the influence of the mass media in his book *Understanding Media* (1969). He coined the oft-repeated phrase "the medium is the message" – the way a message is transmitted can have more impact than its content. Dividing media into "hot" (high definition) forms such as radio, film, and print, and "cold" (low definition) forms such as television and telephone, McLuhan declared that hot media demanded less audience participation than cold ones. The low definition of the TV screen forces the viewer to devote more attention to the medium itself, distancing the audience from the events depicted.

MASS CULTURE

Mass society has brought about mass (sometimes called "popular") culture: a shared set of cultural icons and reference points, in large measure nurtured by the mass media. Typical products of mass culture include celebrities such as the film actor Charlie Chaplin (1889–1977) and the pop singer Madonna (1958–) and phenomena such as soap operas and game shows.

Mass culture has been the subject of heated intellectual debate since the 1950s. A key issue is the extent to which it is profit oriented – the sophisticated marketing of Disney cartoons and rock supergroups calls into question whether they are commercial or cultural in nature. Another debate focuses on the "leveling" characteristics of mass culture. Before mass culture, there was "high culture," funded by the patronage of a wealthy elite, and low-level, localized "folk culture." Mass culture achieves mass penetration by being relevant to all sectors of society.

BUSH BABY Global brands guarantee a gradual homogenization of the world's cultures.

ECONOMICS
Society's invisible mechanism

Today's business executive is a sophisticated version of the prehistoric trader who swapped beads for berries or meat for pots. All economic systems have evolved from these ancient transactions, and for centuries they appeared to be such an organic process that there seemed to be no need to study them separately. Economics was just a subdivision of politics, philosophy, law, and other disciplines.

Only in the 18th century did thinkers start to consider economics as a separate system of ideas. In 1758, François Quesnay (1694–1774), leader of the Physiocrats – a group of French philosophers who were the first to call themselves "economists" – published his pioneering work *Tableaux Economiques*, arguing that land is the source of all wealth, and therefore agriculture, fishing, and mining the only productive occupations. Manufacturing, according to the Physiocrats, did not create wealth, it merely transformed or redistributed the output of the productive class.

This elementary economic theory was taken up by Adam Smith (1723–90), the Scotsman often dubbed the "father of economics." In *An Inquiry into the Nature and Causes of the Wealth of Nations* (1776) – one of the most influential books ever published – Smith laid out a coherent explanation of the way economies work, laying the foundations for what became known as "classical economics."

Smith disagreed with the Physiocratic view that wealth lay in the land and could never be created. He declared that it was labor that created wealth, and that the value of a product is largely determined by the amount of work put into it. A lumberjack adds value to trees by felling and sawing them; the carpenter buys the wood and resells it at a higher price, having added value to it by crafting it into furniture.

Smith's model of a free-enterprise economy is often summarized in a familiar phrase coined by the Physiocrats: "laissez faire," French for "leave (people) to do (as they please)." Laissez-faire capitalism funded the Industrial Revolution, and variants have remained the basis of most Western economies ever since.

MALTHUS AND POPULATION

Worries about the size of the world's population are nothing new. In *An Essay on the Principle of Population* (1798), the English economist Thomas Malthus (1766–1834) painted a gloomy picture of a world in which the number of people will always increase faster than the amount of food available. Eventually population growth is checked by famine, disease, or war. Malthus argued: "That the increase in population is necessarily limited by the means of subsistence. That population does invariably increase when the means of subsistence increase and...the actual population is kept equal to the means of subsistence by misery and vice."

Malthus could not have foreseen the developments in transportation and food technology that were to mean food can be transported across continents relatively cheaply. Nor could he have predicted that birth rates would fall as standards of living rose in the developed world. He would probably be astonished to find that the planet was feeding some 6 billion mouths today, but he might not be surprised by the starvation diet of much of the less developed world, or by the advent of killer diseases such as AIDS.

CLASSICAL ECONOMICS

FATHER OF THE SCIENCE Adam Smith stands over his masterpiece *The Wealth of Nations*, which had already made his name throughout Great Britain.

Adam Smith argued for a free-enterprise, competitive market economy, with as little government interference as possible. Left alone, he said, a "natural" economic order always asserts itself to ensure the efficient allocation of resources. Every individual will act in order to make a profit, mainly by producing goods that other people want to buy. Greed (pushing up prices) merely stimulates competition, inspiring others to enter the market with cheaper goods, leading to a natural redistribution of wealth. Smith therefore deplored monopolies, cartels, import tariffs, and other ways of distorting or preventing the operation of the free market.

What is more, the theory continues, when each individual is left to act in his or her own interest, he or she ends up helping everybody else. Small increases in individual wealth add up to a general increase in the wealth of the community: as Smith put it, every man is "led by an invisible hand to promote an end which was not part of his intention."

CAPITALISM

Any economic system in which companies or individuals produce and exchange goods and services using markets is a capitalist one. The term embraces a wide range of economic models, but they all share one defining characteristic: the land, factories, and machinery used to produce goods and services are privately owned.

Both producers and consumers have the freedom to pursue their own interests – to choose what to make and what to buy – and here, the mechanism of supply and demand comes into play. Manufacturers seek both to supply what consumers demand and to stimulate more demand by inventing new products, skillfully advertising them or just dropping their prices.

In the 20th century, especially in Eastern Europe, communist governments imposed a very different economic system. The means of production, distribution, and exchange were all owned by the state. Prices and levels of production were set by government committees instead of being regulated by the market.

The experiment of these planned economies could not be sustained, and in the 1980s and

MAKING A PROFIT OUT OF SAND A group of 19th-century workers adds value to the raw material of sand by blowing it into beautiful glass.

HANDMADE VALUE A cabinetmaker buys wood and skillfully crafts it into furniture, for which he charges a great deal more than the wood originally cost him. It is his own labor that has created wealth.

1990s the system collapsed. Fully fledged capitalism took its place, as entrepreneurs rushed to fill the yawning gaps between supply and demand. The transition from centrally planned to market-driven systems proved more difficult than many at first predicted. In addition to encouraging free trade, demolishing regulations gave crime syndicates a free hand.

LAWS OF ECONOMICS

Gresham's law

"Bad money drives out good." If a government issues debased currency containing cheap metal, instead of gold or silver, the old "pure" currency disappears from circulation, because people want to hoard the old money or exchange it overseas, and pass on the new. Named after Sir Thomas Gresham, a 16th-century English entrepreneur.

The law of diminishing returns

"In any venture, there comes a point at which further investment ceases to bring a worthwhile profit." Drillers for oil may abandon a site while it still contains oil because the investment needed to extract it is greater than any potential revenue. First stated by the French economist Anne Robert Jacques Turgot (1727–81).

Say's law

"Supply creates its own demand." Every time industrial or agricultural output rises, so does income and therefore the amount of money available to buy goods. Gluts, therefore, are self-liquidating. Named after the French economist Jean Baptiste Say (1767–1832).

Parkinson's law

"Work expands to fill the time available." The more time workers have to complete their task, the less efficient they become. Named after the British economist C. Northcote Parkinson (1909–), who proposed this law in 1955.

The iron law of wages

"Wages are always set at subsistence level." If earnings fall below it, workers will be fit neither to work nor to reproduce; if earnings rise above it, the working population grows, and increased competition for jobs forces wages back down to subsistence levels. Created by the 18th-century French school of economists, the Physiocrats, but often attributed to the English economist David Ricardo (1772–1823).

STOCKS & SHARES AND LIMITED LIABILITY

SEE ALSO: *Internationalism, Economics*

SMALL PART OF A BIG ENTERPRISE A certificate confirms that the holder owns 333 shares in the Union Freight Railway Company.

A healthy capitalist economy depends on entrepreneurs – people willing to take a risk by carrying on a business operation with the expectation of making a profit. Entrepreneurs generally need to raise money to help finance new businesses or make changes to an existing one, and the usual way to do that is by raising a small amount of money from many investors. In return for taking a share of the company, investors receive a share in the profits, or dividend. They can sell shares in successful companies to other investors at a premium, and markets for shares – stock exchanges – exist in the world's major trading centers.

By building a "portfolio" consisting of a range of shares in different companies, it is possible to spread risk, setting off losses on poor shares against profits on successful ones. Shares and financial instruments such as options and futures, which help to spread risk even farther, are the financial fuel of world enterprise.

If, however, taking a share in or becoming a director of a company entailed liability for all its debts, there would be few takers: most people would be held back by the risk of losing all their personal property. What is more, they could be personally sued for damages incurred by the company. The first half of the 19th century saw the rapid evolution of the idea of limited liability: restricting each shareholder's personal liability, in the event of bankruptcy, to the amount he or she has paid for the original shares.

If a company goes bankrupt, the shareholders cannot be called on to meet its debts. What is more, the law treats a company as a separate legal entity, capable of entering contracts and pursuing litigation as if it were a private individual. Shareholders and employees are therefore not responsible for the legal actions of the company – although directors are obviously expected to follow legal advice at all times. If shares make business financially possible, limited liability makes it feasible. The concept is the basis of almost every company in the world today, and without it, the enterprises that generate much of the world's wealth could not exist.

MIDMORNING BREAK Investors and dealers laze around in the New Orleans Cotton Exchange in 1873. Edgar Degas (1834–1917) recorded this moment while visiting relatives in the U.S.

RENT

HISTORY MAKERS: *David Ricardo (1772–1823)*

SEE ALSO: *Economics, Industrialization*

Renting things is a familiar part of daily life. Individuals rent houses and telephone lines; businesses rent offices and equipment. In common parlance, rent is a regular payment made to someone else for the use of that person's property. But for an economist, the term has a specialized meaning: "economic rent" is the difference between the cost of producing a good that is in limited supply and the price obtained for it.

Economist David Ricardo eloquently outlined the theory in the 18th century by pointing out that the price of grain (which was, at the time, controversially high) was not, as many people believed, caused by greedy landlords charging exorbitant rents to tenant farmers. High rents were, in fact, determined by high grain prices: the supply of land and the yield of the crops that were grown was more or less the same, so when food prices went up, so did the economic rent from each bag of wheat. Landlords were merely taking their share of the enhanced

LIVING ON A MARGIN Flower sellers make a low economic rent, and as a result are never likely to become millionaires. The difference between what the flowers originally cost and how much they sell for is too small.

profits. This simple case study developed into a sophisticated theory that is crucial to the study of economics, and has many practical uses: for example, in determining wages and prices. If a chef is willing to work for $25,000 a year, and is paid $30,000, she is receiving $5,000 per year in economic rent. If her customers pay $20 for a meal which costs (or is worth) $15, the economic rent on each meal is $5.

The earning patterns of celebrities such as pop stars demonstrate the workings of rent clearly: given that a pop singer's supply of talent always remains roughly the same, her meteoric jump in wages after rising to fame is attributable to a large increase in the economic rent element of her earnings.

TEMPLE TO MAMMON Clients deposit and withdraw money, while visitors admire the architecture of the newly built Bank of England in 1808.

CENTRAL BANKING

SEE ALSO: *Marxism, Totalitarianism, Capitalism*

Banks started out as places where people could deposit money and valuables. But as large-scale commerce developed, so too did the functions of banks – lending money, issuing bank notes, and providing methods of settling debts on paper such as bank drafts, bills of exchange, and checks. As banks grew more numerous during the 17th and 18th centuries, so did the need for a "banker's bank" to act as a clearing house to settle debts between financial institutions.

At the same time, governments needed institutions to do their banking and take responsibility for managing national finances, executing monetary policy, handling revenues, and paying bills. The first central bank was the Bank of England, founded in 1694 in order to lend the government £1.2 million to finance a war with France.

Other nations followed suit, including the United States in 1791; this initiative did not last, however, and the U.S. was without a central bank from 1836 to 1913, when the Federal Reserve was founded. The Banque de France, the Bank of Japan, the German Bundesbank, and others followed. Today it is inconceivable that a nation should be without a central bank. The new nations that emerged from the Soviet Union immediately formed their own banks.

INDUSTRIALIZATION
A revolution at work

It is no accident that economics developed in the mid-18th century. Adam Smith (1723–90) and his contemporaries were struggling to analyze the mechanisms underlying the sweeping economic and social transformations that historians were later to call the Agricultural and Industrial revolutions. These "revolutions" were linked. Agricultural methods improved first, partly as a result of a series of good harvests across Europe. Industrial growth helped to stimulate an increase in population in Europe from about 1760. There were new mouths to feed and a rapid growth in demand for raw materials. Finally, businessmen spent the fortunes they made in manufacturing towns to buy land to which they eagerly applied industrial methods.

Two plants symbolize the Agricultural Revolution: the hedge and the turnip. Land reforms, especially enclosure in England, introduced the familiar pattern of well-drained fields and hedges, facilitating the rotation of crops. At the same time, the German and Dutch practice of planting winter root crops spread across Europe. These hardy crops provided fodder to keep livestock through the winter and helped to break up the soil for resowing in the spring. Finally, new labor-saving machines, such as mechanical threshers and seed drills, brought increases in productivity.

The Industrial Revolution was born of technical innovations: new methods of making iron and weaving cloth, new ways to transport goods, and the replacement of muscle power with machines. In terms of economics, however, what drove the Industrial Revolution was not steam or coal, but the investment of capital on a scale never seen before. Landowners invested the profits of the Agricultural Revolution in factories, mines, turnpike roads, and canals; merchants invested the proceeds of international trade – including the slave trade, which was then at its peak.

Industrialization had several results. Mechanization increased productive capacity and therefore output, which meant, eventually, a rise in income and living standards. Higher living standards and the increased availability of work led to an increase in population, and so in demand for goods. Production increased to meet it – and so the cycle continued. The revolution, too, continues: the experience of countries in Southeast Asia is in many ways similar to that of Europe and North America in the 18th century.

MASS PRODUCTION

The average 18th-century gunsmith made about six guns a year, lovingly building the weapon, piece by handmade piece. Yet in 1798 Eli Whitney (1765–1825), the inventor of the cotton gin, signed a contract to supply 5,000 muskets a year to the American government. He would achieve this mammoth task by using machines to turn out the components that made up the musket, assembling them all at the end of the process.

By designing a product made of identical, interchangeable parts, and dividing the manufacturing process into simple, mechanized steps, Whitney had invented mass production. The idea soon spread. Ten years later, in England, Marc Isambard Brunel (1769–1849) established what was probably the world's first production line: 43 machines which, in a fixed series of operations, transformed pieces of wood into ship's pulleys. In 1913 Henry Ford (1863–1947) devised the moving assembly line. Magnetos for the Model-T Ford passed on a conveyor belt before a line of stationary workers who added one piece at a time to the component; the system was later extended to the car itself.

The immense savings in manpower and time brought by mass production techniques have made manufactured goods cheap and plentiful. The practice is now ubiquitous.

MEN AND MACHINERY Workers slot in components on a Model-T at Henry Ford's factory in Detroit.

MARKET FORCES

SPOILED FOR CHOICE A late 19th-century lady's ability to choose from a vast array of hats was a result of fierce competition among hat makers and shopkeepers.

In most developed countries, the basic economic challenge – to make, price, and sell goods that people want – is left to "market forces." These nebulous determinants of prosperity were first dissected by the English economist Alfred Marshall (1842–1924).

The biggest mover of markets is consumer choice – people deciding how to spend their incomes. Price is the market's key regulator. The price of an item rises when demand is high (so rationing supplies) and falls when supply is greater than demand (eliminating gluts). Western governments generally interfere with market forces only to safeguard the consumer. One aspect of this is enforcing trading standards – making sure that toys are safe or that food is clean. Another is to prevent businesses from conducting activities that hinder the competition on which a free market depends. Monopolies (when a company's exclusive control of a product allows it to fix the price) are regulated by law. Some industries are also checked to detect cartels, or companies acting together to fix prices.

URBANIZATION

Before the Industrial Revolution, wool weaving was carried out by workers at home using simple machinery. The equipment used by the new cotton mills, with their steam engines and waterwheels, was far too large to fit in a cottage – so workers had to come to the factories.

In Britain, small towns and cities experienced enormous, unplanned growth. Throughout the 19th century, city workers crowded into unsafe tenements, often without sewerage or fresh water. Cholera, diphtheria, and other diseases flourished. By 1850, child mortality in Britain's industrial towns had become extremely high, with half of all children dying before the age of five.

It became clear that cities had to be better managed. Municipal corporations and private companies took responsibility for installing water and sewerage in the towns. A few "model villages" were built for their workers by concerned entrepreneurs. The first of these, created in 1853 by Sir Titus Salt (1803–76), was Saltaire, near Bradford in the north of England: a complete village, with churches and schools, for workers in his nearby mill. Forty years later, George Cadbury (1839–1922), a Quaker chocolate magnate, funded the construction of one of the first garden cities – Bournville, near Birmingham. It is now generally accepted that building, especially in towns and cities, should be regulated.

PUBLIC HOUSING Couples stroll in front of the newly constructed Palmerston Building – apartments designed for workers in the 19th century.

TIMELINE

Britain's Industrial Revolution was the earliest and was also a model for what happened elsewhere.

1800–09
Average steel exports reach 33,000 tons.

1800
11m tons of coal are produced.

1801
National income from mining, building, and manufacturing reaches £54.3m.

1839
970 miles of rail track are built.

1840
Labor force building railroads reaches 100,000.

1847
Labor force building railroads reaches 300,000.

1850–59
Steel exports are on average 1.2m tons.

1851
National income from mining, building, and manufacturing reaches £179.5m.

1880
15,500 miles of rail track are in operation and 156.4m tons of coal are produced.

MACROECONOMICS
Keynes's new economic order

During the 1930s, economic depression sent world trade into the doldrums and brought mass unemployment to the developed world. Market forces and laissez-faire had failed to keep the world economy in equilibrium. While economists searched for an explanation, politicians wanted a solution. The Cambridge economist John Maynard Keynes (1883–1946) provided both, in his revolutionary book *The General Theory of Employment, Interest and Money*.

Keynes's argument was that market forces could not be relied on to provide work for all, nor could they guarantee that savings were invested in industry. There would be periods when demand for goods fell below supply, causing managers to lay off workers and private investors to hold onto their money. The result: self-perpetuating decline. Laissez-faire was no longer a viable policy, and governments should be prepared to intervene to stabilize economies. In recessions, this meant fueling consumer demand by cutting taxes and creating jobs through a program of public works funded by public borrowing. In the resulting boom, governments should trim demand and counter inflation by raising taxes, using the budget surplus to pay off borrowings. Many of Keynes's ideas were foreshadowed by the "New Deal" policy of President Franklin Roosevelt, introduced in 1933.

Keynes's ideas were very influential, not least because he was the first macroeconomist, dealing with what he called "aggregate" (large-scale) factors to produce his model of how economies work. He showed how nations act as economic entities.

Governments can use various tools to prime the economic pump, boosting demand and creating more wealth and more jobs. The most important of these is increasing the amount of money in the economy by lowering interest rates, encouraging people to spend or invest their money instead of hoarding it.

In the decades after World War II, a mixture of Keynesianism and laissez-faire capitalism proved very effective, producing steady growth, low inflation, and rising living standards. Budget deficits, national debt, and public borrowing were familiar features of the world economy. But in the late 1960s, inflation and unemployment both rose. Keynesianism was no longer a panacea: monetarism began its rise to favor.

TRADE CYCLE

Classical economics had no explanation for the cyclical variations in trade which could send economies into uncontrolled rapid expansion ("boom") and equally dramatic decline ("bust"). They were viewed as the inevitable price of material progress. Keynesianism was supposed to provide a cushion against the worst of these ups and downs, but trade cycles remain a major feature of the world economy.

Many of the mechanisms are obscure, but the basic pattern seems doomed to repeat itself: prosperity ushers in high employment, high wages, big profits, and investment. This leads to an increase in costs and prices, and to higher interest rates as banks try to attract savers and ration loans. So consumers have to tighten their belts and buy less. Supply of goods exceeds demand, prices fall, business goes into decline, and money is hoarded instead of invested. Depression comes when factories shut and unemployment rises.

BUST Boarded-up stores are a symbol of a town in the midst of the recession in the early 1990s that followed the boom of the 1980s.

Recovery starts when obsolescence forces consumers to replace their worn-out goods; this time, they take advantage of cheap interest rates and easy credit offered by cash-rich banks. In the factories, surpluses have been liquidated. With recovery comes growing enthusiasm for investing in new industries, some of them started by those made unemployed during the recession. A new trade cycle is under way.

THE CYCLE OF SUPPLY AND DEMAND The more goods are bought, the more manufacturers produce. But when too many goods are produced, demand falls, and workers are laid off.

The more workers are paid, the more they spend and the more they buy.

ECONOMETRICS

If governments are to follow Keynesian principles and occasionally intervene to adjust their economies, they need some way to analyze the effects of their policies. Econometrics – the marriage of economics and mathematics – seeks to do just that, applying statistical methods to test economic policies and to make forecasts. It also checks and adjusts forecasts in the light of experience.

Economists have an armory of equations and assumptions describing how employment, prices, wages, investment, and other factors relate to each other. Policy-makers combine them to assess, for example, the effects of a cut in interest rates on the housing market.

Econometrics is a minefield. It is impossible to conduct controlled experiments to collect data or to field-test policies. Economic predictions are notoriously hard to make: they depend on the actions of people whose behavior is often irrational. No fiscal measures can create what politicians call the "feel-good factor" – a general optimism that somehow results in freer consumer spending. What is more, when governments receive bad economic forecasts, they do everything in their power to invalidate them.

GOLD STANDARD

BULWARK AGAINST UNCERTAINTY German savers during the depression of the 1920s were prudent to exchange paper money for gold, which has an internationally recognized standard value.

All paper money can, at least in theory, be exchanged for a fixed amount of precious metal held at the issuing bank. The French livre, the Italian lira, and the Spanish peseta are all originally derived from the Roman libra, which was equivalent to 12 ounces of copper.

The "gold standard" which prevailed for most of the 19th century extended this principle to foreign exchange. Trading nations gave their currencies a fixed value in terms of gold, and agreed to settle debts by the actual exchange of bullion. If market forces drove exchange rates up or down, the "gold point" – at which bankers found it cheaper to send bullion than notes – was reached.

The system worked until the depression of the 1930s, when most governments came off the gold standard, seeking more control over exchange rates. It was replaced by a new de facto standard, the U.S. dollar (itself fully convertible into gold until 1971). Now money markets are stabilized by complex formulas such as the EU's Exchange Rate Mechanism. The drive to a European single currency is in part an attempt to establish a new world "supercurrency" to rival gold and the dollar.

SEE ALSO

Liberalism · · · · · · · · · · · · · · · · ◄

Social cost · · · · · · · · · · · · · · · ►

Postindustrial society · · · · · · · · · ►

BALANCE OF PAYMENTS

SEE ALSO: *Monetarism, Macroeconomics, Global economics*

Trade is international, and foreign trade is a vital part of most nations' economic performance. In order to assess the relative contributions of imports and exports, every country periodically publishes its balance of payments – a balance sheet showing the value of all its international transactions. A country that imports more than it sells abroad has a net inflow of goods, and a corresponding outflow of cash; the opposite applies to a country that exports more than it imports.

Countries are said to have a "current account" for exports and imports, other foreign transactions and government works, and a "capital account" which tracks the movement of capital in and out of the country. For many countries, "invisible" items (buying and selling services) are more important than trade in tangible goods. The banking and insurance services of the City of London, for example, make a vital contribution to the United Kingdom's balance of trade.

The balance of payments is a critical index of economic strength, carefully examined by international investors and bankers to assess the creditworthiness and financial stability of a nation. Because payments for imports are made in the currency of the exporting country, it has a direct effect on foreign exchange rates.

On the exchange markets, therefore, French purchases of American goods translates into a higher demand for dollars, making the dollar stronger and the franc weaker. One thing remains certain, however: world trade is always perfectly balanced, for one nation's surplus is, by definition, another's deficit.

POOR PAY THE PRICE A Romanian family makes do in one room, without water. Poverty is often linked to reduced life expectancy and health problems – social costs that are hard to calculate.

SOCIAL COST

SEE ALSO: *Socialism, Industrialization*

Some of the costs of economic growth cannot be measured in terms of national income. Unwelcome side effects of such growth include pollution, congestion, over-population, and social problems. A country's automobile industry might be a key source of earnings, but the costs of handling the ensuing social and environmental consequences – from building roads to policing traffic and treating medical conditions associated with breathing traffic fumes – have to be borne by society in general.

Many social costs are passed on to the the consumer in a way that distorts the workings of the marketplace. For

example, farmers boost yields by making intensive use of pesticides and nitrate fertilizers. These chemicals drain off agricultural land, foul the rivers, and eventually find their way into reservoirs. But the farmers do not pay to clean up the water supply and make it fit to drink; that burden falls on the consumer in the form of increased water bills. Organic farmers, who pollute the environment far less, do not benefit from this hidden subsidy – and this contributes to the high cost of organic produce.

Economists struggle to assess social costs, and statistical conventions do not help them. A chemical plant could make a sizable contribution to the gross national product, but there is no way to debit its poisoning of a nearby lake, killing fish and destroying a leisure amenity. A free health service is easy to cost, but the value of the working days it prevents from being lost to illness is harder to quantify. The job opportunities provided by out-of-town shopping malls are undeniable, but they should be offset against the inner-city decay to which the malls contribute – but again, the latter is hard to calculate and the relationship is not direct. The allocation of these kinds of social costs is still in its infancy.

GUEST WORKERS Turkish nationals wait to pass through German immigration. Hard currency sent home by workers like these gives a vital boost to the balance of payments of many developing nations.

THE AFFLUENT SOCIETY

HISTORY MAKERS: *John Kenneth Galbraith (1908–)*
SEE ALSO: *Postindustrial society*

Economics is primarily concerned with the allocation of resources and goods that are scarce. Oil is subject to economic constraints and highly priced because it is in finite supply, but air is free because it is in unlimited supply. If there arose a surplus of air in, say, India and a shortage in China, air would become an economic commodity, like tin or wood.

In many countries – dubbed "affluent societies" by the Canadian-born economist John Kenneth Galbraith – scarcity is no longer a major concern, and the vast majority of the population enjoys a good standard of living. Nevertheless, businesses continue to increase the production of goods every year, relying on aggressive advertising, niche marketing, and expanded consumer credit to stimulate an artificial demand.

Conspicuous consumption – the ostentatious buying of nonessential goods and services for the status they

THE GOOD LIFE Swimming pools and tennis courts compete for space with houses in a Californian suburb. Luxuries like these are key status symbols in the "affluent society."

confer – assumes an excessive economic role. This, says Galbraith, diverts resources away from the public sector, where they could be used in the general interest. The result is a combination of private affluence and public squalor: too many private goods like cars and dishwashers and neglected public assets like transportation, schools, and parks.

EQUILIBRIUM

SEE ALSO: *Economics, Inflation, Monetarism*

Economic systems sometimes behave like natural ones. For example, they always seek a perfect balance. Just as a body of water always tries to find the same level, so economies seek "equilibrium"; just as nature abhors a vacuum, so economies abhor imbalances such as gaps between supply and demand, imports and exports, or investment and employment.

The most fundamental equilibrium is that of supply and demand. The classical economic theory is that when the "demand price" – the price consumers are prepared to pay – matches the "supply price" charged by producers, supply and demand reach a stable balance. Market conditions may

sometimes cause the cost of the product to vary, but the "equilibrium price" will always prevail.

The same principle applies in other areas of economics. The equilibrium wage, for example, is one at which the demand for labor is matched by supply. Some commentators blame large-scale unemployment on disequilibrium caused by workers' refusal to accept lower wages when demand for labor slumps. Equilibrium is reached only when the labor pool has diminished enough to drive wages up again, or lower wages encourage firms to take on more workers. Followers of the English economist John Maynard Keynes (1883–1946) blame such unemployment on another disequilibrium: the failure of planned investment to match savings.

MIXED ECONOMY

SEE ALSO: *Marxism, Sociology, Economics*

Both theory and experience demonstrate that markets are, on the whole, efficient at regulating economies. They perform the essential task – that of marrying supply and demand – reasonably well. But if market forces are allowed free rein, they may not act in the interest of society – and they will sometimes create economically damaging conflicts.

Few governments today would seek to impose a planned economy, where all business is directed by officials of the state, and private property and free enterprise are forbidden. But all governments have to intervene to trim the market's worst excesses. Under such a system, called a "mixed economy," the state takes action to stabilize the trade cycle and the exchange rate, and to manage economic change – for example, by subsidizing technological invention or helping to train the workforce. Governments may also use tax and welfare systems as a gentle way of redistributing wealth.

INFLATION

SEE ALSO: *Conservatism, Economics, Macroeconomics*

When demand for an item exceeds supply, the price rises. When demand persistently exceeds supply, the price rises persistently. Wages rise to keep up with prices, sparking off further price increases, and the real value of money starts to fall. At least, that is one way to explain inflation, the combination of spiraling prices and shrinking money that is the bane of modern economies. Economists find various scapegoats for inflation, among them too much money in circulation, wage increases unrelated to increases in output, and the simple expectation that prices will rise.

Gentle inflation, of up to about five percent a year, can stimulate the economy: investment in plant and machinery is brought forward to avoid future price increases, house prices are given a boost, and consumers (anticipating a fall in the purchasing power of their money) take out loans

MONEY FOR SALE A street vendor sells defunct Brazilian currency in Rio. The government had to keep printing new money to keep up with hyperinflation in the 1970s and 1980s.

for immediate spending. However, higher annual rates can have a devastating effect, whittling away savings and pensions, eroding investments and profits, bringing social and industrial unrest, and even destroying governments.

The cure is painful. The basic policy is to curtail economic activity, reducing output and employment, while imposing strict controls on credit and income. This is inevitably unpopular with the electorate, but it is less destructive than allowing runaway inflation. Many Western governments imposed such austerity measures in the 1980s as an antidote to the high inflation of the previous decade.

Hyperinflation is a more serious version of inflation. Probably the most notorious example is the German economy in the 1920s. In late 1923, paper money halved its value every hour. Wages were set and paid daily. The price of a newspaper was 200,000 million marks. In 1924 the Reichsmark, worth 1 million old marks, was introduced to supplant the mark. The period 1922–23 saw prices rise 10 billion-fold and the currency in circulation expand more than 7 billion-fold.

POSTINDUSTRIAL SOCIETY

HISTORY MAKERS: *Daniel Bell (1919–)*
SEE ALSO: *Internationalism, Economics*

MAKING A MODERN LIVING In a postindustrial society, workers in service industries, such as window cleaning, are in demand.

Two hundred years later, the Industrial Revolution is still taking place. Many of the world's less developed countries continue to make the change from a rural economy to an industrial one. But the economies of nations with a long manufacturing history are moving on. They are, in the phrase coined in the early 1970s by American sociologist Daniel Bell, "postindustrial."

According to Bell's theory, developed economies (led by the United States) are shifting from agriculture and manufacturing to services. The emphasis has moved from the blue-collar workers of industry to white-collar workers: professionals, administrators, and providers of services such as health, education, communications, and banking.

The vital commodity of the postindustrial order is information. The most important economic activities are the acquisition of data, its processing (with the aid of ubiquitous computers), and its interpretation by professional mediators – accountants, journalists, and specialist advisers. In practical terms, this means businesses should give higher priority to research and development (R&D), and indeed most of the highest-performing economies spend generously in this area.

GNP AND GDP

SEE ALSO: *Economics, Industrialization*

The United States is richer than Kenya; Germany is richer than Greece. But how do we know? To assess the wealth of an individual is simple: value his property and investments, find out his bank balance and ask him to turn out his pockets. The wealth of a nation, vitally important for political and economic calculations, is much harder to gauge.

One approach is to add together the wages people earn, the rents earned by properties, and the profits of business over a fixed period – usually one year. This is known as the gross domestic product (GDP). For the gross national product (GNP), economists add to the GDP the income from national assets abroad, and subtract the outflow of cash from foreign-owned assets.

This information can be analyzed in many ways. One of the most important ones is to divide the GDP by the population, which gives a rough measure of the standard of living. By this criterion, the wealthiest country in 1995 was Switzerland, with $36,399 per head, and the poorest was Sudan, with an estimated $63 per head.

MONETARISM

HISTORY MAKERS: *Ronald Reagan (1911–), Milton Friedman (1912–), Margaret Thatcher (1925–)*

SEE ALSO: *Conservatism*

The monetarist school of economics, based on the theories set out by the American economist Milton Friedman (1912–), believes that two major factors determine output, jobs and prices – the quantity of money in the economy and the rate at which it circulates. These can be regulated easily by changing interest rates. High interest rates drain money from the system by making borrowing expensive and saving (which reduces the pool of money available for consumer spending) attractive; low interest rates make loans cheap and bring more investment in industry.

Monetarist economists are critical of the economic systems proposed by followers of the English economist John Maynard Keynes (1883–1946). Keynesians believe that economies can be adjusted and tuned with a range of tools – governments can set prices and limit wage rises, and can stimulate or choke demand by regulating credit; above all, the state should pursue an active fiscal policy to secure full employment, imposing high taxes in times of boom and spending its way out of depression.

Monetarists argue that such policies are based on inherently unreliable economic forecasts and play down the role of market forces, creating instability and inflation. The monetarists prefer a laissez-faire doctrine, and urge governments to hand control of the money supply to central banks with one instruction: keep increases in supply in step with growth in national output. But even avid monetarist politicians in the 1980s found this hard to do.

GURU OF THE RIGHT Milton Friedman's monetarist theories were tried by Margaret Thatcher in her first term of office in the early 1980s – with disastrous results. Only after a policy about-face did Britain begin to regain its economic equilibrium.

WORLD ECONOMIC INSTITUTIONS

World Bank Founded in 1945 to help finance reconstruction after World War II. The World Bank uses money borrowed on the international markets to arrange financing for development projects in the world's poorer countries.

IMF (International Monetary Fund) A sister institution of the World Bank, the IMF lends money to help solve short-term national balance of payments difficulties, especially those in less developed countries caused by the need to repay commercial bank loans. The IMF also lends money for the purpose of restructuring weak national economies.

OECD (Organization for Economic Cooperation and Development) Intergovernmental organization made up of the world's most advanced industrial nations. Members of the OECD seek ways to work together and to help less developed countries.

OPEC (Organization of Petroleum Exporting Countries) Committee of oil-producing countries which sets prices and production levels.

G7 (Group of Seven) Canada, France, Germany, Italy, Japan, the United Kingdom, and the United States – a group of industrialized countries whose ministers meet regularly to discuss issues of mutual concern.

GLOBAL ECONOMICS
A small world

A car drives down a street in Jordan. It was designed in Germany and assembled in Turkey. Its engine was made in Mexico, its windows in France, and its door panels in Korea. Its chassis is Polish, and its headlights are English. The vehicle was built by Italian machine tools using Chinese bolts. This fictional (but feasible) automobile is a product of the global economy – one in which goods, money, and jobs can be moved around the world with little restriction.

Globalization started to emerge as an economic force in the 1980s, contributing to a general expansion of Western and Pacific Rim economies. It consolidated itself during the economic uncertainty and recession of the 1990s, as multinational companies such as Siemens, Glaxo, and Mitsubishi moved plants and offices around the world to take advantage of low labor costs, government grants, or access to cheap raw materials. At the same time, technical advances made it possible to transmit complex data via fax or e-mail in seconds. Better air travel meant that goods could be sent from one corner of the Earth to another quickly and cheaply.

This coincided with a series of political initiatives to free up international trade. The North American Free Trade Agreement (NAFTA), which came into force on January 1, 1994, has a program to establish free movement of goods and services between Canada, Mexico, and the United States by 2009. The Maastricht Treaty of 1993 set up the European Union, which also aims to abolish trade barriers between its 12 member states. Above all, after eight years of negotiations, the General Agreement on Tariffs and Trade (GATT), was signed in 1994. The 125 participating nations agreed a new code of conduct for international commerce and agreed to reduce tariffs through multilateral negotiations.

The perceived unevenness of the economic playing field has made some countries apprehensive, leading to calls for renewed trade protection. The Japanese, who owe much of their economic success to protectionist policies, face a tariff-free future with some nervousness; Westerners blame cheap Asian labor for job insecurity and wage freezes. But globalization has already changed the rules of the economic game and can be as much a source of opportunity as a threat.

AID

In the age of global economics, national fortunes are intertwined. Each country is a small part of the larger picture of world trade, so it makes economic sense for the richer countries of North America, Europe, the Far East, and Australasia to help the poorer countries of Africa, Asia, and South America escape from the vicious circle of poverty. The right sort of aid, it is hoped, will help poorer countries to prosper and play a fuller role in international trade, and eventually become valuable export markets and efficient suppliers for the richer countries.

Much aid is given on a multilateral basis, through institutions such as the World Bank and the regional development banks of Asia, Africa, and Latin America. However, bilateral aid – given directly from one country to another – usually goes hand in hand with trade: donations or loans are conditional on the money being spent on goods and services from the donor country.

Another aid route is to undertake to carry out specific projects, such as providing power and water supplies, as a means of boosting order books at home. Military aid is inevitably linked not only to the purchase of equipment from the donor, but also to the donor's strategic interests; it may, for example, be offered in exchange for the right to maintain military bases in the recipient nations.

Humanitarian and political motives also rank high in aid donations. Disasters such as earthquakes, floods, and famine in less developed countries bring both national and individual donations. Many Western countries increase or withhold aid to denote approval or disapproval of foreign regimes; the oil-rich countries of the Middle East, such as Saudi Arabia, sponsor their poorer neighbors' development, partly out of Muslim solidarity and partly in order to secure allies.

SUSTAINABLE DEVELOPMENT

Developing countries experienced an economic crisis in the 1980s. A sharp fall in the price of main export commodities such as cocoa and copper coincided with a rise in interest rates, and their governments could no longer service loans they had secured from Western banks in the previous decade. The World Bank and the Western governments agreed to provide further support in return for "structural adjustments" – major changes to debtors' economies, including lower government spending and an expansion of exports. Funding was often linked to huge developments, such as hydroelectric schemes that damaged the environment while affording few benefits to local people.

The sometimes draconian nature of these solutions spurred on the search for an alternative. Economists from developing countries argued that the solution lay in self-reliance in food production, regional cooperation, and better marketing. "Sustainable development" – a phrase coined at a 1972 United Nations conference – became the term for a range of policies.

By giving priority to the world's poor and recognizing the fragility of the environment, sustainable development is not just a policy for less developed countries, but a global ideal. The 1987 Tokyo Declaration called on the world's nations to adopt sustainable development as an overriding goal of national and international policy, and the 1992 Earth Summit at Rio de Janeiro produced Agenda 21 – a program stressing the link between environment and development. By asking the world's powers to focus their attention on conservation, economic efficiency, and the wellbeing of individuals, sustainable development has set itself an ambitious and exciting agenda.

HOME-GROWN TALENT Sustainable development aims to safeguard local traditions, protect natural resources, and build on native culture and expertise to create a new and viable economic base for developing nations.

CONSUMERISM

BRAND AWARENESS Multinationals such as Coca-Cola and McDonald's can be just as vulnerable to consumer pressure as local organizations.

Consumers have rights that protect them from being exploited or cheated. What is more, governments set strict standards for certain types of goods. The U.S. Food and Drug Administration (FDA), for example, approves medicines and makes sure they are properly labeled, checks that cosmetics are safe, and enforces food production and hygiene regulations.

This type of protection has a long history, going back to the market regulations of ancient Rome. Modern consumerism, however, was born in the mid-1960s, when the American lawyer Ralph Nader (1934–) successfully argued that vehicle design and manufacturing techniques were responsible for many injuries and deaths on the road, and forced manufacturers to incorporate several safety measures. Nader became a consumers' champion, spearheading controversial campaigns on food, occupational hazards, and many other issues.

Today's consumer organizations follow Nader's initiative, subjecting goods and services to rigorous tests and publishing their findings as a service to potential purchasers. They are also a powerful lobbying force, capable of influencing legislation and molding regulations.

PEOPLE POWER A long-term consumer boycott was one of the factors that contributed to the end of apartheid and the coming of majority rule in South Africa.

SEE ALSO
Internationalism
Sociology
Macroeconomics

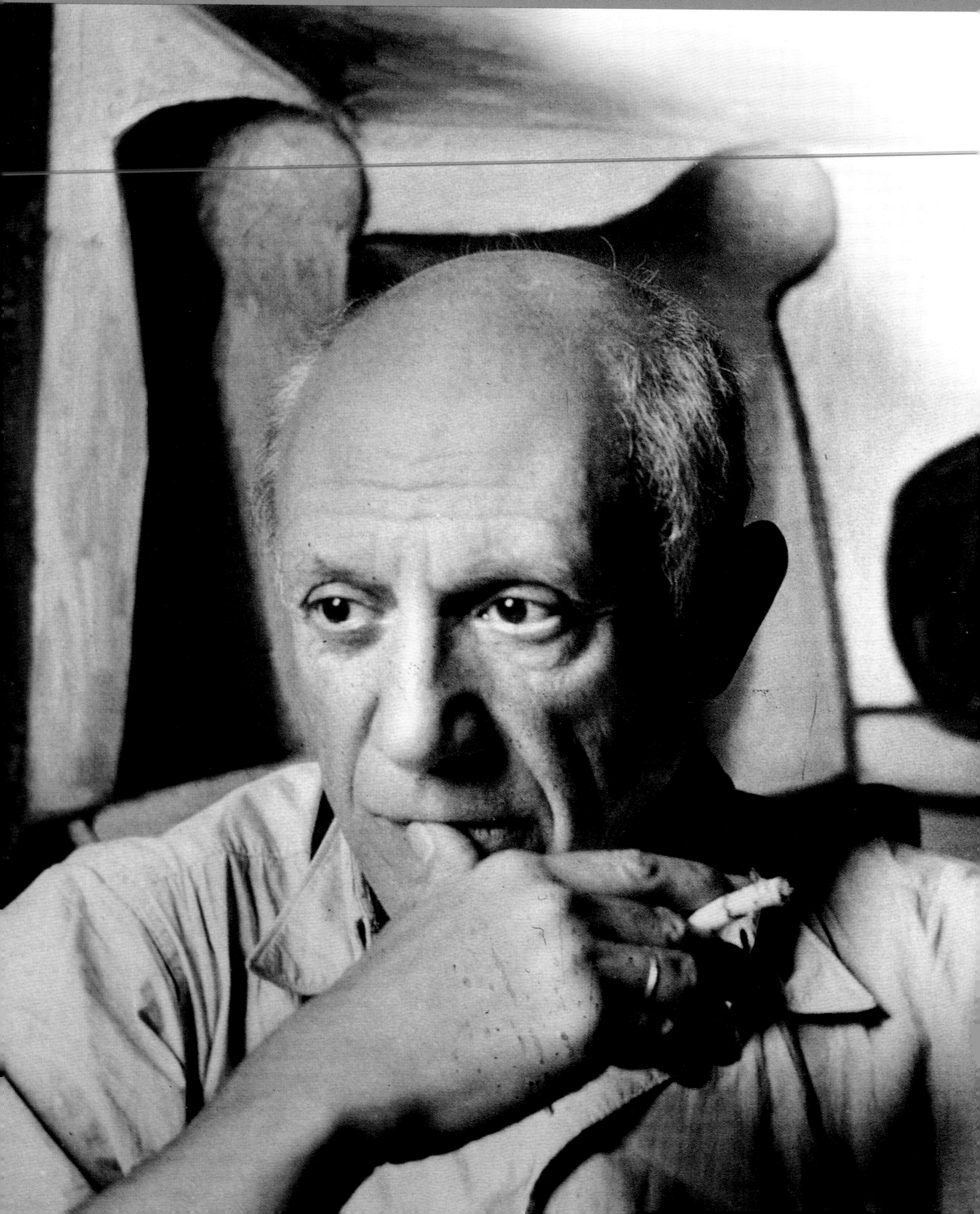

The Arts

From film to literature, the arts world has been shaken by repeated change and innovation.

From the Romantics of the 19th century to the present, the arts world has seen a series of movements and counter-movements. The first half of the 20th century alone spawned more new artistic movements than all previous periods added together. Many factors have driven this constant innovation, among them the growth of the middle classes, a general increase in leisure and wealth, and scientific and technical discoveries. But perhaps the most essential ingredient to this mix has been the notion of individualism.

The idea of individual genius is not a new one: the Greeks recognized the gifts of Aeschylus and Aristophanes. But during the Middle Ages, the work of the individual became subsumed in a grand design, such as Chartres Cathedral. Artist and craftsman were interchangeable. The stamp of the individual was not important; the glorification of God, or occasionally a rich patron, was.

A change in attitude began during the Renaissance. Vasari published his *Lives of the Artists* (1550), which proclaimed the genius of Michelangelo, Leonardo da Vinci, and Raphael. But the writer whose work irrevocably changed Western attitudes to the arts and to artists was the French Enlightenment thinker Jean Jacques Rousseau. Rousseau's *Confessions* (1782–89), a posthumously published warts-and-all autobiography, proclaimed the artist as hero, rebel, and above all individual. The Romantics embraced this novel idea and honed it. Since then, it has entered the public consciousness – from Lord Byron to the contemporary British conceptual artist Damien Hirst, creative people are expected to behave badly, and their work is expected to shock the "bourgeoisie," who are in fact their very audience. This need to shock has created another important 20th-century notion – the "avant-garde" – a group of people who are ahead of their time in their work, lifestyle, and thought.

Art has continued to do what it has always done – either to reflect the outer world refracted through the vision of an artist or to reveal the inner workings of his or her mind. What has changed is the artist's need to show himself to be different, to rebel against conventions and question tradition, and come up with something no one has ever done before. This approach has certainly opened our eyes and ears to whole new ways of perceiving the world, but endless novelty can eventually become wearing. Good craftsmanship, by contrast, lasts forever.

FROM REBEL TO AUTOCRAT Pablo Picasso in his studio, 1949.

NEOCLASSICISM
Art for the "Age of Reason"

In the mid-18th century the buried Roman cities of Herculaneum and Pompeii were excavated, and the extraordinary finds fired the imaginations of the leaders of European taste and fashion. Never before had the art and architecture of the ancient world been studied with such care and accuracy. And never before had the ruins of Greece and Rome been so accessible to a wide audience, because the peace prevailing across most of Europe at that time meant that, for the first time in centuries, travel was safe. For the wealthy, the "Grand Tour" became *de rigueur*. The new style they took home with them – to France, England, and Germany – was dubbed neoclassicism.

Under the impetus of Neoclassicism, grand houses and buildings began more than ever to take on the aspect of temples. The interiors were sprinkled with classical motifs, such as columns, pilasters, pediments, urns, friezes with low-relief sculptures of toga-clad revelers, and contemporary paintings depicting scenes from Greek and Roman mythology. The architecture was well proportioned and symmetrical – the product of carefully defined geometry and rules. The vogue for Neoclassical style soon swept across the Western world – including the newly liberated United States: indeed, it was the first truly international style.

But Neoclassicism was not simply an architectural style: it was a way of thinking. It was an expression of harmony, educated taste, discipline, morality, and the cool reason of the Enlightenment. It also expressed the order of social hierarchy. With its echoes of the grandeur of ancient Rome, it was a fitting style for the ruling classes, who saw themselves as heirs to the patricians, senators, and emperors.

For about a century after 1750, Neoclassicism was the dominant style – and it has remained a lasting influence to this day. Often cited as the opposite to Romanticism, it was in fact frequently its bedfellow, and many patrons saw no difficulty in embracing both simultaneously.

GEORGIAN BATH

The city of Bath, in southwestern England, was a spa town in Roman times. During the Georgian era (1714–1830), it became a popular summer resort for wealthy families. Bath developed as England's second social capital; the summer season became a giddy round of balls, assemblies, gatherings for tea, dinner, and card games – all spiced with gossip and flirtation. Social life was carefully orchestrated by the Master of Ceremonies of the Assembly Rooms, notably Richard "Beau" Nash (1674–1762), who was an early guardian of Bath's respectability and fashionable taste.

To accommodate its visitors, Bath was remodeled between 1727 and the 1790s in elegant and ingenious style, principally by the father-and-son team of architect-developers John Wood the elder (c.1705–54) and the younger (1728–82). They adapted the neoclassical style to an urban environment, creating tall row houses in curving forms to match the contours of the landscape. Instead of designing the facade of each house individually, the entire block was treated as a grand, integrated design.

WINCKELMANN

By the middle of the 18th century, Rome had become a vital cultural crossroads, a meeting point for many of the greatest European artists and intellectuals of the day. A leading figure in Rome was the German writer and archaeologist Johann Joachim Winckelmann (1717–68). He was a librarian to Cardinal Albani, a major collector, and after 1763 he was the Pope's superintendent of antiquities.

Winckelmann brought a new depth of understanding to classical art. He championed above all the Greek sculptors, believing them to be unmatched as interpreters of nature. He pointed to the spiritual quality of Greek art: its "noble simplicity and quiet grandeur," and its felicitous sense of proportion. Winckelmann believed that the modern world could attain the greatness of the Greek civilization by imitating it, and his ideas and writings, especially *Geschichte der Kunst des Altertums* (History of Ancient Art, 1764), helped to spread the ethos of neoclassicism.

HIGH-MINDED Johann Winckelmann's passion for antiquity set a fashion in Europe that lasted well into the 19th century. His death, however, was sordid: he was murdered for a handful of gold coins in Trieste.

THE GRAND TOUR

A LEARNING EXPERIENCE Tourists admire the Piazza del Campidoglio and Cordonata in Rome in a painting by Canaletto (1697–1768). Canaletto's photographic accuracy made him a favorite with visitors looking for a souvenir of their travels on the continent.

"A man who has not been to Italy is always conscious of an inferiority," declared the English writer and critic Dr. Johnson (1709–84). Classical studies were so highly valued in the 18th century that traveling to Italy was considered an indispensable part of every English gentleman's education.

By the 1780s, as many as 40,000 young Englishmen went abroad each year to embark on what was called the "Grand Tour" – a journey that could last as long as five years. Traveling by coach, carriage, riverboat, and litter – and usually accompanied by a tutor to instruct them in history, geography, mathematics, and languages – the "tourists" progressed through France to Italy, stopping to study the great works of the Renaissance and the classical past. Venice, Florence, Rome, and Pompeii were essential stopping points.

The gentlemen studied art, foreign customs, and methods of government; they made sketches, wrote diaries, and bought paintings and antiques – many of dubious authenticity – as trophies to decorate their grand houses back at home. Many of the paintings can be seen today in British museum collections.

The Grand Tour made a considerable contribution to establishing the taste for neoclassicism, as well as a general appreciation of fine art. But not all the participants were civilized by it. Spending as much as £4,000 a year – when a worker's annual wage was £30 – many of the tourists preferred to pass their time in gambling dens, drinking parlors, and brothels. For some families, indeed, the Grand Tour was simply a convenient way to allow their unruly sons to let off steam a safe distance from home.

SEE ALSO

Revolution · · · · · · · · · · · · · · ◀
The Enlightenment · · · · · · · · · · ◀
Romanticism & subjectivity · · · · · ◀
Romanticism · · · · · · · · · · · · · · ▶

THE GRECIAN LOOK

Neoclassicism took another twist at the close of the 18th century when the Greek Revival brought a more severe approach to design. The idea was to re-create the esthetic climate of ancient Greece by adopting purer, less ornamented styles. This had a parallel impact on women's clothes.

Across Europe, the standard daytime outfit for well-to-do young women was a simple white dress, which was believed to evoke the clothing of ancient Athens. The waistline came up to just beneath the bosom, and the dress fell directly to the feet without any elaboration or fullness. Made of silk, muslin, lace, and gauze, with short sleeves and a low-cut neck, it was a lightweight and delicate garment, complemented by plain, slipperlike shoes and perhaps a lace bonnet over hair pinned up and curled. Jewelry – if worn at all – was similarly delicate. Although flimsy almost to the point of transparency, the unfussy simplicity of this outfit was equated with the moral virtue of the Greeks. The style favored slim women; those of more robust build, or who felt the cold, must have rejoiced when the Grecian look fell from favor in the 1820s.

"…light as a woven cloud, walks Mme. Recamier, virgin of good taste in her ever white toilette!"

Edmond (1822–96) and Jules (1830–70) de Goncourt, diarists

HISTORY PAINTING

ARTISTIC LICENSE Jacques Louis David's enormous canvas re-imagines the Greek warrior hero Leonidas at the battle of Thermopylae.

During the 17th and 18th centuries, a number of academies of art were established in European cities: the French Académie Royale was founded in 1648; London's Royal Academy in 1768. They were all based on the academies of art set up in Florence and Rome toward the end of the Renaissance to promote the study of "fine art" and to train artists in drawing, anatomy, geometry, and history.

Students studied the rules of composition and drew from both plaster casts and live models. Morally uplifting history painting was deemed the highest form of artistic expression for painters, and artists were encouraged to produce scenes from classical history and mythology. Landscape painting and portraiture were considered less worthy of esteem.

But it was not until the end of the 18th century that neoclassical art showed its full potential in the paintings of its greatest exponent, the French artist Jacques Louis David (1748–1825). At the same time, the Italian sculptor Antonio Canova (1757–1822) attempted to match the skills of Greek and Roman sculptors, producing marble works on classical themes and achieving considerable artistic – and financial – success.

THE SYMPHONY

ENCHANTED EVENINGS The Queen of the Night descends from the heavens in a set design for Mozart's opera *The Magic Flute*. This production in 1816 at the Berlin Opera House was designed by the great neoclassical German architect Karl Friedrich Schinkel (1781–1841).

When people of the 19th century looked back on the music of the second half of the previous century, they saw the emergence of the orchestra in a prototype of its modern shape, and of music as an art form in its own right. They referred to the music of that era as "classical." This was not a reference to any connection with ancient Greece or Rome, but to contrast it with later, "romantic" music. The term "classical music" has stuck, but is now used more generally. (Confusingly, "neoclassical music" refers to early 20th-century music that harked back to the 18th-century composers.)

The music of the late 18th century, performed in the grand neoclassical palaces of Europe, did not reflect the cool symmetrical sobriety of the surroundings. By contrast, this era saw the rapid evolution of European musical expression into forms charged with emotional power, individuality, invention, and technical complexity. A big breakthrough was the elevation in status of the four-movement symphony – and two Austrian composers, Joseph Haydn (1732–1809) and Wolfgang Amadeus Mozart (1756–91), are given the credit for this. Haydn wrote 104 symphonies which show huge variety and ingenuity.

For a long while, Haydn's reputation as a composer of symphonies was eclipsed by the younger, more mercurial Mozart. In fact, they held each other in great mutual esteem. Mozart wrote 41 symphonies altogether, of which the last three (Nos. 39–41) – all written in less than six weeks in 1788 – rank among his greatest achievements.

EMPIRE STYLE

In the pre-Revolutionary France of Louis XV and Louis XVI, the aristocracy adopted neoclassicism with gusto. It might have died with them – but just as the *ancien régime* equated itself with the patrician class of ancient Rome, the revolutionaries who swept it aside identified themselves with the Romans of the republican era. During the *Directoire* (1793–99), a new form of neoclassicism became the adopted style. It was transformed under Napoleon – who likened himself to Emperor Augustus – into the distinctive and more luxurious Empire Style, seen particularly in furniture and fixtures.

Empire Style had all the elegance and composure of pre-Revolutionary neoclassicism, but was animated by a racy pizzazz expressive of a new world order. The dominant colors were black (or dark brown) and gold – ebony, mahogany, blackened bronze, or black stone were offset by ormolu (gilt-bronze) decorations and mounts, such as plaques and ornate animal feet. Typical decorative motifs included lion's heads, burning torches, palmettes, lyres, the letter N (for Napoleon) – and, after the French invasion of Egypt in 1798, sphinxes, palm trees, papyrus leaves, and stylized lotuses. The main promoters of this style were Napoleon's favorite designers Charles Percier (1764–1838) and Pierre-Leonard Fontaine (1762–1853).

STYLE FIT FOR AN EMPEROR This stool, *c.*1810, exemplifies the Empire Style, which brought martial and revolutionary motifs into furniture design.

ROMANTICISM
Emotion and imagination

The discipline and formality of Neoclassicism could account for only one side of human nature. In the late 18th century, many people – inspired by writers such as Jean Jacques Rousseau (1712–78) and Edmund Burke (1729–97) – began to think that to be a truly modern person you needed to break free of the rules that constrained society, and to give expression to the emotions and imagination. This movement was labeled Romanticism, a term derived from the lurid medieval tales of myth, magic, and the supernatural that were called "romances" because, originally, they were written in the language used every day – *Romanz* – instead of Latin.

The roots of Romanticism, however, had grown concurrently with Neoclassicism. In the 1740s, for instance, an enthusiasm for medieval times had led to fake "ruins" being built in the grounds of Neoclassical houses. The same mood also inspired a vogue for sensational Gothic novels, such as *The Castle of Otranto* (1764) by the English novelist Horace Walpole (1717–97). In Germany, in a movement of the 1770s called *Sturm und Drang* (Storm and Stress), writers such as Johann Wolfgang von Goethe (1749–1832) and Friedrich Schiller (1759–1805) produced works promoting passion and imagination while rejecting the neoclassical virtues of reason and decorum.

After the 1780s, the romantic mood began to take over – in music, poetry, painting, and architecture. The young fashionable set adopted informal behavior, allowing their emotions to flow freely – even to tears – at performances of music and poetry. They exulted at views of landscape that they felt expressed the elemental power of nature. Romanticism remained a force in the arts until the end of the 19th century.

LANDSCAPE PAINTING

During the 18th century, writers, painters, and designers searched for the "picturesque": uncontrived natural landscapes with features – such as an ancient tree or a ruin – that created a mood for reverie. In previous eras, landscape was simply a backdrop in paintings, but now it became the subject of the painting itself.

One of the great innovators in this field was the English painter Joseph Mallord William Turner (1775–1851). A man of consummate gifts, he readily assimilated the techniques of the Old Masters. By the age of 32 he had become successful enough to paint what he chose. Taciturn and independent, he traveled widely, pushing ever farther his experiments in reproducing the effects of light to a point where he began to paint not the landscape so much as the feelings it evoked within him.

German painter Caspar David Friedrich (1774–1840) was master of a darker, awe-inspiring mood of landscape. Strong contrasts, a palette of penumbral colors, and a polished technique help to give his paintings a dreamy, mystic quality, tinged with unease.

VISIONARIES

The Romantics' interest in the world of the imagination opened the door to the more mysterious, irrational world of dreams and visions. The Swiss painter Johann Heinrich Fuseli (1741–1825) specialized in haunting, dreamlike images painted with frenetic emotion, and set in theatrical lighting.

The English writer, artist, and mystic William Blake (1757–1827) claimed to be guided by visions. His independence, eccentricities, revolutionary passions, and impoverishment led many of his contemporaries to write him off as crazy. His best-known poems appeared in two collections, *Songs of Innocence* (1789) and *Songs of Experience* (1794). He illustrated his own texts, and those of others, with naive but powerful engravings that resonate with mystical, symbolic meaning.

Blake lived in a world in which everything was imbued with the sublime. But he also suffered the stress of grappling with the very nature of reality; for him the imagination was "the real and eternal world of which the Vegetable Universe is but a faint shadow."

PERSONAL VISION Toward the end of his life William Blake illustrated Dante's *Divine Comedy*, the story of a pilgrim's visit to heaven and hell. In *The Inscription over the Gate of Hell* (1824–27), the guide Virgil leads Dante, the pilgrim, into hell.

THE LAKE POETS AND BYRON

THE POETIC IMAGE Lord Byron's uncompromising spirit, short life, and lack of respect for social convention have made him the archetype of the "romantic poet."

In Britain, the potential variety of Romantic poetry was signaled by the publication of *Lyrical Ballads* (1798) by William Wordsworth (1770–1850) and Samuel Taylor Coleridge (1772–1834). The book was like a manifesto, demonstrating ways in which poetry could be liberated from the constraints of traditional rules and forms. A central feature of Romantic poetry was a new attitude toward nature. Wordsworth, Coleridge, and Robert Southey (1774–1843) all lived for a while in the Lake District of northwestern England, and were labeled "the Lake Poets."

A younger set of English poets emerged in the wake of Coleridge and Wordsworth – including Percy Bysshe Shelley (1792–1822), John Keats (1795–1821), and George Gordon, Lord Byron (1788–1824). By living intensely and dying young, they did much to enhance the bittersweet public image of the Romantic poet. Byron in particular propelled the poet to celebrity status. Readers lapped up his long works – notably the autobiographical *Childe Harold's Pilgrimage* (1812–18) and *Don Juan* (1819–24). His death – from fever while fighting for Greek independence against the Ottoman Turks – only added to his mystique.

TIMELINE

1774
Johann Wolfgang von Goethe publishes *The Sorrows of Young Werther*, a tragic tale of an archetypal romantic hero.

1789
The French Revolution is supported by many artists and writers, and is later seen as the symbolic beginning of the romantic era.

1798
William Wordsworth and Samuel Taylor Coleridge publish *Lyrical Ballads*, which marks a turning point in English poetry.

1816
John Keats's first sonnets are published.

1818
Mary Shelley, wife of the poet Percy Bysshe Shelley, publishes the Gothic novel *Frankenstein, or the Modern Prometheus*.

1830
Hector Berlioz composes the *Symphonie Fantastique*, and Felix Mendelssohn composes the *Hebrides* overture.

1840–65
London's Houses of Parliament are rebuilt in neo-Gothic style.

1876
Richard Wagner's Festival Theater in Bayreuth opens with the first complete performance of *Der Ring des Nibelungen*.

SEE ALSO
Revolution · · · · · · · · · · · · · ◄
The Enlightenment · · · · · · · · · · ◄
Romanticism & subjectivity · · · · · ◄
Neoclassicism · · · · · · · · · · · · · ◄

OVERTURES AND CONCERTOS

ROMANTIC HERO The Romantic composers of the 19th century hailed Ludwig van Beethoven (1770–1827) as their most important precursor. His vast talent, turbulent personality, and the tragedy of his deafness all contributed to his posthumous glamor.

The test of romantic music was whether it could convey moods – especially strong feelings and passions. The German composer Felix Mendelssohn (1809–47) struck early success with his overture to *A Midsummer Night's Dream*, mood-setting incidental music for Shakespeare's play which he wrote as a prodigiously talented teenager.

Music could also portray impressions of a landscape: one of Mendelssohn's most enduringly popular works is the *Hebrides* overture (1830), also known as *Fingal's Cave*. This was inspired by a boat trip to the Scottish island of Staffa, whose peculiar clusters of basalt columns are said to be part of a causeway laid by the mythical warrior-giant Fingal.

The French composer Hector Berlioz (1803–69) took this idea one step farther: he believed that music could be made to tell a story – as a kind of opera without words. His *Symphonie Fantastique* (1830) tells the story of a young musician who tries to poison himself with opium to assuage his disappointed love. He enters into a delirious nightmare in which he dreams that he kills his loved one, is led to execution, and ends up at a witches' sabbath. It is an imaginative extrapolation of Berlioz's own desperate love for an English actress, Harriet Smithson.

Berlioz, who shared some of the tempestuous characteristics of Byron, set part of the poet's *Childe Harold's Pilgrimage* to music as the symphony *Harold en Italie* (1834). This began as a concerto commissioned by the great virtuoso violinist Niccolo Paganini (1782–1840), a man of such breathtaking talent and stamina that he was popularly rumored to be in league with the devil. This image fitted romantic attitudes perfectly – as did the format of concertos composed as vehicles for soloists to give expression to their talent. Unfortunately, Paganini rejected *Harold en Italie* as too easy for him.

ORIENTALISM

In 1827, the French artist Eugène Delacroix (1798–1863) painted *The Death of Sardanapalus*, an enormous canvas depicting a scene of violence and sensuality. Sardanapalus, king of Assyria, lies impassively on his bed as his harem is put to the sword prior to his own suicide. Five years later, Delacroix traveled to Spain, Morocco, and Algeria and was impressed by their light and color, but above all by their exotic qualities, which he interpreted in his later paintings.

This fascination for things Oriental was a central theme of Romanticism. Although connected vaguely to the European expansion of empire, it was not based on any true understanding of the East: it was a fantasy, of a kind inspired by the recently republished Arab story cycle, *The Thousand and One Nights*. In France, painters such as Horace Vernet (1789–1863) and Jean Léon Gérome (1824–1904) depicted an imagined Arab world of harems, desert caravans, and slave markets, spiced with eroticism and savagery. In Britain Orientalism took on a Mogul theme, reflecting links with India.

FANTASY WOMEN Portraying women in an exotic setting such as a harem gave artists license to explore erotic fantasy and fetishism. Several Orientalist painters, such as Jean Léon Gérome, kept a collection of props in the studio to help make their sets appear realistic.

WAGNER

SHRINE TO MUSICAL GENIUS With the help of Ludwig II of Bavaria (1845–86), Richard Wagner established a permanent home for his opera at Bayreuth, which still holds the celebrated Wagner Festival every year.

All the passion and imaginative élan of romantic music came to a head in the operas of the German composer Richard Wagner (1813–83). As a young man, he reacted to the constraints of traditional music teaching. "For me," he wrote later, "music was a spirit, a noble and mystic monster, and any attempt to regulate it seemed to lower it in my eyes."

He found the narrative power that he sought in European myths. Wagner's operas were saturated with powerful mood-setting music and linked by repeated musical themes, called *leitmotiven*, which represented main characters or aspects of the plot. Mixing narrative, drama, theatrical staging, and sublime music, Wagner intended to produce a total work of art – a *Gesamtkunstwerk*.

His greatest work is the cycle of four long operas called *Der Ring des Nibelungen* (1848–74). This recounts a complex Norse-Germanic myth involving dwarfs, giants, gods, and heroes. His work plumbs strange psychological depths, sometimes tender, sometimes savage, sometimes deeply sensual. The prelude to his opera *Tristan and Isolde* (1856–59), a tale of impossible love, rises to a magnificent crescendo that is unmistakably representative of orgasm. The grandiose, megalomaniac tendencies of his music later struck a chord with the Nazis.

THE GOTHIC REVIVAL

The term Gothic was coined during the Renaissance as a derogatory description of medieval architecture. At a time when classical architecture was held up as the ideal model, the soaring arches and tracery windows of medieval cathedrals were dismissed as barbaric – like the Goths who had destroyed the Roman Empire.

In the middle of the 18th century, various designers began to take a new, more kindly look at medieval architecture – particularly Gothic churches and cathedrals. By the early 1800s, a trickle had turned into a flood. The styles of the medieval world were plundered indiscriminately; rooflines were castellated and pierced by spires, while interiors became luxurious improvisations on ecclesiastical themes.

Some later enthusiasts for the neo-Gothic interpreted Gothic architecture as the only truly Christian style – as opposed to classicism, which had been conceived by pagans. New churches across Europe were built in this style. Neo-Gothic was also associated with national heritage. Thus when the Houses of Parliament in London were rebuilt in 1840–65, neo-Gothic was considered appropriately British and godly.

GÉRICAULT AND DELACROIX

The vanguard of Romantic painters was led in France by Theodore Géricault (1791–1824). His *Raft of the "Medusa"* caused a sensation in 1819. The subject matter was a *cause célèbre* of the day: the French frigate *Méduse* was shipwrecked off West Africa, and 150 of its hapless crew were abandoned on a raft by the incompetent officers who had taken to the lifeboats. For art lovers, it was a shock to see a horrifying contemporary event as the subject of a painting – especially when portrayed with such dynamism and passion.

When Géricault died at the age of 33, his young and impulsive disciple Eugène Delacroix (1798–1863) took up his cause. Breaking the rules of composition, and using a painterly interpretation of nature, he challenged accepted Neoclassical principles of art.

REPORTAGE Delacroix's emotional painting *The Massacre at Chios* (1824) expressed his own anger at the way Greece was left alone to struggle for liberation from Turkish occupiers.

REALISM
Reflecting the rougher side of life

Many forces of change were at work in the first half of the 19th century. Europe was recovering from the dislocation of the Napoleonic Wars; industrialization was breaking up traditional communities and creating new urban ones; scientific discoveries and technological innovations were altering people's perceptions of the world. Smoldering discontent was met with political repression, engendering a radicalism that flared up in 1848 in revolutionary disturbances across Europe.

Romanticism was no longer an appropriate response to this new climate: it was too escapist, emotional, elitist. Artists and writers with a finger on the pulse wanted instead to portray the contemporary world as they saw it, and sometimes – but not always – they wanted to express the mood of revolutionary zeal. They adopted the label realist for this approach.

The desire to portray the real world was not new: many authors of earlier eras had attempted to create the illusion of a documentary account. However, the realism of the 19th century had a particular hue. Even if not overtly political, it reflected a concern for the social problems of the age. This concern sometimes led to depictions of the squalid sides of life, which had not previously been thought of as a proper subject for art. Such work came as a shock to society and was frequently castigated as scandalous.

THE NOVEL COMES OF AGE

The novel was a major beneficiary of the technological and social changes of the early 19th century – notably the improvements in the printing and distribution of literature, and the rapid growth of readership. While all kinds of fiction were now being produced – from sensational thrillers to sentimental romances – realism proved a vein that appealed to the more challenging writers and their readers. Previously, ordinary contemporary society had been almost completely overlooked as a suitable setting for fiction. Realism seemed fresh, and thoroughly modern.

Part of the appeal of realism was the concept that ordinary people – people like the readers – could be the subject of fiction. The driving forces of the narrative tended to be the characters' psychological development. The details of setting and dialogue were carefully reproduced; events described were plausible.

French novelists were at the forefront of this development, led by Stendhal (the pen name of Marie Henri Beyle, 1783–1842) and carried forward by Honoré de Balzac (1799–1850) and Gustave Flaubert (1821–80). Russia produced two of its great novelists in this realist era – Leo Tolstoy (1828–1910) and Fyodor Dostoyevsky (1821–81).

REALIST PAINTING

POLITICAL SATIRE The witty work of Honoré Daumier (1808–79) depicts the French Emperor Napoleon III skewered by his own laws. Daumier's experience as a professional cartoonist gave his paintings a political edge.

"Beauty is in nature and is to be found in reality, in every sort of form," said the painter Gustave Courbet (1819–77), "but the artist has no right to add to that expression. Touch it, and you risk altering its nature – and in the end you weaken it."

Courbet's agenda was to paint images of the world as he saw it, without adornment, without the intervention of the traditional conventions of art. When his *Funeral at Ornans* was shown at the Paris Salon of 1850, it caused a sensation. It is a grim work, painted in earthy colors and depicting a scene from the artist's home village near the Swiss border. But it is also on a monumental scale and includes over 30 life-size figures. No one before had had the bravado to elevate this kind of subject matter to such a size. Critics railed at the vulgarity of it all; others detected political subversion. Courbet – irascible, arrogant, and forthright – was indeed an activist and ended his life in exile for taking part in the 1871 Paris Commune, but he declared that he was simply portraying a real and solemn event taking place in the lives of ordinary people. His combative stance was as much an inspiration to later artists as his determination to paint truthful images of contemporary life.

The French painter Jean-François Millet (1814–75) worked on the land in his youth and later specialized in scenes of farm laborers, reflecting a sympathy for peasant life and an understanding of its hardships. His best-known painting, *The Angelus* (1858–59), depicts a working couple in a field stopping to pray on hearing the tolling of the evening prayer bell and was extremely popular in his lifetime.

AMERICAN REALIST PAINTING

Although directly influenced by developments in Europe, art in the United States began to take on a distinctive American identity during the 19th century. The American landscape was a key element in this: "All nature here is new to art," declared Thomas Cole (1801–48), the founder of the Hudson River school of painters. This loosely defined group of talented artists set out to depict the grandeur and majesty of the American landscape, but the mood was essentially romantic.

It was the next generation – notably Thomas Eakins (1844–1916) – who brought realism to American art. Eakins was gifted with supreme technique and powers of observation, and he sought to depict reality with absolute fidelity. His group portrait *The Gross Clinic* (1875) shows the distinguished surgeon Dr. Samuel Gross supervising an operation – a telling combination of portraiture and the celebration of science in an entirely plausible setting.

The other great painter of this era, Winslow Homer (1836–1910), made his name through work produced during the Civil War (1861–65). He went on to paint genre scenes from rural life before turning to marine subjects.

"BETWEEN ROUNDS" A pause in a sweaty boxing bout is a subject 19th-century audiences would have found surprising from a fine artist such as Thomas Eakins.

SEE ALSO

Socialism · · · · · · · · · · · · · · · · · ◀
Industrialization · · · · · · · · · · · ◀
Romanticism · · · · · · · · · · · · · · · ◀

THE BIRTH OF PHOTOGRAPHY

HISTORY MAKERS: *Louis Daguerre (1789–1851), William Henry Fox Talbot (1800–77)*

SEE ALSO: *Post-Impressionism, Modernism*

In 1839 the French artist Louis Daguerre announced the invention of the daguerreotype – a photographic image produced on a copper plate covered with silver and treated with iodine vapor. It was the solution to an old problem.

For centuries people had known about the phenomenon whereby the image of, say, a landscape can be projected onto paper when light passes through a small hole or lens. It had been employed in a boxlike piece of equipment called a *camera obscura* (dark chamber), which artists used to make accurate tracings of buildings or landscape. The phenomenon posed an intriguing challenge: could this projected image somehow be captured? The answer clearly lay in finding some kind of light-sensitive material that would preserve the image.

Daguerre had cracked it. But he was not alone in his efforts. In England, William Henry Fox Talbot had been working independently on the same problem, and in 1841 he announced the invention of the calotype (beautiful image). This was achieved by a different method. First the view was caught on treated translucent paper, producing a negative image. Then the negative was laid over sensitized paper and

PICTURE BOX The first camera manufactured for sale to the public was this daguerreotype device made under licence from Louis Daguerre by the Paris firm of Alphonse Giroux. The plates it exposed were large – 8½ by 6½ inches (21 by 16 cm). It is mounted on a tripod made at about the same time that was used by William Henry Fox Talbot.

exposed to light, thereby producing the positive image. As it turned out, Fox Talbot's method proved to be the foundation of modern photographic processes. The daguerreotype produced a clear and permanent image, but each photograph was a one-off; with the calotype method, it was possible to make any number of prints from the negative.

Multiple prints were what the public wanted. For the first time, ordinary people could have life-like images of themselves, their families, even distant relatives, and at little cost. Photographic studios sprang up around the world. During the 1860s, the word cartomania was coined to describe the craze for photographic studio portraits in the small carte-de-visite format.

Photography also posed esthetic questions. Here was a method of producing accurate images of the world – in the manner to which painters such as the Frenchman Gustave Courbet (1819–77) aspired. Would this make the artist redundant?

Some artists used photography as an aid to realism, content that it could not rival painting for color and texture. Others dismissed it as incapable of matching an artist's gift for interpretation, which helped to focus minds on the significance of this interpretation. Yet others realized that selecting a photograph's subject matter was an artistic act. Some of the earliest photographs were artistically rendered landscapes; and pioneers such as the Englishwoman Julia Margaret Cameron (1815–79) quickly demonstrated the full artistic potential of portrait photography.

THE GREAT EXHIBITION

HISTORY MAKERS: *Prince Albert (1819–61), Joseph Paxton (1801–65)*

SEE ALSO: *Imperialism, Arts and Crafts, Museums*

GIANT GREENHOUSE The "crystal palace" in which the Great Exhibition was held was designed by English architect Joseph Paxton.

In 1851 Britain staged the Great Exhibition – the first of the prestigious international trade exhibitions. The setting was a vast hall made of glass and steel, erected in Hyde Park in central London. Dubbed the "crystal palace" by the press, it covered 9 acres (3.6 hectares).

Exhibits included locomotives, printing presses, furniture, textiles, porcelain, mass-produced sculpture, toys, and photographic equipment – plus oddities such as a rubber cloak that could be inflated as a boat.

At the end of the exhibition, the crystal palace was dismantled, to be re-erected later in south London. The show was a triumph of organization – visited by around 6 million people, from all social backgrounds. But not everyone was happy. People were impressed by the vast number and variety of exhibits, but many also noted their esthetic impoverishment. It was a turning point in 19th-century attitudes to design.

THE PRE-RAPHAELITES

HISTORY MAKERS: *William Holman Hunt (1827–1910), Dante Gabriel Rossetti (1828–82)*

SEE ALSO: *Realism, New Art*

In 1848 the English artists William Holman Hunt, Dante Gabriel Rossetti, John Everett Millais (1829–96), and four others formed the Pre-Raphaelite Brotherhood (or PRB, as they labeled themselves). They claimed to take their inspiration from the purity of expression in art before the Italian painter Raphael (1483–1520), but in practice the PRB were only nominally influenced by early art. What distinguishes them is their subject matter – usually religious, medieval, or symbolic – their polished technique, and their intense colors.

Realism can be seen in the precision of their observation and treatment of their subjects. For instance, one of Millais's most celebrated paintings, *Christ in the House of His Parents* (1850), shows the boy Jesus working with his hands in his father's carpenter's shop – a treatment that caused outrage at the time.

ETHEREAL BEAUTY Jane Morris, wife of William Morris, posed frequently for Dante Gabriel Rossetti. Her glamorization in paintings like *La Ghirlandata* (1873) had a huge impact on Victorian notions of female beauty.

ARTS AND CRAFTS

HISTORY MAKERS: *Philip Webb (1831–1915), William Morris (1834–96)*

SEE ALSO: *The Great Exhibition*

"Masses of sordidness, filth and squalor, embroidered with patches of pompous and vulgar hideousness": the reaction of William Morris to industrial products of the kind shown at the Great Exhibition in 1851 was characteristically passionate and uncompromising. Morris – poet, artist, craftsman, and socialist reformer – saw industry as a pernicious evil and endeavored to turn back its progress. His main complaint was that industry dehumanized people, both in work and through its products. He looked back to the handmade crafts of the medieval world – all, he felt, stamped with the personality of their creators.

In 1861 Morris set up a workshop specializing in hand-crafted furniture, paintings, stained glass, textiles, carpets, and wallpapers. The aim was to manufacture affordable products that were both beautiful and functional. But his products were too expensive to reach the general public, and he needed wealthy clients to sustain the project.

Morris worked alongside a number of highly talented designers and artists who shared his views – including members of the Pre-Raphaelite Brotherhood. He himself was a gifted designer. Taking his inspiration from nature, Morris had an unmatched talent for pattern in textiles and wallpaper. Many of his gracefully proportioned interlacing floral designs are still popular today.

Toward the end of the century, a distinctive style of Morris-influenced furniture and decoration emerged, rationalized by designer Philip Webb, and developed by others such as the furniture-maker Gustav Stickley (1857–1942) in the U.S. After 1888, the style took the name Arts and Crafts.

Morris himself believed his lasting reputation would rest on his poetry, to which he devoted most of his attention toward the end of his life.

USEFUL BUT ALSO BEAUTIFUL The "Saville" armchair was produced by William Morris and Co. in *c.*1890.

MUSEUMS

HISTORY MAKERS: *Hans Sloane (1660–1753), James Smithson (1765–1829), Augustus Franks (1826–97)*

The 19th century was the great age of the museum. In many of the world's capitals, they were set up as repositories for the increasing numbers of possessions in the national domain. The British Museum, founded in 1753, moved into a new, purpose-built home in the 1840s. The Musée du Louvre in Paris made its royal collections – dating from the 16th century – increasingly accessible to the public. The Smithsonian Institute, now the largest museum in the world and spread over 14 sites, was founded in Washington, D.C., in 1846 with a bequest left by the Englishman James Smithson.

These vast collections came from many sources in addition to straightforward acquisitions or donations: they included war booty and treasures from archaeological sites abroad. The growth of museums corresponded to an increased public interest in knowledge as a result of the spread of education, but they were also expressions of national pride.

IMPRESSIONISM
Painters of modern life

During most of the 19th century, the eyes of the art world were turned toward Paris. The great public interest in the arts engendered fierce passions and loyalties: exhibitions, plays, and concerts could cause rapture and outcry in equal measure. It was a hothouse for new ideas.

In 1863 a group of young painters met when training at the studio of Gabriel-Charles Gleyre (1808–74). They included Claude Monet (1840–1926), Auguste Renoir (1841–1919), Alfred Sisley (1839–99), and Jean-Frédéric Bazille (1841–71). Monet introduced them to an older painter, Camille Pissarro (1830–1903), whom he had met in 1859. Also associated with the group were Edouard Manet (1832–83), Edgar Degas (1834–1917), and Paul Cézanne (1839–1906), but they pursued somewhat different agendas.

Realism, as pioneered by Gustave Courbet (1819–77), was still the main focus of avant-garde artists. However, this new group of artists had grown tired of the suggestion that Realism had to reflect the plight of the poor. There was a whole world out there – a middle-class world of urban scenes, people in bars and cafés, or picnicking by the river – which was just as real. And this was the world that the artists inhabited.

They also objected to the attempts of the earlier Realists to demonstrate that ordinary life could be as timeless and monumental as academic history painting claimed to be. Their concept of reality was that it belonged to the moment, and was constantly changing. Realism, if it was to be modern and free of the past, had to reflect this. The group worked closely through the 1860s and evolved a technique of painting using rapid brushstrokes and bright colors.

In 1874 the group mounted a joint exhibition of work by some 30 like-minded artists. It included a sketchy oil painting by Monet of a sunrise over a harbor which he called *Impression: Sunrise* (1872). It caught the attention of a critic, Louis Leroy, who referred to the group mockingly as "Impressionists." The name stuck.

The 1870s were the great decade of Impressionism, during which the artists produced much of their best work against a backdrop of hostile criticism and poverty. But their integrity was rewarded in the following decades by growing understanding, financial success, and respectability. During the 1880s, however, they pursued their careers in different ways, and Impressionism evolved into diverse strands.

THE SALON DES REFUSÉS

In France, the bastion of establishment art was the Royal Academy of Painting and Sculpture, founded in 1667. Every year the Academy held an exhibition of new painting and sculpture called the Salon. The exhibits were chosen by a committee from the thousands submitted by hopeful artists. The Academy had an immense hold on public taste, and also on patronage: it was hard for any artists to make a living unless their work was shown in the Salon.

In 1863, so much new art was rejected by the Academy that there was a public outcry. Napoleon III felt obliged to step in and ordered an exhibition of the rejected work called the Salon des Refusés. This included paintings by a number of artists who later became famous, including Manet, Pissarro, and Cézanne. The exhibition was praised by a few devotees, but otherwise castigated by critics and the public, and became the subject of mocking cartoons in the press.

An uneasy relationship between the avant-garde and the Academy continued. The Impressionists, who never claimed to be rebels, were happy to exhibit at the Salon in the 1870s when accepted. But the Academy was increasingly sidelined by the growth of independent galleries, particularly after the Salon des Indépendants was established in 1884 for modern artists who did not wish to be associated with Academy taste.

FLEETING IMPRESSIONS

To outraged critics and offended members of the public, the paintings at the first Impressionist exhibition in 1874 simply looked unfinished – like preliminary sketches, not ready for public viewing. In fact, this was no accident: the Impressionists admired the sketches from nature of earlier painters because they possessed the spontaneity that finished paintings lacked.

During the 1860s, the Impressionists worked at techniques that would give their paintings immediacy – to capture the fleeting moments of reality. Renoir and Monet had a particularly profitable summer in 1869, when they worked side by side at La Grenouillère (The Froggery), a pleasure resort on the River Seine near Paris. They painted quickly, reproducing the dappled effect of light reflected on choppy water with a mosaic of dabs of bright color. Instead of using traditional methods of graduated shades of color to build up shapes, they used blocks of pure color set side by side. By loading the brush heavily with paint, the brushstrokes created a textured finish. In addition, the Impressionists abandoned black – a color rarely found in nature – and used blue instead.

Capturing the effect of light was central to the Impressionists' aims. This preoccupied Monet to the end of his long life. In the 1890s he carried out a series of studies of the same subject under different light conditions at various times of day.

LUMINOUS LANDSCAPE Monet was fascinated by the effects of light throughout his career. He painted two long series of paintings – *Haystacks* (1890–92) and *Rouen Cathedral* (1892–94) – which show how color changes with the height and strength of the sun in the sky.

DEBUSSY

By the end of the century, the Impressionists' efforts to evoke on canvas a particular moment in time had caught the attention of writers and composers. The composer whose work is most often cited as Impressionist is Claude Debussy (1862–1918). He abandoned the traditions of thematic progression in his music in favor of more vague evocations of atmosphere. One of his most celebrated pieces is *La Mer* (1905), a set of "symphonic sketches" that conjure up the sea. The Impressionistic intentions can be seen from the titles of the three movements: *From Dawn to Midday on the Sea, Play of the Waves,* and *Dialog of the Wind and Sea.*

TIMELINE

1863
At the Salon des Refusés, Edouard Manet's *Déjeuner sur l'herbe* causes a public outcry.

1863–64
Claude Monet, Auguste Renoir, and Alfred Sisley meet.

1869
During the summer, Monet and Renoir develop the Impressionist technique as they paint together at La Grenouillère on the River Seine.

1874
At their first joint exhibition, Claude Monet's *Impression: Sunrise* is picked on by a hostile critic, who coins the term Impressionism.

1878
Renoir has great success at the salon with his *Madame Charpentier and Daughter*, marking gathering recognition for the Impressionists.

1886
The last of the eight Impressionist exhibitions in Paris is held.

1894
Claude Debussy writes the Impressionistic opera *Pelléas et Mélisande.*

1926
Monet, the last survivor of the great Impressionists, dies aged 86.

SEE ALSO

The birth of photography ◄
Post-Impressionism ►
Modernism ►

POST-IMPRESSIONISM
Beyond representative art

By the time of the eighth and last Impressionist exhibition in 1886, even the key artists in the movement had begun to feel that Impressionism had its limitations. Nonetheless, Impressionism had had an immense impact, both in terms of its techniques and in the way that it had emancipated art: because its skills did not require technical polish, the way was open to artists without formal training. And the public was better prepared to see the merits of new forms of expression.

Subsequent developments were diverse, but most of them can be seen in the light of Impressionism, or as a reaction to it, so they are grouped together under the heading post-Impressionism. Many of the new strands in art were already evolving during the 1860s alongside Impressionism, but their impact was not felt until after the great decade of Impressionism in the 1870s.

Paul Cézanne (1839–1906), for example, exhibited at the first impressionist exhibition in 1874, but his work soon took a tangential path. He worked steadily and virtually alone at a revised way of seeing the world, breaking down its surfaces into flat areas and looking at how a subject could be reshaped as a frankly two-dimensional image on a canvas. Because of his influence on Cubism and abstract painting, he has been referred to as "the father of modern art."

The late 19th century was an age of -isms, many of them now rarely used: neoimpressionism, cloisonnism, synthetism, luminism. This was because a wide variety of talented artists – predominantly French – were looking for the successor to Impressionism. Toward the end of the century, a revival of interest in the world of imagination was largely inspired by French poets such as Paul Verlaine (1844–96) and Arthur Rimbaud (1854–91), working in the wake of their countryman Charles Baudelaire (1821–67). It was romanticism with a new face, and a new name: Symbolism.

VERLAINE AND RIMBAUD

"The poet makes himself a visionary through a long, immense, and reasoned derangement of all the senses, all forms of love, of suffering, of madness; he seeks himself, he exhausts all poisons in himself to keep only the quintessences . . . the poet is the true Stealer of Fire," wrote Arthur Rimbaud. Paul Verlaine and Rimbaud together carried out this strategy.

Rimbaud wrote some of his best work at the age of 15. Aged 17, he went to Paris to seek out Verlaine, who had already acquired a reputation as a poet. Verlaine, a married man, fell under Rimbaud's spell and eloped with him to London and then to Brussels, where they dabbled in drugs, debauchery, and sensory exhaustion in pursuit of visionary wisdom. Their relationship ended with Verlaine shooting Rimbaud in the wrist in a Brussels street – for which Verlaine spent two years in prison. After this, Verlaine went through a period of repentance, during which he wrote some of his best poetry. For his part, Rimbaud gave up writing to begin a new life as a trader in East Africa. He left behind a large body of work, almost all written before he was 20.

VAN GOGH AND GAUGUIN

SIMPLE LIFE Vincent van Gogh lived in this little room in Arles after moving there in order to set up a colony of artists. In addition to painting the surrounding countryside of Provence, van Gogh used the simple everyday objects where he lived as motifs.

Two of the most influential post-Impressionist painters were virtually self-taught. The Dutch painter Vincent van Gogh (1853–90) tried his hand as an art dealer in London and a missionary among Belgian miners before devoting his life to art. Encouraged by his brother Theo, an art dealer with contacts among the Impressionists and the avant-garde, van Gogh developed a highly personalized style using thick layers of paint.

In 1888 van Gogh settled in Arles, where Paul Gauguin (1848–1903) came to stay with him. Gauguin left after a violent dispute, following which van Gogh cut off part of his own ear. After a spell in an asylum, van Gogh's painting became more frenetic, revealing a close identification with the turbulent forces of nature. Ill, impoverished, and haunted by

madness, van Gogh shot himself in 1890, aged 37. He had sold just one painting in his life. Soon after his death, however, his work became widely known and admired, and van Gogh came to represent the archetype of the misunderstood artist driven by his art to the limits of sanity. His work became a key influence on the expressionist movement in the early 20th century.

Gauguin was French but raised in Peru. He was a stockbroker until 1883, when he abandoned both job and family to paint. A major influence in his early development was the painter Emile Bernard (1868–1941), whom he met in Brittany. Bernard is credited with developing the technique of cloisonnism, in which images are broken up into areas of color surrounded by bold outlines, rather like stained glass.

Gauguin painted from memory, and his work became increasingly stylized and highly colored, with symbolic undertones. These were combined with sensual exoticism in the last decade of his life, most of which was spent in Tahiti and other islands of the South Pacific. Although championed by the symbolists, he died in poverty in the Marquesas Islands.

SLOW MOTION The sequential photographs of Eadweard Muybridge (1830–1904) showed how animals and humans really moved for the first time. They were hugely influential on artists, notably Edgar Degas (1834–1917), who used them for his racetrack paintings.

THE IMPACT OF PHOTOGRAPHY

"Photography is a marvelous discovery," wrote the photographic pioneer Nadar (Gaspard-Felix Tournachon; 1820–1910), "a science that has attracted the greatest intellects, an art that excites the most astute minds – and one that can be practiced by an imbecile." By the 1860s, photography had come into its own. Inexpensive portrait photographs touched the lives of virtually everyone; cheap views of landscapes were sold as souvenirs – the forerunners of picture postcards.

War photography began with Roger Fenton (1819–69) in Crimea (1853–56), to be followed by harrowing scenes of the American Civil War (1861–65) by Matthew Brady (1823–96) and his team. These brought home the brutal realities of war – or at least its aftermath, for early photographic technology required long exposures.

Photographic equipment remained cumbersome until the development of celluloid film and the first Kodak box camera by George Eastman (1854–1932) in 1888.

SEE ALSO

Impressionism · · · · · · · · · · · · · ◄
New Art · · · · · · · · · · · · · · ►
Modernism · · · · · · · · · · · · · ►

RODIN

When Auguste Rodin (1840–1917) exhibited a statue of a male nude entitled *The Age of Bronze* at the 1877 Paris Salon, critics accused him of cheating by making a cast of a living model. Rodin's sculptures were unprecedentedly realistic and had a naturalistic look rarely seen in sculpture since classical times. Singlehandedly, he blew fresh life into sculpture in France, which had become mired in a trend toward sycophantic historical public sculpture.

Although largely sponsored by the state, Rodin was always controversial. The marble statue called *The Kiss* (1886) shows a couple kissing deeply: it is brazenly sexual and at once classical and totally modern. But Rodin was not simply realistic: his sculptures have a graceful poetry and a rugged finish. His habit of leaving part of a sculpture unfinished, in the manner of Michelangelo, also gives it the freshness of work-in-progress. These deft touches help to impart a sense of emotion and drama, as in *The Burghers of Calais* (1894), a group portrait of the six citizens who volunteered to be hostages to Edward III of England in 1347 in order to stop the siege of the city.

Rodin's masterpiece was to be a pair of bronze doors called *The Gates of Hell* (1880–1917), commissioned for the Musée des Arts Décoratifs in Paris. An ambitious project incorporating 186 figures, it was never completed, but one of his best-known sculptures, *The Thinker* (1879–1900), emerged from it.

THE KISS The naturalness of its execution and the urgency of its subject make this one of Rodin's most memorable works.

SYMBOLISM

THE SPHINX'S KISS Fernand Khnopff's *Caresses* (1896) mixes sensuality and myth, exploring the same areas of the human psyche that Sigmund Freud (1856–1939) in Vienna was investigating at the same period.

Symbolism provided the dominant flavor for the avant-garde during the final two decades of the 19th century. It covers an immensely varied body of output. The common thread was a reaction against realism: as in the Romantic era, the world of the imagination returned to center stage – and the way to express this was not direct portrayal but evocation.

The movement was led by poets, and in 1886 Jean Moréas (1856–1910) produced a manifesto called *Le Symbolisme*. Stéphane Mallarmé (1842–98), one of the leading proponents of Symbolism, declared that the aim of the poet was "to paint not the thing, but the effect it produces" – which could apply equally to the work of like-minded painters and composers. The music of Claude Debussy (1862–1916) and the poetry of Charles Baudelaire (1821–67), Paul Verlaine (1844–96), and Arthur Rimbaud (1854–91) helped set the mood, and the effect produced ranged from gentle evocation of mood to powerful images of religious mysticism, sensuality, and eroticism.

The Symbolist painters drew on a vast variety of techniques, old and new. Paul Gauguin's (1848–1903) art evolved out of the stylized technique called cloisonnism, while Odilon Redon (1840–1916) painted dreamy images in watery, softly colored tones. Gustave Moreau (1826–98), by contrast, had a much more classical approach, painting biblical and antique scenes set in misty Byzantine palaces, rendered with a jewel-like combination of academic precision and suggestion. Pierre Puvis de Chavannes (1824–98) invented scenes from the classical world in a naive style, setting a dreamlike mood by using bleached colors; Jean Delville (1867–1953) painted polished and highly colored images of writhing bodies succumbing to beauteous demons. In his calm, matter-of-fact depiction of the bizarre, Fernand Khnopff (1858–1921) suggested a fevered inner world of suppressed sexual tension.

Symbolism ended up being more a mood than a movement, with contributions from hundreds of highly individualistic minds. It survived as a current of art until about 1910.

THE NABIS

In 1888, a young member of Paul Gauguin's short-lived Synthetist movement called Paul Sérusier (1865–1927) painted *Landscape: The Bois d'Amour*, which was all but abstract. The painting fascinated a group of artists who saw it as a kind of portent for art of the future, and they renamed it *The Talisman*. This encouraged Sérusier to form a secret society of like-minded painters, which he named the Nabis, meaning "prophet" in Hebrew. They included Maurice Denis (1870–1943), a leading light in the Symbolist movement; Pierre Bonnard (1867–1947); and Edouard Vuillard (1868–1940).

Their common agenda was to explore how three-dimensional reality could be interpreted on a flat surface, in the manner of Cézanne. As Denis put it: "A picture – before being a horse, a nude, or an anecdotal subject – is essentially a flat surface covered with colors arranged in a certain order." This concept prefigured much of early 20th-century art. The work of Sérusier and Denis had a religious and mystical quality. Bonnard and Vuillard were more concerned with patterning and painterliness; they adopted a distinctive post-Impressionist style. The Nabis exhibited together during the 1890s, but the group dispersed after 1900.

ORDERED CHAOS Edouard Vuillard's *In the Room* (1904) shows how a riot of pattern and color making up a cozy interior can be arranged into a harmonious two-dimensional design.

POINTILLISM

MODERN TIMES Georges Seurat was fascinated by contemporary life – especially the leisure activities of the bourgeoisie. In *La Grande Jatte* (1884–86), people enjoy a Sunday afternoon by the River Seine.

To imitate the effect of the way that the eye perceives light, the Impressionists devised a technique using dots of bright color. During the 1880s, a French painter called Georges Seurat (1859–91) promoted the view that this dotted technique had a scientific base, and that the Impressionists had not gone far enough. By pushing the technique to its logical conclusion in the studio, he believed, Impressionism could better imitate light and, furthermore, acquire the monumental qualities of classical art.

Using color theories of the chemist Eugène Chevreul (1786–1889) and others, Seurat devised a technique of painting using only the pure colors of the spectrum arranged in thousands of tiny dots, which become mixed by the eye when viewed from a distance.

TIMELINE

1883–84
Georges Seurat paints *Bathers, Asnières*, the first of his great pointillist paintings.

1884
Paul Verlaine publishes his book of essays *Les poètes maudits* (The Accursed Poets), associating poetic genius with doom.

1886
The last Impressionist exhibition takes place in Paris. Jean Moréas publishes *Le Symbolisme*.

1888
Paul Gauguin meets Emile Bernard in Brittany and adopts the cloisonnist technique. Later that year he visits Vincent van Gogh at Arles.

1889
Paul Sérusier forms the Nabis with Maurice Denis, Edouard Vuillard, Pierre Bonnard, and others.

1890
Vincent van Gogh commits suicide at Auvers-sur-l'Oise, near Paris. Henri de Toulouse-Lautrec scores an overnight success with his *Moulin Rouge* poster.

1891
Paul Gauguin goes to Tahiti.

1900
Maurice Denis paints *Homage to Cézanne*, acknowledging the debt of the Nabis to Cézanne.

1903
Gauguin dies in the Marquesas Islands in the South Pacific.

NEW ART
Decadence and eroticism

The arrival of the 20th century produced feverish activity in the arts on both sides of the watershed year of 1900 as people looked for new ways to express modernity. During the 1890s, people could look back on a century of extraordinary technological change. They now lived in a world of international telephone links, electric lighting, automobiles, portable cameras, and even moving films. In London the world's first electric underground rail system was under construction. In Paris the plans devised by Baron Georges Haussmann (1809–91) and begun in the 1880s had radically modernized the city. Meanwhile in Brussels – a great center for the avant-garde since the 1880s – the large, rapidly expanding middle class was seeking a new look for architecture, free of the endlessly recycled modes of the past. They found their answer in Art Nouveau.

Art Nouveau dovetailed neatly with symbolism, but in both lay traces of decadence and the luxuriously morbid frame of mind identified as *fin de siècle* (end of century). Beyond 1900 lay a new order: on the one hand, bright and breezy, materialistic and optimistic, the *Belle Epoque* of the Edwardian era; on the other, strident and challenging. This was the era of art manifestos and secession, brashly proclaiming new visions for art and the world. Fauvism, Cubism, Expressionism, and Futurism crowded in one upon the other, shunted along by a succession of mold-breaking concepts and inventions: the psychoanalysis of Sigmund Freud (1856–1939); the theory of relativity (1905) of Albert Einstein (1879–1955); the birth of powered flight (1903).

But as the years passed, the optimism of the turn of the century faded in an increasingly uneasy political atmosphere of imploding empires, colonial jostling, burgeoning nationalism, and revolution. The writing was on the wall, but when World War I came, nobody predicted that it would shake European civilization to its very foundations.

"FIN DE SIÈCLE"

Symbolism and Art Nouveau can be seen as the tail end of the Romantic movement, which had meandered through the whole of the 19th century. Romanticism had always had its darker side: a morbid interest in decay and death, the occult and supernatural.

In the late 19th century, this tradition was reawakened, influenced by the French poets Charles Baudelaire (1821–67), Arthur Rimbaud (1854–91), and Paul Verlaine (1844–96), and fostered by the Symbolists. The novelist Joris Karl Huysmans (1848–1907) wrote the great hymn to this mood, *A Rebours* (Against Nature, 1884), the story of a recluse, who luxuriates in rarefied art, worships the artificial, and yearns for new sensations and perverse pleasures.

In England the Aesthetic Movement developed in the 1870s, promoting the idea of "art for art's sake" – art without meaning beyond its own beauty. Among its champions were the painter James McNeill Whistler (1834–1903) and writer Oscar Wilde (1854–1900). Wilde's trial and conviction for homosexuality in 1895 seemed to some to confirm a descent into moral turpitude.

TRAGIC LOVE *Tristan and Isolde*, a Celtic myth about an unstoppable passion that ends in death, was perfect material for the fashion for decadence epitomized by the illustrations of Aubrey Beardsley (1872–98).

HOW SIR TRISTRAM DRANK OF THE LOVE DRINK

ART NOUVEAU

In 1896 a shop opened in Paris called La Maison de l'Art Nouveau, stocking a variety of new painting and design products in the current fashionable style. The term "Art Nouveau" had been used by the Belgian designer Henri van de Velde (1863–1957) in 1894, but now it stuck – in English and French at least. In German and Dutch it was called *Jugendstil*, after a magazine called *Jugend*. In Italy it was known as *Stile Liberty*, after Liberty's of London (founded in 1874), one of the main outlets and patrons of the style. But all these names described the same phenomenon: a new style in the decorative arts and architecture incorporating motifs of organic inspiration – peacocks, lilies, flowing hair – with sinuous, interlacing lines. By the time of the Paris Exhibition of 1900, Art Nouveau was the height of fashion.

Early practitioners such as Victor Horta (1861–1947) had referred to Art Nouveau as *Style Anglais*, acknowledging their debt to William Morris and the Arts and Crafts movement. Further inspiration came from Japanese design, traditional Celtic interlacing patterns, and the sensuous asymmetry of 18th-century rococo. In 1892–93, Horta designed the very first Art Nouveau building, the Hôtel Tassel in Brussels. Horta was an *ensemblier*: he designed everything in this private mansion, including furniture, down to the coat hooks and door handles. His work was cool, cerebral, and stylish. Some architects and designers, however, took Art Nouveau to the limits of extravagance, piling on organic and zoomorphic forms, as seen for example in the Paris metro stations (from 1900) of Hector Guimard (1867–1942). Hostile critics condemned the excesses of the style as a disease.

Art Nouveau at its best maintains a delicate balance between elegance and excess, a duality exploited in the jewelry of René Lalique (1860–1945), in which flowing organic forms are wittily set against erotic or brutal motifs, such as outspread claws. In the United States, Art Nouveau's greatest champion was Louis Tiffany (1848–1933), famous in particular for his lamps of iridescent Favrile glass.

Art Nouveau also had a more restrained, rectilinear mood exemplified by the Scottish designer Charles Rennie Mackintosh (1868–1928). His work became a major influence on the Modernist movement.

FLOWING ELEGANCE Many of Art Nouveau's most celebrated products, such as the glassware of Emile Gallé (1846–1904) and the furniture of Louis Majorelle (1859–1926), came from specialist craft workshops.

THE VIENNA SECESSION

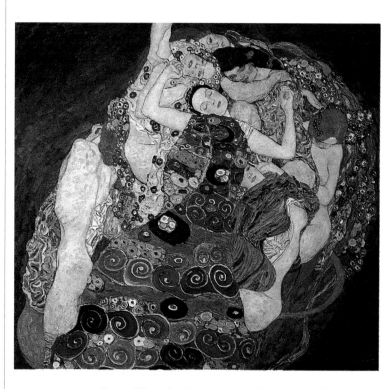

WANTON WOMEN Gustav Klimt, the Austrian artist who was one of the leading members of the Vienna Secession, injected a barely suppressed eroticism into his paintings – like this one, *The Girls*, painted in 1912–13.

A number of "secessions" took place in Europe around the turn of the century, as groups of radical artists and designers proclaimed their departure from the mainstream. The Vienna Secession is the best known, mainly because of its triumvirate of individualistic and talented painters. Gustav Klimt (1862–1918) created murals and paintings that combined original composition with a mosaiclike decorative quality. His disciple Egon Schiele (1890–1918) turned his gifts to powerful and disturbingly cruel drawings of nudes. Schiele and the third major artist associated with the group, Oscar Kokoschka (1886–1980), became important figures in the Expressionist movement.

The Vienna Secession was not just a painters' movement; it also embraced architecture and interior design. In 1898, Joseph Olbrich (1867–1908) built a remarkable exhibition hall for the Secession, a cubelike building with corner towers surmounted by an ironwork dome. The Palais Stoclet (1905–11) in Brussels by Josef Hoffmann (1870–1956) is even more uncompromising – a medley of strident rectangular forms. The work of Charles Rennie Mackintosh was a major influence, especially after he exhibited at the Vienna Secession Exhibition in 1900. The architecture of the Vienna Secession was a vital link in the chain connecting Art Nouveau to modernist architecture that emerged after World War I.

SEE ALSO

Romanticism ···············
Arts and Crafts ············
Modernism ················

FAUVISM

HISTORY MAKERS: *Henri Matisse (1869–1954), Maurice de Vlaminck (1876–1958), André Derain (1880–1954)*

SEE ALSO: *Impressionism, German Expressionism*

In 1905, at the avant-garde Salon d'Automne in Paris, the critic Louis Vauxcelles saw a sculpture surrounded by wildly colorful paintings and declared: "Tiens! Un Donatello parmi des fauves!" ("Look! A Donatello among wild beasts!"). The creators of the paintings rather liked the comparison to wild beasts, and the name stuck – Fauvism became their label.

The story goes back to 1901, when Henri Matisse, a gifted artist in post-Impressionist styles, met two younger painters, André Derain and Maurice de Vlaminck. Over the next five years, they explored new ways of painting, using expressive brushwork and increasingly non-naturalistic color.

The Fauves had a powerful influence on Expressionism, but their work contained little of its emotional

WILD STYLE At the height of his Fauve period, André Derain painted *The Pool of London* in 1906. Later in life, he was one of many leading contemporary artists to design scenery and costumes for the French-based Ballets Russes.

vehemence. Matisse himself was interested in reproducing the stately mood of classical art. His *The Joy of Life* (1906) had a pastoral beauty, but its vivid pinks, yellows, and oranges and simplified drawing added up to something shockingly new, and the painting confirmed Matisse as a leader of the avant-garde. However, Matisse soon went on to explore new areas, and the movement had effectively disintegrated by 1908.

CUBISM

HISTORY MAKERS: *Pablo Picasso (1881–1973), Georges Braque (1882–1963)*

SEE ALSO: *Modernism, Abstract art & minimalism*

Spanish artist Pablo Picasso, who settled in Paris in 1901, had already enjoyed some success with his highly distinctive Blue and Rose Period paintings when in 1907 he painted a large, radically new canvas called *Les Demoiselles d'Avignon*.

It marked the beginning of a new direction, in which Picasso attempted to reassess visual reality. He swept aside traditional rules of perspective to show different views of a subject simultaneously, fracturing reality into

THOUGHT OUT Picasso's *Les Demoiselles d'Avignon* has been called the first modernist painting. His approach was analytical: "I paint objects as I think of them, not as I see them."

sets of interconnected planes. He collaborated with a like-minded French painter, Georges Braque, and they exhibited together in 1908 at the Salon d'Automne. Louis Vauxcelles once again produced a label for the style: Cubism.

Picasso and Braque initially applied their cubist technique to nudes, still lifes, and portraits, using primarily somber colors. Later they were more playful, using brighter colors, collages, and even "found objects."

THE BALLETS RUSSES

HISTORY MAKERS: *Sergei Diaghilev (1872–1929), Igor Stravinsky (1882–1971), Anna Pavlova (1885–1931), Vaslav Nijinsky (1890–1950)*

SEE ALSO: *New Art, Modernism*

The new currents in art, dance, theater, design, and music came together in Paris in 1909 when the Russian impresario Sergei Diaghilev launched his Ballets Russes. Diaghilev's company brought a new style of ballet to the stage.

Diaghilev's team included many of the great names of 20th-century ballet, such as Michel Fokine (1880–1942), Anna Pavlova, and Vaslav Nijinsky. He

commissioned music from leading avant-garde composers, such as Erik Satie (1866–1925), Maurice Ravel (1875–1937), and Igor Stravinsky, creator of the ballets *L'Oiseau du Feu* (The Firebird, 1910) and *Le Sacré du Printemps* (The Rite of Spring, 1913).

The success of the Ballets Russes depended upon lavish productions – and on dynamic dancing that overturned many of the traditions of classical ballet. Their productions were often controversial, with several opening nights ending in uproar. The company disbanded after Diaghilev's death in 1929, and many of its leading talents went to work in the United States.

ALL-STAR PRODUCTION Nijinsky choreographed and also danced in the Ballets Russes' *L'Après-midi d'un faune* (Afternoon of a Faun) in 1912. Music was by Claude Debussy (1862–1918) and design by the Russian Leon Bakst (1866–1924).

GERMAN EXPRESSIONISM

HISTORY MAKERS: *Vasily Kandinsky (1866–1944), Emil Nolde (1867–1956), Paul Klee (1879–1940), Franz Marc (1880–1916), Ernst Kirchner (1888–1938)*

SEE ALSO: *Modernism, Fauvism*

While the Fauves were painting with lavish color in France, a similar movement was developing in Germany.

ANIMAL MAGIC Franz Marc, co-founder of *der Blaue Reiter* with Vassily Kandinsky, believed that painting could reveal the spiritual reality of nature. He painted *The Little Yellow Horses* in 1912. He was killed at Verdun in World War I.

Die Brücke (The Bridge) was a Dresden-based group founded by Ernst Ludwig Kirchner and Karl Schmidt-Rottluff (1884–1976) in 1905, and later joined by Emil Nolde (real name, Hansen). Its members used physical distortion and raw color; emotional stress was one of their themes.

In 1911 a second group of Expressionists formed *der Blaue Reiter* (The Blue Rider) in Munich. Their approach was more diverse and lyrical. They showed a particular interest in naive, folk, and children's art, an influence seen especially in the delicate images of the Swiss-born painter Paul Klee. Russian-born Vasily Kandinsky made an important step toward abstract art with a series of non-representative canvases called *Improvisation* (1911–13).

Expressionism had a parallel in the theater – a revolt against realism which produced highly charged, distorted work. This trend came to maturity with such works as the *Gas* trilogy (1917–20) by the German Georg Kaiser (1878–1945).

FUTURISM

HISTORY MAKERS: *Filippo Tommaso Marinetti (1876–1944)*

SEE ALSO: *Totalitarianism, Modernism*

The Futurist Manifesto was published by the Italian poet Filippo Tommaso Marinetti in Paris in 1909. "A screaming automobile that seems to run like a machine-gun," he declared, "is more beautiful than the *Victory of Samothrace* [a Greek classical sculpture in the Louvre]." Futurists adored the modern age and yearned for a brilliant future of machinery, dynamism, and speed. They saw that the world was set on a collision course to war and welcomed the prospect of a cataclysmic clash capable of blasting away the cobwebs of the past.

The movement's legacy comes from its painters, who attempted to represent movement and dynamism using techniques adapted from Cubism and Symbolism. The Italians Giacomo Balla (1871–1958) and Umberto Boccioni (1882–1916) were leading figures.

Futurism came to an end during World War I, but it was later taken up by the Italian fascists. Its revolutionary zest, and its expression of a world view beyond art, had a major impact in its day.

MODERNISM
Out with the old, in with the new

By 1918, all the fervor and bluster of the prewar arts scene seemed like a distant bubble. The world had changed: the European economy was in tatters, and the old patrician regimes – the source of great patronage of the arts in the past – had been torn apart by the war or, in the case of Russia, by revolution. The horrors of the war had provoked a disgust for much of the old cultural baggage of the past, which was held partly responsible for the conflict.

In the immediate aftermath of the war, there were three main reactions. One was a sense of deep anger and disillusionment, expressed in the arts by a general taste for iconoclasm; this had built up a head of steam over the preceding decades, but boiled over after 1918. The nihilistic Dada movement was popular for a while before its anarchic tenets were formalized in Surrealism, which rejected the traditions of conscious perception in favor of the workings of the unconscious mind.

The second response was a sense of relief and joy, and a desire to live life to the full after the war's dramatic lesson in mortality. This mood produced Art Deco, the racy style of the happy-go-lucky Jazz Age, a fitting backdrop for bare-limbed flappers of the Roaring Twenties in their skimpy Chanel-inspired dresses and pearls, and men in snappy lounge suits – drinking cocktails, going to the movies, driving in their cars, and dancing the Charleston.

The third reaction was a more focused, constructive attitude. Before the war various artists, designers, and architects had begun to grapple with the challenge of producing work that could express – or even precipitate – a new world order. Artists with this in mind now headed boldly down the path to geometrical abstraction. Designers and architects followed a parallel course toward a cleaner, less cluttered style. The solutions that they arrived at have been loosely labeled Modernist – and so profound was their influence in the fields of architecture and design that the term retains its currency at the end of the century.

THE BAUHAUS

Out of the ashes of postwar Germany rose the most dynamic and influential of all 20th-century art schools. The Bauhaus was founded in 1919 by the avant-garde architect Walter Gropius (1883–1969), who remained its first director until 1928. Gropius wanted to show how art, design, technology, and architecture could be brought together under one roof and encouraged to crossfertilize. The products were to be modern, beautiful, and accessible to the masses.

This utopian agenda owed much to the legacy of the Arts and Crafts movement, but instead of looking back to the past, the Bauhaus was uncompromisingly modern. Design had to correspond to function.

Gropius gathered around him a formidable team of some of the brightest designers and artists of the day. These included the artists Vasily Kandinsky (1866–1944) and Paul Klee (1879–1940), both of whom had been associated with the German Expressionist group *der Blaue Reiter* before the war. The Hungarian painter, sculptor, and designer László Moholy-Nagy (1895–1946) was put in charge of the metal workshop. Staff included the architect Ludwig Mies van der Rohe (1886–1969), who took over directorship of the Bauhaus in 1930, and the designer Marcel Breuer (1902–81), who produced the first tubular steel chair.

The Bauhaus was created out of two existing schools (for fine art and for arts and crafts) in Weimar, but in 1926 it moved to a purpose-built home in Dessau. These buildings, designed by Gropius, were a showpiece of Bauhaus thinking. They were at the forefront of building technology, with glass curtain walls suspended from a steel frame, creating well-lit and functional interior spaces.

MASS APPEAL The Bauhaus aimed to make good design available to ordinary people, so all its products were made with mass production in mind.

CRAFT MEETS ART Strong colors and bold abstract shapes are hallmarks of Bauhaus style.

Bauhaus products were not widely appreciated by the German public, who preferred the comfort of familiar styles. For the Nazis, the modernist image and socialist politics of the Bauhaus were anathema, and they closed down the school within months of coming to power in 1933. The leading lights of the Bauhaus then scattered, and many ended up in the United States.

The U.S. already had its own trends in modern architecture and design. With the added impetus of Gropius, Mies van der Rohe, and Moholy-Nagy, it was set to become the world leader in architecture and design after World War II.

DADA

During World War I a lively arts scene developed in the Swiss city of Zürich, home to a number of refugee artists, musicians, writers, and revolutionaries. Out of a mood of disillusionment with politics and the culture of the establishment emerged an artistic movement that set about challenging and mocking everything – from bourgeois comforts and pretensions to the basic concepts of European art. It was nihilistic and anarchic, and thrived on producing baffling events, products, and literature which – their progenitors liked to claim – had no meaning or value whatsoever. The movement was given the name Dada, a child's word for a hobbyhorse, chosen at random from a dictionary.

At the Cabaret Voltaire in Zürich in 1916, Dada emerged as a mainly literary concept under its founder, the German Hugo Ball (1886–1927). He produced staged "manifestations," poetry made up of gibberish, and music consisting of rude noises and squawks. The Alsatian artist and writer Jean Arp (1888–1966) was also part of this group; he created collages made of haphazardly dropped pieces of colored paper.

The idea and mood of the Dadaists caught on, and after the war Dada groups were set up in other cities, such as Cologne, Paris, Barcelona, New York, and Berlin. But few of its products survive; its main spokesman after 1918, the Romanian poet Tristan Tzara (1886–1963), declared it to be more a state of mind. But its effect was profound, causing writers, artists, and painters to reassess the traditions upon which all their esthetic judgments were founded and to redefine art in general.

ANTI-ART One of the most influential Dadaists was the French artist Marcel Duchamp (1887–1968) whose series of "readymades" – ordinary industrial products exhibited as art – included *Bicycle Wheel* (1913). A readymade was art simply because the artist chose it, called it art, and displayed it in a gallery. Duchamp's gesture has had a profound impact on much of the art of the 20th century.

TIMELINE

1913
French writer Marcel Proust publishes the first volume of his influential novel *A la recherche du temps perdu* (Remembrance of Things Past).

1917
The magazine *De Stijl* is first published, in Leiden, the Netherlands.

1916
Dada begins at the Cabaret Voltaire, Zürich.

1922
James Joyce's *Ulysses* is published in France and promptly banned as obscene in the U.S. and England.

1924
André Breton publishes the First Surrealist Manifesto.

1925
The Exposition Internationale des Arts Décoratifs et Industriels Modernes takes place in Paris, eventually giving rise to the term Art Deco.

1927
The *Jazz Singer* is launched as the first "talkie," ending the era of silent films.

1933
The Bauhaus is closed by the Nazis; its staff disperses abroad.

SEE ALSO

Poststructuralism . . . . ◀
Arts and Crafts . . . . ◀
New Romantics . . . . ▶

AMERICAN ARCHITECTURE

Notwithstanding the powerful forces of innovation in Europe, some of the most original and inventive architecture in the early part of the 20th century came from the United States. Indeed, many of the Bauhaus precepts had been foreshadowed in the U.S. before World War I. The invention of the elevator (1857) had permitted the building of the first skyscraper in New York in the 1870s; thereafter, skyscraper design – assisted by steel and concrete building techniques – became the focus of some of the most daring building of the time. One of the leading figures in this development was Louis Sullivan (1856–1924): by the 1890s he had begun to shake off the legacy of historical influences in architecture and was moving toward Modernism. Europe, however, had to wait until 1928 for its first skyscraper, the Torengebouw in Antwerp.

Frank Lloyd Wright (1867–1959), one of the most original and influential architects of the 20th century, worked in Sullivan's Chicago office in the 1890s. Inspired by Sullivan's dictum "form follows function" and by Japanese design, he developed a style of private dwelling which he called a prairie house. This involved low, sleek profiles of intersecting rectangles and horizontal lines, balconies and cantilevered roofs, asymmetrical ground plans, and high-quality craftsmanship.

FATHER OF THE FORM Frank Lloyd Wright shows his apprentices the blueprint of a new design. Wright called his style of architecture organic Modernism. He believed buildings should reflect the spirit of place in their design and materials.

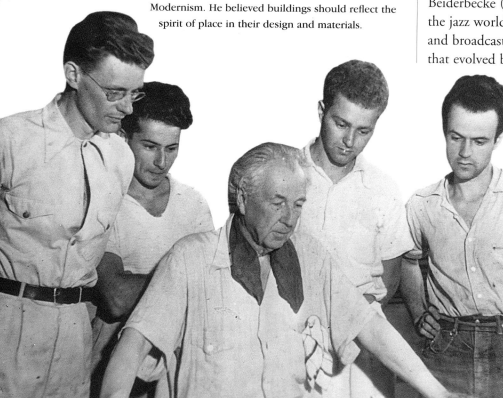

JAZZ

Jazz evolved out of the spirituals sung by black slaves on the plantations of the Southern states, which in turn were influenced by a blend of African and European folk music. Jazz instruments were those of the military band – trumpet, clarinet, trombone, drums – plus piano, banjo, and double bass. The essential features were a syncopated rhythm and improvisation by band members. The music's self-expression and spontaneity seemed so exactly to reflect the decade's mood that the 1920s were dubbed the Jazz Age.

The original home of jazz was New Orleans, which developed its distinctive Dixieland style at the turn of the century, exemplified by the ragtime piano compositions of Scott Joplin (1868–1917). By the 1920s, jazz had moved north to Chicago, where it was popularized by artists such as Louis Armstrong (c.1898–1971) and Bix Beiderbecke (1903–31). By the end of the decade, the center of the jazz world was New York, where the music was recorded and broadcast on radio. Swing developed in the 1930s and from that evolved big band jazz with orchestras of 20–30 players fronted by virtuoso soloists or singers.

Despite the arrival of rock and roll in the 1950s, jazz continued to develop and grow new branches – the daring drug-driven improvisations of "bebop," the sophisticated cool jazz of the 1950s and 1960s, and the feather-light "free jazz" played by the likes of Ornette Coleman (1930–) and John Coltrane (1926–67). It has also been a major influence on 20th-century classical music – notably the work of Maurice Ravel (1875–1937), Igor Stravinsky (1882–1971), Dmitri Shostakovich (1906–75), Béla Bartok (1881–1945), and Aaron Copland (1900–90).

"EMPRESS OF THE BLUES" The emotional power of vocalist Bessie Smith (1894–1937) took the United States by storm in the 1920s. She was the first in a line of jazz divas to make heartbreak her artistic territory.

DE STIJL

In 1922 the Dutch designer and artist Theo van Doesburg (1883–1931) taught at the Bauhaus and had a major impact on its evolution. Van Doesburg was already the founder and main theorist of a radical Dutch group which took on the name of its magazine *De Stijl* (The Style), first published in 1917. The group included the architect-designers Gerrit Rietveld (1888–1964) and J.J.P. Oud (1890–1963). The project of De Stijl was to adapt the ideas of a member of their group, painter Piet Mondrian (1872–1944), to architecture and design.

Mondrian had spent several years in Paris during the Cubist era. During the war years in neutral Holland, he worked to develop the Cubist idea and came to the conclusion that the Cubists had not gone far enough. They had headed down the path of abstraction, but failed to follow it to its logical conclusion. In a series of paintings, Mondrian gradually moved away from representation, and after 1917 abandoned any attempt to represent the visual world. He ended up with compositions of geometric, rectilinear shapes, painted in primary colors and non-colors (black, white, and sometimes gray) – an approach that he termed neoplasticism. Mondrian aimed to encapsulate a sense of universal harmony.

THE WORLD ACCORDING TO MONDRIAN It is almost impossible for the layperson to tell the difference between paintings produced by Mondrian in 1920 and those he did 20 years later. His persistent fascination with the same limited themes led to his eventual estrangement from his colleagues in 1924 when he refused to accept diagonal lines.

ART PHOTOGRAPHY

By the beginning of the 20th century, photography was still held to be inferior to painting. It took the avant-garde artists of the 1920s – notably the Dadaists – to give photography artistic cachet. The Dadaist Man Ray (1890–1976) produced semi-abstract images, manipulated in the darkroom, which he called photograms. The German-born artist John Heartfield (Helmuth Herzfelde, 1891–1968) used collages of cutout photographs – a technique he called photomontage – to create shocking juxtapositions, often bearing political messages.

SOCIAL COMMENT The work of Tina Modotti (1896–1942) combined strong composition with social or political messages. *Once Again* (1929) highlights the situation of Mexican women condemned to an endless cycle of childbearing and rearing.

But another significant development during this era was the growing acceptance that conventional photographic images could hold their own as art – and on their own terms, quite independent of painting. This was largely the result of work in the United States, and of Alfred Stieglitz (1864–1946) in particular. At his 291 Gallery in New York, he exhibited not only contemporary photographs, but also the latest work by European painters such as Picasso and Matisse, and as a result placed photography squarely among the avant-garde. Stieglitz and associates, such as Edward Steichen (1879–1973), Paul Strand (1890–1976), Ansel Adams (1902–84), and Edward Weston (1886–1958), did not attempt to make photography compete with painting. Instead, they demonstrated what it could do simply through craftsmanship and the selection of subject matter. Their landscapes, portraits, and details of nature – of fruit, seashells, gnarled trees – showed how the camera could eloquently transmit the photographer's vision.

ART DECO

TWENTIETH-CENTURY CHIC The flamboyant lines of Art Deco have a modern, abstract edge. This illustration is by the Russian artist Erté (Romain de Tirtoff; 1892–1990), who worked as a designer on many Hollywood films after 1925.

In 1925 a major exhibition took place in Paris entitled the Exposition Internationale des Arts Décoratifs et Industriels Modernes. The art on show exhibited a sleek and robust style – a machine-age, cubist version of 1890s Art Nouveau, in which the wisps and florid curls of the earlier movement had been replaced by chevrons, zigzags, and hard-edged curves. The new look was called the *style moderne* at the time, but much later – in the 1960s – it was renamed Art Deco, after the exhibition that provided its public debut.

To begin with, Art Deco was a luxurious style, adapted by designers such as Jacques Emile Ruhlmann (1879–1933) in France for expensive furniture made of macassar ebony, ivory, lacquer, and sharkskin. The discovery of the ancient Egyptian pharaoh Tutankhamen's tomb in 1922 introduced an exotic note, and the style found its way into the new palaces of the day: the cinemas. Huge 4,000-seaters were built – in Europe and the United States – in a variety of fantasy styles, from straightforward Art Deco to Egyptian, Moorish, and Aztec.

In the United States in the 1930s, the style took on the dynamic look known as streamlining, with aerodynamic curves and closely packed horizontal lines inspired by the design of locomotives. Many new buildings borrowed from the idiom of the great ocean liners, with railings, balconies, curved glass windows, and portholes. Streamlining motifs also found their way onto radios, vacuum cleaners, and refrigerators. But despite its appropriation by mass-market products, Art Deco retained a note of glamor throughout the 1920s and 1930s.

SURREALISM

Surrealism grew out of Dadaism, but was significantly different. Whereas Dadaists attacked established culture in a casual and essentially negative way, Surrealism claimed a coherent world view. Influenced by Sigmund Freud (1856–1939), the Surrealists gave primacy to the unconscious mind. They saw the unconscious, untainted by the legacy of taught culture, as a way of achieving a more truthful sense of reality – a surreality.

The French poet André Breton (1896–1966) published the *First Surrealist Manifesto* in 1924, and initially Surrealism was envisaged primarily as a literary movement. Breton was joined by other poets such as Paul Eluard (1895–1952) and Louis Aragon (1897–1982). They experimented with automatic writing – creating prose and poetry by writing down whatever flowed from the brain when in a receptive state.

Surrealism was also adapted to theater and movies, but it is best known for its effect on painting. At first, many Surrealist artists, notably the Spaniard Joan Miró (1893–1983), painted doodlelike images. Miró evolved a language of organic shapes that have strange, semifamiliar resonances. The most celebrated Surrealist painter is Miró's fellow countryman Salvador Dali (1904–89), creator of hallucinatory images of arid landscapes filled with melting clocks, dead trees, and sagging body parts.

FRUIT OF THE SUBCONSCIOUS In the work of Belgian Surrealist René Magritte (1898–1967), repressed or forgotten images break disturbingly into the everyday world, which is rendered in a precise style like that used by commercial artists in advertising.

A REVOLUTION IN SCULPTURE

FREE FLOW English sculptor Barbara Hepworth (1903–75), creator of this fluid bronze, was at the forefront of 20th-century sculpture's investigation of abstract form. She had a close working friendship with Henry Moore.

In the first two decades of the 20th century, a giant leap occurred in sculpture. Cubism provided the main impetus. During the era of synthetic cubism, Picasso experimented with new three-dimensional ideas, using paper, tin plate, string, and found objects. This gave a new sense of mass to sculpture: the spaces within the structures were exploited and made to bear almost as much meaning as the solid areas.

After 1917 the Russian Vladimir Tatlin (1885–1953) began to create similar assemblages. He saw his work as more than sculpture: it was a fusion of art and architecture expressive of the aspirations of the new revolutionary industrial class of Russia. He called his movement Constructivism.

The American sculptor Alexander Calder (1898–1976), working in Paris, was inspired by Constructivist ideas and the semi-abstract shapes created by Surrealist painters. He developed delicate sculptures, made of sheet-metal components suspended from rods and wires, which moved in a breeze.

The Romanian Constantine Brancusi (1876–1957) worked in Paris after 1904. He initially produced solid carved sculptures, but later created streamlined virtually abstract forms, for instance, *Bird in Space* (15 versions after 1923). The British sculptor Henry Moore (1898–1986) likewise took organic ideas, such as the reclining nude, to the borders of abstraction.

MODERNIST WRITING

The major shift in 20th-century writing has been the devaluing of the objective narrative voice – the basis of 19th-century realists' work – in favor of subjective perception. It was the most significant common thread in the body of experimental writing that emerged after World War I and which has been gathered under the heading "Modernism."

The pattern for new writers was set by the Frenchman Marcel Proust (1871–1922), in whose multivolume *A la recherche du temps perdu* (Remembrance of Things Past) the protagonist's perception of reality is filtered through the subjective experience of memory. Two seminal works of modernist writing appeared in 1922, the year Proust completed his work. In *The Waste Land* by the American-British poet T.S. Eliot (1888–1965), a personal crisis is linked to a sense of the decline of European civilization. The poem is deliberately fragmented, its language varying from the elevated to the everyday. In *Ulysses*, the Irish novelist James Joyce (1882–1941) depicted the inner musings and sensations of his characters through a kaleidoscope of the images, impressions, and emotions that temper thought processes.

Joyce's experimental way of rendering thought patterns – "stream of consciousness" – was used widely by subsequent writers, notably the English novelist Virginia Woolf (1882–1941). Her novel *To the Lighthouse* (1927) describes a family vacation on the island of Skye, viewed through the interior reflections of the characters. The American writer William Faulkner (1897–1962) also used the technique to great effect in *The Sound and the Fury* (1929).

The confines of the individual's interior world were hauntingly portrayed by the Czech Franz Kafka (1883–1924). *The Trial* and *The Castle* (written 1911–14, published posthumously) portray interior landscapes in which the protagonists are trapped in bureaucratic labyrinths.

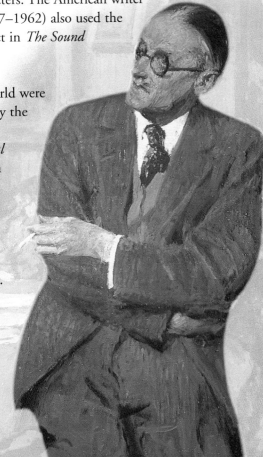

WRITER ABROAD James Joyce wrote *Ulysses* – which recalls his native Dublin in loving detail – in Paris, where it was also published. The novel was banned in England and the U.S. because of its openness about sex.

INTERNATIONAL STYLE

The tenets of the Bauhaus were picked up by numerous architects in Europe and the United States, and evolved into what became known as the International Style following the publication of an architectural book with that title in the U.S. in 1932. The main features were: the absence of ornament; clean, rectilinear shapes; horizontal bands of windows; flat rooflines; asymmetrical elevations and ground plans; open and spacious interiors; and a predilection for white. The overall effect was one of unprecedented lightness and transparency.

The Swiss architect Le Corbusier (Charles Edouard Jeanneret; 1887–1965) was a major innovator. He strove to reinterpret living habits in terms of architecture, on the level of both individual dwellings and whole cities. His trademarks are the use of supporting pillars, flat roofs, and reinforced concrete.

In the U.S. after the late 1930s, Mies van der Rohe and Walter Gropius – working primarily in glass and steel – were given opportunities to realize their Bauhaus theories on a scale that had been denied to them in Europe. By this time, the International Style was being widely adopted by many other practitioners and applied to factories and offices, as well as some private homes. The style was accepted for commercial buildings, where sharp-edged modernity was considered appropriate; with private dwellings it was more controversial, and was frequently condemned as unsightly and pretentious. After World War II, however, the International Style became so familiar that it was long considered the only style of modern architecture – seen particularly in apartment buildings. The pared-down look suited mass production in an era when a large number of new buildings was needed quickly.

THE MOVIES

By the late 1920s, the movies had become a multimillion dollar business. Audiences could be treated to a mixed program of news reel (introduced in 1908), comedy shorts, and full-length features. In around 1912, the film studios had begun to recognize the pulling power of certain actors such as Lillian Gish (1896–1993) and created the "star system."

Close-ups, panning, tracking, and other camera techniques, as well as the varied tricks of editing such as cross-cutting and flashbacks, demonstrated the

THE MAN WHO MADE THE WORLD LAUGH
"Moving pictures need sound as much as Beethoven symphonies need lyrics," said Charlie Chaplin.

capabilities of film to create a language substantially different from that of the theater. This was developed and exploited by the major directing talents of the era, among them the American D.W. Griffith (1875–1948) and the Russian Sergei Eisenstein (1898–1948). At the end of the silent era, the French director Abel Gance (1889–1981) produced one of the most extraordinary and powerful epics in the history of the cinema: his cut of the unfinished *Napoléon* (1927) lasted nine hours.

Movies were also adopted by several art movements, with some notable results. These include the Expressionist film *The Cabinet of Dr. Caligari* (1919) and the Surrealist one *Un Chien Andalou* (1928), by Salvador Dali and his compatriot Luis Buñuel (1900–83).

SPIRIT OF MODERNISM Notre-Dame-du-Haut, Ronchamp, the chapel designed by Le Corbusier in the early 1950s, exhibits the architect's departure from the glass-and-metal regime of International Style toward more sculptural forms.

NEUE SACHLICHKEIT

General disillusionment in Germany after World War I produced a distinctive voice among a small group of artists, who formed a loosely defined movement which, in 1925, was christened Neue Sachlichkeit (New Objectivity). Its main artists were Max Beckmann (1884–1950), Otto Dix (1891–1969), and George Grosz (1893–1959). Through their work, they criticized and satirized bourgeois attitudes, official corruption, establishment values, and urban vice. The political attitudes of these artists guaranteed disapproval by the Nazis, who labeled them degenerate, persecuted Dix, and forced Beckmann and Grosz to flee Germany.

Neue Sachlichkeit is foreshadowed by the brutal, cartoonish realism of Honoré Daumier in the 19th century. The artists' desire to portray the real world, however grotesquely, ran counter to the thrust of much of modernist art, which concentrated on exploring the inner world of the imagination.

THE SEAMY SIDE OF LIFE The color and tawdriness of Berlin nightlife kept the pen and brushes of George Grosz busy throughout his life.

ATONAL MUSIC

BREAKING NEW GROUND Arnold Schoenberg stands over a string quartet as they tackle an atonal piece of music. Alban Berg, composer of the opera *Wozzeck* (1925), sits in the background.

European composers in the early years of the century were wrestling with the direction of classical music in the wake of Richard Wagner (1813–83). Wagner had sown the seeds of future development by his use of chromatic notes. Most classical music of the 19th century had been written around a tonality based on a chosen key (G sharp minor, for example), which consists of its own scale of eight notes. Chromatic notes are dissonant sounds introduced from outside that scale.

The angular appeal of these chromatic notes provided the clue to the way forward for the Austrian composer Arnold Schoenberg (1874–1951). Rejecting tonality, he devised a system of writing that gave equal importance to all 12 notes of the octave (including the sharps and flats), thus freeing music from the constraints of the key. He called this effect pantonality (all tones), but it is generally referred to as atonality. It produced some novel and wildly controversial effects, as seen in his *Three Pieces* (1909) for piano, which established Schoenberg as the *enfant terrible* of modern music. Hostility only encouraged him further. To avoid the anarchy which this direction threatened, however, after 1917 he began to devise a systematic approach called 12-note composition, or serialism: each note was introduced in a chosen order (the note-row, or series), and then had to remain in that order or shape – albeit inverted or transposed – throughout the piece.

He and two pupils in Vienna, Anton von Webern (1883–1945) and Alban Berg (1885–1935), worked together on the system. In 1933 Schoenberg had to flee from the Nazis; he went to the United States, where serialism had a major influence on music of the postwar era.

ABSTRACT ART & MINIMALISM
Hedonism vs. puritanism

After the end of World War II, the so-called free world had a new leader, the United States, and soon the U.S. also became the world's main cultural influence. In part this was due to the economic might of America, enjoying the spoils of its technological and industrial supremacy. To many living in a depressed and threadbare Europe, things American seemed bright and fresh. But it was also due to the fact that so many leaders of European culture had been forced by the Nazis and the war to flee their homelands: Gropius, Mies van der Rohe, Breuer, Moholy-Nagy, Mondrian, Ernst, Dali, Schoenberg – the list is as long as it is impressive. In the U.S. these émigrés found fertile ground in which to further their careers – ground prepared for them by native design talent, notably that of Frank Lloyd Wright, and by an avant-garde that included Duchamp and challenging semi-abstract painters such as Georgia O'Keefe.

The desire for a new kind of art had been brewing in the United States since the 1930s, especially through the work of government-funded projects such as the Federal Art Project, designed to keep several thousand artists off the breadline. Many of them had experimented with the current trends of European art – such as surrealism and De Stijl-influenced abstraction. By the end of the war, they were on the verge of creating two authentically American trends of their own. One was abstract expressionism, the other was minimalism – which in some ways were polar opposites. It was to the U.S., and especially to New York, that the eyes of the avant-garde now turned.

NATURE AND ART Wood and stone work together in *Head* (1960) by the Scottish artist William Turnbull (1922–).

ABSTRACT EXPRESSIONISM

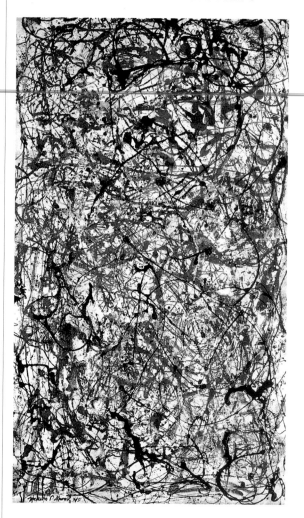

MIND'S EYE *Black and White* (1948) by Jackson Pollock illustrates the process of painting.

The abstract expressionists can be seen as heirs to the legacy of the German expressionists and the surrealists – painters of the subconscious. Jackson Pollock (1912–56) was one of the artists working under the aegis of the Federal Arts Project in New York during the 1930s. Influenced at that time by surrealism, he took an increasing interest in the actual process of painting. Around 1947 he began to abandon representational painting completely: instead he dribbled, splashed, and threw paint at the canvas. In a way, Pollock's work can be seen as the logical fusion of the abstraction of Kandinsky and the "automatic" work of surrealists such as Ernst. What was new was the raw quality of personal expression; the painting was not some preplanned image, but the unmanipulated record of a painting performance. This new form of art was labeled "abstract expressionism," and Pollock's approach to it was called "action painting."

COLOR FIELD

A more meditative strand of abstract expressionism is known as color field. Its leading exponent was the Russian-born American artist Mark Rothko (1906–70). In the early 1950s he began to experiment with rectangular blocks of color, produced on a large scale with a distinctive, painterly style. Despite limiting his paintings to three or four tones, he managed to extract a powerful, luminous quality from the colors. Rothko's work has a haunting sense of monumentality, which he equated with mystical experience.

Fellow American Helen Frankenthaler (1928–) achieved similarly luminous effects by pouring paint onto unsized canvas to create flat areas of staining. Other practitioners developed a more controlled finish – notably Barnett Newman (1905–70), whose canvases were broken up by the precise, vertical stripes that he called "zips."

HARMONY OF HUES The soft, floating quality of Mark Rothko's work is unmistakable. *Untitled* (1969) is one of many works that are simple colored rectangles on a different-color background.

MINIMALIST ART

BRINGING THE OUTDOORS IN Using rocks from the Swiss mountains, in the mid-1970s Richard Long (1945–) created a still space within the gallery.

Contemporaneously, another rather different movement was developing in the U.S., owing its inspiration to the more analytical and clinical legacy of De Stijl, the geometric abstraction of the Russian suprematist Kasimir Malevich (1878–1935), and the tenets of modernist architecture. It has been called minimalism, because its products have been stripped back to the minimum of materials and the minimum of artistic manipulation.

Minimalist art represents a rejection of the highly personalized, emotional indulgence of the abstract expressionists. Its most characteristic exponents produced "sculpture." The forms of the work are usually symmetrical and geometric, or based on mathematically calculated proportions. The American Donald Judd (1928–94) produced work such as *Untitled* (1965), a ramp made of perforated steel; fellow American Carl André (1935–) created his famous *Equivalents* (1966) out of a set of firebricks. Set on the floor – a novel position for sculpture – these works invite contemplation about space and volume; but in the 1960s they were also burningly controversial and posed fundamental questions about the nature of art and creativity.

Minimalism was also expressed in painting, seen for example in the "black paintings" (1959–60) of Frank Stella (1936–), and the so-called hard-edged paintings of Ellsworth Kelly (1923–).

SEE ALSO

German Expressionism ········ ◀
Modernism ················ ◀
New Romantics ············· ▶

Neo-Dada

BACKWARD ICON Jasper Johns's series of American flag paintings, including *Flag on Orange Field* (1957), subverts notions of patriotism.

While the art world argued over the relative merits of abstract expressionism and minimalism, there were artists who took something from both, but were satisfied with neither. After all, both of these trends had defined themselves within somewhat limited parameters. Where was that anarchic, irreverent, and no-holds-barred spirit so successfully tapped by Dada and surrealism?

Robert Rauschenberg (1925–) took a broad view of the visual arts, attempting to "unfocus" the viewer's visual perceptions.

In 1959 he produced his provocative *Monogram*, an assemblage consisting of a stuffed angora goat with a tire around its middle, standing on a collage-style painting. It was baffling, witty, and iconoclastic – a Dada-like gesture. Rauschenberg later went on to produce his "combine paintings," mixing silkscreened readymade photographs of contemporary subjects with abstract painting.

Meanwhile, Jasper Johns (1930–) produced paintings of familiar images – the American flag, targets, maps of the United States – but applied to them the rich textural surface and painterly qualities of abstract expressionism.

As a term, neo-Dada had a short-lived currency: Rauschenberg and Johns had only passing affinities with Dada. But their impact was more durable than the term: despite the claims of the abstract expressionists and minimalists to be the beacons for the future, it was Rauschenberg and Johns who led the way toward the next major artistic movement: Pop Art.

JUNKYARD ELEGANCE Robert Rauschenberg used a mixture of found objects, including old clock faces, paint, and canvas to create *Reservoir* (1961).

Happenings and Performance Art

In the early 1950s, at the influential Black Mountain College in North Carolina, the composer John Cage, the artist Robert Rauschenberg, and others staged performances that were unscripted, unrepeatable, and often impenetrable. It was not theater, cabaret, or dance: it was multimedia performance, transient and ephemeral – yet capable of transmitting notions that could not be conveyed in any other way. As John Cage put it, it was "purposeless purposefulness: it was purposeful in that we knew what we were going to do, but it was purposeless in that we didn't know what was going to happen in the total."

These "happenings" were among the earliest examples of a trend that developed further in the 1960s and was later formalized into "performance art." Performances often took place in non-art environments (such as an industrial site) could last any length of time from seconds to days or months, and did not necessarily require an audience at all.

THE "NOUVEAU ROMAN"

LADY OF LETTERS Marguerite Duras (1914–) experimented with the *nouveau roman* and brought its elliptical style to the cinema with her screenplay for *Hiroshima Mon Amour* (1960).

In the postwar era, writers struggled to find a voice that could carry forward the experimentation of the modernists of the interwar years and also reflect the state of the contemporary world. In France a group of writers evolved what became known as the *nouveau roman* (the new novel). Its main exponents were Nathalie Sarraute (1920–), Alain Robbe-Grillet (1922–), and Michel Butor (1926–).

Guided by existentialism – and notably by its emphasis on the inadequacies of communication – the writers re-examined our perception of the world. They concluded that traditional novel-writing, as devised in the 19th century, rests on artificial premises: plot, character development, logical chronology, the objective author are all contrivances. By contrast, real life is perceived through the window of individuality, with all the distortions and minute but influential impressions that this entails. Sarraute in particular was interested in what she called tropisms: the numerous spontaneous and involuntary responses of people to the stimuli of ordinary surroundings. The *nouveau roman* builds an image of the world by producing a kaleidoscope of impressions – some highly detailed, many seemingly irrelevant. The reader has to figure out what they all add up to.

MINIMALIST MUSIC

A key figure in the American avant-garde was the composer John Cage (1912–92). Formerly a pupil of Schoenberg, during the early 1950s he began to take new leaps into experimental music, producing work, for instance, for "prepared piano" – "prepared" by sticking nails, bolts, and pieces of paper into the strings. He was determined to demonstrate a completely new vision of the nature of sound, and the potential of music to take on board a hugely extended range of sound. He hoped to "unfocus" the listeners, to let them become sensorially more aware, in the way that Zen Buddhists unfocus their minds in meditation to achieve ultimate awareness. His *Imaginary Landscape No. 4* (1954) called for 24 performers to twiddle the knobs of 12 radios for four minutes, producing an arbitrary, yet selective set of noises. More controversial still, his *4'33"* (1952) instructs a performer to open the lid of the piano and then sit in silence for four minutes and 33 seconds, to draw attention to ambient sounds largely emanating from the audience itself.

During the 1960s, two new American composers emerged to combine a classical training with Cage's experimentation, plus the influences of non-Western music, such as Balinese gamelan, Indian sitar, and African drums. Steve Reich (1936–) and Philip Glass (1937–) worked together for a while, producing music noted for its limited ambit, with its repeated phrasing advancing in tiny, almost imperceptible stages. Later the two composers diverged, and their work became ever more complex and polished, and less minimalist.

LESS IS MORE Steve Reich performs his own composition at London's Albert Hall. Drums help to reinforce the repetitive phrasing of minimalist music.

POPULAR CULTURE
Art for the mass market

The influence of American culture in the postwar era was not limited to the fine arts. Indeed, American popular culture – an expression of the United States' economic power, consumerism, and democracy – had greater impact. In the U.S., ordinary people had spending power. An increasingly important group was the young – the "teenagers" – who were affluent enough to attract the attention of advertisers, record producers, and filmmakers. American-style consumerism spread across the Western world. Despite prejudices and fears for their own cultural integrity, European countries were happy enough to buy it in Hollywood films, rock and roll, denim jeans and Coca-Cola. The United States seemed to be the place where things were happening.

By the 1960s, Europe was reawakening and began to contribute its share of innovation. France had developed its own highly influential cinema, dubbed the New Wave. With the Beatles, the Rolling Stones, and other groups, Britain became a key source of "pop music," and London emerged as a major center for the fashion and design of the "Swinging Sixties." But British pop music was heavily influenced by American music, and even the Beatles had to succeed in the U.S. before they could hope to hold the world stage.

The phenomenon of the American consumer culture also had an impact on the art world. Artists began to comment on it, borrow from it and imitate it. Popular culture thus became both "high art" and "low art" at the same time.

THE KING With the voice of an angel and the looks of a Greek god, Elvis Presley's hip-swinging entrance onto the music scene in 1953 set teenage hearts aflutter across the United States. His music brought together gospel, country and western, and rhythm and blues.

ROCK AND ROLL

The term rock and roll was adopted in about 1953. This was a marketing ploy to distinguish the music from rhythm and blues – a style that was the preserve of black artists – and make it more palatable to white audiences – a paradox, since rock and roll was black slang for sexual intercourse. Rock and roll caught on, propelled forward by a burgeoning record industry, jukeboxes, and the by then ubiquitous radio. It has been a major influence in the evolution of popular music in subsequent decades, spawning the broader-based electronic music called simply rock. That in turn divided into various strands such as jazzlike progressive rock and the more melodic folk rock.

HOLLYWOOD AND THE NEW WAVE

DIRECTOR'S CUT The French New Wave idea of the director as a film's *auteur*, or author, was in stark contrast to the director's role in the Hollywood studio system. Truffaut's *Jules et Jim*, released in 1962, became an instant classic of the genre.

The years 1930–49 were a golden age for Hollywood – an era when the major producers consolidated their power over the industry, and nurtured stars such as Ingrid Bergman (1915–82), Humphrey Bogart (1899–1957), and Cary Grant (1904–86). After World War II, the American film industry still had the structure, finance, and innovation to produce films of considerable cultural impact. But television was gaining ground rapidly, siphoning off cinema audiences, and forcing Hollywood to make technical changes – such as the wide screen and stereophonic sound.

In the late 1950s and 1960s, new centers of cinematic excellence began to emerge, most notably in France. The French directors Jean-Luc Godard (1930–), François Truffaut (1932–84), and Claude Chabrol (1930–) were the key directors of the *Nouvelle Vague* (New Wave) of French cinema. This loose term correlates broadly to the *nouveau roman*, and certainly Godard's innovative films, such as *A Bout de Souffle* (Breathless, 1959), use a similarly fragmentary approach. But in practice the New Wave directors produced a disparate body of work.

THE BEAT GENERATION

It was the American writer Jack Kerouac (1922–69) who coined the term beat to describe people leading the bohemian lifestyle that was popular in the 1950s in parts of the United States. It was a joke about the way that like-minded folk were drifting to San Francisco, where they were "beatified" as "Franciscans." Like the bohemian artists of Paris, the beats led easy-going lives; they experimented with new forms of art and literature, with sexual freedom, Zen Buddhism, and drugs. Their flirtations with subversive politics led to the Russian-inspired name, "beatnik" (as in "sputnik").

The main beat poet was Allen Ginsberg (1926–). His free-form poem *Howl* (1956) combined slang, jazz rhythms, and an edgy sense of angst. Other beats were the poets Lawrence Ferlinghetti (1919–), Gregory Corso (1930–), and Gary Snyder (1930–), and the novelist William Burroughs (1914–).

BEAT BROTHERS Jack Kerouac and Neal Cassady enjoyed a close friendship. Kerouac pioneered a fresh and freely expressive style in his books, such as *On the Road* (1957) and *The Dharma Bums* (1958).

CARTOONS

Experiments with animated drawings found their way on to film in the very earliest days of the movies. From the start, screen cartoons borrowed the skills of the comic-strip illustrators. One of the first commercially successful cartoons, *Gertie the Dinosaur* (1909), was made by Winsor McCay, the creator of *Little Nemo in Slumberland* (1905), which is often seen as the first modern comic strip.

The screen cartoon remained primitive until Walt Disney (1901–66) applied his talent to the subject in the 1920s. He first introduced the cartoon mouse Mickey in *Steamboat Willie* (1928). At this time no cartoons ran for more than 10 minutes – but Disney was convinced that cartoons had the power to entertain an audience for the duration of a feature-length movie. *Snow White and the Seven Dwarfs*, first shown in 1937, was full length – and it was a prodigious commercial success. Disney went on to release other full-length features such as *Pinocchio* (1940) and *Dumbo* (1941). Always well aware of the broader marketing potential of his creations, Disney also created the pioneering Disneyland theme park (1955) in Anaheim, California.

SEE ALSO

Poststructuralism · · · · · · · · · · ◄
Modernism · · · · · · · · · · · · · · ◄
Abstract art & minimalism · · · · · ◄

POP ART

HISTORY MAKERS: *Richard Hamilton (1922–), Roy Lichtenstein (1923–), Andy Warhol (1926–87), Claes Oldenburg (1929–)*

SEE ALSO: *Modernism*

In 1956 the British artist Richard Hamilton produced a collage entitled *Just what is it that makes today's home so different, so appealing?* It bore similarities to the surrealist collages of Max Ernst, but what was different was its content: here was a mixture of consumer products and familiar advertising features, juxtaposing popular glamor with domesticity. Hamilton said he wanted to produce art that was "popular, transient, expendable, low cost, mass produced, young, witty, sexy, gimmicky, glamorous, and big business." This statement might almost be a manifesto for "Pop Art," which subsequently developed as the major art movement of the 1960s in Europe and the United States.

Pop Art explores the relationship between art and popular culture. The commonplace nature of the subject matter and the depersonalized industrial techniques used to create the art raise the question of where the line should be drawn between commercial art and fine art. As in the work of Marcel Duchamp, Pop Art suggests that selection is a key element in artistic statement. But the Pop artists go farther by suggesting emblematic meaning in their work, or by using marginally painterly techniques. For example, the American artist Roy Lichtenstein paints a blown-up comic strip that imitates the dotting of the three-color printing process.

The most famous of the American Pop artists was Andy Warhol, whose background as a commercial artist was a major influence on his work. His studio, the Factory, was a hive of creativity where he and other artists, often in collaboration, created paintings and films and staged "happenings."

A few Pop artists produced three-dimensional works in the same vein. The Swedish-born Claes Oldenburg made soft sculptures – out of sailcloth or vinyl stuffed with kapok – of everyday objects like hamburgers, egg beaters, and ice cream cones. They challenge the very idea of art and simultaneously imply that there is artistic value in the ordinary things that surround us.

POP ICON Andy Warhol mass-produced images of the screen goddess Marilyn Monroe using the technique of silk screen printing.

OP ART

HISTORY MAKERS: *Viktor Vasarely (1908–), Bridget Riley (1931–)*

SEE ALSO: *Abstract art & minimalism*

PRISONER OF ART In common with that of many minimalist and proto-minimalist painters such as Mondrian, Bridget Riley's work has changed little since she found her niche. The most important innovation was her introduction of color to her paintings in the late 1960s.

A small but well-publicized movement in painting developed during the 1960s. It explored the effects of optical illusion, using geometric shapes, sharply defined lines, and contrasting colors. Contemporaneous with the success of Pop Art, it was jokingly labeled "Op Art."

The Hungarian Viktor Vasarely, working in Paris from 1930, was an early proponent – producing careful compositions of geometric shapes. But the best-known Op artist of the 1960s was the British painter Bridget Riley. Her precise techniques and carefully planned colors had something in common with the minimalist painters: but the work's impact is very different, causing the eye to swim and see apparent kinetic motion, an effect that can be disturbing or strangely soothing. Op art is unusual in that it makes no claims for its content beyond the trick that the patterning plays on the eyes.

CONCEPTUAL ART

HISTORY MAKERS: *Joseph Beuys (1921–86), Sol Lewitt (1928–), Joseph Kosuth (1945–)*

SEE ALSO: *Poststructuralism, Modernism*

Like so many aspects of modern art, conceptual art can trace its origins back to Marcel Duchamp. The basic idea of conceptual art is that the object itself, such as a painting or sculpture, is not as important as the concept behind it. This concept may be obscure, complex, intriguing, or utterly banal. The task of the artist is to put the idea across through whatever medium will best convey it – performance art, installation, written text, video, painting, or a multimedia

ARTISTIC IRONY Joseph Beuys's work *Art and Capital* (1979) pokes fun at the relationship between money and the art world.

combination of these. The materials used are simply props, in themselves worth nothing. Indeed, conceptual art is in principle a rejection of art objects, although financial necessity may make the sale of such props desirable.

Conceptual art has its pitfalls. The concept has to be valid to deserve the effort of both artist and viewer: it is the artist's job to show that the methods applied to convey it are the most appropriate and that the concept cannot be expressed better in any other way.

Successful conceptual art should convince the viewer of its integrity as an expression of an idea. But if it is clear that the concept could have been expressed more effectively – for example, in a few words rather than in an elaborate installation – the viewer might be entitled to feel let down.

KINETIC ART

HISTORY MAKERS: *Alexander Calder (1898–1976)*

SEE ALSO: *Modernism*

Since the American artist Alexander Calder introduced an element of movement into his

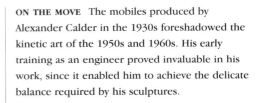

ON THE MOVE The mobiles produced by Alexander Calder in the 1930s foreshadowed the kinetic art of the 1950s and 1960s. His early training as an engineer proved invaluable in his work, since it enabled him to achieve the delicate balance required by his sculptures.

"mobiles" during the 1930s, a number of artists have explored the sculptural possibilities of motion – using motors, electromagnetic forces, and water power, as well as the breeze.

One of the pioneers of kinetic art in the 1950s was the Hungarian-born French artist Nicholas Schöffer (1912–), who specializes in what he calls "spatio-dynamic" towers involving Plexiglas sheets, moving parts, music, and lighting. The Greek artist Takis (Takis Vassilakis, 1925–) uses electromagnets and ordinary magnets in abstract metallic installations; the magnets set up alternating movements of attraction and repulsion. Some of the most endearing kinetic sculptures were created by the Swiss artist Jean Tinguely (1925–91), who, through his peculiar and humorous machinelike constructions, parodies the world of machine technology.

NEW ROMANTICS
A world of pick and mix

In any period of history a broad range of stylistic influences is in play: some are fresh and new, but rapidly prove ephemeral; others are still embryonic and the province only of the avant-garde; yet others are retrospective or nostalgic echoes of the past. It is hard to judge – without the distance of time – by what currents of contemporary taste one's own era will be marked. A century ago, for example, Art Nouveau had to compete with Arts and Crafts, Neoclassicism, and the prototype Modernism of Louis Sullivan.

Many of the predominant trends of the 20th century were heralded by manifestos and guided by rules. The Futurists, Modernists, and Abstract Expressionists were all convinced of the rightness of their chosen path. Since the 1970s, the trends in art, architecture, and design have been rather less dogmatic and more open to suggestion. The mood broadly parallels Romanticism, set against the more rigid strictures of Neoclassicism.

But contemporary art has become a complex issue, the result of the perpetual questioning and battering it has suffered since the beginning of the century. What is art? Who can judge it? As artists and critics perform their arcane dances around each other, the public looks on perplexed; many people have suffered a loss of faith.

POSTMODERN ARCHITECTURE

The reaction to the straitjacket of modernist architecture began to emerge in the 1970s, when a new generation of architects started to take a less dogmatic approach to design. In part, this was influenced by developments in building technology that allowed for a greater variety of shapes, structures, and surface textures. But it was also a response to what was perceived as a missed opportunity in the Modernist ethic. Buildings could be treated as sculptural forms – and all the more so if one dared to break the old Modernist commandment that form must follow function.

Leaders of Postmodernist architecture include the Spaniard Ricardo Bofill (1939–), the Italian Aldo Rossi (1931–), and the American Michael Graves (1934–). Between them they draw on a variety of historic styles – Neoclassical, Art Deco, and so on – sometimes used on the same building.

FANTASY FORTRESS Designed by architect Terry Farrell (1938–), Vauxhall Cross on the south bank of the River Thames in London epitomizes the mood of postmodern architecture. Built in 1990–93 to house the British secret service, it is anything but unobtrusive – appropriate perhaps for a millennial Bond.

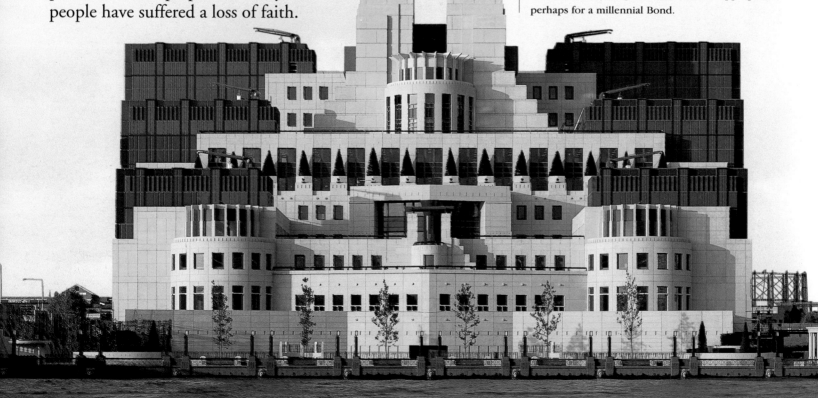

INSTALLATION ART

GLOWING IN THE DARK The work of American Dan Flavin (1933–), unlike that of many installation artists, is sensual rather than conceptual.

Multimedia installations are essentially a postwar phenomenon, but they can trace their history back to the new freedoms in sculpture and art concepts achieved by Picasso, Duchamp, the Dadaists, and the Surrealists. Being neither sculpture nor painting, installations represent an entirely new medium: physical environments to be walked through or around. Sometimes they also include music and video presentations. Most installations are prepared for particular gallery spaces, and are temporary exhibits, later dismantled. For example, Joseph Beuys's *Plight* (1985) was an installation prepared for a London gallery – a grand piano set in two rooms composed of large rolls of felt.

Some installations may be seen as a form of land art. In 1969, the Bulgarian-American Christo (Christo Javacheff, 1935–) wrapped a section of the coast of Australia in 11,120 sq. yards (9,300 m²) of plastic sheeting; in 1983 he surrounded 11 small islands off Florida in 670,000 sq. yards (560,000 m²) of pink fabric to create a waterlily effect as a homage to Monet. Installations are rarely more ambitious.

LAND ART

In his *Mile Long Drawing* (1968), Walter de Maria (1935–) drew two parallel lines across the Mojave Desert in the southwestern United States. The only precedents for this kind of gesture are from the ancient world, such as the Nazca lines in the Peruvian desert created some 5,000 years ago. Art based around natural forms that already exist in the landscape, called land art, was taken up by a number of artists in the late 1960s and 1970s and still flourishes today. Unlike much of the art of that era, land art has changed and developed, gaining adherents from subsequent generations.

Land art combines conceptual art and minimalism with a romantic's awe of nature. It can be seen as a reaction to the limitations of gallery-based art – but since galleries are still the main window on art, land art faces a problem of presentation. Some practitioners have met this problem by creating installations or by exhibiting photographs of their creations.

TRICKS OF NATURE The British artist Andy Goldsworthy (1956–) creates transient works of art and then photographs them. Land artists often produce work that can be described as beautiful – both delighting the senses and pleasing the mind.

WORLD MUSIC

Pop music has always been open to new influences. In the 1970s Caribbean reggae became popular and proved highly influential. The eclectic spirit of the 1980s and 1990s also caused music promoters and the public to open their ears to new sounds from abroad: traditional West African praise singing, club music from Algeria, Bulgarian chants, folk music from Colombia.

Only certain strands of this "World Music" proved commercially successful in their own right – usually the most rhythmic, conforming to Western tastes in popular music. Some were tailored and adapted to suit Western styles of music, while the more inventive composers and musicians in the West absorbed some of the features of these unfamiliar sounds into their own music. The result was a valuable trade of influences – and, perhaps more significant, a reversal of a postwar trend. Previously Western culture – especially American consumer culture – had been exported to the rest of the world. Now the rest of the world returned the favor.

It is possible that this new trend in global cross-fertilization signals a shift in the history of Western culture – and one that will evolve further in the new millennium.

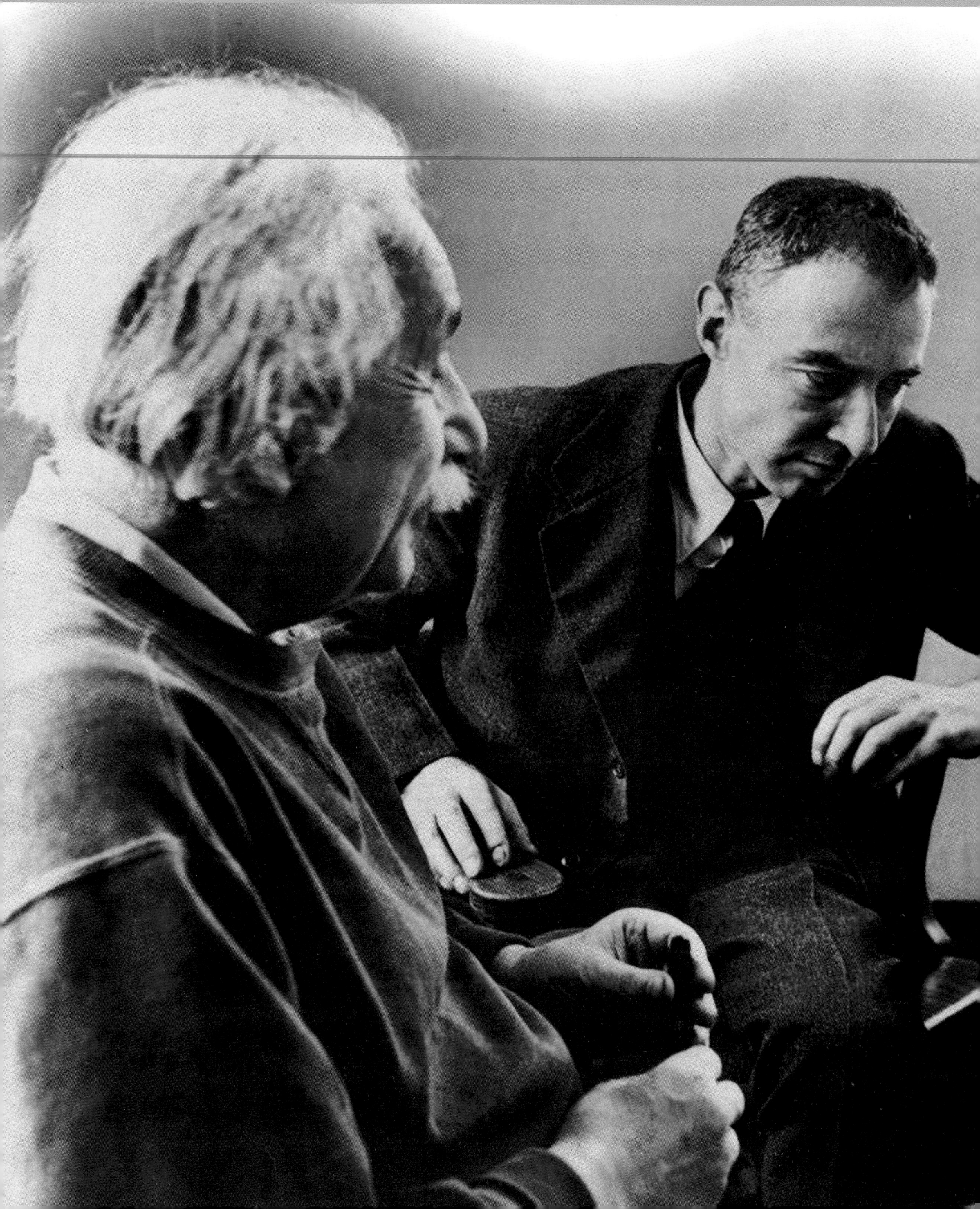

Science

The search for answers to the question "how?" has led the human imagination to the farthest reaches of outer space.

In a very literal sense, science has shaped the world in which we live. Modern life would be unrecognizable without inventions such as cars, telephones, satellites, skyscrapers, and computers. But science has also affected humans far more profoundly: it has altered the way we think about ourselves.

One word could sum up the key scientific notion of the past 250 years: scale. Our appreciation, at one end of the spectrum, of the vastness of the universe and at the other end, of the infinite minuteness of subatomic particles has had a permanent effect on our understanding of our place in the scheme of things.

From the medieval notion of humanity made in God's image at the center of an ordered universe, we have moved to the realization that we are all made up of the same matter as the stars in the sky and the Earth beneath our feet. And furthermore, we may only have arrived at our current state of consciousness through a series of random mutations.

This change of attitude did not happen overnight. Before the Scientific Revolution of the 17th century, "natural philosophy," as science was then called, was simply a number of "certainties" inherited from the ancient Greeks – for example, that the heavens were made up of seven crystal spheres. But new inventions, such as the telescope and the microscope, began to expose the hidden complexities of the universe; and new empiricist techniques – for example, Newton's experiments with light – showed that the world was not always quite what it seemed.

By the end of the 19th century, it seemed that very soon, using the magic of science, we could know everything and so reinforce our position as masters of God's universe. A whole new age of industry had been built on scientific discovery – the combustion engine, the railroad, electricity.

But the atom bombs dropped on Hiroshima and Nagasaki in 1945 marked the high-water mark of that optimism. We have indeed become masters of our planet, masters of destruction – using the tiniest particles known to us, we created the fastest catastrophe the world has ever witnessed.

Today we are seeing a backlash against science. It is blamed for our precipitous flight into the future pursued by the ancient familiars of pestilence, famine, and war. Global warming, chemical warfare, the threat of nuclear fallout, weird diseases such as the ebola virus: all these are biproducts of the scientific quest to go one step farther. Yet it is also through science and the application of the still-mysterious human brain that these problems may some day be resolved.

ATOMIC GENIUS Albert Einstein and Robert Oppenheimer chat at Princeton University, New Jersey, in 1951.

PRIME MOVERS
Machines to move things and people

The Industrial Revolution was made possible by machines that multiplied the force of human muscles. First water power, then steam, drove the mills and factories that transformed life in Britain at the end of the 18th century. Matthew Boulton (1728–1809), the industrialist whose partnership with the engineer James Watt (1736–1819) produced the first steam engines, told King George III: "I sell, Sire, what all the world desires – power."

The steam engine, like all subsequent prime movers, converts heat into work according to rules codified in the laws of thermodynamics. But the inventors of the steam engine knew nothing of thermodynamics, proceeding by trial and error. The first steam engines – more accurately "atmospheric engines," since it was the pressure of the atmosphere that drove the piston – were used to pump water from mines. Watt was the first to use engines to provide rotary motion; his "rotative engine" of 1783 made possible the development of the factory system in England.

The effects were profound. Within 30 years, more people in England worked in trade, manufacturing, and handicrafts than on the land. Cities grew explosively: Manchester's population was 25,000 in 1772, 181,000 by 1821, and 455,000 by 1851. Railroads made their first appearance in the 1820s and the first crossing of the Atlantic by steam ship was in 1838. Within half a century of Watt's patent, the French scientist Sadi Carnot (1796–1832), discoverer of the laws of thermodynamics, was able to write: "To rob Britain of her steam engines would be to rob her of her coal and iron . . . to ruin her prosperity, to annihilate her power."

But steam did not conquer all. Steam-powered road vehicles had limited success. A lighter prime mover was needed, and it appeared in the internal combustion engine, in which fuel is burned inside the cylinders rather than under a boiler. In 1859 French engineer Etienne Lenoir (1822–1900) developed a stationary gas engine, improved in Germany by Nikolaus Otto (1832–91), who adopted the four-stroke cycle in which the fuel is compressed before being ignited. More than 200,000 Otto engines had been sold by 1900.

WATER POWER

NATURAL POWER A traditional "undershot" waterwheel, driven around by the force of a moving stream. Wheels such as this were used across Europe – often to power mill machinery – from the first century BC on.

Waterwheels provided the best source of power before the age of steam. In the last quarter of the 18th century, the British engineer John Smeaton (1724–94) showed that "overshot wheels," in which the water flows over the top to fill a series of buckets and turn the wheel by gravity, were nearly three times as efficient as "undershot wheels," in which paddles dip into a flowing stream. But the future for water power lay with turbines, developed largely in France. The name came from the Latin word *turbo*, a top, and like tops turbines spin fast as water flows past their blades. In 1838 the French engineer Benoit Fourneyron (1802–67) produced a turbine just 12 inches (30 cm) wide and spinning at 2,300 revolutions per minute, which was able to produce 60 horsepower from a water drop of 380 feet (115 m). Today turbines are used to generate electricity in hydroelectric plants.

STEAM ENGINE

SCHOOLBOY'S HOMEWORK James Watt's first experiments with steam were in his mother's kitchen. His steam engines later powered many of the factories that sprang up during Britain's Industrial Revolution.

The first practical steam engine was developed by a British blacksmith, Thomas Newcomen (1663–1729), in 1712. Steam was introduced into a cylinder below a piston, and condensed by a jet of cold water. This process created a partial vacuum, and atmospheric pressure acting on the top of the piston drove it down. The engine was slow, at 12 strokes a minute, and unsuitable for rotative motion, but served well to drive pumps for draining mines.

James Watt realized that constant heating and cooling of the cylinder was inefficient, and introduced a separate condenser into which the steam could be exhausted and condensed. He also introduced steam rather than cold air above the piston. Efficiency was increased by a factor of three. Watt next made his engine double-acting, so that the downward as well as the upward stroke delivered power and, using a sun-and-planet gear of his own devising, he created rotary motion. His engines were powerful and reliable, and their low efficiency did not matter because coal was cheap and plentiful.

HIGH ACHIEVER This locomotive from 1829 pulled one of the first steam trains. The tall smokestacks meant that bridges had to arch high over the rail tracks to give the engines room to pass.

THERMODYNAMICS

The science of heat engines began in 1824 with Sadi Carnot, whose *Reflexions sur la puissance motrice du feu* (On the motive power of fire) first showed that any heat engine has a theoretical maximum efficiency. Carnot showed that the efficiency of a steam engine depended on the temperature difference between the hottest steam and the cooling water. In a series of experiments, James Joule (1818–89) showed that energy cannot be created or destroyed, only converted from one form to another. Codified by Hermann von Helmholtz (1821–94) in 1847, this became the first law of thermodynamics. It means, among other things, that a perpetual motion machine is impossible.

Unfortunately for engineers, although work can be converted entirely into heat, the opposite is not true. When heat is used to do work, something is always lost. The portion lost is measured by the system's "entropy" – a term coined in 1850 by the German physicist Rudolf Clausius (1822–88). In practice, this means that no heat engine can ever convert its fuel into work at 100 percent efficiency. This is the second law of thermodynamics, and it underlies all energy conversion processes. The two laws can be summed up very simply: the first law says you can't win, the second that you can't even break even.

TIMELINE

1712
Thomas Newcomen's steam engine is erected at Dudley Castle, Worcestershire.

1779
James Watt's rotative steam engine is built for the Birmingham button manufacturer James Pickard – the first factory powered by steam.

1884
Charles Parsons develops his first steam turbine in Gateshead.

1885
Gottlieb Daimler and Karl Benz independently develop motor vehicles propelled by gasoline-fueled internal combustion engines.

1892
In Germany, Dr. Rudolph Diesel patents the compression ignition engine, a form of internal combustion engine in which gas is compressed to raise the temperature enough to ignite fuel without the need for spark plugs.

1926
Liquid-fueled rocket launched by Robert Goddard at Auburn, Massachusetts.

1937
Frank Whittle of British Power Jets Ltd. gives his experimental jet engine its first run.

SEE ALSO
Romanticism
Chemistry
Ecology

ELECTROMAGNETIC INDUCTION

Two mysteries – electricity and magnetism – were united and explained by the work of Michael Faraday (1791–1867). He knew from the work of the Danish physicist Hans Christian Oersted (1777–1851) that an electric current could deflect a compass needle. Faraday concluded in 1821 that this was because circular lines of magnetic force were produced around the wire by the current, and proved it with a device that caused a magnet to rotate around a wire – the first electric motor.

He then investigated whether a moving magnet could produce a current. In August 1831, he wound two coils of wire around an iron ring, connecting one to a battery and the other to a galvanometer, to detect any current. He found that current flowed in the second circuit, but only when the current in the first was switched either on or off. This was the basis of the transformer, and the principle of electromagnetic induction. At the same time in the United States, Joseph Henry (1797–1878) made the same discovery.

In October 1831, Faraday set up a copper disk between the poles of a magnet and rotated it. When wires were touched to the center and periphery of the disk, a current flowed. This was the first generator. The discovery meant that any prime mover could be used to generate electricity, until then available only from batteries.

> ### "What glorious steps electricity has taken in the days within our remembrance."
>
> *Michael Faraday, scientist*

ELECTRIC DISCOVERIES Michael Faraday experiments in his laboratory. His pioneering work on electricity – he developed an early electric motor as well as creating the first generator – paved the way for electric lighting.

INTERNAL COMBUSTION ENGINE

HORSELESS CARRIAGE Wilhelm Maybach takes the wheel of an early Daimler automobile, in 1886. The practical gasoline engine created by Maybach and Gottlieb Daimler made possible the development of a new form of transportation that transformed the world in the 20th century.

In 1680 the Dutch physicist Christiaan Huygens (1629–93) invented an engine in which a charge of gunpowder was ignited in a cylinder, driving a piston along it. The device was impractical, but the principle was sound. In 1859 the French engineer Etienne Lenoir (1822–1900) made it work, igniting a mixture of coal gas and air inside the cylinder of an engine with a spark from an induction coil.

Lenoir's engine was really a modified steam engine – slow, heavy, and inefficient. What transformed it was the four-stroke cycle, first outlined by Alphonse Beau de Rochas (1815–93) and put into practice by the German engineer Nikolaus Otto (1832–91) in 1876. The first downward stroke of the piston drew fuel into the cylinder; the second, upward, stroke compressed it; ignition then took place, driving the piston down on the third stroke; and finally the fourth stroke expelled the exhaust gases. A heavy flywheel was used to smooth out the jerky motion that this created, and the result was a practical engine. All modern car engines use the same principle.

One final change made the internal combustion engine mobile. This was achieved by the German engineers Wilhelm Maybach (1846–1929) and Gottlieb Daimler (1834–1900), who substituted a mixture of gasoline and air for the gas vapor used by Otto. Gasoline was an unwanted byproduct of the oil industry, notorious for its flammability. Following Maybach's development in 1893 of the carburetor – a device for mixing fuel and air in the engine – gasoline proved the perfect fuel.

STEAM AND GAS TURBINES

The steam turbine created by Irish engineer Charles Parsons (1845–1931) had a sensational debut. In 1896 he packed four turbines into a tiny ship, the *Turbinia*, and the following year the boat – capable of 34½ knots, or nautical miles per hour (about 65 km/h) – outstripped the British Royal Navy's finest ships at the Naval Review.

Parsons had developed his first turbine in 1884, using steam to turn a shaft as it flowed over a series of fanlike blades along its length. He saw that a single set of blades would not extract a worthwhile amount of energy from the steam and designed a series of blades that grew larger along the shaft.

In the steam turbine, fuel is burned outside the engine to create the steam; in the gas turbine, fuel is burned inside the turbine, expanding to drive the blades around. The Swiss firm Brown Boveri made the first practical gas turbine in 1936. By that time, Frank Whittle (1907–96) in England and Hans Pabst von Ohain (1911–) in Germany were developing a gas turbine with an exhaust strong enough to power an aircraft. Von Ohain had one flying first, in August 1939; Whittle's first jet engine flew in May 1941.

LEGACY OF POWER Charles Parsons was an industrialist as well as an inventor. Descendants of his 1896 steam turbine are used in modern electricity generating plants.

POWER OF FLIGHT Wilbur and Orville Wright's first flying machines used a homemade gasoline engine.

AERODYNAMICS AND FLIGHT

The principles of aerodynamics were established by the English scholar Sir George Cayley (1771–1857), who in 1849 built a glider that made a manned flight with one of Cayley's servants aboard. But Cayley was frustrated by the lack of a prime mover light enough to fly. That was first available around 1900, when improvements to the gasoline engine produced a weight-to-power ratio of about 9 pounds (4 kg) per horsepower. Americans Orville (1871–1948) and Wilbur Wright (1867–1912) – brothers who ran a bicycle shop in Dayton, Ohio – built their own engine and attached it to a biplane, also of their own design, called *Flyer I*. On December 17, 1903, Orville made the first powered flight, while Wilbur watched. This momentous achievement went virtually ignored by the world.

ROCKETS AND SPACE TRAVEL

The idea of space travel by rocket owes its origins to the Russian schoolteacher Konstantin Tsiolkovsky (1857–1935). He saw that leaving the atmosphere would require a multistage rocket, able to shed most of its mass and leave only a small final stage to enter orbit. Robert Goddard (1882–1945), an American professor of physics, showed that liquid fuels could provide the necessary thrust, proving it in a series of test flights which began in 1926. Scientists in 1930s Germany built the first ballistic missile, the A4. After 1945 bigger rockets were built; in 1957 the U.S.S.R. launched Sputnik, the first manmade object in Earth orbit. In 1961 Soviet astronaut Yuri Gagarin (1934–68) orbited the Earth in *Vostok I*, becoming the first man in space.

SKY TRIAL Robert Goddard gets ready to test his gasoline and liquid-oxygen-fueled rocket, on March 16, 1926. It flew 185 feet (56 m).

ASTRONOMY
The forces that make up the universe

By 1800, astronomers had begun to grasp the immensity of the universe. The force that shaped the universe, gravitation, had been described by the English physicist Isaac Newton (1642–1727) in 1687, and in 1846 the Frenchman Urbain Leverrier (1811–77) used Newtonian mechanics in calculations that successfully predicted the existence, and the position, of the planet Neptune.

In 1838, the distance to one of the nearest stars, 61 Cygni, was worked out by the German astronomer Friedrich Bessel (1784–1846). He found that it was 64 billion miles (103 billion km) away – 9,000 times the width of the solar system. By 1900, the distances to about 70 stars had been determined, and it was clear that the solar system was little more than a dot lost in the immensity of space. In 1868 the English astronomer William Huggins (1824–1910) discovered that the stars were moving away from us, because their light was shifted in frequency by the Doppler effect, the same phenomenon that makes a train whistle change in frequency as it passes. In the late 1920s, the American astronomer Edwin Hubble (1889–1953) studied this "red shift" for a number of galaxies and found that the faster the galaxies were receding from the Earth, the farther away they were. Hubble showed not only that the universe is even bigger than suspected, but also that it is constantly expanding, the galaxies moving farther apart from one another as time passes.

Hubble's discovery implied that the universe must have originated at a definite moment in the past, from a single point. Roughly when that must have been can be worked out from the ratio between the speed of the galaxies and their distance from us, the so-called Hubble constant. Different values for the Hubble constant have been found, giving ages for the universe ranging from about 12 to 20 billion years.

UNIFORMITARIANISM

The creation story was used by biblical scholars to work out the age of the Earth, sometimes with surprising precision. In 1656, for example, an Anglican archbishop, James Usher, declared that Creation had taken place at 8 P.M. on October 22, 4004 BC. These beliefs were shattered by the theory of uniformitarianism, put forward first by the Scottish naturalist James Hutton (1726–97) in 1785 and confirmed in the 1830s by British geologist Charles Lyell (1797–1875).

Hutton's view was that the complex shape of the Earth, its mountains, valleys, and seas, could be explained by forces that we see about us today, such as mountain-building, erosion, and the buildup of sediments on the sea bed. Since all these processes were exceptionally slow, it meant that the Earth must be much older than the Creation story implied. Hutton's views, which appeared to point to an eternal Earth and hence to atheism, were derided. Half a century later, Lyell

TO BOLDLY GO The *Cosmic Background Explorer* was launched in November 1989 to investigate the remains of the radiation emitted during the Big Bang.

came to the same conclusions independently, and argued them so cogently in his *Principles of Geology*, published between 1830 and 1833, that they became accepted. The modern science of geology had been born.

GRAVITATION

The basic force that shapes the universe is gravity, one of the four fundamental forces of nature. Newton's universal law of gravitation, formulated in 1687, states that two bodies attract each other with a force that is proportional to the product of their masses and which falls off with the square of the distance between them.

Although it is a weak force compared with those that hold atoms together, gravity is the sculptor responsible for the shape of the universe. Newton's law had the beauty of universality – it applied to the apple falling from the tree just as precisely as it did to the motions of the planets. Newtonian mechanics was so successful for so long that it led to the belief that, given enough data, the behavior of every particle in the universe could be predicted in advance and its future foretold – the principle of determinism.

SPINNING IN SPACE The great mass of matter that makes up a galaxy is held together by the force of gravity.

CATASTROPHISM

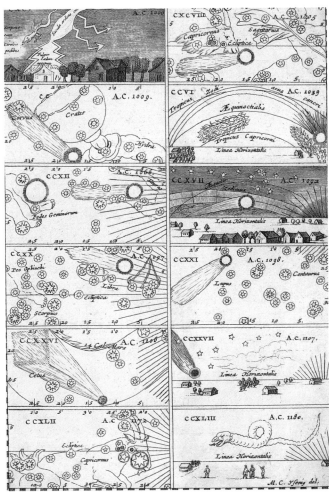

IT CAME FROM OUTER SPACE The possibility that the meteorites which whizzed through the night sky might land on Earth seemed about as likely as the return of dragons to some 19th-century satirists.

The geological record shows that life on Earth has suffered five major setbacks, in which many species died. The greatest of these was 250 million years ago, when 70 percent of all species then alive disappeared; the best known, 65 million years ago, when the dinosaurs were wiped out. The most likely explanation for these extinctions is a global catastrophe caused by the impact of some huge object from space.

The surface of the Moon and Mars show that steady bombardment does occur, though cratering is less evident on Earth because geological activity has tended to cover it up. The idea of catastrophism runs counter to Lyell's uniformitarianism, but does not negate it. It simply means that to the steady changes of geology must be added the occasional violent shift accomplished by an impact.

TIMELINE

1610
Galileo identifies Jupiter's moons, using the newly invented telescope.

1687
Newton's law of gravitation is published.

1799–1825
Pierre Simon de Laplace publishes a five-volume work, *Celestial Mechanics*, using Newtonian mechanics to explain the solar system.

1916
Einstein's general theory of relativity is published.

1929
Edwin Hubble shows the link between red shift and distance, establishing the size of the universe.

1931
Karl Jansky discovers radio waves in space.

1948
George Gamow predicts the existence of the microwave, discovered by Arno Penzias and Robert Wilson in 1964.

1996
First definite evidence of planets around other stars is collected.

SEE ALSO

Physics ················ ▶
Evolution ·············· ▶

THE BIG BANG

The discovery by American astronomer Edwin Hubble (1889–1953) that the universe is expanding implied an astonishing thing. It was that if we could run time backward, we could retrace the universe's history back to a point – perhaps 15 billion years ago – when all matter was contained in a single point. The "Big Bang" theory holds that it was an explosion at this point that created both matter and time, simultaneously setting the clock ticking and the universe expanding.

The theory had many originators, starting in 1927 with the Belgian mathematician Georges Lemaître (1894–1966), but it came to prominence after World War II with the Russian-born physicist George Gamow (1904–68). It was given a boost by the discovery in 1964 by the German-born Arno Penzias (1933–) and the American Robert Wilson (1936–) that there is a background of low-level microwave radiation throughout the universe. This radiation is the dying echo of the Big Bang, the remainder of the intense heat generated by the vast initial explosion. Its existence had been predicted by Gamow.

Detailed examination by Cosmic Background Explorer (COBE), the telescope in orbit around the Earth that is operated by NASA, has determined the characteristic temperature of this radiation very precisely, and shown that it varies fractionally from place to place. The hotter patches are the parts of the explosive cloud of gas that had become more concentrated and where stars and galaxies would form – a primeval "lumpiness" which led to the universe we see today.

The Big Bang theory made another prediction that has proved accurate. The relative abundances of hydrogen, helium, deuterium, and lithium found in the universe are exactly those to be expected if the Big Bang had occurred. Today, most cosmologists accept that the universe did come to life in a single, vast explosion.

ON THE JOB MAINTENANCE NASA astronauts service the Hubble Space Telescope. The space shuttle launched the HST into orbit around the Earth in 1990. Above the distortions of the Earth's atmosphere, it can take much clearer pictures of distant stars than an earthbound telescope can.

> *"It is the most persistent and greatest human adventure in human history, this search to understand the universe, how it works and where it came from."*
>
> Murray Gell-Mann (1929–),
> American theoretical physicist

Inflation

The American physicist Allan Guth (1947–) has proposed a small but crucial modification to the Big Bang theory. He suggests that 10^{-33} seconds after the Big Bang, the universe went into a period of super-rapid expansion called inflation. At the end of this period, which lasted only a fraction of a second, the universe was still only 4 inches (10 cm) across. After that, expansion continued at a rate equal to the speed of light.

This enormously rapid expansion "inflated" a tiny part of the infant universe into everything we can see. Inflation implies that not one but countless universes may have been created and are now separated into a patchwork of regions that cannot communicate with one another.

Black holes

What is left behind when a star dies? High-mass stars die by blowing themselves apart in supernova explosions, sometimes leaving behind incredibly dense cores called neutron stars, made of material so compacted that a thimbleful would weigh 100 million tons. This star is so called because its very atoms are crushed and reduced to neutrons.

For even larger stars, the end is still more extreme. If the mass of a burned-out star's core is more than three times that of the Sun, its collapse produces an object called a "black hole." This term was coined in 1967 by American physicist John Wheeler (1911–) to describe objects so dense that nothing, not even light, can escape from them. If the Earth were compressed until it became a black hole, it would be roughly the size of a ping-pong ball.

The British physicist Stephen Hawking (1942–) has suggested that many small black holes might have been produced during the Big Bang. Detecting a black hole is tricky, because it cannot be seen, but its presence can be inferred from the behavior of other objects nearby which are subject to its gravitational attraction. Gas from neighboring stars is dragged into a revolving disk that surrounds the black hole. The gas heats up as it plunges into the disk, shedding a brilliant light and sending out X-rays. It is these X-rays that astronomers trace in order to find black holes.

SEEING THE PAST The light from these distant galaxies – captured by the powerful lenses of the Hubble Space Telescope – may have been traveling through space for as long as 14 billion years. Scientists have determined that in this image we see the galaxies shortly after their formation, and that some of them came into existence within a billion years of the Big Bang.

OPEN OR CLOSED UNIVERSE

SAILING THROUGH SPACE Ever since the Big Bang, all the galaxies that we know of have been slowly flying apart in an infinitely long separation.

Will the expansion of the universe go on forever? That depends entirely on how much matter it contains. If the average density of matter in the universe is low, then the gravity associated with it will be low and there will be little to stop the universe from continuing to fly apart. Even infinitely far into the future, galaxies will continue to separate until we are left alone with only our immediate galaxy for company.

This condition is known as the open universe: it will end in the "Big Chill," when everything is infinitely far apart and infinitely cold. But if the density of matter is above a critical level, then the expansion will eventually stop and go into reverse. The universe will start contracting again, ending in a "Big Crunch" when all the galaxies come together. This model is called the closed universe.

In between these two conditions is one in which matter is present in just the right amounts to allow the galaxies barely to keep moving apart. For a number of reasons, including the fact that it requires no arbitrary changes to Einstein's equations, this is the model most cosmologists favor. But the density of matter needed to bring it about – about three hydrogen atoms per cubic meter of space – is well above the density that we can actually observe.

For this reason (among others) astronomers believe that there is probably about 10 times as much invisible matter in the universe as there are visible stars and galaxies. This "missing mass" could be in the form of dead stars too dark to see, or of exotic particles which we cannot detect. Until we know whether or not it is there, we cannot say whether the universe is open or closed, and whether it will end in a Big Chill or a Big Crunch.

STELLAR EVOLUTION

The fuel that keeps the Sun and other stars burning is hydrogen. The process is nuclear fusion, in which hydrogen atoms combine to produce helium. The British physicist Arthur Eddington (1882–1944) was the first to suggest this in 1930, and the details were worked out by the American physicist Hans Bethe (1906–) in 1939.

Every second, the Sun is turning 4.2 million tons of matter into energy; ultimately it will run out of fuel and die, but that will not happen for at least another five billion years. When it does happen, the core of the Sun will contract, generating heat through gravitational collapse that will raise the temperature to 180 million°F (100 million°C. That will be high enough for the helium atoms to fuse, generating more heat that will cause the Sun to expand into a "red giant," a hundred times larger than it is today. Finally, the outer layers will fly off to form a planetary nebula (a fragmented mass of gas and dust), while the center contracts to a small "white dwarf" star. This life cycle lasts about 10 billion years, and is followed by all stars whose mass falls in the range 0.06 to 1.4 times the mass of the Sun.

Smaller stars never get hot enough for nuclear reactions to start, and so evolve into "brown dwarfs." Bigger ones follow a shorter and more violent course. Those between 1.4 and 4.2 solar masses burn normally for only about a million years before becoming red giants, then get so hot that helium atoms can fuse, producing a range of much heavier elements. Such stars are the forges in which the heavy elements, such as iron, are born. Ultimately they explode as supernovas, hurling their debris into space to condense into new stars and planets. Stars even more massive than this may produce black holes.

STAR NURSERY A cluster of stars at different stages of evolution light up a corner of the sky. The top left star is a red supergiant.

CONTINENTAL DRIFT

EARTH'S WRINKLES The San Andreas Fault in California was created by the meeting of two tectonic plates.

The idea that the continents have moved about the Earth's surface occurred to the German meteorologist Alfred Wegener (1880–1930) in 1912. He noticed that the edges of the continents seemed to fit together like a jigsaw puzzle, and proposed that in the past they had formed a supercontinent, which he called Pangea. His argument was strengthened by the similarities in geology – such as fossils and glacial deposits – that appeared on continents thousands of miles apart. But his theory gained little support at the time.

Sentiment changed dramatically in the 1960s. The mapping of the ocean floor, which had been going on since the 1950s, had shown that rock appeared to be spreading outward from the midline of the long mountain chains that run down the center of the Pacific and Atlantic oceans. On one side of this midline, the magnetic orientation of the rock matched that of rock in the equivalent position on the other side. The conclusion was that new rock was being formed along the mid-oceanic ridges by liquid rock rising from below, solidifying, and slowly driving the continents apart.

But if new rock is constantly appearing, it must also be constantly disappearing. This, according to the theory of plate tectonics, occurs along subduction zones – areas where the crust is being pushed down into the Earth. Most, but not all, of these zones lie around the edge of the Pacific. The process is slow – the continents of Europe and North America are separating about as quickly as a fingernail grows – but it means that over tens or hundreds of millions of years, continents will have moved by thousands of miles. It also means that all the crust under the oceans is recycled every 200 million years.

The theory has proved one of the most revolutionary this century. It explained why so many earthquakes and volcanoes were centered in the so-called Ring of Fire around the Pacific – these are subduction zones, where one plate is sliding below another. Other earthquakes, such as those along the San Andreas Fault in California, occur where two plates are sliding uneasily alongside each other. Where plates collide head on, as in the Himalayas, great mountain ranges are thrown up. The Earth's crust is now believed to be made up of some 15 plates of various sizes, which "float" on the semiliquid rock below.

EXTRATERRESTRIAL INTELLIGENCE

The discovery that we are surrounded by countless numbers of stars has encouraged a search for life elsewhere in the universe. The Milky Way alone contains 100 billion stars, and it is only one of hundreds of millions of galaxies. For the Sun to be the only one of those stars which contains a solar system with a planet that is habitable is literally unimaginable, say supporters of the Search for Extraterrestrial Intelligence (SETI).

But so far no evidence has been found. The only viable technique is to listen, using radio telescopes, in the hope of overhearing some signal sent out by an intelligent race elsewhere. Efforts began in 1960, and since then dozens of searches have been carried out. All have drawn a blank.

Sceptics argue that the universe is the way it is only because if it were not, we would not be here to observe it. If it were much younger, for example, we would not be here. If the laws of physics were different, carbon would not be abundant, and carbon-based life would never have evolved. Thus it seems to these scientists that the universe is only big enough for one form of intelligent life to have evolved. Others see this as a return to human-centered science, rejected when the cosmology of Ptolemy was overthrown by Copernicus and Galileo.

FUEL FOR FANTASY The possibility of other forms of life in the universe has fired the imaginations of all kinds of artists, from serious novelists to comic-strip writers and filmmakers.

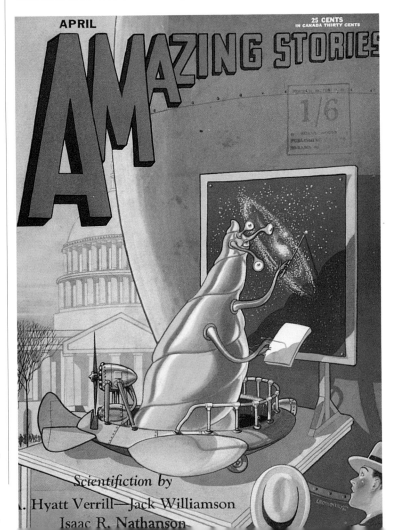

CHEMISTRY

Studying the smallest particles of matter

For a thousand years, alchemists tried to convert base metals into gold. From about the 7th century until the 17th, this hopeless task was pursued first in Islamic countries and later in Europe. The alchemists produced no gold – although the more unscrupulous pretended that they had – but they did produce more useful things, including nitric acid and sulfuric acid. By the 17th century, alchemists were discredited and changed their name to chemists, and alchemy became chemistry. The standard-bearer was the Irish scientist Robert Boyle (1627–91), author of *The Sceptical Chymist*, published in 1661. He ridiculed the accepted notion that all materials were composed of the same four elements: earth, air, water, and fire.

At the beginning of the 19th century, the English chemist John Dalton (1766–1844) revived the idea of "atoms," a word coined by the Greek philosopher Democritus (*c*.460–*c*.370 BC) in about 450 BC to describe the smallest indivisible particles of matter. Dalton asserted that each element was made up of particular kinds of atoms, which could combine to form compounds. The basic difference between atoms was in their weight. In 1813 the Swedish chemist Johan Jakob Berzelius (1779–1848) suggested the symbols for atoms that are still in use, based on the initial letter of the Latin name supplemented by a second letter where necessary. Berzelius also made the first systematic attempt to measure atomic weights. The concept of atoms and molecules – a grouping of two or more atoms – gave chemists a tool to work with, but their physical reality remained elusive.

Throughout the 19th century, rivals to Dalton's theory existed, and only at the beginning of the 20th century did "atomism" finally triumph. By then the Russian chemist Dmitri Mendeleyev (1834–1907) had created his periodic table to order the elements. Molecules were too small to be observed, and chemists were obliged to deduce their structures. Their chemical formulae could be worked out using analytical methods, but the discovery of their three-dimensional shapes had to wait for the development of X-ray crystallography, a technique that used the diffraction of X-rays to work out the structure of crystals.

LAVOISIER

REVOLUTION'S VICTIM Antoine Lavoisier was a scientific radical, but was beheaded by the French revolutionaries because he had worked as a government tax collector.

French scientist Antoine Lavoisier (1743–94) was the first to show that when elements such as phosphorus and sulfur were burned, they increased in weight. To test the hypothesis that they were taking up something from the air, he heated tin and lead in closed containers, until a layer formed on the metals' surface.

He knew that this layer – he called it calx (actually metallic oxide) – weighed more than the metals: but when he weighed the vessel after heating, it weighed the same as before. If the calx was heavier, this meant that something else was lighter – perhaps the air. When he opened the stopper, air rushed in, and after that the whole apparatus did weigh more.

From this he was able to show that combustion involved a combination of the material burned with some part of the air, and that mass was not gained or lost by the system as a whole. One simple experiment had established the nature of combustion and the law of conservation of mass. Lavoisier concluded that air consisted of two gases: oxygen, which supported combustion, and another – azote (later renamed nitrogen) – which did not.

SACRIFICE TO SCIENCE Air pumps were used to aid understanding of the respiratory system in living things. In this painting by Joseph Wright of Derby (right), if the experiment to create a vacuum succeeds, the bird will die.

BROWNIAN MOTION

In 1827 the Scottish botanist Robert Brown (1773–1858) was examining some pollen grains in water under a microscope when he noticed that they were moving about in a random fashion. He thought that they must be alive, but tried the same experiment with grains of dye, with the same result. Brown had no explanation, but in the 1860s the Scottish physicist James Clerk Maxwell (1831–79) found one. Maxwell's molecular theory of gases suggested that it was the movements of the water molecules acting on the tiny pollen grains that made them move. In 1905, Albert Einstein (1879–1955) worked out the theory mathematically, and three years later the French chemist Jean Perrin (1870–1942) used it to calculate the size of the molecules – the first physical evidence of molecules.

ATOMIC WEIGHTS

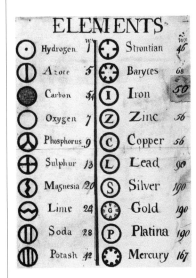

ELEMENTS

Hydrogen 1   Strontian 46
Azote 5   Barytes 68
Carbon 54   Iron 50
Oxygen 7   Zinc 56
Phosphorus 9 Copper 56
Sulphur 13   Lead 90
Magnesia 20   Silver 190
Lime 24   Gold 190
Soda 28   Platina 190
Potash 42   Mercury 167

WEIGHTS In 1808 Dalton calculated atomic weight relative to hydrogen.

The first systematic study of the weight of atoms was made by John Jakob Berzelius, who published tables of atomic weights in 1814, 1818, and 1826. He took oxygen as his standard, because there were so many compounds which contained it, and gave it the value 100. By isolating each element in a compound and weighing it, he deduced the compound's formula and calculated many atomic weights with a reasonable degree of accuracy.

In 1811 the Italian chemist Amedeo Avogadro (1776–1856) had advanced the notion that a given volume of any gas contains the same number of particles. They might not be single atoms, but could be combinations of atoms – molecules. This emerged as a useful way of calculating atomic weights after Avogadro's countryman Stanislao Cannizzaro (1826–1910) championed it at the 1860 Chemical Congress in Karlsruhe.

The chemical measurement of atomic weights reached its peak in the hands of the American chemist Theodore Richards (1868–1928), who with his associates spent nearly 30 years in the early 20th century establishing the atomic weights of 60 elements with unprecedented accuracy.

TIMELINE

1808
John Dalton puts forward the idea that all elements are composed of atoms.

1814
Johan Jakob Berzelius draws up the first table of atomic weights.

1869
Dmitri Mendeleyev publishes his first periodic table.

1896
Antoine Henri Becquerel discovers radioactivity.

1905
Courtaulds Limited introduces viscose rayon – artificial silk.

1910
The mass spectroscope is used by J.J. Thomson to measure the mass of atoms of different elements.

1913
Henry Moseley clarifies the periodic table by introducing the concept of atomic number.

1919
Ernest Rutherford transmutes elements by bombarding their nuclei with subatomic particles.

1932
John Cockroft and Ernest Walton split the atom.

SEE ALSO

Astronomy · · · · · · · · · · · · ◀
Physics · · · · · · · · · · · · · · ▶
Medicine · · · · · · · · · · · · · ▶

VITALISM

The idea that living things differ fundamentally from the inanimate, following different scientific laws and controlled by a "vital force," is a scientific heresy with a long pedigree. One of the first to put it forward was the German chemist Georg Stahl (1660–1734).

Vitalism was influential in the early years of the 19th century, with many chemists arguing that the organic compounds characteristic of life could not be produced without a vital force present in plants and animals. In 1828 the German chemist Friedrich Wöhler (1800–82) used ammonia and cyanic acid from organic sources to make urea – normally a product of the kidney. But he did not claim to have disproved vitalism.

Vitalists argued that fermentation could not take place without the presence of living yeasts. But Eduard Büchner (1860–1917), a German chemist, disproved this in 1896 by grinding up yeasts so small that they contained no living cells, and showing that they could still cause fermentation. Büchner's "ferments" – now known as enzymes – were chemicals containing no vital force. Yet in spite of these demonstrations, vitalism has never died; many people prefer to believe that living things are more than chemical machines.

PERIODIC TABLE

As the number of elements grew, chemists looked for ways of organizing them in a systematic way that reflected both their atomic weights and their properties. The French geologist Béguyer de Chancourtois (1819–86) and the English chemist John Newlands (1837–98) both produced tables ordering the elements by atomic weight, but credit for the correct classification of the elements rightly went to the Russian Dmitri Mendeleyev (1834–1907).

Although he did not produce his table until 1869, with an improved version in 1871, Mendeleyev was so sure of its value that he did not hesitate to leave gaps where he felt elements had yet to be discovered, or place known elements out of strict order if their properties suggested this. He left three gaps, announcing the properties of the elements which would one day fill them. They were discovered – gallium in 1875, scandium in 1879, and germanium in 1886 – exactly as he had predicted: his fame was assured.

CHEMICAL ORDER Dmitri Mendeleyev drew up the elements in his periodic table in rows of increasing atomic weight and columns of similar properties.

PERKIN'S MAUVE AND SYNTHETIC CHEMISTRY

SCIENTIFIC DRESS SENSE Cloth in the delicate new color of mauve – created using the first synthetic dye, mauveine – was enthusiastically embraced by fashionable 19th-century ladies and their dressmakers.

At the age of 18 in 1856, the English chemist William Perkin (1838–1907) discovered the first synthetic dye – an event generally held to mark the birth of the chemical industry.

Perkin was working under the German scientist August Hofmann (1818–92) at the Royal College of Chemistry in London. Hofmann had wondered aloud if it might be possible to synthesize the drug quinine from coal tar, a byproduct of the coal-gas industry. At Easter 1856, working in a laboratory he had rigged up at home, Perkin tried to create quinine by oxidizing aniline and produced a black precipitate. As he was about to throw it away, he caught a purplish glint, added alcohol, and produced a beautiful purple.

He sent it to John Pullar and Son of Perth, a firm of Scottish dyers. "If your discovery does not make the goods too expensive, it is decidedly one of the most valuable that has come out for some time," wrote Robert Pullar in reply. To Hofmann's horror, Perkin resigned from the college, set up a plant to produce the dye, and was in production by 1857. English buyers proved sceptical at first, but the French dyers were enthusiastic, naming the color "mauve" (from the French word for the madder plant, the source of a vegetable dye of similar color) and the chemical, mauveine. Perkin became rich enough to sell up and return to chemistry full time by the age of 35.

RADIOACTIVITY AND ISOTOPES

In 1896, the French physicist Antoine Henri Becquerel (1852–1908) accidentally found that uranium salts emitted strong radiation. He had discovered radioactivity.

The English chemist William Crookes (1832–1919) then found that purified uranium split into two substances, one much more radioactive than the other. Later, Becquerel showed that the feebly radioactive form, if left alone, increased in radioactivity. The New Zealand-born scientist Ernest Rutherford (1871–1937) and the English chemist Frederick Soddy (1877–1956) suggested that the radioactive elements transformed themselves as they emitted radioactivity. Some of the transformed elements seemed to be chemically identical to existing elements. In 1913 Soddy argued that elements can exist in more than one form, chemically identical but differing in mass: he called them "isotopes."

ULTIMATE SACRIFICE Polish scientist Marie Curie (1867–1934) was poisoned by her prolonged researches into radioactivity and died of radiation poisoning. With her husband Pierre (1859–1906), she discovered new radioactive substances, including radium.

X-RAY CRYSTALLOGRAPHY

The German physicist Wilhelm Röntgen (1845–1923) discovered X-rays in 1895 when he found that some form of unknown radiation from a cathode-ray tube could create a glow in luminescent materials, even through thick sheets of cardboard. In seven weeks of furious activity, he worked out the rays' fundamental properties, but unaware of what they really were, called them "X" for unknown. The discovery provided the first way of observing the skeleton through the soft tissues.

Chemists and physicists immediately began studying X-rays, investigating whether they behaved like light. One way of doing that was to observe whether they could be diffracted – bent – by passing through a finely divided grating. This works only if the spacing of the lines on the grating is roughly the same as the wavelength of the radiation, and the penetrating power of X-rays suggested they were of short wavelength. It occurred to the German physicist Max von Laue (1879–1960) that crystals, with their evenly spaced lines of atoms, might have the right sort of spacing to diffract X-rays. In 1912 he tried it with a crystal of zinc sulfide, and found it worked. The English scientist William Bragg (1862–1942) and his son Lawrence (1890–1971) used X-ray diffraction to work out the structure of unknown crystals in 1915, inventing the powerful technique of X-ray crystallography. X-rays also helped clear up confusion in the periodic table. In 1914 the English physicist Henry Moseley (1887–1915) made use of the fact that different elements emit X-rays of different wavelengths to put the elements in their final order, leaving spaces in the appropriate places.

COLORFUL DESIGN
The plastic catalin, used for this radio c.1940, was often cast in bright shades; made at low temperatures, it did not discolor.

PLASTICS, MANMADE FIBERS

The plastic age began in 1862, when the British chemist Alexander Parkes (1813–90) created cellulose nitrate by exposing cellulose, the structural material of wood, to nitric acid. Improved by the addition of camphor and named celluloid, it was used for toys, wipe-clean collars and cuffs, and ping-pong balls.

The first entirely synthetic plastic was Bakelite, made by the Belgian-born chemist Leo Baekeland (1863–1944) in 1905 by mixing phenol and formaldehyde. A resinous material that could be shaped by heat and pressure, Bakelite was used in telephones and radio sets. In 1930 chemists in Britain, Canada, and Germany found that methyl acrylate could be polymerized to produce a clear plastic, Perspex. In Britain, ICI (Imperial Chemical Industries) chemists also discovered polyethylene (Polythene) in 1935, while the American chemist Wallace Carothers (1896–1937) at Du Pont in the United States synthesized nylon the same year by reacting adipic acid with hexamethylenediamine.

PHYSICS
The secrets of the atom

By the end of the 19th century, it was plain that the idea proposed by the English chemist John Dalton (1766–1844) in 1808 that the atom was a single indivisible particle was wrong. Already one subatomic particle, the electron, had been discovered, and research by New Zealand-born Ernest Rutherford (1871–1937) between 1906 and 1908 showed how extraordinary an object the atom really was. His experiments involved firing helium atoms at thin foils of gold or platinum. Most went straight through, but a few were deflected, as if they had hit something solid. Rutherford concluded that the atom consisted of a tiny core, the nucleus (since shown to occupy only one hundred-thousandth of an atom's volume) surrounded by electrons.

Rutherford's atom was a brilliant step forward, at last beginning to explain the properties of the elements. The nucleus of the atom, he argued, consisted of protons carrying a positive electric charge that was balanced by the negative charge of electrons, which danced in a kind of orbit around the protons. Then, in 1934, the British physicist James Chadwick (1891–1974) discovered another particle, the neutron, which had the same mass as the proton, but no charge. He deduced that protons and neutrons together make up the nucleus.

Simplicity in science seldom lasts long. Chemists had been happy with atoms, then with atoms made up of two particles, and now had to accept the idea of three. But it did not stop there. In 1930, the British physicist Paul Dirac (1902–84) had suggested, on the basis of a mathematical analysis, that each particle should have a matching "antiparticle" equal in mass, but opposite in charge. Two years later, the American Carl Anderson (1905–91) discovered the "anti-electron," or positron, proving Dirac right. The particle menagerie began to grow, challenging physicists to create a model that incorporated them all and also explained how matter was constructed. Scientists have continued that process up to the present day, using particle accelerators of ever-increasing energy to smash particles together and observe the results.

It is the theorists who have taken the lead. Their models suggest the possible existence of new particles which the experimenters then set out to find. Today's model of the atom, based on quarks and gluons, is known as the standard model and has so far satisfied all experimental tests. But if history is any guide, it is unlikely to prove the final word.

QUANTUM THEORY

There are national styles in science, and in the 19th century, British scientists emphasized the continuity of matter and energy, while Germans preferred to think in terms of particles. The Scottish scientist James Clerk Maxwell (1831–79) treated radiation of energy from hot objects as a wave phenomenon, but in 1900 the German physicist Max Planck (1858–1947) suggested that it was not emitted continuously, but in the form of "quanta" – discrete packets of energy. Planck's idea was used by the German-born physicist Albert Einstein (1879–1955) in 1905 to explain why metals exposed to light eject electrons. Einstein also suggested, in the same year, that light was made up of particles called photons.

In 1913, Danish scientist Niels Bohr (1885–1962) used Planck's quantum theory to explain the spectra of light emitted by atoms. He suggested that the electrons orbiting the atomic nucleus could occupy only certain orbits, and that shifting from one to another would be characterized by emission of radiation of a fixed frequency – the spectra of the elements. Bohr was able to explain the spectrum of the simplest element, hydrogen.

UNCERTAINTY PRINCIPLE

Niels Bohr had limited success in explaining the properties of any atom larger than hydrogen. Scientists soon replaced physical models with mathematical ones. In 1924, the French physicist Louis de Broglie (1892–1987) suggested that radiation was both a wave and a particle. Quantum mechanics – new mathematical treatments – were developed to predict the behavior of atoms and their particles. The Austrian scientist Erwin Schrödinger (1887–1961) treated the electron not as a discrete particle, but as the probability of finding a particle at any point. The German scientist Werner Heisenberg (1901–76) introduced the uncertainty principle, which asserted that it is impossible to know both the position and the velocity of an electron at the same moment.

This idea has profound implications. Imagine a microscope capable of making an electron visible. It would have to shine light or other radiation on the electron, but that would affect the electron. We cannot observe it without changing it. There is a limit to physical inquiry – the behavior of matter is not deterministic, but statistical.

CERTAIN GENIUS Atomic scientists pose at a gathering in 1932. Seated, left, is James Chadwick, discoverer of the neutron; seated center, holding a pipe, is Ernest Rutherford; behind him are Lise Meitner and Otto Hahn, who later achieved the first nuclear fission.

SPECIAL THEORY OF RELATIVITY

MASTER OF TIME Albert Einstein's special theory of relativity transformed scientists' view of the relationships between time, matter, and space.

In 1905, Einstein put forward his special theory of relativity. In it, he assumed that light traveled through space in the form of photons. He also asserted that the speed of light in a vacuum is invariant and is independent of the speed of its source. His equations showed that mass increases with velocity, and that time is foreshortened by velocity – two paradoxical conclusions that have nevertheless been verified by experiments in which subatomic particles are accelerated close to the speed of light. Einstein did not disprove the laws of motion developed by Isaac Newton (1642–1727) – these work as long as velocities are moderate. But under extreme conditions they fail, and then only the special theory gets the answers right.

TIMELINE

1900
Max Planck resolves difficulties in the interpretation of atomic spectra with the quantum theory.

1905
Albert Einstein publishes his special theory of relativity.

1907
Herbert McCoy and William Ross describe isotopes.

1913
Niels Bohr explains the atomic spectrum of hydrogen by applying quantum theory to the atom.

1925
Wolfgang Pauli's exclusion principle asserts that in an atom no two electrons can be in the same quantum state.

1930
Paul Dirac predicts the existence of antiparticles.

1934
James Chadwick discovers the neutron.

1939
Otto Hahn and Lise Meitner discover nuclear fission.

1964
The quark is postulated by Murray Gell-Mann.

SEE ALSO

The Enlightenment · · · · · · · · · · ◀
Philosophy of science · · · · · · · · ◀
Chemistry · · · · · · · · · · · · · · · ▶

NUCLEAR FISSION

BOMB THEORISTS Robert Oppenheimer (left), Enrico Fermi (center), and Ernest Lawrence used nuclear fission to power the first atom bomb in 1945. Nuclear fusion made an even more powerful bomb possible.

Following the discovery of the neutron by the English physicist James Chadwick in 1934, scientists investigated elements by bombarding their atoms – using the neutron as a missile. What usually happened was that a new isotope of the element was created, often an unstable one that quickly disintegrated. The Italian physicist Enrico Fermi (1901–54) bombarded uranium and produced a new element.

In Germany Otto Hahn (1879–1968) and Lise Meitner (1878–1968) tried to identify the new element. They thought that Fermi had produced radium, but analysis failed to confirm it. Then Meitner realized that an entirely new kind of nuclear disintegration was occurring. The neutrons were splitting the uranium nucleus in two and creating not radium but radioactive barium, a much lighter element. She called the process fission.

In fact, Meitner and Hahn had discovered that the uranium nucleus was unlike any other. It was so large that it was on the verge of splitting into two, like a huge drop of liquid; the merest tweak was enough. What made the discovery so significant was that fission produced a lot of energy – and in splitting the uranium nucleus it released two or three fresh neutrons, each capable of causing successive fissions in nearby atoms. Given enough uranium, the process would be self-sustaining and explosive, producing an extremely powerful bomb.

THE ATOM BOMB

The discovery of nuclear fission came in 1939 on the eve of World War II. On both sides, physicists were making anxious calculations. Uranium has two isotopes – chemically identical forms differing fractionally in mass and with different radioactive properties. Scientists realized that natural uranium could not be used in a bomb, because only 0.7 percent of it consists of the uranium-235 isotope – the one that is fissile, or capable of being split. Most of the neutrons released by fission would be captured harmlessly by atoms of the non-fissile isotope, uranium-238, and the chain reaction would stop before it had started. Only if the two isotopes could be separated would a bomb be feasible. There was, however, another possibility. If uranium-238 is exposed to a flux of neutrons, it is converted into a new element, plutonium-239, which is also fissile.

Working in England, the Austrian-born physicist Otto Frisch (1904–79) calculated uranium-235's critical mass – the smallest mass capable of sustaining a nuclear chain reaction. He showed that it was just a few pounds – a feasible weight for a portable bomb. In Germany physicists calculated a much greater critical mass, making a bomb in their opinion impracticable. The "Manhattan Project" was launched in the United States to create not one bomb, but two: one based on uranium-235, the other on plutonium-239. The first atom bombs were dropped by the U.S. Air Force on Hiroshima and Nagasaki in Japan in 1945.

In the 1950s an even more powerful bomb was developed. Instead of splitting a heavy atom into two, the hydrogen bomb combined two light elements (isotopes of hydrogen) to create a heavier one, a process called fusion. In both fission and fusion, the elements that are produced weigh fractionally less than the starting materials, so mass is "lost" – or rather it is not lost, but converted directly into energy, according to Einstein's equation $E = mc^2$.

Nuclear weapons have proved to be among the most influential discoveries of all time. They have changed the nature of defense by introducing the concept of deterrence, the threat that any attack will be met by a withering response.

POWER OF THE ATOM UNLEASHED The center of the Japanese port of Nagasaki was reduced to rubble, and 75,000 people were killed or wounded on August 9, 1945, when the U.S. dropped the second of its two atomic bombs. The first had been dropped on Hiroshima three days earlier.

ANTIMATTER

The existence of antiparticles – proposed by British physicist Paul Dirac (1902–84) in 1930 – raises, in theory at least, the possibility of a bomb even more powerful than the atom bomb. When a particle meets its antiparticle, they annihilate each other – and the total mass of both is converted directly into energy. To make such a prospect possible in practice, however, some means would have to be found of storing antimatter out of contact with ordinary matter.

Although the first antiparticle was discovered in 1932, and was followed by many others, combining the antiparticles to create antimatter was not achieved until 1996 by scientists in Geneva, Switzerland. By combining positrons with antiprotons, a few atoms of antihydrogen were briefly created before they were annihilated by collisions with ordinary matter. The experiment, a technical tour de force, confirmed the existence of a material which had been the stock-in-trade of science fiction since Dirac had first postulated the existence of the positron more than 50 years before.

CREATION'S NEGATIVE Antimatter was first made – from antiparticles – in 1996 in this particle accelerator at the European Laboratory for Particle Physics in Switzerland.

QUANTUM ELECTRODYNAMICS

PERFORMANCE SCIENTIST Richard Feynman, whose work on quantum electrodynamics with Julian Schwinger and Shin'ichiro Tomonaga won the 1965 Nobel Prize for Physics, was a compelling lecturer.

Relativity, quantum theory, and electromagnetism came together in the early 1930s in a synthesis known as quantum electrodynamics, or QED. The theory can be applied to predict the behavior of atoms and electrons, but it does not deal with internal atomic structure. It is, in a sense, the ultimate chemical theory, since chemistry is involved with the behavior of atoms. When the British theoretical physicist Paul Dirac made the first steps in QED in 1928, he claimed with only slight exaggeration that his relativistic quantum-mechanical equation for the electron explained most of physics and all of chemistry.

The problem with Dirac's equations was that when solved approximately they gave good results, but when attempts were made to become more precise, they failed. The equations kept throwing up infinities, which was absurd. This frustrated many great physicists, including Dirac; the theory seemed to be right, but when pressed, it produced nonsensical answers. The difficulty was solved by the Japanese physicist Shin'ichiro Tomonaga (1906–79) and the Americans Julian Schwinger (1918–94) and Richard Feynman (1918–88) in the late 1940s. Their method allowed quantum electrodynamics to make very precise calculations, and it has proved a successful theory. For example, the response of an electron to an external magnetic field is measured by a quantity known as Dirac's Number. The theory calculates this number to be 1.00115965246; experiment finds it to be 1.00115965221, an astonishingly close agreement – equivalent, in Feynman's words, to measuring the distance between New York and Los Angeles to within the thickness of a human hair. Quantum electrodynamics is, said Feynman, "the jewel of physics – our proudest possession."

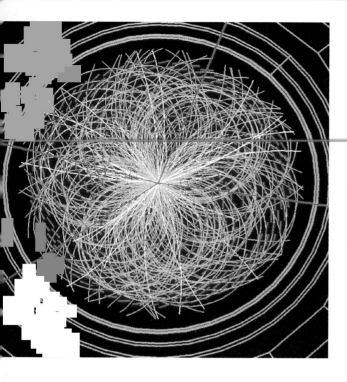

HIGGS BOSONS

SECRETS OF MASS A computer simulation shows (red lines) four Higgs bosons – a theoretical particle that binds other particles into the Higgs field, where they acquire mass – and other particles (blue lines) as scientists believe they would look after a violent collision between two protons.

The mystery of mass is one of the greatest puzzles faced by physicists. Why do the particles that make up matter differ so greatly in mass, and where does mass come from? The electron and the muon, for example, are two particles that are identical except that the muon is 200 times heavier.

The Scottish physicist Peter Higgs (1929–) came up with a proposal to explain this, and indeed the origin of all mass. He suggested that a field exists that gives particles mass. This he called the Higgs field. He based the theory on the way in which the gravitational and electromagnetic fields work: a heavy mass lifted to a higher position acquires potential energy because of its changed position in the Earth's gravitational field. If Higgs's proposal that all particles acquire mass by their interaction with the Higgs field is right, then differences in mass are a function of how strongly a particle couples to the field.

The electromagnetic field is created by particles of light, or photons. The gravitational field is believed to be the result of a particle called the graviton. If the Higgs field exists, scientists reason that it must have its own particle – and this theoretical particle has been named the Higgs boson. By calculation, physicists know what this particle is like, but they have not found one yet.

To find subatomic particles, scientists break atoms up by smashing them into each other at very high speeds. The greater the speed, the more violent the collision and the smaller the particles that can be detected. The scientists use vast chambers called particle accelerators, in which the atoms are accelerated through great distances, but no existing accelerator is large enough to create a collision violent enough to detect the Higgs boson.

UNIFIED FIELD THEORY

Many attempts have been made to discover a single theory that describes all natural forces. Albert Einstein (1879–1955) spent most of his later years in an attempt to unify his general-relativistic explanation of gravity with electromagnetism, but without success. The aim of those who search for a unified theory is to find an underlying principle, or set of equations, which would both explain the multiplicity of subatomic particles and, when the appropriate approximations were applied, yield Einstein's equation for gravitation and the equations for electromagnetism proposed by the Scottish physicist James Clerk Maxwell (1831–79). No such theory yet exists: string theory is the closest approach so far.

A SINGLE FORCE Sheldon Glashow (1932–) proposed a grand unified theory of elementary particles in 1974. He argued that the three subatomic forces – the strong, the weak, and the electromagnetic – were in reality parts of a single force.

STRING THEORY

Ultimate theories of matter are plagued by infinities. Ways of dealing with them were found in the theory of quantum electrodynamics, but this theory does not incorporate gravity. Any "theory of everything" has to include gravity, so some method must be devised for eliminating infinities. In frustration, some theorists wondered what would happen if particles were treated not as points, but as extended strings.

In string theory, the particles consist of tiny loops, so small that for the purpose of much scientific observation they are essentially equivalent to points. The beauty of the string theory is that it reduces to Einstein's general theory of gravitation, without raising any of the usual problems with infinities. This has led many physicists to believe that it may contain at least an element of the truth. It remains to be seen whether string theory can predict the existence of known subatomic particles, or of particles yet to be discovered. If it can, then its position would be enormously strengthened.

> ### "All science is either physics or stamp collecting."
>
> *Ernest Rutherford (1871–1937), British physicist*

QUARKS

As subatomic particles proliferated, physicists found themselves in the same position as chemists before the Russian scientist Dmitri Mendeleyev (1834–1907) produced his periodic table in 1869. They urgently needed some classification of the particles to bring order out of confusion.

In 1964 the American physicist Murray Gell-Mann (1929–) came up with the idea of quarks, ultraelementary particles from which others could be constructed. His idea was that every baryon – the class of elementary particles to which the proton and the neutron belong – could be made up of three quarks. He called them quarks after the line "three quarks for Musther Mark" in the novel *Finnegan's Wake*, by the Irish writer James Joyce (1882–1941), published in 1939.

Gell-Mann's scheme was designed for economy of explanation: he wanted a way of explaining the baryonic jungle in the simplest way. He did not spell out whether he meant his ideas to be taken literally or metaphorically. In fact, experiments have since shown that quarks are real, and almost all the varieties that Gell-Mann outlined have been discovered.

PARTICLE DANCE Quarks are grouped in triplets in this computer simulation of a silicon nucleus. Each trio is either a positively charged proton (two pinks, one green) or an uncharged neutron (two greens, one pink). Clouds of gluons – another type of subatomic particle – hold the quarks together.

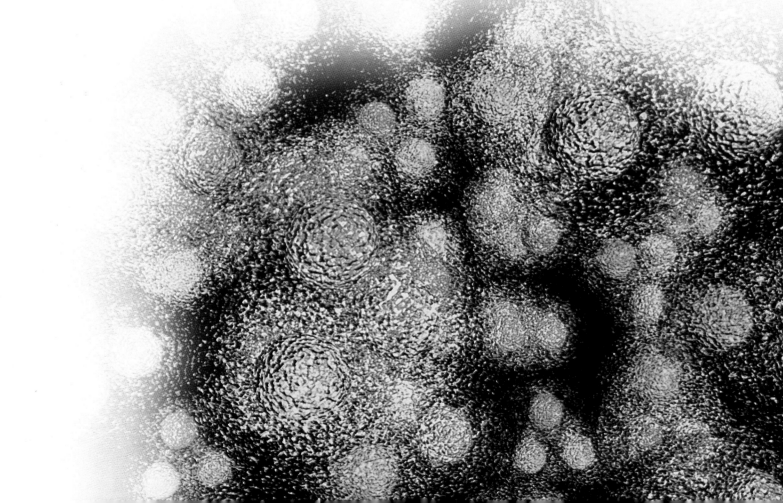

THE FOUR FORCES

Just four forces are responsible for the behavior of matter. Gravity – the attraction between different masses – has been studied since the time of the English physicist Isaac Newton (1642–1727). It is the weakest of the forces, and the least well understood, but it is the force that sculpts the cosmos.

Electromagnetism, explored by the Scottish physicist James Clerk Maxwell (1831–79) in the 19th century, is the force experienced by charged particles. It is the best understood: the theory of quantum electrodynamics makes very precise calculations possible. The two other forces, the so-called strong and weak forces, operate within the nucleus of an atom. The strong force holds the nucleus together, while the weak force controls processes such as radioactive decay.

The forces differ enormously in strength and in the distances over which they operate. The strong force is by far the most powerful: if its value is set at 15, then the electromagnetic force has a value of 0.0073, the weak force a value of 10^{-12}, and the gravitational force a value of 10^{-35}. The strong force within nuclei would dominate all physical phenomena if it were not so short range, but at distances between particles of more than 10^{-13} centimeters it ceases to operate. The electromagnetic force operates by means of the charges on particles which tend to cancel out over long distances. The weak force has an even shorter range than the strong force. But the force of gravity – negligible at short range – does operate over great distances.

FRACTALS

In 1926 the English scientist Lewis Richardson (1881–1953) asked what sounds a simple question: how long is the coast of Britain? He showed that the answer depends entirely on the length of the ruler. Using a ruler 1 yard (about 1 meter) long will produce a quite different answer from using one only 1 inch (2 cm) long, because the shorter ruler will go in and out of all sorts of tiny crevices ignored by the longer one.

Many years later, Richardson's insight inspired the Polish-born mathematician, Benoit Mandelbrot (1924–), who found that the smaller the ruler used, the greater the coastal length, without limit. A coastline is not like a circle or a square or a straight line; its ragged shape repeats itself on every scale from the largest to the smallest. Mandelbrot gave such shapes the name fractals, and showed that they could be generated on computers from quite simple equations.

> *"Fractals describe the roughness of the world, its energy, its dynamical changes and transformations."*
>
> *John Briggs (1945–), science writer*

THEORETICAL WORLDS Computer-generated fractal images derived from equations float like planets in an undiscovered mathematicians' galaxy. Most fractals are "self-similar" – each part, no matter how small, resembles the whole. A snowflake has this quality. The word fractal comes from the Latin *fractus*, meaning fragmented.

CHAOS

In 1959 the American meteorologist Edward Lorentz (1917–) was using a computer to forecast the weather. He programmed the machine to predict the latitude of westerly winds, using a set of equations with 12 variables, and it produced variations rather like those of real weather. One day, trying to repeat the calculations, he re-entered some figures the computer had printed out some time before and set it running again. This time, the numbers bore no relation to the previous run. He suspected the computer had gone wrong, but on checking the calculations, found something much more interesting. The new calculations closely matched the old ones at first, but then diverged, the differences doubling in size every four days of forecasting until all resemblance disappeared.

Lorentz saw that tiny changes in the initial values, caused by rounding off the last decimal place, were altering the whole calculation. Instead of being deterministic, the equations were behaving chaotically. If this truly represented the atmosphere, Lorentz realized, long-range weather forecasting was impossible. In a phrase that has become famous, he declared that the flap of a butterfly's wing in Brazil could set off a tornado in Texas.

Today it has been realized that many natural and manmade systems behave chaotically, from the growth of populations to the flow of a river and the prices on a stock market. Science has long assumed that nature is deterministic. The French astronomer Pierre Simon, Marquis de Laplace (1749–1827), declared at the beginning of the 19th century that if he knew the precise state of the universe at any starting point, and the laws that governed it, he could predict everything that would happen in future. Chaos theory asserts that he was wrong.

CHAOTIC PATTERN The Lorentz Attractor – developed by Edward Lorentz in the 1960s – is a three-dimensional graph of two spirals, representing the solution to three equations, one of whose variables is time. The spiral shape develops as time passes, never repeating exactly but remaining within a simple overall pattern.

SYMMETRY

NATURAL BEAUTY Symmetry is widely found in nature and, whether in the shape of a leaf or of a well-proportioned face, is pleasing to the human eye. Yet physicists have discovered that symmetrical patterns do not occur in certain subatomic activities that are governed by the weak force.

Though ragged, the shapes of nature seem to express an underlying symmetry. Crystals, the shapes of animals, and the leaves of trees, even the bilateral symmetry of the human body, imply that symmetry is intrinsic. Until 1956 it was believed that this symmetry was reflected right down to the subatomic level: every particle had an antiparticle, for example, and a spinning particle is just as likely to spin one way as the other. In particle physics, this concept is called the conservation of parity. This means that the laws of physics are identical in right- or left-handed sets of coordinates; nature does not make any fundamental distinction between right and left.

The concept was overturned late in 1956 by Tsung Dao Lee (1926–) and Chen Ning Yang (1922–), two Chinese physicists working in the United States. They suggested that parity might not be conserved in so-called weak interactions – processes involving the weak force – such as the process known as beta decay. Another Chinese physicist, Chien-Shiung Wu (1912–), proved that they were right: nature is left-handed.

EVOLUTION
The secret of life's diversity

The great diversity of life on Earth and the web of interdependence between different species have long been used by believers as powerful evidence for a Creator. Surely, they argue, such an elegant and complex system, each part perfectly matched to its purpose, could only have arisen by design. It was the greatest triumph of 19th-century science, Charles Darwin's theory of evolution by natural selection, that gave the lie to this argument of design.

Many philosophers, from Aristotle on, had wondered whether organisms had evolved one into another. But it needed two profound shifts of understanding to make a theory of evolution credible. The first was the discovery of fossils and the evidence they provided of species that had once lived but were now extinct, first suggested by a Swiss naturalist called Charles Bonnet (1720–93) in 1770. Twenty years later, an English land surveyor, William Smith (1769–1839), discovered that different layers of rock through which he was digging a canal contained different fossils. In 1800 the French naturalist Georges Cuvier (1769–1832) classified the known fossils, finding that while many belonged to surviving families of plants and animals, others did not. He attributed these extinctions to periodical catastrophes.

The second underlying idea was the discovery that the Earth was not simply a few thousand, but millions or billions of years old. That made it possible to believe that slow changes to a species – too slow to observe in a lifetime – might over eons of time transform it entirely. In 1859 Darwin published *On The Origin of Species*, which suggested the mechanism by which this change might come about. The idea alarmed Victorian society and scandalized the church, for it suggested that all the infinite variety of life could be explained by the operation of chance acting on the small variations between one member of a species and another.

Darwin's idea, "the single best idea anybody has ever had" according to the American philosopher Daniel Dennett, lacked a mechanism. Darwin could show that change had occurred, and why it had occurred, but could not explain how. Knowledge of the laws of inheritance, of genes, and of genetic mutations provided this apparatus. Brought together as the Modern Synthesis in the 1940s by the work of several biologists, the combination of Darwin and Mendel has proved an enduring theory which still underpins all biology.

LAMARCKISM

The first scientific theory of evolution came from the French naturalist Jean Baptiste de Lamarck (1744–1829) in 1809. He proposed that the characteristics acquired by a creature during its lifetime could be transmitted to its descendants – the "inheritance of acquired characteristics." He took as an example the giraffe, then newly discovered by Europeans and something of a sensation. He imagined an ordinary sort of antelope feeding on the leaves of trees, constantly stretching its neck and standing as tall as it could to reach ever higher ones. Over a lifetime, legs, neck, and tongue would extend, an advantage the creature could then pass on to its offspring. In the course of not very many generations, the antelope would have become a giraffe.

Lamarckism is an attractive idea, appealing strongly to the notion that by improving ourselves we can improve the lot of our children, and of all mankind: but it is false. It can be easily disproved experimentally, as the German biologist August Weissman (1834–1914) showed by cutting off the tails of generations of mice, and proving that the final generation grew tails just as long as the first.

The final nail in the coffin of Lamarckism came from the discovery (also by Weissman, in 1883) that the germ cells, which produce sperm and eggs, separate at an early stage in the embryo and remain unchanged throughout life. No mechanism has ever been found by which these cells could take up changes acquired by other cells of the body during life.

MENDELIAN GENETICS

Gregor Mendel (1822–84), an Austrian monk, became interested in the mechanisms of inheritance in the 1860s. Sensibly, he chose to study a simple system, the pea, which he could grow in the monastery garden.

By crossing a line of peas with round seeds with a line whose seeds were crinkly, he could explore how these characteristics were inherited. He did the same with a variety of different characteristics, and found a surprising result. When a wrinkled pea is crossed with a round one, for example, the result is not a pea halfway between the two, but a round pea. But when these round peas in turn were sown and used to fertilize each other, the crinkly form returned. For every three plants producing round peas, one produced crinkly ones.

Mendel deduced that each parent pea possessed particles, which we now call genes, that carry the characteristics of roundness or crinkliness. The next generation gets one from each parent, but the one for roundness dominates the one for crinkliness, while the other is recessive. Both genes remain in the pea, and in the next generation, they can combine in just four possible ways. Three of these would produce round peas, and one, crinkly – explaining both the reappearance of the "lost" characteristic, and the three to one ratio he observed.

DARWIN AND NATURAL SELECTION

In 1831 Charles Darwin (1809–82) joined HMS *Beagle* as companion to its captain, Robert FitzRoy, and sailed off on a five-year voyage around the world. On the journey, he collected specimens of every species he encountered and began to ask himself questions about how they had evolved. More than 20 years after his return – and then only because Alfred Wallace had independently reached the same conclusions – he published his theory of evolution by natural selection.

Darwin argued that in each species there were small variations between individuals. Some were larger, or had beaks of slightly different shapes, or could run faster, than others. For most of the time, these differences did not affect the chances of an individual surviving. But when times were hard, even a small difference might enhance the chances of survival. That meant that species possessing the advantage had a greater chance of passing it on, because they would on average have more offspring. In this way, the whole population would eventually share the characteristic and over time evolve into a distinct species.

Darwin was vague about how this last step took place, as well he might be; even today the mechanisms of speciation are a subject of debate. But his idea of natural selection provided a means of explaining both the variety of nature and its exquisite fitness for purpose.

RETIRING RADICAL Twenty years passed between Charles Darwin's original observations and the publication of his groundbreaking work *On The Origin of Species*. This was because Darwin was aware that his theories would cause a furor, and he was not a naturally combative personality.

EVOLUTION OBSERVED

SPECIALIST BEAKS The Galapagos finches with different beaks adapted to different conditions confirmed for Darwin his theories of evolution.

Darwin was able to show changes in species from the fossil record, but could not show those changes happening in real time. His observations in the isolated Galapagos Islands led him to speculate that plants and animals adapted to the demands of their environment. He was particularly intrigued by the number of variations in the beaks of finches. He speculated that as food supplies adjusted to changing environments, finches with different-shaped beaks waxed and waned. Some developed powerful beaks specialized for cracking hard nuts, while others had fine-pointed beaks suitable for other sources of food.

Over the past 30 years, biologists have been observing evolution in these finches. Their studies have shown conclusively that changes in the environment, such as drought, do indeed alter the bird population.

THE GENE

The Austrian geneticist Gregor Mendel (1822–84) had no idea what his "particles" of inheritance were, but observations of cells in the 1880s showed that when they split, threadlike structures form and divide equally between the newly developing cells. German botanist August Weissman (1834–1914) decided that these structures, given the name chromosomes (colored body) because they could be made visible by staining with dyes, must be the carriers of the hereditary instructions. They came in pairs, obeying Mendel's rules, but there were far too few of them to account for the huge variety of inherited characteristics.

Experiments by the American geneticist Thomas Hunt Morgan (1866–1945) at Columbia University, using the fruit fly *Drosophila melanogaster* (the laboratory mouse of genetics), showed that the chromosomes were in fact packages containing many of Mendel's particles, which were given the name genes in 1909 by the Danish biologist Wilhelm Johannsen (1857–1927). Morgan's experiments, which involved breeding flies with different characteristics, began to show the location of genes for specific characteristics on the chromosomes.

DNA

In 1868, chemical analysis of white blood cells by the Swiss chemist Johann Miescher (1844–95) showed that in the nucleus was a phosphorus-containing substance very different from protein: Miescher called it nuclein. Further work showed it to be acidic, so it was renamed nucleic acid. Miescher had an inkling that this molecule might carry the hereditary message, though few agreed. Chemical analysis showed that nucleic acids – of which there are two sorts, deoxyribonucleic acid (DNA) and ribonucleic acid (RNA) – were rather monotonous molecules. DNA was made up of just four basic building blocks, called bases – adenine, cytosine, guanine, and thymine – while in RNA thymine was replaced by uracil. Most biologists thought that proteins, which were more complex molecules, were better candidates for the genes.

In the late 1940s and early 1950s at Cambridge University, Alexander Todd (1907–), a Scottish organic chemist, worked out the chemical constituents of DNA. He showed that it consisted of a backbone of alternating sugar and phosphate groups, with the four bases attached to each sugar opposite the phosphate. In the early 1950s, several groups of scientists started to search for the actual shape of the molecule. Success went to biologists Francis Crick (1916–) and James Watson (1928–), working at Cambridge, using X-ray crystallographic images taken by British scientist Rosalind Franklin (1920–58) at King's College, London. In 1953, in one of the seminal discoveries

DNA MOLECULE DNA's capacity for storing genetic information underlies the reproduction of all life on Earth.

of the 20th century, they showed that DNA consists of a double-helix, two intertwined spirals linked by pairs of bases. This structure fitted both the chemical and the X-ray data and, what is more, suggested how hereditary information might be passed on when a cell divided.

The discovery of DNA as the hereditary material provides a mechanism for evolution. Experiments show that the recipe it carries can be modified by the process of mutation; sometimes errors seem to arise spontaneously, but chemicals and radiation can also cause mutation. In many cases, such mutations prove fatal, but some may provide species with the characteristics needed to guarantee better survival. So it is the mutation of DNA that provides the variation on which the environment works in the process of natural selection.

DNA MODEL Francis Crick (left) and James Watson shared the 1962 Nobel Prize for their discovery of the structure of DNA.

ETHOLOGY

In the 1930s, partly in response to the American emphasis on the behavior of animals in laboratory situations, biologists in Europe developed a more natural approach. Ethology, founded by the Austrian Konrad Lorenz (1903–89) and the British zoologist Niko Tinbergen (1907–88), sought to study how animals behaved in their natural surroundings. The subject is concerned with how animals respond to stimuli – from other animals and from their own bodies – and what those responses mean to other animals. This approach has become the basis of all modern nature films.

Behaviorism, which represents the opposite pole, was developed by the American psychologist John Broadus Watson (1878–1958) in the early 20th century. His aim was to show that what people do is largely determined by conditioning, not by their own free will. Experiments with animals in captivity showed that behaviorism could explain how they learned new skills, but it has had limited application to human psychology.

IMPRINTING Konrad Lorenz's first discovery as a scientist occurred when he was given a one-day-old duckling that followed him around as if he was its mother.

PUNCTUATED EQUILIBRIUM

The evidence of the fossil record, with its apparently sudden changes, led the evolutionists Stephen Jay Gould (1941–) and Niles Eldridge (1943–) to suggest their theory of punctuated equilibrium in 1972. While orthodox Darwinians see all change as gradual, Gould and Eldridge argued there appeared to be long periods of stasis interrupted by bursts of rapid change.

Punctuated equilibrium did seem to explain a puzzling feature of the geological record. If Darwin was right that species evolved slowly, then there ought to be a continuous gradation of intermediate forms found among fossils, and this is not generally seen. If species evolved in spurts, then intermediate forms would exist for such a short time that their absence from the record would be unsurprising.

The defenders of Darwinism argue, however, that this is not a problem. Suppose, as the American evolutionist George Ledyard Stebbins (1906–) suggests, that mice were subject to a tiny selective pressure to increase in size. The process is too slow to observe, yet eventually mice would be the size of elephants. Stebbins calculated that this would take 12,000 generations – say 60,000 years. That is a long time, but by the standards of paleontology, it is almost instantaneous, and the fossil record is too blunt an instrument to measure so short a period.

GENETIC CODE

Once the structure of DNA had been determined, the next step was to figure out how it stored the huge amounts of genetic information needed to create living things. DNA is made of nucleic acids, but the actual materials of life are proteins, complex molecules assembled from a repertoire of amino acids. This was known by 1905 through the work of Emil Fischer (1852–1919) in Germany, but until about 1940 it was not known how many amino acids there were. The answer was that the entire range of proteins could be made from about 20 amino acids, arranged in different orders. The unique properties of each protein, and the three-dimensional shape it adopted, depended on the order of the amino acids. The first such chain to be "sequenced" – that is, to have the complete order of its amino acids worked out – was insulin, by the English biochemist Frederick Sanger (1918–) in 1951.

In 1957, the British scientist Vernon Ingram (1924–) demonstrated that just one amino acid out of its proper place made a protein behave differently. He showed that the fatal condition sickle-cell anemia was caused by the substitution of valine for glutamic acid at position six on the hemoglobin beta chain.

Four years later, in 1961, Englishman Francis Crick (1916–) and South African-born Sidney Brenner (1927–) performed experiments in which they deliberately damaged the DNA of bacteriophages – viruses that infect bacteria. They found that knocking out one or two base pairs generally prevented the phages from growing. But if they knocked out three base pairs, the phages grew. This suggested that the DNA code was made up by the order of the bases, and that it consisted of a series of three-base groups, or "three-letter words." Removing one or two prevented the code being read, since it had to be read in groups of three. Removing three made a change in the protein, but it did not make nonsense of the code.

There are four "letters" in the DNA code – those of the four bases. If these four letters are arranged in all available combinations, 64 three-letter words can be made. Since there are only 20 or so proteins to be coded, the code is ample to carry the recipe for all the amino acids. The entire code was worked out by 1967, and it was clear that it was universal – all living things use the same code for translating their genes into proteins. For the first time, scientists were close to understanding the mystery of how characteristics were handed down and how cells were programmed.

LIFE-CARRYING THREADS Chromosomes, which consist of DNA, are the structures in the nucleus of cells that bear the genetic code. The information they carry governs the inheritance of characteristics from one generation to another.

GENE THERAPY

GIANT STEP A space suit allows a boy born with a genetically malfunctioning immune system to brave outdoor germs. Amending the genes can cure the disease.

When a link has been made between a gene defect and a disease, the possibility arises of trying to cure the disease by inserting the correct DNA sequence into the cells that are malfunctioning. Diseases caused by a single misplaced base pair, such as cystic fibrosis, seem to offer the best prospects, although early trials in patients in Britain and the United States produced only modest signs of success.

The first evidence that gene therapy might work came in 1990 from trials in which children born without a functioning immune system were given the gene for the enzyme adenosine deaminase (ADA). The absence of the enzyme prevents the immune system from working, leaving those born without it vulnerable to infection and condemned to life inside a plastic "bubble." But in the United States and Italy, such children given the ADA gene showed clear signs of improvement and in several cases were able to lead a normal life.

GENETIC ENGINEERING

Even a simple bacterium contains several hundred genes, each of them made up of thousands of DNA bases. The idea of providing a complete list of these genes, never mind of finding a way to alter them, initially seemed impossible. But in the 1970s, starting with the experiments performed by the American microbiologist Hamilton Smith (1931–), a range of enzymes was found that could be used to cut a length of DNA at a precise, known position. This suggested it would be possible to alter the DNA by splicing in new sections.

The enzyme that cut DNA produced a jagged, or "sticky," end. Fragments of DNA cut with this enzyme were inserted into circular sections of DNA called plasmids – found in bacteria – that had also been cut with sticky ends. The inserted length of DNA interlocked with the plasmid and became part of it – and, as a result, the bacterium was programmed to produce the protein coded by the inserted DNA. The first such experiments were carried out by American biochemists Herbert Boyer (1936–) and Stanley Cohen (1922–) in 1973. Within a decade, the method was being used to create proteins such as the human growth hormone from bacteria reprogrammed to make the human protein and grown in culture dishes.

This technique is not restricted to bacteria. Many crop plants have now been genetically engineered by inserting genes – for instance, to make the plants more resistant to pesticides so that large areas of land may be sprayed without the need to distinguish between crops and weeds. In 1997, British scientists managed to clone a sheep – called Dolly – using genetic engineering.

ANIMAL DONOR In tests, pig organs have been modified so that they bear signals declaring them to be human. The hope is that the organs would not be recognized as foreign if they were transplanted into human patients, creating a new source of organs to meet the increasing demand for transplants.

HUMAN GENOME PROJECT

At least 3,000 human diseases are known to be hereditary, passed from parents to their children by defects in the genes. Even diseases such as cancer or heart disease have a strong genetic component. During the 1990s, a large number of genes for common conditions were worked out, as biologists explored

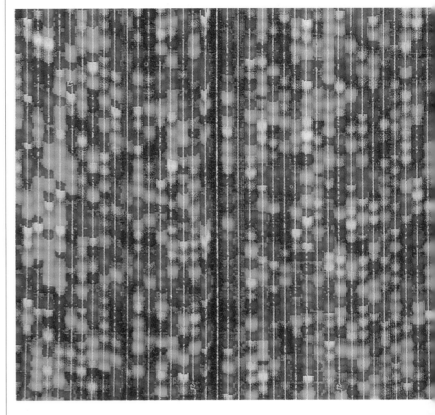

FRAGMENT OF THE HUMAN CODE Humans are made up of more than 100,000 genes, coded by three billion base pairs. Scientists are attempting to log all of them and produce a definitive blueprint of the body.

the full human complement, or genome. The Human Genome Project is an international effort to produce a map showing where all known genes lie along the DNA, which is split between 23 chromosomes. After that, the aim is to go on to sequence the entire genome. The first complete genomes to be produced were of simpler organisms, such as the bacteria *Mycoplasma genitalum* and *Haemophilus influenzae*, elucidated in the mid-1990s. The full human genome is expected to take well into the next millennium to work out.

MEDICINE

The struggle to prevent and cure disease

The patient at the beginning of the 19th century was little better off than he or she had been in the ancient world. The circulation of the blood had been discovered in 1603 by the Englishman William Harvey (1578–1657), and vaccination by his countryman Edward Jenner (1749–1823) in 1796, but in 1800 surgery remained primitive, anesthetics were nonexistent, and the cause of common infectious diseases was still a mystery.

It was growing prosperity in the 19th century that allowed doctors to begin a more systematic exploration of disease. Better instruments – such as the stethoscope, the hypodermic syringe, and the thermometer – emerged at the same time as new ideas in biochemistry, physiology, and the transmission of disease. The greatest contribution of all was the simplest: the provision of clean water and effective sewerage in cities removed one of the greatest sources of disease at a stroke.

The 19th century saw rapid advances in the understanding of respiration, nutrition, the digestive system, and above all microbiology. Effective treatments did not immediately follow; many drugs enjoyed a vogue, but their effectiveness was never proven. Not until the discovery of sulfonamides and antibiotics in the 20th century did bacterial diseases begin to lose their terror; however, viral diseases still lack comparably effective treatments today.

As threats from infectious disease diminished and life expectancy increased, other diseases emerged: heart disease, cancer, and the dementias. These degenerative diseases, though well understood in many cases, have proved hard to prevent or cure.

VACCINATION

In the 18th century, it was common knowledge in the west of England that milkmaids who contracted cowpox (*Variola vaccinae*) never caught the deadly smallpox. A farmer, Benjamin Jesty, decided in 1774 to infect his wife and child deliberately with material from a cowpox pustule, using a stocking needle. When they subsequently proved immune to smallpox, Edward Jenner took an interest.

In 1796 Jenner put the theory to the test by inoculating an eight-year-old boy, James Phipps, with cowpox and then, six weeks later, with smallpox. The boy proved immune. Jenner went on to inoculate 23 other people, publishing his results in 1798. Within three years, 100,000 people in Britain had been inoculated, and a disease that had replaced plague as the worst epidemic was at last brought under control.

THE GERM THEORY

The French chemist Louis Pasteur (1822–95) was responsible for demonstrating that many diseases were caused by microbes too small to see. Pasteur's initial breakthrough came in 1864 when he proved that the fermentation of wine and beer was accomplished by yeasts that could be killed by heating (pasteurization).

In the 1870s, the German doctor Robert Koch (1843–1910) isolated the microbe responsible for anthrax in cattle – a rod-shaped bacterium or bacillus. Koch went on to isolate the bacilli responsible for tuberculosis and cholera. Pasteur decided to use a weakened form of the anthrax bacillus as an immunization against the disease.

He produced an enfeebled version of the microbe by culturing it at high temperature. In 1881 he injected it into 24 sheep, a goat, and six cows. Two weeks later, he injected this group, plus a control group of unvaccinated animals, with pure anthrax. When he returned after two days, he found the vaccinated animals well and the unvaccinated ones dead or dying. He named the process vaccination, after the disease *Variola vaccinae* which had inspired Jenner's successful experiment.

ENEMY OF DISEASE Louis Pasteur concentrated on preventing illness rather than curing it. He saved many lives in the Franco-Prussian War of 1870 by insisting that doctors should boil instruments and steam bandages.

ANTISEPTIC SURGERY

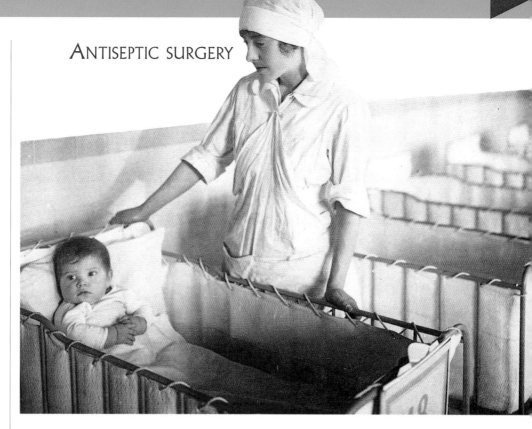

A CLEAN, SAFE PLACE Joseph Lister's methods of "antisepsis" transformed hospitals from breeding grounds for disease into places of healing.

In the 1860s anyone entering a hospital for surgery was, according to the physician Sir James Simpson (1811–70), the inventor of chloroform, "exposed to more chances of death than was the English soldier on the field of Waterloo." Hospitals were crowded; new patients were often put in dirty beds; surgeons wore the same, unwashed operating coat – sometimes for many years. Patients who died on wards when their wounds became infected were said to be victims of "hospital disease."

Joseph Lister (1827–1912), an English surgeon at Glasgow Royal Infirmary, had already come to the conclusion that the infections might be caused by an airborne dust when in 1864 he came across Louis Pasteur's work on the role of microorganisms in fermentation. Lister set about finding a practical means of protecting wounds from infection by microbes. He chose carbolic acid, a derivative of coal tar, as a cleansing agent. On August 12, 1865, he operated on James Greenlees, an 11-year-old boy with a compound leg fracture – one in which the bone has broken tissue and skin, and which presents a great risk of infection. Lister cleaned the wound with a solution of carbolic acid in linseed oil and protected it with a mixture of the acid and putty – intended to hold the acid firmly in place over the wound – before applying a dressing. The treatment was a success: six weeks later, the boy's leg was healed.

In 1867 Lister called for the general use of antiseptic methods in hospitals. At first, he was ignored, but during the 1870s and 1880s his theories became widely accepted.

SEE ALSO

Philosophy of science ········ ▶
Physical anthropology ········ ◀

ANESTHESIA AND PAIN RELIEF

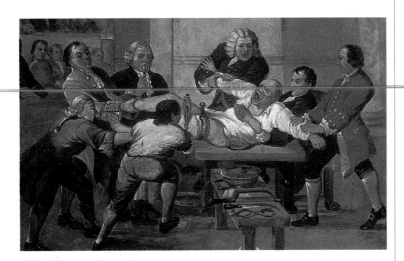

OPERATING AGONY A man endures the horror of having his leg amputated without pain relief. Surgery before anesthesia was a grim business. With no means of dulling the pain, surgeons had to work as fast as they could.

The first successful public use of anesthetics during surgery came in 1846 when William Morton (1819–68) used ether to knock out a young man at Massachusetts General Hospital while a tumor was removed from the patient's neck. In England, chloroform – pleasanter to inhale and more potent – came into use in 1847. The first local anesthetic was cocaine, developed by Karl Koller (1857–1944) in Vienna from an extract of the coca plant that had been chewed by Peruvian Indians for centuries. It was effective but caused addiction; safer substitutes such as novocaine followed.

A source of pain relief for conditions such as arthritis, headache, or toothache was discovered in 1758 by the Reverend Edward Stone (1702–68) of Chipping Norton, Oxfordshire, England. Guided no doubt by folk traditions, he found that twigs of the white willow tree (*Salix alba*) could relieve the pains of the rheumatism to which he was a martyr. Unfortunately, his discovery was ignored. It was not until 1895 that the active ingredient, salicylic acid, was turned into an effective drug by Felix Hoffman, a chemist at the Bayer company. He found that, by modifying it to make acetyl salicylic acid, he could produce a powerful painkiller with fewer damaging side-effects. He named it aspirin.

TRADITIONAL WAY During an influenza outbreak in 1917, boys wear bags containing camphor to ward off the fever. Folk remedies gave way to more scientific treatments as doctors gained a fuller understanding of the medical and social factors lying behind such epidemics.

EPIDEMIOLOGY

When cholera struck Soho, London, in August–September 1854, a local anesthetist named John Snow suspected that it was caused by contamination of the water supply. Most of the cases came from a small area around a pump on Broad Street (now Broadwick Street). Desperate for a way to stem the rush of cases, officials responsible for the area agreed to his suggestion that the pump handle should be removed. The epidemic ended within three days, but an inquiry at first exonerated the pump. Later, a more detailed investigation, carried out by a committee that included Snow, overturned this conclusion. The investigators interviewed local people and found that of 137 who had drunk water from the pump, 80 had caught cholera; of the 297 who had not used it, only 20 had fallen ill. It was the first success for epidemiology – the technique of searching for the cause of a disease by comparing the habits of those who suffer it with those who do not.

Epidemiology has been used to trace the causes of heart disease, cancer, and many other conditions. It is responsible for the conclusion that smoking is a cause of lung cancer, and that diet may influence the development of heart disease.

"The cholera is the best of all sanitary reformers, it overlooks no mistake and pardons no oversight."

The Times, 1849

CHEMOTHERAPY

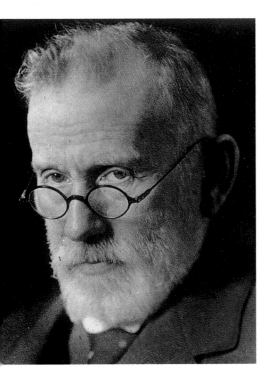

WONDER DRUG The firm that manufactured Paul Ehrlich's antisyphilis shot distributed 65,000 free treatments worldwide. Ehrlich was widely honored for his work. He won the 1908 Nobel Prize for Physiology or Medicine with the Russian Ilya Mechnikov (1845–1916).

The discovery, by Frenchman Louis Pasteur (1822–95) and German Robert Koch (1843–1910), that diseases are caused by germs raised the possibility of curing them with chemicals that would kill the microbes but leave the patient unharmed. Paul Ehrlich (1854–1915), a German bacteriologist, was the first to show that this was possible. He was an expert in the use of dyes to stain bacteria for examination, and reasoned that if a dye could color bacteria while leaving other cells unchanged, it might form the basis of a drug. He found that a dye that he had developed, tryptan red, could destroy the trypanosomes that cause sleeping sickness.

Looking for something better, he began synthesizing all the arsenic-containing compounds he could, testing them one after another. By 1907, he reached number 606, dihydroxydiamino-arsenobenzene hydrochloride. But it did not do well, and he set it aside. Two years later, an assistant found that the compound was effective against spirochetes, the cause of the sexually transmitted disease syphilis. Ehrlich confirmed the result and launched compound 606 as Salvarsan, the first "magic bullet" that could cure a disease. It was not, in fact, a very good drug, requiring many painful injections to effect a cure, but until then no cure at all had been possible, and many syphilitic patients had ended up in asylums with "general paralysis of the insane" – the terminal condition of a horrible disease.

VITAMINS

The success of Pasteur's germ theory led to the belief that all diseases were caused by microbes, parasites, or toxins. All that was needed for good health, it was believed, was avoidance of these infectious agents, and a diet containing carbohydrates, fats, proteins, and mineral salts. However, in 1906, the English biochemist Frederick Gowland Hopkins (1861–1947) found that rats denied milk failed to flourish, and concluded that "astonishingly small amounts" of some substances in food were needed to sustain good health.

In 1912, Casimir Funk (1884–1967), a Polish-born chemist working in London, isolated an active material in rice husks needed to prevent the disease beriberi in pigeons. He called it a vitamine, for "vital amine," believing that it and other similar substances were all amines – organic compounds of nitrogen derived from ammonia. The final e was dropped in 1920 when it was found that not all vitamins are amines.

Vitamins are now known to be compounds that are vital in trace amounts to the functioning of an organism, yet cannot be synthesized by it. Vitamins are species-specific; vitamin C, for example, which humans obtain from fruit and vegetables, is not essential to most other animals.

MEAL IN A BOTTLE Schoolchildren are encouraged to drink milk because it is one of the most concentrated nutritious foods available. It contains vitamin A and some B vitamins as well as protein, calcium, and zinc.

ANTIBIOTICS

The first "wonder-drug" against bacteria was Prontosil, developed by the German chemist Gerhard Domagk (1895–1964). While investigating dyes in 1932, he found that an orange-red dye had a powerful effect against streptococcus infections in mice. Its value was proved in the most dramatic way when Domagk's young daughter fell desperately ill with a streptococcal infection. He injected her with large amounts of the dye, Prontosil, and she made an instant recovery. Later it was found that only part of the molecule, sulfanilamide, was needed for the antibacterial effect. The sulfa drugs, as they were called, proved wonderfully effective against several diseases, including some types of pneumonia.

In the late 1930s, the Australian pathologist Howard Florey (1898–1968) and the German-Jewish chemist Ernst Chain (1906–79), working together in Oxford, read an intriguing paper written a decade earlier by the British scientist Alexander Fleming (1881–1955). In it he detailed the way a mold, *penicillium notatum*, appeared to have a powerful antibacterial effect. They found it difficult to isolate the active ingredient from the mold, but extracted enough to run tests on mice. On May 25, 1940, they inoculated eight mice with fatal doses of streptococci, gave four penicillin, and left the other four untreated. The results were convincing. By the following morning, the mice that had not had penicillin were dead, while those that had were alive and well.

But Florey and Chain could not produce enough and turned to the United States, where mass-production methods were developed in time to save many Allied soldiers in World War II. Since then, antibiotics have proved the single greatest weapon against infectious disease.

FLUKE RESULT Alexander Fleming first discovered the antibacterial properties of the *penicillium notatum* mold by accident in 1929. But he believed that it would not work when mixed with blood, so after reporting his results, he turned to other problems.

MEDICAL IMAGING

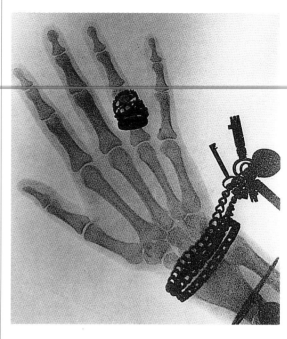

SECRETS REVEALED The extraordinary sight of a living person's skeleton photographed by X-ray was a novelty in 1896 when this picture of a woman's hand, complete with ring and bracelets, was taken.

Few inventions have been incorporated into medicine as rapidly as the discovery of X-rays in 1895 by Wilhelm Röntgen (1845–1923). Within a few months, doctors were using the new technique to study bone fractures, and the German surgeon Georg Perthes quickly put it to therapeutic use by treating a malignant tumor.

The development of the computer transformed radiography in the 1960s by allowing an entire cross-sectional image of a patient's body to be built up stage by stage and then displayed. Similar techniques were developed with radioactive sources (positron emission tomography, or PET scanning) and magnetic resonance imaging (MRI). The view they provide of the internal organs without the need to operate is transforming medical practice.

HOMEOPATHY

At the beginning of the 19th century, a German doctor called Samuel Hahnemann (1755–1843) was hounded for 12 years from one town to the next across Europe. His crime was to give his patients free drugs according to the system of diagnosis and treatment he had developed after years of experiment. He called his system homeopathy. It is based on the concept of curing "like with like," a notion that goes so far against the grain of commonsense that it has taken until the end of the 20th century for it to be accepted by some practitioners of conventional medicine.

By giving patients substances that in a healthy person would create the symptoms of a disease, homeopaths hope to stimulate the body's immune system to fight off illness. For example, someone with a fever might be given belladonna, a herb which would normally stimulate fever. In a large enough dose, belladonna is a deadly poison, but a crucial part of homeopathy is the concept of the infinitesimal dose. Hahnemann found that diluting the dose seemed to make the medicine more powerful. Homeopathic remedies can be as weak as a million parts to one.

Homeopathy has yet to be convincingly proved by rigorous testing. But the scientific establishment's antipathy to alternative medicine has meant that very few trials have ever been carried out. Nevertheless, many conventional doctors now use homeopathy to complement their normal practice.

BOX OF TRICKS The contents of a homeopathic medicine chest have changed little over the past 100 years.

HORMONES

MAKING THE 1960s SWING The contraceptive pill, created from synthetic hormones, probably had a more profound effect on Western society than any other medical discovery in the last 250 years.

Cells in complex organisms communicate with one another in two ways: through the nervous system and through hormones, chemical messengers carried by the bloodstream to distant tissues. The term hormone was coined in 1905, from the Greek *hormao*, meaning to excite or arouse.

Hormones control a host of functions, including growth, sexual development, and the levels of different chemicals in the body. The first hormone to be found, before such materials even had a name, was epinephrine, which was synthesized by Friedrich Stolz (1860–1936) in 1901. Many diseases are caused by hormone deficiencies, of which the most common is a form of diabetes. The cause of this fatal disease was discovered by two Canadian researchers, Charles Best (1899–1978) and Frederick Banting (1891–1941), in 1921. They found that it was the absence of insulin that caused the disturbance of glucose metabolism in the disease. Daily injections of insulin have since allowed millions of diabetics to lead a normal life.

The sex hormones were identified in the 1920s and 1930s. The discovery that the female menstrual cycle was controlled by hormones opened up the possibility of a new form of contraception, and in the 1960s the pill was launched.

COMPUTERS
Intelligent machines

As soon as people began counting, they looked for ways to make the process simpler. Pebbles (*calculi*, in Latin) were mounted on wires to form an abacus, a device invented in 450 BC and still in use in some parts of the world. Logarithms, invented by the Scotsman John Napier (1550–1617) in about 1600, made multiplication and division simpler and were the basis of the slide rule. Although many calculating devices were made, the idea of using machines to carry out logical operations is more recent. The principles were discovered by the English mathematician George Boole (1815–64), who in 1854 published a book in which he applied algebra to logic. He used algebraic symbols based on the functions "and," "or," and "not" to found the field of symbolic logic.

In 1936, the British mathematician Alan Turing (1912–54) showed that a machine could theoretically not only compute but also handle logical statements and manipulate symbols. Meanwhile, the German engineer Konrad Zuse (1910–) built a computer using electrical switches to combine binary numbers. His third prototype, Z3, was programmed using old pieces of film. It worked, though slowly. For his next computer Zuse wanted to use electronic valves, which would be a thousand times faster, but he found no backers.

Unaware of Zuse's work, the United States and Great Britain were working on computers during World War II. At the Bletchley Park code-breaking center, just north of London, a team built the first computer to use valves. It proved Turing's contention that computers were not limited to calculations. Meanwhile, the U.S. Ballistics Research Laboratory had commissioned a computer to calculate the trajectory of shells. ENIAC (Electronic Numerical Integrator and Calculator) used 18,000 valves, 70,000 resistors, 10,000 capacitors, and 6,000 switches. It was fast, at 5,000 additions a second, but hard to program and had no internal memory. This last barrier was surmounted in 1948, with Manchester University's Mark 1 stored-program computer.

The first generation of computers used valves; the second, beginning in about 1955, transistors; and the third, from about 1960, integrated circuits. In 1970, the California company Intel designed the first microprocessor, or "computer on a chip." This revolutionized the business by

THE DIFFERENCE ENGINE

"PRINCESS OF PARALLELOGRAMS" Ada, Countess Lovelace (1815–52), wrote the most important contemporary commentary on Charles Babbage's *Sketch of the Analytical Engine*. The complex computer language ADA is named in her honor.

The Victorian inventor Charles Babbage (1791–1871) was the first to try to develop a general-purpose computer. He began in 1821 with the Difference Engine, a vast machine with 25,000 parts. Its task was to work out and print mathematical tables. Numbers were inscribed around the edges of a series of wheels on vertical axles. When turned, the axles performed the process of addition through gears and linkages, with a special device for "carrying" a digit to the next column when two numbers added up to more than nine.

By 1832, a seventh of the machine had been completed, but by then Babbage's mind had turned to an even more ambitious idea, the Analytical Engine. It was to be the first general-purpose computer, able to perform addition, subtraction, multiplication, and division, which could be programmed in any sequence. The Analytical Engine was never constructed, but a series of designs have survived. They show that he had anticipated the architecture of the electronic computer. His engine had a separate store, or memory, to record numbers; a mill that could manipulate them just as the processor of a computer does; and a program, in the form of punched cards.

TURING AND VON NEUMANN

Alan Turing, a British mathematician, defined the nature of a computer even before one was built. He set out to discover if there were a mechanical process that could be applied to any mathematical statement in order to determine if that statement were provable. To do so he designed an imaginary machine capable of following instructions to carry out a series of mathematical operations. He realized that it was the instructions that determined the outcome, so a machine could in principle carry out any logical operation of which a human was capable. It did not need to be restricted to mathematics: it could play chess or work out anagrams. In 1945, Turing wrote a report that proposed building an electronic calculator.

The same year, the American mathematician John von Neumann (1903–57) was outlining the basic structure of a computer. It consisted of four elements: a memory, a unit for calculations, a control unit to direct operations, and units for putting data in and getting results out. He decided his computer should work serially because it was simpler than designing a machine in which more than one operation went on at once. Until recently, all digital computers followed this pattern.

BINARY NOTATION

More than 5,000 years ago, the Babylonians used a system of numbers based on 60 – it is the origin of the familiar 60-second minute and 60-minute hour. The German mathematician Gottfried Leibniz (1646–1716) developed the first general exposition of positional number systems – including the binary system, which uses the base two. In this system, each successive position in the number – rather than representing tens, hundreds, thousands, and so on, as in the decimal system – represents 1s, 2s, 4s, 8s, 16s, and so on. The binary number 10101 consists of one one, no twos, one four, no eights, and one 16 – total 21. Binary notation is ideal for computers because it is simple to record by a switch that is capable of only two positions – off (0) or on (1).

CAN COMPUTERS THINK?

Attempts to build computers with human intelligence have been going on since the 1950s. None has so far come close to matching the human brain over the whole range of intelligence. Yet in limited areas computers can think as well as humans can. There are chess programs, such as IBM's *Deep Blue*, that can win a game with even the world chess champion and leave average players floundering.

What has proved harder to produce is programs that can build up a picture of the world and behave accordingly. Learning language, recognizing objects, and building relationships with other people are all beyond the capabilities of computers. But most experts in artificial intelligence believe that this is not an unsurmountable barrier, and that there is no reason why computers could not match human intelligence.

CONTROL CENTER Bletchley Park was the nerve center of Allied code-breaking during World War II. The first electronic programmable computer, the 1,500-valve Colossus Mark 1, became operational in December 1943 and was used to break the codes known as Fish, the cipher used for communications between German high command, including Hitler himself, and generals in the field.

SEE ALSO

Philosophy of mind · · · · · · · · · · ▶

Philosophy of science · · · · · · · · ▶

Psychology · · · · · · · · · · · · · ▶

ECOLOGY
Earth's natural communities

The word ecology was coined in 1866 by the German zoologist Ernst Haeckel (1834–1919), known as the "German Darwin." He defined it as "the relation of the animal both to its organic as well as its inorganic environment." The root was the Greek word *oikos,* meaning a home or a place to live. Haeckel's message was that plants, insects, animals, and the setting in which they live cannot be understood in isolation from one another. Everything connects in a complex network of relationships. But ecology remained little more than a word until 20th-century scientists began to put some substance behind the original concept.

In the 1920s the German biologist August Thienemann introduced the idea of trophic levels, the steps on the food chain occupied by different organisms. At the base are green plants, converting the energy of the Sun into food for herbivores. They in turn are eaten by carnivores. The British ecologist Charles Elton (1900–) spent 20 years studying animals in meadows, woods, and water near Oxford, and came up with the idea of ecological niches (the roles occupied by individual organisms). He also showed that Thienemann's trophic levels form a pyramid, with the greatest number of species at the bottom – such as grasses – narrowing to just a few top predators – such as foxes – at the summit.

The rise of ecology blew apart the comfortable divisions into which scientists had split the natural world. While it began as a branch of biology, by the 1960s ecology had taken on political significance. Worries about population, pollution, and the shrinking wilderness could be explored only by using the concepts of the ecologists. One small change to an ecosystem – such as the elimination of an apparently insignificant species – could have profound effects on the whole. This was music to the ears of social critics such as Theodore Roszak, who described ecology in 1973 as "a subversive science" with a sensibility that was "holistic, receptive, trustful, largely non-tampering, and deeply grounded in aesthetic intuition."

Since then, ecology has become as much a slogan as a science. Its concepts are used by environmentalists to fight their battles, while its emphasis on the whole appeals to critics of reductionism, the basic scientific method.

SILENT SPRING

KILLER CHEMICALS Agricultural workers using pesticides to wipe out insects have to wear protective clothing because the sprays can be lethal to humans.

In the 1940s and 1950s, the chemical industry produced new, powerful pesticides to control insects and plant diseases. Among them was the insecticide DDT, which killed the lice that carry typhus, and the mosquitos that spread malaria. Millions of lives were saved by DDT, but it had a flaw. It persisted in the environment, even building up in human fat and mothers' milk.

The alarm was sounded in 1962 by Rachel Carson (1907–64), a biologist who spent years working for the U.S. Bureau of Fisheries. Her book *Silent Spring* (1962) documented pesticide build-up in the environment, and is credited with launching the environmental movement. DDT was later banned worldwide.

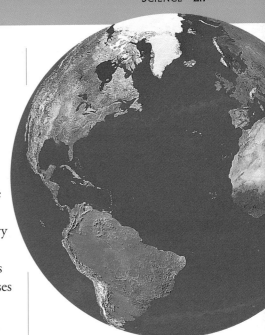

GREENHOUSE EFFECT

The Sun's energy alone is not enough to keep the Earth as warm as it is now. Temperatures are kept up by a natural phenomenon known as the "greenhouse effect." Without it, the Earth's surface would be 68°F (38°C) colder.

Once the Sun's rays reach the Earth's surface, it warms up and radiates energy. This type of warm energy is absorbed by carbon dioxide and water vapors in the Earth's atmosphere and remains there. The effect was first explained by the Swedish chemist Svante Arrhenius (1859–1927) in 1896. The amount of carbon dioxide in the atmosphere has risen from 290 parts per million (ppm) at the end of the 19th century to more than 350ppm today. If continued, this will accelerate natural global warming, because more of the Earth's energy will be absorbed by the extra carbon dioxide.

FACTORY FUMES Carbon dioxide belched into the air by factories and agricultural burning has helped increase the temperature of the Earth's atmosphere by almost 1°F (0.5°C) in the past 100 years.

OZONE HOLE

In 1982, scientists working in the Antarctic noticed that the layer of ozone high in the atmosphere was getting thin. A new instrument confirmed their finding. Ozone, a form of oxygen, forms a shield preventing damaging ultraviolet light from reaching the Earth, so the news was serious.

One scientist unsurprised by this discovery was Sherwood Rowland (1927–) from the University of California. More than 10 years before he had calculated what became of gases called chlorofluorocarbons (CFCs) used in refrigerators and aerosol cans. At sea level, CFCs persist forever, but as they rise through the atmosphere, they are broken up by ultraviolet light, releasing chlorine. Rowland found that the chlorine eventually destroyed ozone.

INVISIBLE POLLUTION Garbage is regularly shipped out from scientific bases in Antarctica, but even the Earth's wildest continent has fallen victim to the scourge of pollution.

GAIA

Ecologists customarily think big, but few think as big as the British scientist James Lovelock, originator of the Gaia hypothesis, named after the ancient Greek Earth goddess. He claims that the whole Earth functions as a single organism. All its living systems conspire to keep conditions habitable for the others. Like a living creature, the Earth may become sick – for example, with air pollution – and will try to fight off the infection. The idea is both a powerful metaphor and a scientific theory, and has been adopted enthusiastically as part of the "New Age" culture. Scientists, however, remain sceptical.

SEE ALSO

Modern spirituality · · · · · · · · · · ◄
Industrialization · · · · · · · · · · · · ◄
Global economics · · · · · · · · · · · ◄
Astronomy · · · · · · · · · · · · · · · ◄

INDEX

Note: Words and page numbers in **bold** type indicate major sections on a topic. The index should be used in conjunction with the cross-references in the text.

ACKNOWLEDGMENTS

t = top, **b** = bottom, **c** = center, **l** = left, **r** = right

1 AKG London; 2–3 Louvre, Paris/Giraudon/Bridgeman Art Library; 4–5 Vatican Museums & Galleries, Rome/Bridgeman Art Library; 6 **t** Sygma, **b** AKG London; 7 **t** © ADAGP, Paris and DACS, London/Private Collection/Bridgeman Art Library, **b** Roger Malloch/Magnum Photos; 8 **t** Justus Gopel/AKG London; 9 **t** Michael Holford, **b** Robert Harding Picture Library; 9–10 Ancient Art & Architecture Collection; 10 **t** Staatliche Glypothek, Munich/E.T. Archive, **bl** British Museum/E.T. Archive, AKG London, **br** AKG London; 11 **t** Hilbich/AKG London, **b** Museo e Gallerie Nazionali di Capodimonte, Naples/Giraudon/Bridgeman Art Library; 11–12 T. Jackson/Robert Harding Picture Library; 12 **l** AKG London, **r** Michael Holford; 13 **t** AKG London, **b** British Library, London/Bridgeman Art Library; 13–14 AKG London; 14 **t** Bibliothèque Nationale, Paris/Bridgeman Art Library, **bl** Joe Cornish, **br** British Library, London/Bridgeman Art Library; 15 **t** AKG London, **bl** National Gallery, London/Bridgeman Art Library, **br** Museo Nazionale del Bargello, Florence/Erich Lessing/AKG London; 16 **t** Mary Evans Picture Library, **b** Museo delle Scienze, Florence/AKG London; 17 **t** Château de Versailles/Lauros-Giraudon/Bridgeman Art Library, **cl** Louvre, Paris/Giraudon/Bridgeman Art Library, **cr** AKG London, **b** Trinity College, Cambridge/Bridgeman Art Library; 18–19 Ernst Haas/Magnum; 20 AKG London; 20–1 Private Collection/Bridgeman Art Library; 21 **t** Louvre, Paris/Erich Lessing/AKG London, **b** Louvre, Paris/Giraudon/Bridgeman Art Library; 22 **l** Château de Fontainebleu/Giraudon/Bridgeman Art Library, **r** AKG London; 23 **l** Schloss Charlottenburg, Berlin/Bridgeman Art Library, **r** AKG London; 24 **l** Louvre, Paris/Giraudon/Bridgeman Art Library, **r** Bibliothèque Nationale, Paris/Giraudon/Bridgeman Art Library; 25 **t** & **b** AKG London, **c** Musée de l'Armee/AKG London; 26 **l** Hulton Getty, **r** Tretyakov Gallery, Moscow/Bridgeman Art Library; 27 **t** Harry Gruyaert/Magnum, **b** Jon Jones/Sygma; 28 **l** Sir John Soane Museum, London/Bridgeman Art Library, **r** AKG London; 29 Mary Evans Picture Library; 30 Corbis-Bettmann/UPI; 31 **tl** Corbis-Bettmann, **tr** Corbis-Bettmann/UPI, **b** Corbis-Bettmann/Reuters; 32–3 Corbis-Bettmann/UPI; 34 © ADAGP, Paris and DACS, London 1997/Giraudon/Bridgeman Art Library; 35 Corbis-Bettmann/UPI; 36 **l** Mary Evans Picture Library, **r** Corbis-Bettmann; 37 **t** Robert Harding Picture Library, **b** Mary Evans Picture Library; 38 **l** Corbis-Bettmann/UPI, **c** Cornell Capa/Magnum, **r** AKG London; 39 **l** Ben Edwards/Impact Photos, **c** Michael Mirecki/Impact Photos, **r** John Arthur/Impact Photos; 40–1 Tate Gallery/AKG London; 41–2 AKG London; 43 **t** © Elizabeth Banks/London School of Economics/Bridgeman Art Library, **b** Fine Art Society, London/Bridgeman Art Library; 44 Tretyakov Gallery, Moscow/AKG London; 45 **t** & **br** AKG London, **bl** Private Collection/Bridgeman Art Library; 46 **l** Private Collection/Bridgeman Art Library, **r** Magyar Nemzeti Galeria, Budapest/Bridgeman Art Library; 47 **t** & **b** Private Collection/Bridgeman Art Library, **c** AP/AKG London; 48–9 **t** AKG London, **b** Harrison Forman/Popperfoto; 50–1 India Office Library/E.T. Archive; 51–3 **t** ET Archive; 52–3 **b** L'Illustration/Sygma; 54 Popperfoto; 55 **l** Bundesarchiv Koblenz/E.T. Archive, **r** Musée Carnavalet, Paris/E.T. Archive; 56 **t** Nolde-Stiftung-Seebüll, Neukirchen/Christie's Images/Bridgeman Art Library, **b** E.T. Archive; 57 **t** L'Illustration/Sygma, **b** Hulton Getty; 58 **t** E.T. Archive, **b** C Spengler/Sygma; 59 **t** Matsumoto/Sygma, **b** AKG London; 60 Corbis-Bettmann/UPI 61 **l** Paul Lowe/Network, **r** Corbis-Bettmann; 62 Hulton Getty; 63 **t** Popperfoto, **b** E.T. Archive; 64 **t** Shell Art Collection/National Motor Museum, **b** AFP; 65 **t** Peterson/Gamma/Frank Spooner Pictures, **b** Witness Memory; 66 Sygma; 67 **tl** & **r** Keystone/Sygma, **b** Sanchez Garcia/Sygma; 68 Corbis-Bettmann/UPI; 69 Keystone/Sygma; 70–1 Magnum; 72–3 Christie's Images; 72 Musée du Louvre, Paris/AKG London; 73 **t** AKG London, **b** Erich Lessing/AKG London; 74 **t** AKG London, **b** Mary Evans Picture Library; 75 **t** Jason Hawkes/Tony Stone Images, **b** AKG London; 76 Roudnice Lobkowicz Collection, Czech Republic/ Bridgeman Art Library; 77 **r** Musée de Louvre, Paris/AKG London, **t** SMPK, Nationalgalerie/AKG, **b** Offtl. Kunstsammlung, Basel/AKG; 78 **l** Ancient Art & Architecture Collection, **r** AKG London; 79 **t** Ca d'Oro, Venice/Bridgeman Art Library, 79 **b**–80 Mary Evans Picture Library; 81 **t** Museo de la Abadia, Montserrat, Catalonia/Index/Bridgeman Art Library, **b** Wallace Collection, London/Bridgeman Art Library; 82 Vatican Museums & Galleries, Rome/Bridgeman Art Library; 83 National Museum of American Art, Smithsonian Inst./Bridgeman Art Library; 84–85 **t** AKG London, **b** Humphrey Spender/Bolton Museum & Art Gallery; 86 **t** Ronald Grant Collection; 87 **t** Tony Stone Images, **b** Jan Kopec/Tony Stone Images; 88 **l** Rafael Valls Gallery, London/Bridgeman Art Library, **r** © DEMART PRO ARTE BV/DACS 1997/Museo Dali, Figueras/Bridgeman Art Library; 89 **t** Scott Camazine/Science Photo Library, **b** Corbis-Bettmann/Hulton Getty; 90 Zoe Dominic; 91 AKG London; 92 **l** Charles Thatcher/Tony Stone Images, **r** Leonard Lee Rue III/Oxford Scientific Films; 93 **t** Musée d'Orsay, Paris/Lauros-Giraudon/Bridgeman Art Library; 93 **b**–94 AKG London; 95 **l** Alain Le Garsmeur/Impact, **r** AKG London; 96 **l** Victoria & Albert Museum/Bridgeman Art Library, **r** Fitzwilliam Museum/AKG London; 97 **l** Mary Evans Picture Library; 97 **r**–98 **l** Hulton Getty, **r** Corbis-Bettmann; 99 **l** Corbis-Bettmann/UPI, **r** Sue Cunningham/Tony Stone Images; 100 Brian Harris Harris/Impact; 101 **l** Mark Penney Maddocks/E.T. Archive, **r** J.P. Laffont/Sygma; 102–3 Corbis-Betttmann/UPI; 104 Mary Evans Picture Library; 105 **l** Mary Evans Picture Library; 105 **r** E.T. Archive; 107 Musée des Beaux Arts, Rouen/E.T. Archive; 108 Collections of the Library of Congress/Photo Assist; 109 **t** Sophie Barker/Camera Press, **b** Bill Potter/Camera Press; 110 **l** Mary Evans Picture Library, **r** © DEMART PRO ARTE BV/DACS 1997/Ex-Edward James Foundation, Sussex/Bridgeman Art Library; 110–111 Mary Evans Picture Library/Sigmund Freud Copyrights; 111 Mary Evans Picture Library; 112 **l** Musée Carnavalet, Paris/Giraudon/Bridgeman Art Library, **r** K & B News Foto, Florence/Bridgeman Art Library; 113 **l** Rorschach H., Rorschach-Test © Verlag Hans Huber AG, Bern, Switzerland, 1921, 1948, 1994, **r** Detroit Institute of Arts, Michigan/Bridgeman Art Library; 114 **l** FPG/Robert Harding Picture Library, **r** Galleria Degli Uffizi, Florence/Bridgeman Art Library; 115 **tl** Terry Vine/Tone Stone Images, **tr** Sheila Terry/Science Photo Library, **b** Corbis-Bettmann; 116 Mary Evans Picture Library; 117 **t** Corbis-Bettmann, **b** © The Munch Museum/The Munch-Ellingsen Group/DACS 1997/Gamma/Frank Spooner Pictures; 118 **t** Corbis-Bettmann/UPI, **b** AP/AKG London; 119 Hulton Getty; 120 **t** Gamma/Frank Spooner Pictures, **b** John Maier/Still Pictures; 121 **t** Popperfoto, **b** Hjalte Tin/Still Pictures; 122 Christie's Images/Bridgeman Art Library; 123 **tl** Mary Evans Picture Library, **tr** AKG London, **b** Museo de Arte, Ponce, Puerto Rico/Bridgeman Art Library; 124 **t** AKG London, **b** Musée des Beaux-Arts, Pau/Bridgeman Art Library; 125 **t** Victoria & Albert Museum/Bridgeman Art Library, **b** AKG London; 126 **l** Museum of London/Bridgeman Art Library, **r** Corbis-Bettmann; 127 Mary Evans Picture Library; 128 Hulton Getty; 129 **tl** Brian Harris/Impact, **tr** Corbis-Bettmann, **bl** Gert Schutz/AKG London, **br** AKG London; 130 **t** Barry Lewis/Network, **b** Gilles Peress/Magnum; 131 Alon Reininger/Contact/Colorific!; 132 **t** Barry Lewis/Network, **b** K. Rodgers/Hutchison Library; 133 Hulton Getty; 134 Crispin Hughes/Hutchison Library; 135 **t** Mary Henley/Impact, **bl** Sarah Errington/Hutchison Library, **br** Robert Aberman/Hutchison Library; 136–7 Magnum; 138 Roy Miles Gallery, London/Bridgeman Art Library; 139 **t** Christie's Images/Bridgeman Art Library, **b** Mansell Collection; 140 **t** Louvre/Giraudon/Bridgeman Art Library, **b** Musée Carnavalet, Paris/Bridgeman Art Library; 141 **t** AKG London, **b** Victoria & Albert Museum/Bridgeman Art Library; 142 Kunsthalle, Hamburg/Bridgeman Art Library; 143 **t** Stapleton Gallery/The Bridgeman Art Library, **b** Tate Gallery/E.T. Archive; 144 **t** AKG London, **b** Fine Art Society/Bridgeman Art Library; 145 **t** AKG London, **b** Musée des Beaux Arts, Bordeaux/Giraudon/Bridgeman Art Library; 146 Musée d'Orsay/Reunion des Musées Nationaux; 147 **t** AKG London, **b** Philadelphia Museum of Art, Pennsylvania/Bridgeman Art Library; 148 Science Museum/Science & Society Picture Library; 149 **t** Woodmansterne/William Morris Gallery, **b** Guildhall Art Gallery/AKG London; 150 Phillips Collection, Washington DC/Bridgeman Art Library; 151 Musée d'Orsay, Paris/Giraudon/Bridgeman Art Library; 152 Private Collection/Bridgeman Art Library; 153 **t** Musée d'Orsay, Paris/Erich Lessing/AKG London, **b** NMPFT/Science & Society Picture Library; 154 **t** Musées Royaux d'Art et d'Histoire/AKG London, **b** Museum of Fine Arts, Budapest/Bridgeman Art Library; 155 **t** Art Institute, Chicago/AKG London, **b** © ADAGP, Paris and DACS, London 1997/Pushkin Museum, Moscow/AKG London; 156 **l** Narodni Galerie, Prague/Bridgeman Art Library; 157 **l** Private Collection/Bridgeman Art Library, **r** Narodni Galerie, Prague/Erich Lessing/AKG London; 158 **t** © Succession Picasso/DACS 1997/Museum of Modern Art, New York, acquired through the Lillie P. Bliss Bequest, **b** Tate Gallery/E.T. Archive; 159 **t** Staatsgalerie, Stuttgart/Erich Lessing/AKG London, **b** AKG London; 160 **l** Max Jones Files/Redferns, **r** Christie's Images; 161 **l** Visual Arts Library, **r** © ADAGP, Paris and DACS, London/AKG London; 162 **t** Michael Ochs Archives/Redferns, **b** Popperfoto; 163 **l** © 1997 ABC/Mondrian Estate/Holtzman Trust/Tate Gallery/AKG London, **r** AKG London; 164 **l** © Sevenarts 1997/Bridgeman Art Library, **r** © ADAGP, Paris and DACS, London/Private Collection/Bridgeman Art Library; 165 **l** © Alan Bowness, Hepworth Estate/Visual Arts Library, **r** © ADAGP, Paris and DACS, London 1977/National Gallery of Ireland, Dublin/Bridgeman Art Library; 166 **t** Popperfoto, **b** © ADAGP, Paris and DACS, London 1997/Bridgeman Art Library; 167 **t** Fred Dolbin von Benedikt/AKG London, **b** © DACS 1997/Private Collection; 168 **l** © William Turnbull 1997. All rights reserved DACS, **r** © ARS, NY and DACS, London 1997/Private Collection/Bridgeman Art Library; 169 **t** © Richard Long, **b** © ARS, NY and DACS, London 1997/National Gallery of Art, Washington/AKG London; 170 **t** © Jasper Johns/DACS, London/VAGA, New York 1997/Ludwig Museum, Cologne/AKG London, **b** © Robert Rauschenberg/DACS, London/VAGA, New York 1997/AKG London; 171 **t** Leon Herschtritt/Camera Press, **b** Henrietta Butler/Redferns; 172 Corbis-Bettmann; 173 **t** AKG London, **b** © Carolyn Cassady; 174 **t** Camera Press, **b** © ARS, NY and DACS, London 1997/Private Collection/Bridgeman Art Library; 175 **t** © ADAGP, Paris and DACS, London 1997/Christie's Images/Bridgeman Art Library, **b** © DACS 1997/Christie's Images/AKG London; 176 Mark Fiennes/Arcaid; 177 **t** © ARS, NY and DACS, London 1977/Werner Zellieu, Ileana Sonnabend Collection, New York/AKG London, **b** © Andy Goldsworthy; 178–9 AKG London; 180 **l** The Science Museum/Science & Society Picture Library, **r** AKG London; 181 **t** Waterhouse & Dodd, London/Bridgeman Art Library, **b** Science Museum/Science & Society Picture Library; 182 **t** Hulton Getty, **b** Royal Institution/Science & Society Picture Library; 183 **l** Science Museum/Science & Society Picture Library, **c** Hulton Getty, **r** NASA; 184 NASA/Science Photo Library; 185 **l** NASA, **r** Mansell Collection; 186 NASA/Science Photo Library; 187–8 **t** NASA; 188 **b** Royal Observatory, Edinburgh/AATB/Science Photo Library; 189 **t** David Parker/Science Photo Library, **b** Mary Evans Picture Library; 190 **l** The Science Museum/Science & Society Picture Library, **r** Erich Lessing/AKG London; 191 **t** Science Photo Library, **b** The National Gallery, London; 192 **t** © ADAGP, Paris and DACS, London 1977/Private Collection/Fine Art Photographic Library, **b** Novosti/Science Photo Library; 193 **t** Science Museum/Science & Society Picture Library, **b** Corbis-Bettmann; 194 Patrice Loiez, CERN/Science Photo Library; 194–5 Professor Peter Fowler/Science Photo Library; 195 AKG London; 196–7 US Navy/Science Photo Library; 196 **l** Lawrence Berkeley/Science Photo Library, **r** Mirror Syndication International/Hulton Getty; 197 **l** CERN Photo, **r** CERN/Science Photo Library; 198 **t** David Parker/Science Photo Library, **b** CERN/Science Photo Library; 199 ArSciMed/Science Photo Library; 200 Gregory Sams/Science Photo Library; 201 **t** James Randkler/Tony Stone Images, **b** Scott Camazine/Science Photo Library; 202 **l** Mary Evans Picture Library; 202–3 E.T. Archive; 203 **t** Dr. Jeremy Burgess/Science Photo Library, **b** AKG London; 204 **t** Philippe Plailly/Science Photo Library, **b** A. Barrington Brown/Science Photo Library; 205 Science Photo Library; 206 **l** Jean-Luc Ducloux/Image Select, **r** Popperfoto; 207 **l** Geoff Tompkinson/Science Photo Library, **r** David Parker/Science Photo Library; 208 Jean-Loup Charnet/Science Photo Library; 209 **t** AKG London, **b** Musée d'Orsay, Paris/AKG London; 210 **t** Royal College of Surgeons/Bridgeman Art Library, 210 **b**–211 **t** Corbis-Bettmann; 211 **b** Hulton Getty; 212 **t** Science Photo Library, **b** St. Mary's Hospital Medical School/Science Photo Library; 213 **t** Hulton Getty, 213 **b**–214 Science Museum/Science & Society Picture Library; 214–15 Hulton Getty; 216 **l** Frans Lanting/Tony Stone Images, **r** Wayne Eastep/Tony Stone Images; 216–17 Mary Evans Picture Library; 217 **l** Peter Harper/Mountain Camera, **r** Worldsat International & J. Knighton/Science Photo Library.